Keeping Archives

Second Edition

Keeping Archives

Second Edition

Editor
Judith Ellis

THORPE

in association with
The Australian Society of Archivists Inc

Keeping Archives
Second Edition

Published 1993 by
D W Thorpe
(a part of Reed Reference Publishing)
18 Salmon Street
Port Melbourne, Victoria 3207
Australia

in association with the
Australian Society of Archivists Inc

First published 1987 by
The Australian Society of Archivists Inc

National Library of Australia Cataloguing-in-publication data

Keeping archives.

2nd ed.
Bibliography.
Includes index.
ISBN 1 875589 15 5.

1. Archives – Administration. I. Ellis, Judith. II. Australian Society
of Archivists.

025.1714

ISBN 1 875589 15 5

Typeset in Century Old Style by D W Thorpe
Page & Cover Design by text-art
Printed in Australia by Impact Printing, Brunswick

Availability
In Australia, Thorpe titles are available directly from the publisher. In New Zealand,
orders should be placed with Thorpe in Wellington. In the UK and EC, contact Bowker-
Saur in London. In the USA, contact R R Bowker in New Providence, NJ. Throughout
Asia, contact Butterworths Singapore.

Contents

Acknowledgments

Editors

Judith Ellis, Sigrid McCausland, Sue McKemmish, Michael Piggott,
Frank Upward. Copy Editor: Kaye Quittner

First Edition Authors

Grateful acknowledgment is made of the following authors' work in the
first edition of *Keeping Archives* as the source of a number of the ideas
and approaches in this edition: Gunnel Bellviken, Averil Condren, Kathy
Oakes, Sigrid McCausland, Sandra Hinchey, Michael Piggott, Clive
Smith (Glossary)

Contributors

Michael Piggott, Frank Upward, Baiba Berzins for their contributions
and comments

Indexing

John E Simkin

Cartoon

Reproduced with the kind permission of Michael Leunig. First published
in the *Age,* 30 May 1992.

Photographs

Australian Archives, ACT Regional Office; Australian Archives,
Canberra; Australian Archives, NSW Regional Office; J G Edgecombe;
Ann Pederson; State Library of NSW

List of Abbreviations

ACA	Australian Council of Archives
AALIA	Associate of the Australian Library and Information Association
AIMM	Member of the Australian Institute of Management
ACT	Australian Capital Territory
AICCM	Australian Institute for the Conservation of Cultural Materials
ARMA	Associate of the Records Management Association (Australia)
ASA	Australian Society of Archivists Inc
ASAP	Australian Science Archives Project
CD	compact disc
EDI	electronic data interchange
EFT	electronic funds transfer
FIAT	International Federation of Television Archives
FIAF	International Federation of Film Archives
ISO	International Standards Organisation
MRMA	Member of the Records Management Association (Australia)
NAP	normal administrative practice
NSW	New South Wales (Australia)
OCR	optical character recognition
PC	Personal Computer
RMIT	Royal Melbourne Institute of Technology
SAA	Society of American Archivists
US	United States
USMARC AMC	United States Machine Readable Cataloguing – Archival & Manuscripts Control
WORM	write once ready many

Preface

Many new and practising archivists have used the principles and methods contained in the first edition of *Keeping Archives* to introduce or operate successful archival programs in a variety of organisations. This edition builds upon the strong foundations provided by the first edition. It also introduces changing concepts and approaches to the management of archives in the context of changing organisational structures, technology-based record formats, and a new look at the nature of recordkeeping and archival responsibilities.

The aim of this book is to augment the approaches of the first edition while recognising the different institutional contexts in which the archivist may be operating. The book continues to provide an up-to-date, practical approach to archives management through revision of the original chapters. New issues relating to the modern organisational context are also explored in chapters on legal responsibilities and issues and managing records in special formats.

Overall, the approach of this book reflects the practice of the majority of archives programs; this is to wait until records have been received into custody before undertaking arrangement and description work, and to wait until day-to-day reference has ceased before acquiring records. To this end, the book provides comprehensive coverage of issues, principles and practices for people in charge of an in-house archives. It is also a useful introductory text for students of archives, and for people employed by a major institutional archives, or an in-house archives.

The 11 writers faced a significant challenge in presenting, within the confines of one volume, a blend of principles and practices subsumed by the title *Keeping Archives*. The phrase 'keeping archives' raises many questions, such as keeping them in what organisational setting, primarily what type of records, and assuming what resources? The broad coverage of this book contrasts with the trend towards specialisation heralded 12 to 15 years ago with the appearance of texts on archives administration in intermediate and smaller organisations, and since followed by titles on local government, business archives, college and university archives, and religious archives.

As art dealers, archaeologists, ecologists, forensic scientists and archivists know, virtually everything has a context. So too does this book. How the chapter authors covered their various large and complicated themes is a product of many factors, including their education and training, reading, interests, and the length, variety and institutional settings of their professional experience.

The introductory chapter sets the scene for principles and practices outlined in the rest of the book. It explores the nature of archives, their meaning and value, and introduces the principles that guide archival practice. It also provides an overview of archival programs with reference to their organisational and professional context. Chapters 2 and 3 provide principles, strategies and techniques for managing and preserving archives. Chapter 4 continues the focus on management techniques by considering the legal responsibilities and issues that may affect archival operations. Chapters 5 to 9 cover the detailed techniques for determining which records will become archives, acquiring them, and establishing physical and intellectual control over them to enable their use in the future. Chapters 10, 11 and 14 look at the strategies and practices for making archives available for use through reference services, educational activities, and created documentation programs. Chapters 12 and 13 focus on the influence of modern technology in archives management, including the use of computers and document imaging as tools for the archivist, as well as the requirement to manage records in special formats.

Repeatedly in this edition, issues and processes are covered from two points of view, those of the collecting archives and the in-house archives. These are two of any number of poles fixing the context of the organisational setting of archival work, and this in turn is one of many factors that shape the practice of our profession. To treat them all fully is beyond the scope of a single volume. With this background, readers should adapt and apply what they read to their own context either within an institutional or organisational structure or an educational or training program.

In reflecting upon the book as it evolved and on the issues that have arisen or become critical since the first edition appeared, one dominating question has emerged. When in the life of a record, increasingly in electronic format, should archivists become involved; involved in selection and preservation, and in documenting the context of record creation? That is, is our core business restricted to gaining custody or to the physical keeping of archives? These major questions reside beneath the text, answered when they (occasionally) surface in discussions of particular chapter themes.

Recent literature on these matters, which has proliferated during the preparation of this edition, challenges the traditional custodial approach to archives management. Collectively, the chapters sit as a reasonably integrated whole between the old world and the new; they have something to offer those grappling with immediate day-to-day challenges of keeping archives, without denying the force of front-end thinking in an era where archivists can become involved with the records long before they are transferred to archival custody. This is especially relevant to appraisal theory and practice.

The contents of neither this edition, nor its predecessor, should be regarded purely as representing *the* Australian approach to keeping archives, the recommendations of the Australian Society of Archivists, or the vision exclusively of the editor. The book represents Australian approaches to the extent that it incorporates Australian illustrations, examples and references, and draws on the richness of Australian archival work as variously experienced by the authors.

Since the first edition, the case for a series-centred system of documentation and control of archives has continued to build. It is now used by almost all government archives and a growing number of university and business archives in Australia. Also, adaptations have occurred in New Zealand, and in 1990 changes at the Public Record Office (London) had reached the stage where Susan Healy could write that its records control system 'resembles the Australian system in many ways, for instance in its respect for the integrity of original series and in its use of finding aids to reconstitute the record group'. The ease with which it incorporates information about functions, and its role in contributing to the development of descriptive standards, vouch for its continued importance. It is beyond the scope of this book to provide a blueprint for developing and implementing a fully-fledged series system. However, the concept of the record series rather than the record group is central to the book, particularly to its coverage of arrangement and description practices.

Archival programs have an integral link to records management programs. While archives and records management programs are brought together in some organisations, and kept separate in others, and while both archivists and records managers are involved in managing records of social and organisational activity, discrete activities and roles can be identified. It is not appropriate for this book to explore the full nature and context of records management programs. However reference is made in some chapters to the links or relationships between archives programs and the records management context or activities.

Understanding the nature of archives and why they are of continuing value and use to our society forms the basis for the practice of keeping archives. This book draws upon the collective skills and experiences of practising archivists working in a variety of organisational settings to provide guidance for the introduction or operation of archival programs. It is hoped that readers can draw upon the principles, strategies and practices contained in this book to meet the challenges of managing archives in their own organisation, and to enhance their own professional development.

Keeping Archives

Second Edition

A method has recently been discovered, of listening to the hidden messages stored in table tops.

A national archive of restaurant tables is presently being assembled and the huge process of transcription has already begun.

Table tops actually record and store in their atomic stucture all conversations conducted during meals.

Public access to these transcriptions will be available under the Freedom of Information Act.

Restaurant tables are of enormous significance for the variety and substance of their recordings

Scientists are presently conducting experiments with mattresses and a major breakthrough is expected very soon.

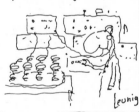

leunig

1 | Introducing Archives and Archival Programs

Sue McKemmish

Introduction

People and organisations create and use records in the course of conducting business and relating to each other. These records are threads in the social fabric of human interaction. They provide

- evidence of activities and interrelationships
- information about associated people, organisations, events and places.

Some records of social and organisational activity are preserved because they are of continuing value to individuals, organisations or society. Records of continuing value are called archives (Figure 1.1).

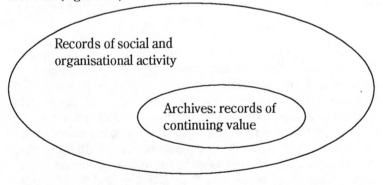

Records of social and organisational activity

Archives: records of continuing value

Figure 1.1 Records and Archives

Archivists transmit knowledge and experience of past and present human interaction to present and future generations. They do this by

- identifying, documenting and preserving archives

- enabling their continuing use.

The rest of this book is about the practice of keeping archives for continuing use. This chapter explores the nature of archives, their meaning and value, and introduces the principles that guide archival practice. It also provides an overview of archival programs with reference to their organisational and professional contexts.

The Nature of Archives

The key to understanding the nature of archives, as defined in Table 1.1, lies in exploring
- the characteristics they share with all records of social and organisational activity
- why they are of continuing value and use.

Table 1.1 What Are Archives?

Archives are documents made or received and accumulated by a person or organisation in the course of the conduct of affairs and preserved because of their continuing value.

Historically, the term has often referred more narrowly to non-current records deposited or selected for deposit in an archival institution.

The word archives is also commonly used to refer to
- the organisation, agency or program responsible for the selection, care and use of records of continuing value
- the repository, building or place dedicated to their storage, preservation and use.

In its singular form, archive refers specifically to the whole body or group of records of continuing value of an organisation or individual, a vital resource also known by the French word *fonds* or the term *archief* common to many European languages.

People and organisations – or more strictly speaking, parts of organisations – create records employing whatever technology is available to them. Therefore, such records can be in any media, eg paper, microform, film, magnetic tape or disk, optical disk, video or audiotapes. They also come in various shapes, sizes and formats, including letters, paper files, diaries, registers, index cards, maps, plans, microfiche, aperture cards, photographs, videocassettes, computerised databases, and electronic mail.

Individuals keep records of their activities and interrelationships with other individuals and organisations. Accounts, receipts, cheque butts, bank statements, payslips, income tax assessments, share certificates, personal computer spreadsheets and wordprocessing files, contracts and guarantees all arise from our financial and legal relationships as consumers of goods and services, employees, shareholders, beneficiaries of public services and taxpayers. Birth, death and marriage certificates, passports and visas, statements of educational qualifications, plans, titles, wills, deeds and employment histories document our status, property rights and other entitlements. Letters, records relating to our membership of unions, clubs and societies, diaries, photographs, home videos, bus tickets, postcards and invitations document our social and community relationships. Most records we quickly discard. Many we keep for longer periods. All capture our experiences, support our memories, go towards forming for each of us a history of a life, but some – our personal archives – we continue to value more highly for these purposes.

Similarly, organisations of all kinds – governments, businesses, community groups, churches, clubs and societies – keep records of their interaction with each other and with individuals. Employee dossiers, client records, accounts and salary databases, share registers, policy and precedent files, the agenda, minutes and papers of decisionmaking or deliberative bodies and processes, drafts and internal memoranda, annual reports, taxation returns, project or research and development files, maps, plans and contracts all document an organisation's legal and financial obligations and entitlements as an employer, provider or receiver of goods and services, debtor or creditor and owner of property. They also document processes showing how transactions take shape, record administrative activities and business dealings, and account for the actions of the organisation. As with personal records, organisational records may be of short- or long-term value to the organisation that created them. Those of continuing value form the organisation's archives.

As these examples illustrate, records are the information by-products of social and organisational activity. They are defined by their contextuality and their transactionality, ie by their creation in the context of social or organisational activity, of human interaction. Records creation refers to the act of accumulating records or incorporating them into a recordkeeping system. For example, the records created by a bank might include

- originals of documents received, eg letters and completed forms from a customer relating to a loan request
- copies of documents made and dispatched, eg advice to the customer about the conditions of the loan and repayment statements
- copies and originals of documents circulating within the organisation, eg instructions to staff on processing and approving loans and reports to the Board on loans approved and their management.

In this example the documents on the customer's file, the instructions maintained by staff in procedural manuals to facilitate their work, or the reports incorporated in the minutes of the Board are records of lending activity created by the bank. Similarly, the customer might create records of her dealings with the bank by keeping copies of letters and forms sent to the bank, documents received from the bank, diary notes about the transaction and an electronic record on a personal computer (PC) spreadsheet package of repayments.

Key attributes of records of social and organisational activity are their links to their creator, the activity itself, and other records accumulated as part of the activity. First and foremost they provide evidence of the activity. Incidentally, they also provide a rich source of information about associated people, organisations, events and places. They are often unique and usually unpublished. They are most likely to be part of an accumulation of records, although they may also be discrete items. Table 1.2 briefly explores the derivation of the concepts of records and archives used in this chapter.

Table 1.2 What's in a Name?

Australian definitions of archives and records have been influenced by two at times contradictory traditions, represented by the eminent practitioners and writers, Jenkinson and Schellenberg.

When Jenkinson, former Deputy Keeper of Public Records in England, developed his classic definition of archives as particular types of documents, he was in fact defining what this chapter terms records of social and organisational activity, for he used the terms records and archives interchangeably. In 1948 he wrote

Archives are the Documents accumulated by a natural process in the course of the Conduct of Affairs of any kind, Public or Private, at any date; and preserved thereafter for Reference, in their own Custody, by the persons responsible for the affairs in question or their successors.

('The English Archivist: A New Profession', in *Selected Writings of Sir Hilary Jenkinson*, Alan Sutton, Gloucester, 1980. p. 237.)

Jenkinson's writings emphasised the evidentiary, transactional nature of archives and the part they play in the conduct of business, and therefore the importance of preserving their integrity and authenticity, powerful concepts which are highly relevant today.

A useful modern definition of the term document, which traditionally has referred to something written or inscribed that provided evidence or information on any subject, is provided by R. A. Brown. He defines a document as

1 some physical thing or medium
2 on or in which data are
3 more or less permanently recorded
4 in such a manner that data can subsequently be retrieved (with the proper equipment).

(*Documentary Evidence in Australia*, The Law Book Company, Sydney, 1988, p. 9.)

The American Schellenberg, an archivist with the National Archives and Records Administration, distinguished between records and archives on the grounds of currency, the act of selection and worthiness for preservation for research purposes. He defined records as

> all books, papers, maps, photographs or other documentary materials regardless of physical form or characteristics, made or received by any public or private institution in pursuance of its legal obligations or in connection with the transaction of its proper business and preserved or appropriate for preservation by that institution or its legitimate successor as evidence of its functions, policies, decisions, procedures, operations or other activities or because of the informational value of the data contained therein.

And archives as

> those records of any public or private institutions which are adjudged worthy of preservation for reference and research purposes and which have been deposited or have been selected for deposit in an archival institution.

(*Modern Archives*, University of Chicago Press, Chicago, 1956, p. 16.)

Schellenberg's demarcation tends to de-emphasise the evidentiary nature of archives by defining them primarily in terms of the acts of selection and transfer of custody.

In this chapter we build on Jenkinsonian concepts of the nature of archives to define records of social and organisational activity and use the term archives to denote records of social and organisational activity of continuing value, rejecting Schellenberg's notion of demarcation based on the acts of selection and transfer of custody.

In an electronic environment records could perhaps be defined as data in the context of activity.

As well as their relevance to the people and organisations that created them, records of social and organisational activity may be of short- or long-term value to the wider community – to other people and organisations or for broader social purposes.

Archives and the Information World

Together with other records of social and organisational activity, archives are a part of a wider world of information which includes oral traditions, the natural and built environment, natural objects, artefacts and works of art. Within this wider world of information, records of activity form one strand of recorded information. Librarians have specialised in another strand, ie materials with an imposed subject matter, basically designed for dissemination.

These are information products brought into being to inform, to perpetuate knowledge, to entertain, or to convey opinions, ideas and feelings. They too can be in any media or format, but they are more likely to be discrete items and they are usually produced in multiple copies, published, broadcast or otherwise distributed via mass communication channels. Examples include monographs, journals, newspapers, magazines, radio and television productions, commercial films, videotapes and sound recordings, novels, plays and anthologies, and commercial databases on-line or on compact disk (CD). Table 1.3 compares the origin, purpose and characteristics of the records or information by-products of activity with those of information products.

The distinction between records of activity and information products is often not clear-cut. Literary manuscripts, eg outlines, notes and drafts of published works on paper or wordprocessing files accumulated by an author in the course of producing a novel, may be considered to be records of activity, information by-products of the creative activity, evidence of the author's 'business at hand'. Copies of the published work are information products, consciously authored and designed for dissemination. Similar distinctions can be made between unedited film and the commercial product or television news broadcast. A certain amount of crossover also occurs between these two strands of recorded information. For example, in the process of drafting and making legislation, records of the activity accumulate, including copies of successive drafts, Bills and Acts. The copies of the published Bills and Acts accumulated on file in the Parliamentary Drafting Office have become part of the records of the activity. Master sets of newspapers accumulated by a newspaper office or master tapes of television productions accumulated by a television station may also be considered to have become records of the publishing or broadcasting activity. On the other hand, records of activity may be incorporated into an information product, eg through the publication of a diary, personal correspondence or selected records of a government or business activity, or the inclusion of a home video in a television news broadcast.

Records of activity often have a special relationship to consciously authored information products. Access to the case records of a government department, the minutes of the Board, a laboratory's records of experiments, or a municipal council's archives provide sources for and a means of verifying or validating the information presented in a published ministerial press release, the company's annual report, the scientific article and the local history book.[1]

Table 1.3 Two Strands of Recorded Information

	Information Products	Information By-Products of Activity
Origin	Consciously authored with imposed subject matter, including products of the imagination, creative mind, artistic spirit	Accumulated or created in the course of doing or transacting business, they are primarily records of, rather than about, social and organisational activity
Purpose	Designed for dissemination or publication; to inform, perpetuate knowledge, convey ideas, feelings and opinions; to entertain; to provide information about their subject	Facilitate activity or interaction of which they are a part; get the business at hand done; provide evidence of the activity and, incidentally, information about associated people, organisations, events and places
Significant relationships	Links to author/producer, subject, publisher/ distributor/broadcaster Usually discrete items	Links to context: their creator, activity, other related records Usually part of an accumulation, larger group of related records
Media/format	Varied depending on available technology	Varied depending on available technology

Archives and Cultural Heritage

Archives are also part of our cultural heritage. They have signifi-cant relationships with other forms of evidence of past and pre-sent human activity, for example oral tradition, artefacts and the built environment. Our understandings of artefacts or the built environment may be enhanced or modified by archives relating to their manufacture and construction, their use and associated peo-ple or events. Similarly, interpretation of the evidence provided by archives may be enhanced or modified by the evidence of the built environment or artefacts. Oral history programs or projects aiming to record oral traditions are often supported by extensive research of other sources, and in turn add another dimension to their interpretation. People gain understanding from different forms of evidence in different ways, eg intellectually, experientially and through sensory perception. In Australia public historians who work outside academia, for historic buildings councils, muse-ums, archaeological surveys and national parks, have helped pio-neer the use of a mix of sources to research past activity and its current relevance. They are demonstrating how much richer our understanding can be if we draw on all available forms of evidence and explore their interrelationships.

The bringing together of archives and artefacts relating to a specific activity in an institution or at an associated historical site may be particularly evocative or appropriate for research purposes, provided proper archival, curatorial and site management programs are established. Locating sources together in this way is not the norm. Although not a general practice yet, it may be possible to document the links between them in the information systems of relevant institutions. Loan of related material for exhibitions is a more common way of demonstrating links.

Archives – Why Do We Keep Them?

Records of activity are valued and used by their creators and other individuals and organisations for a variety of current social and organisational purposes. They enable informed planning and decisionmaking, and support continuity, consistency and effectiveness of human action. They are vehicles of communication and interaction. Society's current recordkeeping requirements or expectations are formalised in our legal system and in ethical codes of behaviour or practice. Records of activity provide evidence of rights, entitlements and obligations, and support the role of law enforcement agencies and the judiciary. In some cases they constitute legal instruments, eg a title or deed, adoption order, or committal document to a mental institution. They also support information reporting, audit, review and accountability mechanisms, including the role of society's watchdogs – Parliament, Royal Commissions, the Ombudsman, administrative appeals tribunals, auditors, and regulatory authorities. Thus, they play a vital social role. Above all they provide for continuity and accountability.

Some records of activity are preserved because of their continuing value to an individual or organisation as well as to society
- as long-term memory, enabling better quality planning, decisionmaking and action by providing for continuity, access to past experience, expertise and knowledge, and a historical perspective
- as a way of accessing the experience of others
- as evidence of continuing rights and obligations
- as instruments of power, legitimacy and accountability, facilitating social interaction and cohesion
- as a source for our understanding and identification of ourselves, our organisations and our society
- as vehicles for communicating political, social and cultural values.

Thus, they form part of the archives of an individual or organisation and more broadly are a part of the cultural heritage of society. For example, the archives of the Westpac Banking Corporation (formerly the Bank of New South Wales) are a vital resource for the Bank itself, but they also form part of the cultural heritage of the nation as the Bank is our oldest financial institution and has played a very significant role in the development of Australia.

Archives are not just made up of the records already in archival custody. In the example cited above, they include records already deposited in the Bank's archives, records identified as having continuing value but not yet deposited, and records yet to be appraised, ie assessed to determine whether or not they are of continuing value. For organisations still in existence, they can even be said to include records yet to be created.

Sometimes particular documents are selected for preservation because of a reverence for their age, or their association with famous events, people, objects or buildings. A few such documents become cultural icons of the sort that can be characterised as 'making us go weak at the knees'. It is easier to think of overseas examples – such as the Magna Carta or American Declaration of Independence – than of Australian ones. Perhaps James Cook's journal of his voyage to Australian shores, or inland explorers Burke and Wills' last letters qualify.

It has been estimated by archivists that less than 10% of records generated are preserved. Many of the records destroyed are no longer considered relevant or useful to their creators or society. However, for essentially economic reasons some records potentially of continuing value will be destroyed, particularly if they are created in large quantities. The overall percentage of records preserved is primarily determined by resourcing levels for archival programs, the ever-increasing quantities of records being created and the costs associated with preservation and future use. Appraisal of records to identify which to preserve is therefore concerned with relative not absolute values. Contextual issues, eg the significance of related purposes, functions and activities, as well as the importance of the records creators, are coming to play an important role. These considerations supplement analysis of the records themselves, such as their origin, form, purpose and use, their informational content and relationships with other records, as explored in Chapter 6. Records of core functions or business activities may be considered more valuable than housekeeping records; records of nuclear waste disposal or oil exploration more significant than records of personnel management. The records of decisionmaking boards or councils may be considered more valuable than those of an advisory committee, or those of headquarters more significant than those of a regional office. Some archivists now identify the key appraisal question as being what should we document as opposed to which records should we keep.[2] As social values change, so too do perceptions of the relevance and usefulness to society of different functions and activities, the importance of various records creators and the value of their records. For example, in our society the great men of history and their actions are no longer regarded as the predominant subjects of scholarship. Historians have become increasingly concerned with ordinary men and women and with grass roots activities. Appraisal decisions inevitably reflect the cultural and social biases of their times.

Archival Principles

For the reasons explored above, the meaning and value of archives derive from the social and organisational context in which they were created and used, and from their links with other records. Used or interpreted out of context, their significance is lost or compromised. Therefore, to provide for their continuing useability, archivists manage archives from their creation in ways which preserve their meaning and value as well as ensuring their long-term physical survival.

Sir Hilary Jenkinson identified the moral and physical defence of the archives as being the archivist's primary duty. By moral defence he meant that archives must be cared for in ways that safeguard their authenticity and preserve their context and links to other records – and hence ensure their useability, their capacity to fulfil the administrative, legal and social roles defined above. By physical defence he meant the physical care and security required for long-term preservation.

Jenkinson's dictum has significant implications for the appraisal and selection of records of continuing value and for issues of transmission, custody and ownership as well as for their management in archival custody.

In their moral defence of the archives, early archivists established two interconnected principles which continue to guide the management of archives today, particularly the processes which document the records and their context and the development of systems for their physical and intellectual control, including their arrangement and description, storage and preservation. This in turn has a significant influence on the construction of archival finding aids and guides.

The two principles are those of provenance and original order. The principle of provenance is closely associated with the notion of *respect des fonds*, ie with respecting the integrity of the whole body of records of continuing value of an organisation or individual. It therefore relates to the preservation of the context of the records, that is their links to purpose, function and activity, to the individual or parts of an organisation which created them, and to other records created by that individual or within that organisation. As defined earlier in this chapter, the term 'created' is here used to refer to the act of accumulating records or incorporating them into a recordkeeping system. Thus, records created within an organisation usually comprise copies of documents made and dispatched, originals of documents received and both originals and copies of documents circulating within the organisation. Historically, *respect des fonds* and adherence to the provenance principle were achieved by keeping the body of records of continuing value of an organisation or individual together physically following transfer to archival custody. The archives of one organisation were not mixed or combined with that of another. In some cases application of the principle of provenance resulted in the records of an organisation being kept physically in ways which reflected organisational structures and recordkeeping practices. In modern systems the context of the records is often preserved 'on paper' or intellectually by describing the archives, their administrative and organisational context, related purposes, functions and activities as well as recordkeeping processes and the interrelationships between records. It is possible to picture records in the centre of an ever-widening series of circles, representing their systems environment, organisational setting, and social context.

The principle of original order involves keeping records in the order in which they were accumulated as they were created, maintained or used, and not rearranging them according to some imposed subject, numerical, chronological or other order. Such rearrangement may suit the needs of one group of users, but not another. It may compromise the integrity of the records and destroy or mask the evidence provided by their original arrangements and juxtapositioning. Keeping records in their original order also facilitates access using their own indexes and registers. Determining original order is not always straightforward. Some records become disordered after they are no longer needed for current purposes. Some have never been kept in a systematic way. This may be particularly the case with personal papers. However, even where records are kept in a systematic and highly organised way, they may be rearranged as changes occur in organisational structures or in the way an organisation does business. What stage in the creation, accumulation, rearrangement and use of records should then be captured in the archival arrangement? This question is increasingly being resolved by using the last active order or order in which the records are found or transferred to the archives as the basis for arranging the records, and describing all stages in guides and finding aids.

The guiding principles for archival work can be contrasted with those which inform the work of librarians. As they have dealt mainly with consciously authored information products with the purpose and characteristics outlined in Table 1.1, librarians have developed collection-building techniques based on knowledge of the publishing world and subject specialisations, sophisticated bibliographic and reference tools ideally suited to the discrete items they manage, and knowledge of their clients' needs and usage of material. Archivists have developed different approaches centred in 'the indissoluble relationship of an activity to its records'.[3] Provenance-based archival systems of arrangement and description preserve context and relationships because they are essential to the integrity and future useability of the archives. In Australia the development of the record series system by Australian Archives represented a substantial achievement in this area, in particular because of its capacity to capture rich contextual information and complex relationships – of records to their creators, between records creators, and between the records themselves – through time.[4] Moreover, the strategies and processes, developed in association with the system to document the records and their contexts, are directed at capturing contextual and records-related information while the records are being created and used for current purposes. The system is now widely used in a variety of modified forms throughout Australia and New Zealand.

To sum up, the meaning of records rests not only in their information content or text. It also stems from contextual information about them, eg who created them, in relation to what activity or as part of what transaction, who authorised them, how they were transmitted and when they were received. Consider also the information conveyed by the form or structure of a letter, title, deed, diploma, will or statement of accounts and the significance of links to other records – eg the relationship between a letter and its reply, the sequence of documents that make up a legal brief, and the accumulation of case notes that record patient treatment. Through the application of the principles of provenance and original order to the arrangement and description of records, archivists have aimed to enable users to interpret archives in context and to allow records to 'speak' to users directly from the past:

> The Archivist's career ... is one of service. He exists in order to make other people's work possible, unknown people for the most part and working very possibly on lines equally unknown: some of them perhaps in the quite distant future and upon lines as yet unpredictable. His Creed, the Sanctity of Evidence; his Task, the Conservation of every scrap of Evidence attaching to the Documents committed to his care; his Aim, to provide, without prejudice or afterthought, for all who wish to know, the Means of Knowledge.[5]

These are noble sentiments expressed by Sir Hilary Jenkinson in 1948 in the language and stereotypes of another age, but nevertheless they capture the spirit of what was then a new profession.

Archives and Users – Bridging the Gap

Archives are consulted by a wide range of direct users, such as historians, genealogists, educationalists, students, journalists, filmmakers, geophysicists, environmentalists, individuals concerned with their rights and entitlements, Royal Commissions and Boards of Inquiry, professional researchers and archivists as well as records creators. These direct users serve as communication channels to indirect users in their wider communities who read the newspaper articles, reports and history books, study the published collections of documents and family trees, watch films and documentaries, learn in the classroom, benefit from the research results or use them to prove rights and entitlements or lobby governments or businesses, visit an exhibition or participate in a workshop.

To enable better retrieval and therefore to provide for more effective continuing use, archivists need to bridge the gap between archives and users more effectively than they have in the past. Although arrangement and description practices based on the principles of provenance and original order have successfully preserved contextual links to records creators and other related records, they have not always captured links to related purposes, functions and activities, or their broader social context. Moreover it has been argued that systems that use these links – in particular the relationship between an activity and its records – to retrieve information about relevant records could provide far better tools for the users of archives.[6] Users approach archives with information needs that are usually presented as a query about a subject, person, place or event. The archivist bridges the gap between the user and the archives by linking the query to information in guides and finding aids about organisations or people who were engaged in activities that would have generated relevant records. For example, a family historian may want to find out more about a relative rumoured to have been placed in a mental asylum in the 1860s. The archivist links this query to the organisation responsible for the activity of committing people to such institutions at that time – and thence to the records created by that organisation. The records of committal will reveal the name of the asylum itself – and this information in turn will lead to the case record of the relative. All of these links – between a user's query based on subject, person, place or event and the relevant activity, the records creator and the records – are not always captured in the archival system of guides and finding aids. In these circumstances the intermediary role of the archivist is critical, as discussed further in Chapter 10.

Archivists can build better bridges, for example by incorporating into their systems purpose, function or activity-based approaches, enhancing provenance-based guides with subject, form of record, name and place indexes, developing guides on selected subjects or themes or for particular types of users. We can also get to know our users and their needs better and develop our understanding of their information-seeking behaviour. We can promote better informed and wider use of archives by a range of user education and public programs as described in Chapter 11.

Archives in the Electronic Age

The electronic age brings new challenges and opportunities for archivists in their moral and physical defence of records of continuing value and in providing for continuing use. In a paper environment, information provided by the content of records, their form and structure, their links to other records and much other contextual information is physically present in the records themselves or their association with other records. This is not the case in electronic systems. For example, in electronic mail systems the form and structure of a document and its links to other documents are not physically present, but result from software applications. One of the greatest challenges for archivists is to capture and preserve the information content and contextual information of continuing value in electronic systems and to provide for long-term accessibility and useability. Non-custodial arrangements in which electronic records of continuing value are kept alive in their organisational and systems context, rather than being transferred to archival custody, are being explored as a possible way of meeting this challenge.[7] In Australia the Australian Archives, the Australian Society of Archivists (ASA) and the Australian Council of Archives (ACA) are jointly playing a pioneering role in exploring ways to meet the challenges and take advantage of the opportunities that electronic recordkeeping provides.

The new technology applied to systems that archivists use to describe records and their contexts has considerably enhanced their capacities and enables more powerful provenance-based retrieval. The application of artificial intelligence and expert systems may provide the means of building into archival systems the inferential process archivists use to link user queries to activities, organisations and people, and thence to the records they generate.

Archival Programs and Their Organisational Context

Archival programs operate in a wide range of organisational contexts and institutional settings, from the archival authorities of federal, state and local government to manuscript libraries, university, school and church archives, community archives and the archives of businesses and other private sector organisations. They can be broadly categorised as

- large centralised government programs which operate in a 'captive field', ie they are given legislative responsibilities for the public records and/or archives of specified agencies of federal, state or local government
- in-house archives which operate in business or community organisations or within individual government agencies (usually under some sort of agreement with the central archival authority) and care for the archives of their parent organisations and related records
- collecting archives which solicit deposits or donations from a number of sources relating to a specific region or location, subject or activity, media or format
- any combination of the above.

Table 1.4 provides examples of these types of archival programs.

Another less common type of archival program is the clearinghouse operation exemplified by the Australian Science Archives Project, which maintains a register of information about the archives of science in Australia and acts as an archival broker, eg arranging the deposit of the archives of individual scientists in suitable collecting institutions. There are also a number of commercial archival operations offering consultancy services ranging from archival processing and documentation of records and their contexts to storage and preservation.

Some archival programs stand alone, ie they are undertaken by dedicated institutions or sections. Ideally, centralised government programs at national and state level should operate independently as do the Australian Archives and most state government archival authorities. Some in-house operations and collecting archives, particularly those associated with the universities, also stand alone in that they take the form of an identifiable administrative unit. Other archival programs are closely associated with state and local libraries, museums or historical societies, typically the manuscript sections of the national and state libraries, some municipal archives and local history collections, and the archival programs of the Australian War Memorial and the Performing Arts Museum (Victoria). In-house programs may be linked to the parent organisation's corporate services, special library, information or records management unit, or the public relations area.

Archives are not usually transferred to an archival institution, building or area dedicated to their preservation until they are no longer needed for everyday business. However, this does not mean that archival programs are concerned with records only after they are transferred. Many archivists now feel it is imperative to be involved even before the creation phase to ensure the preservation and future integrity and useability of records of continuing value. There are increasingly compelling reasons for early appraisal, preservation and action to document the records in their context.

The phenomenal growth in the quantities of records created, particularly since the end of World War II, necessitates early identification of records of continuing value. Delaying appraisal and disposal action until records are semi-current or inactive – ie no longer needed for current purposes – results in totally unmanageable backlogs. The application of modern technology to information and communications systems is revolutionising recordkeeping. Because of the threats associated with the fragile and vulnerable media, hardware obsolescence and the possibility that in some cases records of activity are not actually captured by the system, archivists need to be involved in system design and development. Action to document the records and their context – the records creators and related functions and activities as well as recordkeeping processes and systems – is also much more effective at the time records are being created and used for current purposes. Unless archival skills are applied early, the survival and quality of future archives are jeopardised. This is particularly the case in situations in which records management programs are poorly developed or non-existent.

Archival program activities include
- developing standards and guidelines on records creation and maintenance, eg on archival requirements relating to electronic recordkeeping systems, on media issues such as the use of recycled paper and archival microfilming standards, or on storage conditions
- developing and applying ambit, acquisition or collection policies to define the types of activities and records the program covers
- collection, analysis and incorporation into archival information systems of information about the records and their context in order to meet the needs associated with appraising records, managing records of continuing value, preserving their integrity and providing for their future use
- appraisal action to identify significant functions, activities and records creators, and related records of continuing value
- disposal guidance or regulation, including provision for transfer or deposit at certain times or in specified media
- accessioning records, ie arranging their transfer or deposit and formally accepting them into archival custody

- arranging and describing records already in custody
- storing and preserving records in custody
- implementing access policy
- providing reference or user services
- outreach and public programs.

Most of these activities can involve the archivist with the records long before they are transferred to archival custody. Indeed, as outlined above, in the electronic age we may be moving into a non-custodial role as attempts to transfer electronic records may threaten their integrity and useability.

Archival programs need to be managed with a clear direction and vision. Their success also depends on securing and managing purposefully the necessary resources – money, people and their expertise, appropriate technology, equipment and specially designed accommodation. Chapter 2 deals with these issues in greater detail.

Table 1.4 Examples of Archival Programs in Australia

Type of Program	Example	Acquisition Focus
Centralised Government	Australian Archives (regional offices in all states and territories)	Commonwealth government records
	Archives Office of New South Wales	NSW government records
	State Records (South Australia)	SA and local government records
In-house	Australian Broadcasting Corporation (ABC) Radio Archives	ABC Radio sound records
	Commonwealth Scientific and Industrial Research Organisation (CSIRO) Archives	CSIRO records
	Parliament of New South Wales Archives	Records of both houses, their committees and administration
	City of Melbourne Archives	Council's records
	Marrickville Municipal Council Archival Reference Centre	Council's records
	University of Queensland Archives	University's records
	Royal Perth Hospital	Hospital's records
	Broken Hill Proprietary (BHP) Ltd. Archives	Company records
	Coles Myer Ltd. Archives	Company records
	Westpac Banking Corporate Group Archives and Records	Group's records
	Royal Australasian College of Surgeons Archives	College's records
	Lutheran Church of Australia Archives	Church's records

(cont/...)

	Wesley Central Parish Mission Archives	Wesley Church and Central Parish Mission records
	Guildford Grammar School	School's records
Collecting	Australian War Memorial	Records of the fighting forces
	National Film and Sound Archive	Film and sound recordings
	Latrobe Library (Victoria) — Australian Manuscripts Collection	Records of history and development of Victoria
	John Oxley Library (Queensland) — Manuscripts and Business Records Collection	Records re regional, political, economic and social history of Queensland
	Performing Arts Museum (Victoria)	Records of the performing arts and popular entertainment
	Public Libraries (throughout Australia)	Local history collections
	The Noel Butlin Archives Centre, ANU	Records of business and labour
	Australian Jewish Historical Society (Victoria)	Records re Jews in Australia, New Zealand and the Pacific
	Historical Societies (throughout Australia)	Records re local history
Combined	Archives Office of Tasmania	Records of government, business, community groups and individuals re development and history of the State/Territory
	Northern Territory Archives Service	
	State Archives of Western Australia	
	Geelong Historic Records Centre	Local government, business and community records of Geelong and district
	Botany Municipal Library Service	Botany Council records and records of local community
	Dennis Wolanski Library and Archives of Performing Arts	Sydney Opera House records and records of performing arts, music, theatre and dance
	Charles Sturt University Regional Archives	Records of the University and the Riverina region (including State and local government as well as private records)
	Catholic Diocese of Toowoomba	Diocesan records and records re Southern Queensland

For a more comprehensive listing, see Burnstein Susan et al., *Directory of Archives in Australia*, ASA, Canberra, 1992.

Archival Programs: Relationship to Records Management Programs

Both records managers and archivists are involved in managing records of social and organisational activity. As we have seen, archivists are responsible for the identification and preservation in context of records of continuing value for future use. Records managers are primarily concerned with the complete, accurate and reliable documentation of organisational activity for current purposes. They operate in a complex environment involving the interplay of an organisation's interests, the rights and entitlements of its clients and employees, and its legal and social obligations. They are also concerned with selective retention and destruction of records in circumstances of massive information overload.

A clearer idea of what this role involves can emerge from exploring a particular case, eg managing the records of a community services or health care organisation. In such an organisation the records manager would develop and implement policies, systems and procedures to support

- the capture of complete, accurate and reliable information needed for quality decisionmaking and service delivery, eg in relation to a counselling service, this might involve developing a system that adequately documents client histories and enables counsellors to record their interaction with clients
- communication within and outside the organisation, eg between staff on patient treatment, or between staff and clients about the services being provided
- the retrieval of relevant information, eg to enable decisions to be made about future treatment based on knowledge of the treatment already provided
- authorised access on the one hand and the protection of confidential information and client privacy on the other, eg through the development of appropriate information security procedures
- compliance with legal recordkeeping requirements, eg in relation to drug administration or child protection legislation
- regulated records disposal involving destruction of information no longer needed and the survival of information of continuing value, eg providing for information survival through changes in automated systems and for secure and efficient records storage
- the means of accounting for the organisation's activities and service delivery, both to individual clients and to the general public, eg its financial management via proper accounting systems with audit trails, or the adequacy of case management or patient treatment via the keeping of complete, accurate and reliable records of action.

Although records management skills are applied for the current purposes of public administration or corporate business and archival skills are applied for purposes associated with the future use of records of continuing value, it can be argued that, operating in tandem, records managers and archivists can better serve both current and future purposes.

This is the rationale behind the bringing together organisationally of records management and archival programs, eg at the University of Queensland and Monash University. It also under-

pins the involvement of government archival authorities in records management programs in their own right, ie to serve records management ends relating to the current use of records. Supported on the grounds of economies of scale and the public records expertise of their staff, most government archival authorities are involved to some extent in the following records management programs
- regulatory activity and standard setting
- authorisation of disposal (including destruction, preservation as part of the archives, transfer of custody)
- consultancy, advisory and training services
- secondary storage services.

Such activities are closely linked in the public records tradition to the notion that ethical recordkeeping practices that ensure the completeness, accuracy, reliability and useability of public records, and regulated disposal action that prevents records from being destroyed without proper evaluation, authorisation and documentation are crucial elements in modern democratic societies, providing for public accountability and underpinning freedom of information and privacy legislation. In some companies they are linked to aspects of corporate culture which emphasise the obligations and responsibilities of directors and employees to comply with legal requirements and quality systems standards and to be accountable for their actions in accord with standards of corporate behaviour and business ethics.

Although these activities are not the subject matter of this book, they do form a significant part of the context of some archival programs.

The Archival Profession

Institutions and people have cared for archives in Australia for well over a century. However, the archival profession here is relatively young. Three of the most significant developments in the profession have occurred within the last two decades. First, postgraduate archival education programs have been established at the University of New South Wales in 1973, the University of Melbourne (then the Melbourne College of Advanced Eduction) in 1985, and Monash University in 1988. Second, the Australian Society of Archivists, founded in 1975, has grown and matured as the independent professional body representing archivists. Third, the Australian Council of Archives (initially known as the National Archival Forum) was formed in July 1985 as the national consultative body which represents and promotes the interests of archival institutions in Australia. It provides a framework for cooperative action on a range of matters, including the management of electronic records, the collection and dissemination of information about archival institutions and issues, and the funding of archival programs.

The Australian Society of Archivists Incorporated

Because the profession in Australia is small and scattered over a large continent and many archivists work alone or in small archives, communication and cooperation with other practitioners to share ideas and experience and to act jointly to promote archival goals, develop standards and codes of practice and foster links with the international community are vital.

For these purposes archivists established the Australian Society of Archivists (ASA) in 1975. (Before 1975 the interests of archives and archivists were represented by the Archives Section of the Library Association of Australia, the Business Archives Council and the Sydney Archivists' Group.) The ASA is a national body with a branch in each state (except the Northern Territory). It is governed by a Council of 10 elected members, including the Executive which manages the day-to-day affairs. Each branch elects a committee on an annual basis to organise branch activities. The ASA also has a number of special interest groups which are designed to bring together members with similar interests, affiliations and challenges, namely the school archives, university and college archives, archives of science, medicine and technology, collecting archives, business archives and local government groups. The ASA's Corporate Plan identifies its mission as being 'to promote the keeping, care and use of archives'. Its objectives are presented in full in Table 1.5.

The Society has four categories of membership:

- Professional membership, which is open to any graduate employed as an archivist for two years, or to any graduate also holding a post-graduate professional qualification recognised by the Council who has been employed as an archivist for one year.
- Associate membership, which is open to anyone supporting the Society's objectives.
- Honorary membership which is conferred in recognition of services to the profession or the Society.
- Institutional membership, which is open to archival and other institutions recognised by the Council.

The ASA's activities are designed to involve and attract members. Members receive the ASA's journal, *Archives and Manuscripts*, twice a year and the ASA's newsletter, the *ASA Bulletin*, every two months. The ASA holds an annual general meeting and branches hold regular meetings, including lectures, workshops, visits, discussions and social events, to discuss issues of concern or interest and to bring members together.

Corporate planning targets for 1991–95 include setting up a secretariat, developing a code of ethics, establishing standards for archival education and training and course accreditation processes, joint action with the ACA on electronic records, liaising with related professional groups in the information and

Table 1.5 Objectives of the Australian Society of Archivists Inc.

The ASA's basic objectives are to
1 promote by all available means the preservation and care of archives
2 establish and maintain communication and cooperation amongst archivists, the institutions in which they work and the users of archives
3 establish and maintain standards of archival practice and administration and of professional conduct among archivists
4 establish standards of archival qualifications and professional training
5 encourage research into any area of archival practice and administration and the care and use of archives
6 publish a journal and other material relating to the objects of the Society
7 provide a means of collecting, coordinating and disseminating information relevant to the practice, status and problems of the archival profession
8 promote among the general public and special groups an understanding of the nature of archives and their value
9 encourage the efficient and responsible use of archives
10 promote a professional identify among archivists and to advance their professional standing and welfare
11 cooperate with other organisations and groups having complementary objectives, particularly in the fields of conservation, research and records management
12 provide an authoritative voice on matters of archival concern.

SOURCE: Australian Society of Archivists Incorporated, *Rules*, April 1992, Part 1, Rule 3.

cultural heritage fields to identify shared goals and areas for cooperative action, developing lobbying techniques and resources, creating a national archives policy framework and continuing to build links with the international community and the local region.

The importance of the ASA to individuals and institutions is generally recognised. It is our vehicle for communication, support, learning/teaching, socialising and campaigning.

Conclusion

Understanding the nature of archives and why they are of continuing value and use to our society forms the basis for the practice of keeping archives. This book offers practical information and guidance about archival work and its challenges. Through involvement in the ASA or your institution's membership of the ACA, you can develop strong personal, professional and institutional networks which will provide support in your continuing professional development. Through educational programs, participation in conferences and workshops and the professional literature, you will continue to grow and learn. In turn you will be able to share your ideas and experiences and work cooperatively with colleagues to better meet the many challenges facing our profession, one which is centrally relevant to the evolution of our society.

Endnotes

1 The section on Archives and the Information World builds on concepts presented by Francis Blouin and David Bearman, in particular in Bearman, David, 'Documenting Documentation', in *Archivaria*, 34, Summer 1992, pp. 33–49; Blouin Francis X Jr, 'The Relevance of Archival Theory and Practice for Library Education: An Argument for a Broader Vision', in *Journal of Library Administration*, 7/2–3, 1986, p. 158.

2 Cook, Terry, 'Mind Over Matter: Towards a New Theory of Archival Appraisal', in Barbara L. Craig (ed.), *The Archival Imagination: Essays in Honour of Hugh A. Taylor*, Association of Canadian Archivists, Ottawa, 1992.

3 Blouin, op. cit. p. 158.

4 Scott, Peter J., 'The Record Group Concept: A Case for Abandonment', in *The American Archivist*, 29/4, October 1966, pp. 493–504.

5 Jenkinson, Hilary, 'The English Archivist: A New Profession', in Alan Sutton (ed.), *Selected Writings of Sir Hilary Jenkinson*, Alan Sutton, Gloucester, 1980, p. 258.

6 Bearman, David and Lytle, Richard, 'The Power of the Principle of Provenance', in *Archivaria*, 21, Winter 1985–86, pp. 14–27.

7 Bearman, David (ed.), *Archival Management of Electronic Records*, Archives and Museum Informatics Technical Report No. 13, 1991. On the concept of a non-custodial role for archivists, see in particular Bearman's 'An Indefensible Bastion: Archives as a Repository in the Electronic Age', pp. 14–24.

Further Reading

Introduction to Archives

Acland, Glenda, 'Archivist – Keeper, Undertaker or Auditor', in *Archives and Manuscripts,* 19/1, May 1991, pp. 9–15.

Bradsher, James Gregory (ed.), *Managing Archives and Archival Institutions*, University of Chicago Press, Chicago, 1989. A general text on archival administration.

Craig, Barbara L. (ed.), *The Archival Imagination: Essays in Honour of Hugh A. Taylor*, Association of Canadian Archivists, Ottawa, 1992. State-of-the-art essays on archival issues.

Cox, Richard J, *Managing Institutional Archives: Foundational Principles and Practices*, Greenwood Press, New York, 1992. Advice on basic functions of institutional archival work, building internal and external support, and cooperative opportunities, with case studies illustrating problems and challenges.

Daniels, Maygene, and Walch, Timothy (eds), *A Modern Archives Reader: Basic Readings on Archival Theory and Practice*, National Archives Trust Fund Board, Washington DC, 1984. A collection of 'classic essays' and modern revisions from the archival literature.

Dearstyne, Bruce W., *The Archival Enterprise: Modern Archival Principles, Practices and Management Techniques*, American Library Association, Chicago, 1992. An introduction to theory and practice.

Eastwood, Terry, 'Reflections on the Development of Archives in Canada and Australia', in *Papers and Proceedings of the 7th Biennial Conference of the Australian Society of Archivists Inc.*, Hobart, 1989.

McKemmish, S. & Upward, F., 'The Archival Document: A Submission to the Inquiry into Australia as an Information Society', in *Archives and Manuscripts*, 19/1, May 1991.

O'Toole, James M., *Understanding Archives and Manuscripts*, Archival Fundamentals Series, Society of American Archivists, Chicago, 1990. An introduction to the nature of recorded information, its use and management.

Classic Texts on Archival Principles and Practice

Jenkinson, Sir Hilary, *A Manual for Archive Administration*, 2nd edn, Percy Lund, Humphries, & Co., London, 1966. A revised version of the original 1922 edition in which Jenkinson explored the nature of archives and established standards for archival practice.

Schellenberg, T. R., *Modern Archives: Principles and Techniques*, University of Chicago Press, Chicago, 1956. Application of European archival principles and theory to American practice, in particular to the voluminous modern archives of government.

Archival and Records Management Journals

Archivaria, the journal of the Association of Canadian Archivists.

Archives and Manuscripts, the journal of the Australian Society of Archivists.

Archives and Museum Informatics, a journal which provides detailed analysis and up-to-date information in the areas of archival automation and electronic records.

Archivum, a publication of the International Council on Archives.

The Informaa Quarterly, the journal of the Records Management Association of Australia.

Journal of the Society of Archivists, a British Periodical.

Records Management Quarterly, the journal of the Association of Records Managers and Administrators.

The American Archivist, the journal of the Society of American Archivists.

The Series System

Healy, Susan, 'The classification of modern government records in England and Australia' in *Journal of the Society of Archivists*, 11/1 & 2, January & April 1990, pp. 21–26.

Hurley, C. and Smith, H., 'Developments in Computerised Documentation Systems at the Public Record Office of Victoria', in *Archives and Manuscripts*, 17/2, November 1989, pp. 165–183.

Scott, P., Smith, C. and Finlay, G., 'Archives and Administrative Change', parts 1–5 in *Archives and Manuscripts*, 7/3, August 1978, 9/1, September 1981.

Simes, Cheryl, 'The Record Group is dead – long live the Record Group', in *New Zealand Archivist*, 2/1, reproduced in *Archives and Manuscripts*, 20/1, pp. 19–24.

Australian Society of Archivists, 'Comment on ICA Statement of Principles regarding Archival Description; First Version Revised', Canberra, 1992.

For more information about the Australian Society of Archivists Inc., contact: The Secretary, PO Box 83, O'Connor ACT, Australia 2601

2 | Getting Organised

Anne-Marie Schwirtlich

Caring for Archives

Archives are those records of social and organisational activity preserved because of their continuing value. All programs which care for records are therefore important and play a significant part in the national archival network. Thus, it is important that each member of the archival community, large or small, independent or part of a museum, library, or historical society, be efficiently organised and managed.

Archives by their very nature have value and currency far beyond the lifetime of their custodians, creators and donors. In managing archives we accept that we have long-term legal and moral obligations to the holdings, the donors, the parent organisation, and the researchers. It is not desirable to initiate any archival program on the basis of short-term funding allocation and staffing provisions. Similarly, personal enthusiasm, although commendable, obviously cannot sustain an archival program in perpetuity. The collection and care of archives need to be undertaken in a responsible, responsive, thoughtful and committed way.

The key element of responsible management of the archives is a clear acceptance of long-term obligations to the records, their creators and their users which includes providing

- continuity of care and resources
- continuity of custody.

This chapter reflects these concerns. It outlines the practical considerations and decisions that are involved and discusses some of the tools that are useful in managing archives.

Developing Policies, Plans and Procedures

Regardless of the project or the nature of the work for which you are responsible, you will be more effective and efficient if you plan, systematise and document your work. Since archives deal with material that is unique, valuable and of public interest, it is particularly important for us to be orderly.

Archives work involves performing diverse functions in the context of competing priorities. Therefore, developing policies, plans and procedures to structure the archives and to ensure a consistent and steady approach is important. These tools provide a basis and checklist for work activities so as to ensure that each time a certain task is undertaken it is completed in a uniform and objective way. Aside from ensuring consistency, this is a way of codifying information and setting standards which serve as lucid and informative documents for the people who join or succeed us in our work.

The Archives Policy

The first and fundamental organisational tool is the archives policy. Archival programs may be large government programs, in-house archives, collecting archives, clearing-house operations or commercial archives (see Chapter 1). It is very important that the archives has a clear role within the organisational context of which it is a part and that its objectives should be clearly and concisely set out. The means of achieving this is to draft an archival policy. This document is a broad written statement outlining the purpose, objectives and conditions which define the scope of archival activities, the authority under which they operate and the services offered to clients.

What is the Archives Policy Designed To Achieve?

The archives policy is designed to achieve several things:
- It is a public statement of purpose and objectives for the archives program.
- It defines the scope of the archives collections and establishes general conditions for access to them.
- It provides a legal and authoritative basis for the archivist to exercise all of the powers and perform all of the duties, responsibilities and functions with which he or she is invested by the governing body of the parent institution.
- It facilitates consistency, uniformity and impartiality in the procedures and conditions adopted for the management and use of the archives.

Drafting an Archives Policy

The formulation of an archives policy should be undertaken as soon as possible after the decision to establish an archives program is made and its development should continue for some months after the actual archival work commences. During this formative period it is desirable to perform all archival services, but at a minimal level so that the archivist can develop and test new policies and forms and procedures without being swamped with work. The policy document must be developed in conjunction with, and have the approval of, the governing authority of the parent organisation where relevant, or other interested bodies. This is because it is vital for the policy to have the widest possible support if it is to fulfil its role as the touchstone of all archival activity.

Nature and Components of an Archival Policy

The archives policy must be comprehensive and general, not particular, in its approach. It is analogous with the overall constitution of an organisation as opposed to the more prescriptive by-laws. The archives policy sets out the broad philosophy and limits of the program and establishes the administrative machinery to operate it. Using the policy as a base, the archivist can design specific services and develop procedures and forms for accomplishing the work. The archives policy gives authority and protection to the archives and the archivist and should be cultivated widely.

A comprehensive archives policy will generally contain the following elements, though not all will be relevant to every archival program. It may be necessary to modify this comprehensive model archives policy for the particular circumstances of your individual organisation.

Authority of the Archives Policy Document. State that the archives policy document establishes the framework within which the archives program functions and that all practices and procedures must be in accordance with its provisions. State who should be involved and the general process for amending the archives policy document. The policy should be issued on official letterhead stationery and it should be signed or issued (and dated) by or on behalf of the governing body or chief executive officer.

Authority of the Archives. State the proper name of the archives and its host or parent organisation (if any), and set out the circumstances of the archives' establishment, ie the Archives of the University of the Antipodes was established by Resolution 3 of the University Council on 2 September 1980.

Purpose of the Archives. State the purposes which the archives serves within the parent organisation and in the wider community. In general these purposes fall into three categories: preservation of records, reference use of records, and promotion/appreciation of organisation and community heritage/history.

Definitions. Define selected terms so that all readers will understand the document fully. This section generally includes, but is not limited to, the following terms: records, archives, official and non-official records, active and inactive records, archivist, depositor, access, appraisal and disposal.

Administrative Setting of the Archives Program. Explain the following aspects of the administrative context within which the archives operates:

(a) *Position within the Organisational Context.* Describe the relationship between the archives and the organisational units which supervise or cooperate/liaise with it.

(b) *Relationship with an Advisory Body (if any).* Describe the composition of the Archives Advisory Body, the method for selecting members of the body, and the powers of any advisory group giving advice on the overall direction of the archives program and interpretation of policy.

(c) *Position and Responsibilities of the Archivist.* State that the archives shall be cared for by a professional archivist. Describe the basis of authority delegated to the archivist. State to whom the archivist reports.

(d) *Obligations of Officers and Staff of the Parent Organisation to Cooperate with the Archives Program.* State that officers and staff shall cooperate with the archivist to ensure the following:

- No officer or staff member shall alienate, relinquish control over, destroy or dispose of records of the organisation without proper authorisation.
- Officers and staff are to follow the guidelines and utilise the procedures, forms and supplies authorised by the archives in carrying out its work (see 6 below).
- Officers and staff of the organisation are to seek the advice of the archivist in any matter affecting the quality and quantity of records produced by the organisation (ie record media, types and numbers of copies, computer applications, microfilming, storage location and equipment).

Scope and Nature of Archival Requirements. Define the scope and state the policy considerations for each of the following archival activities:

(a) *Acquisition.* This is an area that will be treated very generally in the overall policy as the details of what will be acquired and the conditions of acceptance are usually explained more fully in a separate acquisitions policy. However, it is necessary to state the responsibilities the archives has for acquiring the records of its parent organisation (by approved disposal schedules) and the records of outside persons or bodies (subject to archival appraisal and legal transfer of custody, title and rights). State that agreements for acquisition oblige the archives to care for records indefinitely and represent a major continuing commitment of resources. State that material acquired by the archives becomes its property to be administered as the archives sees fit, which includes the right of the archives to de-accession or dispose of material deemed non-archival. State that the process and conditions of acquisition must comply with guidelines and procedures devised by the archives (see Chapter 5, Managing the Acquisition Process, for discussion of the more detailed acquisitions policy statement).

(b) *Arrangement and Description.* State that all records brought into archival custody shall be arranged and described according to archival principles to the extent necessary to make them available for research. State that, in general, records that have not been processed cannot be used by researchers.

(c) *Preservation.* State that as the preservation of the archives is the basis for the archives program, every effort shall be made to provide the proper facilities, environment and resources to prolong the life of the records in custody.

(d) *Access to Archives.* The function of access, like that of acquisition, warrants a separate statement explaining in detail the conditions and processes for obtaining access to the archives and its holdings. The archives policy should state whether the archives is available to the public or only to specific groups. State that because of the unique and irreplaceable nature of the archives, all users must apply for an admitting document, usually a reader's ticket, and register their use of records from the collection. State that archival materials will be available for research under conditions that ensure their preservation and which comply with the requirements to respect confidentiality, privacy, and legal agreements with depositors. State that the archives' staff will administer access to the archives and its collections in accordance with sound archival principles, the available resources, their legal and ethical obligations and the physical integrity of the materials (see Chapter 10, Access and Reference Services).

(e) *Community Education.* Many archives have a commitment to promote an awareness and appreciation of the contribution the host institution (library, museum, business) has made, and makes, to the life of the wider community and a statement to that effect could be made here.

(f) *Management and Administration.* State that, in addition to its responsibility to manage the records of depositors, the archives also has an obligation to manage its own resources effectively and to document its work carefully, ie to measure and evaluate its effectiveness and to maintain and care for its own 'archives' documenting its work.

The creation of an archives policy document is a very demanding task, but one which, when successfully completed, is pivotal. The archives policy document forms the foundation of the archives program and becomes the basis for all projects and operations undertaken by, or in the name of, the archives. Within a strong and flexible framework, the archives program can evolve and develop, accommodating change and growth while maintaining a consistent philosophy and direction.

The Nature of the Archives Program

An archives program has several components. Many of these functions are discussed in detail in later chapters which explain the principles underpinning the work, the activities involved and the context in which they are undertaken. This chapter is concerned with the general organisation and balance among these components.

It needs to be emphasised that every archives has priorities. Few archival programs have their resources spread evenly across their functions. Every archivist has to make decisions about the order in which work is undertaken. The orientation of programs is dictated either by policy or by demand.

The general direction of the archives program should be set out in the archives policy. Consequently, work priorities should reflect this direction. For example, the archives of a company would have as its first priority the orderly transfer of the company's records and the comprehensive documentation of these transfers to enable quick retrieval of needed items. Arrangement, description and the preparation of extensive finding aids for the use of the public would not be of primary concern.

Compiling a list of priorities on the basis of the policy is a vital first step. Categorise functions as having either high, medium or low priority. Within each category identify the tasks that are involved and rank them in order of priority. This provides a clear idea of how resources should be committed. Then it is possible to decide what particular projects will get done within the next six months or year.

Organising the workload
• ensures that the most important projects are tackled first
• provides a sense of continuity rather than lurching from project to project

- provides a sense of accomplishment as projects are completed as planned.

Conflicts of priorities can arise. Take the instance of the company mentioned above. If there were a deluge of enquiries from the public, it would cause some diversion of resources from meeting the company's needs to assisting the public. Decisions would have to be made about which was more important and how resources could best be apportioned to meet the demands. Making these decisions requires familiarity with the workload of the archives, with the state of current projects, with those outstanding, and with the likely consequences if any are neglected.

How Do You Start?

Administering an archives involves managing five broad areas
- yourself
- the information needed to manage
- people
- financial resources
- facilities, equipment and stores.

Organising Yourself

Remember that self-management is the first step. Your personal resources, such as time and energy, are non-renewable and must be scheduled and focused on priorities if they are to maximise productivity.

Structure your time and establish a pattern that enables you to be most efficient. The following ideas may be of assistance, particularly if you work alone or with part-time assistance:

(a) Limit the hours that the archives is open to the public. This allows you uninterrupted time to
- process collections and answer research queries
- visit depositors or potential depositors
- schedule appointments and meetings.

(b) Arrange for the telephone to be answered. Telephone calls can be disruptive. Unanswered telephone calls can lead to disgruntled researchers and donors.

(c) Devise form letters for routine correspondence.

(d) Recognise that your metabolism affects your work. If you always feel sluggish after lunch either eat a light lunch or save repetitive and undemanding tasks for after lunch.

(e) Start each day with a clear idea of what you want to accomplish. Distinguish between the urgent and the important. Ensure that preoccupation with the urgent does not prevent achievement of the important.

(f) Attack daunting projects by dividing them into stages. It is easier to start and sustain a large project if you have a picture of the steps involved and can gain satisfaction from completing each step.

(g) Say NO to taking on jobs that are not part of, or of direct benefit to, the archival program.

Organising Your Information Resources

Ensure that the information necessary to support your work and decision-making processes is organised, up-to-date and readily accessible. This essential information will be both published and unpublished and falls into two broad categories

- administrative (helps to structure and coordinate work)
- technical (describes and discusses concepts and techniques for assessing and accomplishing professional tasks).

Table 2.1 itemises the sources of information that should be kept at hand.

Maintain your information in well identified folders, or well labelled shelves and cabinets. Documents, like procedures and instructions, should be current and comprehensive. Remove superseded and outdated documents promptly from your master set and either transfer them to the archives or destroy them.

Publications can pose a storage problem. Browsing through journals will alert you to articles that could be of use. It is possible to photocopy all potentially useful articles and file them. This takes time and the copies occupy space. It may be preferable to create a card or computer index in which you nominate subject headings, for example, 'Photographs', 'Maps', and slot in a card with all citation details for each article of interest.

Information and documentation about your own operations is vital. You must have available accurate and complete data about your administrative and archival activities. Whatever filing system you adopt or inherit, maintain it properly - you should make notes of developments, and file them immediately; and house your files safely and in order.

Developing Forms and Procedures

Developing a management system for an archives involves

- clearly defining each function of the archives
- listing the work activities necessary to carry out the function
- identifying and creating the forms and procedures needed to structure the work
- devising ways of measuring performance
- formulating the information to be distributed to clients using your services
- documenting and reporting your achievements.

Table 2.2 illustrates these steps in developing a management system for the function of arrangement and description.

The level of detail to which you develop your management system depends on the nature and complexity of your operation.

Table 2.1 Information for Managing

Administrative Information

Unpublished
- Organisation charts
- Statements of duties
- Administrative, legal and financial regulations
- Administrative instructions
- Organisation policies

Published
- Texts on budgeting, staffing, raising money

Technical Information

Unpublished
- Archives policy
- Archival procedures
- Archival forms
- Archival instructions
- Consolidated set of archival leaflets

Published
- Bibliographies
- Texts on archives and records management

Before you change anything find out how things are done at the moment. Ideally the status quo will be documented by existing policies, procedures and forms. If there are none, then prepare a document that describes the current practices as they are understood by persons associated with the program. Annotate it to show which systems or methods work properly and suggest improvements for those which do not.

You can then proceed further afield, eg read the available professional literature, consult colleagues and ask for guidance. You can look at how similar organisations do things and at their procedures, forms and systems. Most archival institutions are prepared to explain and to provide you with examples of their procedures and forms. The ASA and other professional bodies with members who work in related areas, such as the Museums Association of Australia, can either give you direct assistance or guide you to sources that will. However, you should not uncritically adopt another institution's archival practices. It is important to think about what you are seeking to do and to know the characteristics, capabilities and limitations of your institution. This enables you to compare your organisation with another and to

Table 2.2 Developing Documentation For Arrangement And Description

Define the Function
* The arrangement and description of archival material in order to discern, preserve (or restore) original order and to document this and key content and contextual points for researchers.

List the Activities Necessary To Carry Out the Function
* Examine new transfers/collections thoroughly
* Determine priority for arrangement and description
* Decide if any items need special storage
* Recommend if disposal of non-archival material is required
* Determine the level of arrangement and description to be undertaken
* Research the life of the person/organisation creating the records
* Identify the record series
* Arrange items – first on paper, then physically
* Inventory and describe the records
* Write the administrative history
* Prepare the finished descriptive inventory/guide

Identify and Create the Tools for Structuring the Work
* Arrangement and description policy and priorities
* Arrangement and description procedures
* Worksheets to record progress/information
* Series description sheets
* Plan for contents of finished descriptive inventory/guide

Measures and Statistics
* Number of series arranged
* Number of series described
* Number of descriptive inventories/guides prepared

Documenting and Reporting
* Keep records in order
* Prepare regular reports

Information for Clients
* Introductory leaflet on the principles of arrangement and description of archives with information about how this might shape their research strategy
* Finding aids: finished descriptive inventories/guides

determine how compatible or useful are its systems and practices.

For example, if you had responsibility for the archives of a small hospital and you were interested in organising your reference work, it would be advantageous to learn how the Mitchell Library organises its reference work. However, it would not necessarily be beneficial to use the Mitchell's forms and procedures. The Mitchell's systems are designed to cope with thousands of public enquiries which are dealt with by several staff, whereas your archives might serve specialist users, ie medical personnel, and have records of a confidential nature. Thus, the Mitchell's systems might be inappropriate for your reference needs.

The lesson is to gather and analyse all available information, and select and adopt only those features that are directly relevant. Test the new form or procedure for a while. When you are confident it is workable, incorporate it into your system.

Likewise, once you have introduced a form or procedure that is suitable, do not assume that it will work as intended. Evaluate its performance in use and be prepared to make modifications as required.

Managing Staff

Archival work is labour intensive, complex and detailed. These factors shape all staffing considerations. Assessment of needs for personnel and of people's capabilities should be made in the light of these factors. Administering staff involves

- recruiting
- training and development
- allocating responsibilities and projects
- staff evaluation.

Before any decision can be made about augmenting staff, it is necessary to know the following:

- Can your organisation acquire staff? If so, on what basis? (Can you afford to pay? Can you accept volunteers? Can you use people enrolled in work experience schemes?).
- Do you have the power to appoint people? If not, who does?
- What, if any, are the procedures for appointing people?

Equipped with this information you can identify whether you need more staff and of what type. To do this you need to assess

- how many staff you have
- what hours or on what basis they work
- what skills/areas of expertise they have
- what the archives program priorities and workload are
- how long/how many people it will take to accomplish various tasks.

A cautionary note: increasing staff is not the solution to all workload problems. An increase in staff entails more time spent on supervision and planning. It can strain accommodation and equipment and be counterproductive. In some situations modification of procedures and priorities will achieve a satisfactory result.

People often think that only paid appointments need to be carefully planned. This is not so. Many small archives depend heavily on volunteer labour. There are two reasons for taking care with any appointment:

* Archives are unique – anybody who works with them must be selected with care.
* Time spent on training is valuable – it should be invested wisely.

If you do recruit staff, you will need to develop

* a list of duties for the position/person
* a list of selection criteria
* an advertisement
* a list of questions you wish to ask applicants.

Formulating these will absorb some time and require close attention. They are important because they focus your requirements, streamline your search, and assist prospective applicants in deciding whether or not they are interested in and suitable for the vacancy. Moreover, they advertise your organising ability and your professional approach.

The list of duties is a schedule of the tasks the position undertakes and the responsibilities it carries. It can also indicate to

Table 2.3 Duty Statement Sample

Position Number: 42
Section: Archives
Supervises: Clerical Assistant

Sunshine Press Limited
Position Title: Assistant Archivist
Branch: Administration
Responsible to: Archivist
Duties: Assist the Archivist in carrying out the archives and records program. In the Archivist's absence assume responsibility for the archives program.

* Appraise records eligible for transfer to archives. Make recommendations on their suitability and any necessary disposal activity (30%)
* Negotiate and document the transfer of records (10%)
* Arrange and describe the archives in accordance with procedures and priorities (25%)
* Prepare finding aids (15%)
* Provide reference assistance to researchers – both public and from within the Press (12%)
* Identify items requiring conservation treatment (3%)
* Assist with other archival and administrative work as required (5%)

Approved: 22 January 1993

Table 2.4 Selection Criteria Sample

Sunshine Press Limited
Selection Criteria: Assistant Archivist (Position Number 42)

Knowledge
- Thorough grasp of archival principles and practices (Essential)
- Working knowledge of records management principles and practices (Essential)
- Familiarity with the principles and practices of conservation (Essential)
- Familiarity with the development and history of Australian printed news media (Desirable)

Attributes/Skills
- Good communication skills, both written and oral
- Ability to undertake and sustain complex research
- Eye for accuracy and detail
- Willingness to accept responsibility

Experience
- Two to three years' archival experience – preferably working with business archives

Qualifications
- Postgraduate Diploma in Archives Administration (or equivalent)
- Professional membership of the Australian Society of Archivists

Approved: 22 January 1993

---

whom the position is responsible and in turn who is responsible to the position. Every position, paid or volunteer, in the archives should have a list of duties. Table 2.3 is an example of a duty statement.

The document listing the selection criteria is the basis on which you will make the choice for filling the vacancy. The selection criteria set out the skills, abilities, knowledge, experience and personal qualities you seek. These criteria must relate to the duties listed on the duty statement and should be compiled before advertising the job. Table 2.4 is a sample list of selection criteria.

It is preferable to advertise vacancies to give yourself the best chance of finding the most suitable person. Choose an appropriate vehicle for your advertisement. Would it be best placed in your own organisation's newsletter? In a local paper? In a national paper? In a specialist journal? In the window of a local shop?

Draft your advertisement carefully. The essential elements of an advertisement are illustrated in Table 2.5.

Take care over the advertisement's presentation and double check the final typed version with your original draft.

Compiling a list of questions to ask applicants, either at a formal interview or over the telephone, enables you to satisfy yourself about a person's suitability. It also enables you to select the best person from a range of applicants when they have all answered the same questions.

Table 2.5 Advertising a Vacancy

Sunshine Press Limited – Brisbane
Assistant Archivist – Permanent Appointment
(Position Number 42)

The Sunshine Press has been Queensland's largest printed news media organisation for 93 years. It is seeking to appoint, on a permanent basis, an Assistant Archivist.

Duties
Appraise, accession, arrange and describe the archives. Provide reference services and identify items requiring conservation treatment.

Qualifications
• Postgraduate Diploma in Archives Administration (or equivalent)
• Two to three years' archival experience
• Professional membership of the Australian Society of Archivists

Salary
$30,000 – $35,000 per annum

Benefits
20 days annual leave; 10 days annual sick leave; eligibility for Sunshine Press Superannuation Scheme; removal expenses

Apply by
19 June 1993

Contact
Barbara Winsome (07) 467 351 for further details, Selection Criteria and Statement of Duties. Applications should be in duplicate, should address the Selection Criteria and should nominate two referees. Envelopes should be addressed to:
Dr Barbara Winsome
Archivist
Sunshine Press Ltd.
GPO Box 4444Z
Brisbane QLD 4001

Table 2.6 lists some of the considerations to keep in mind when framing questions and conducting interviews.

Training New Staff
Having appointed someone who is interested and eager to contribute, it is essential to devote time and care to training. Effective training means that staff
• can competently and independently undertake the projects assigned them
• will not inadvertently or unconsciously damage or destroy material
• will be able to learn and gain satisfaction.
Training can be either practical or theoretical. Remember that

Table 2.6   Framing Interview Questions and Running an Interview

Framing Interview Questions

- Ask questions that are relevant to making the decision about the job. Questions should reflect the selection criteria.
- Keep questions concise.
- Make the questions open ended so that they require more than a one word response. For example, 'How would you try to persuade a notable local family to deposit its records?' and not 'Would you emphasise the benefits of tax deductibility when persuading a notable local family to deposit its records?'
- Vary the approach – ask a direct question, delineate a problem and ask for a solution, prepare a practical exercise.
- Graduate the questions so that the simplest are asked first. This helps everyone to settle down.
- Ask one question at a time.

Running an Interview

Before
- Get to know the statement of duties and selection criteria in detail.
- Frame the questions to be asked. Identify the answer to each question.
- Decide how responses will be rated. For example, will each question carry a certain number of points?
- Select the other people who will sit on the panel. Provide them with the necessary documents (duty statement, applications, selection criteria, advertisement, questions). Decide how to run the interview and for how long each interview will last.
- Schedule appointments.
- Organise interview room and ensure that there will be no interruptions.
- Read applications thoroughly. Make necessary notes.

During
- Introduce every person on the panel.
- Be attentive.
- Be encouraging.
- Be prepared to paraphrase questions and to provide prompts if people are struggling to answer.
- Be prepared to stop and refocus any answers that go off the track.
- Make notes of the responses provided by each interviewee.
- Keep interviews to time and keep to the interview timetable.
- Give the applicant time to ask any questions he or she may have.
- Thank applicant for his or her interest and time.

After
- Document your decision and the basis for it.
- Inform applicants of the interview results as soon as possible.
- Be available to provide feedback on any of the applicants' performances.

you train by example. Do not wonder why your colleagues treat the archives carelessly if you smoke, eat and drink your coffee while working on them.

If people are new to an organisation, training should encompass the technical aspects of the job such as the principles and procedures for doing the work. Training should also cover general or political aspects. For example, how the organisation functions, who are the decisionmakers and who are the people with information. Training needs to be carefully tailored and graduated to suit the needs and capabilities of the person.

When confident that staff can work independently, ensure that all projects and tasks are distributed. This enables people to take responsibility for their work and to vary it. When allocating work, be clear in communicating your expectations. For example, when and how it should be completed and how complex or detailed the work should be. Attempt to roster or share the urgent, unpleasant or tedious work rather than expecting one person to do it all.

Most people want to find their work enjoyable and interesting. They would also like to derive some non-financial benefits such as increased skills or knowledge from it. If you work with volunteers, this is particularly important as their only compensation is the self-satisfaction they gain from their work.

Being approachable, fair, encouraging and appreciative is important for all supervisors – more so for those working in small organisations.

Managing Finance

The funding required to maintain your archives is dependent on your holdings, their condition and your responsibilities. Archives confront three recurring financial problems:
• Will there be funds?
• Will the funds be sufficient and continuing?
• How should the funding be allocated?
Because managing and maintaining archives costs money, the enterprise should not be entered into lightly. If there are no sources of assured income, the enterprise should only proceed after very careful thought. Neither the records nor the archival profession are well served by archives which are established on a flimsy financial basis. There is always a danger that they will close because financial support dwindles or is withdrawn leaving collections unusable and/or vulnerable to dismemberment or loss.

At the same time it is not always possible for a new archives program to have its funding fully sorted out. What must be obtained is the commitment for start-up costs with the clear understanding that the amount requested will lead to an on going obligation for funding. This commitment then becomes the first budget within which to plan your program.

As you are developing your program proposal for funding, consider engaging the services of an experienced archivist to advise you in a consultant capacity. This step, though it may require an initial investment in consultancy fees, is time and money well spent. It is important to develop a clear program proposal with a realistic assessment of required resources before seeking financial support.

Archives can receive funding in three ways:

- From their parent organisation. For example, the Archives of the Corporation of the City of Adelaide is funded entirely by the Corporation.
- By donation/sponsorship/fees.
- By a combination of the above. For example, the Mitchell Library's operations are covered by the State Government of New South Wales. However, the Library also has income from the David Scott Mitchell bequest which it augments by seeking donations from individuals and businesses.

An archives relying solely on the second method of funding is in a precarious situation. It is difficult to plan if one is unsure of how much money will be available from year to year. Relying on donations involves the staff in planning and conducting fundraising activities. This means less time can be spent on caring for the archives.

Institutions soliciting money need to be mindful of the expectations of their patrons. People will give money for worthy causes but they do expect the money to be utilised and progress to be visible. A balance must be preserved between the archives program and the fundraising program. Patrons may need to be reminded that a donation does not automatically carry the right to influence the direction or priorities of the archives.

If your archives falls into the first category identified above, your strategy should be to define your financial environment. For example:

- Is there automatic provision in your organisation's budget for your operations?
- If yes, how much is allocated, on what basis and how can it be increased?
- Who drafts and approves the organisation's budget?
- What is the budgeting cycle?
- What is the procedure for seeking funds?

With this basic information it should be possible to target your requests most effectively.

Regardless of the source of funds, every archives should have a budget. A budget is a document in which calculations, for a specified period, of the amount of money to be expended and raised are presented. Budgets are usually done annually and are divided into categories so that they itemise expenditure and income.

The budget should be completed and submitted to dovetail with your organisation's financial cycle. There are three responses your budget can attract

- it can be accepted and all funds sought provided
- it can be pruned
- it can be ignored.

Never be disheartened by the last two responses. The preparation and submission of a budget highlights the professional approach you have adopted to administering the archives. It also underlines the message that archives require funding. A first budget may have little success. However, it is an excellent public relations tool. People, whether allocating money personally or in an official capacity, are far more likely to give money to a unit with a clear purpose, well-defined needs and proposals which are properly justified. Prepare your budget with an eye to success:

- *Be realistic.* Do not seek money to buy 20,000 boxes if you will only use 200 within the budget period.
- *Be concise.* The budgeting review process is conducted under pressure. The people allocating money do not have time to read wads of paper.
- *Be precise.* Do your homework, seek quotes on prices so that you can cite costs accurately and can show that you have chosen the most economical option.
- *Be lucid.* Do not use jargon. Explain what an item will be used for, especially if it is expensive.
- *Be frank.* Briefly explain what the consequences will be if funds are not provided for activities.

Budgeting and receiving funds are only the beginning of the cycle. Ensure that you use the money responsibly and in accordance with your predicted needs. If you have asked for a specified sum of money to last you for a specified period, it is important to see that it does. Expenditure needs to be monitored and financial records (quotations received, invoices, receipts) properly maintained so that a financial report can be compiled at the end of the budgeting period.

The process of securing finance is often seen as a very dry and tedious one. In fact the success of this vital process can be contingent on two aspects of your operation that are well within your control – the image of the archives and your capability for lobbying the appropriate people.

Managing Facilities, Equipment and Stores

Housing records properly is crucial. Enemies such as heat, light, moisture, mildew and vermin are constantly at work. Once they have preyed on records, the cost to repair the damage will be enormous if it can be accomplished at all. Chapter 3, Preservation, covers these issues in detail.

Unsuitable equipment will, apart from increasing the wear and tear on records, extend retrieval time, possibly cause accidents to staff and will in the end be a bad investment. Money is best invested in proper storage facilities and equipment.

The archivist's first responsibility is to ensure that the records in his or her custody are given the best possible environment and care. Knowledge of optimum storage environments and equipment is vital and can be a matter of life and death for the records. Do a bit of homework before making decisions about facilities and equipment. Read the current literature about planning archival facilities such as the books and articles listed at the end of this chapter. Contact other archivists for information and advice. Visits to major archival institutions will provide useful hints and ideas. The ASA and the Australian Institute for the Conservation of Cultural Materials (AICCM) can give advice and act as an intermediary for making contacts.

Any decisions about where and how to house and service a particular archives are ultimately dependent on the nature of the holdings and activities as well as resources available at the time and in the foreseeable future. Therefore, this chapter cannot give advice on specific accommodation or equipment as the individual choices and decisions will vary between institutions. However, some general guidelines for planning archives facilities may be useful.

The criteria to use when selecting accommodation are discussed in the following section. Before you start this process be prepared:

- Know what your current needs are.
- Forecast your needs for the next five years.
- Identify the features you want and those you must avoid for preservation or security reasons.
- Familiarise yourself with what accommodation is available.
- Realise that you may need to be extremely patient and persistent.

When looking for accommodation you must be well versed in your requirements both present and near future. Remember that you need space not just for storage; room must also be allocated for administrative work, to allow researchers to consult items, and to enable staff to undertake work on archives. Ask yourself the following questions:

- How much and what types of material are in custody now? In five years?
- Does any of the material have special storage needs?
- How many staff are there now? In five years?
- How many researchers visit per week, month, year?
- What kind of equipment (computers, microfilm/microfiche readers etc) are we using now? What space does it consume? What equipment will we need or use in five years time?

Table 2.7   Characteristics of Accommodation for Archives

Sites

Desirable
Near most of your researchers or good transport; room for expansion

Avoid
Proximity to strategic targets, dangerous industries or utilities, floodplains, unstable earth zones, direct sun or wind

Building

Desirable
Constructed using fire- and vermin-resistant materials, large open spaces, good load-bearing capacity, limited points of access, mostly above ground, few windows, good loading/unloading facilities, air conditioning

Avoid
Several separate buildings, totally below ground, extensive internal partitioning

Position within building

Desirable
As above

Avoid
Attics or basements, widely separated rooms, potential hazards such as water pipes, chemical stores, heating/air conditioning plants, proximity to kitchens and bathrooms

Next, look for areas you consider acceptable in terms of size, location and suitability. Identify vacant or under-utilised areas on the premises of your organisation and inspect them. Assess their suitability. Table 2.7 indicates features of sites and buildings that you need to take into account. If yours is a community organisation, find out whether your local council has vacant buildings or areas which could be used. If your organisation is in a position to pay for accommodation, have a preliminary discussion with real estate agents and monitor advertisements in the papers.

The size and complexity of holdings determines the amount and the sophistication of equipment needed. Equipment used in archives falls into four categories

- administrative
- storage/repository
- reference/outreach
- conservation.

It may be more satisfying to obtain new equipment, but for most equipment it is not imperative. Word processing equipment, shelves, filing cabinets, ladders, desks, tables and chairs and trolleys may be borrowed, begged or bought second-hand. As long as the item functions and is safe (particularly ladders and shelving), it is perfectly acceptable. If buying second-hand, it is also preferable to buy the product of a well-known company which is still in the retail market. This means that spare parts and servicing can be obtained. It is also wise to buy a basic model rather than a highly accessorised model as there are fewer components that can go wrong.

If you are relying on gifts, loans and second-hand purchases, your most valued asset will be an extensive network of contacts. For example, people who can be vigilant in finding items you need, who can be relied upon to lend you items and who will devote their time and skills to repairing or modifying the items you acquire.

Written Specifications for Work, Equipment and Supplies

Exercise great caution when building or fitting out an archives facility. As the archivist it is your responsibility to specify your requirements, not only for the type and quality of the work or equipment but also for its maintenance and support and for the security of the archival holdings while the work or installation is underway (See Table 2.8). Without such specifications you have no legal recourse for correcting faulty work or shoddy supplies. Do not pay the bills until you are satisfied.

Table 2.8 Some Points to Include in a Specification Brief

- Dimensions – Height, width, depth, length
- Material
- Use
- Performance – Load, speed
- Description of the work to be undertaken
- Special conditions or requirements
- Drawings
- Time limit
- Supply and installation
- Service, spare parts
- Schedule of payment

The Archives Facility

Archives facilities fall into two categories – a purpose-built building, planned specifically to fit the requirements of a particular collection, or an existing building or part of one which is to be converted for archival use. Designing and building an archives facility is a very specialised and challenging task and one that will usually only be undertaken by very large and well-established archival institutions. Therefore, this chapter will not include any discussion of this task. Rather, it will focus upon selecting and adapting existing buildings and spaces for archival use.

Once you have identified your needs and assessed the suitability of the areas you are likely to be offered, you are then in a position to state your case. Decide whether it would be most appropriate to outline it in person or to prepare a submission. If you decide on the former, give the person making the decision a concise statement of your requirements and follow the meeting up with a letter confirming the substance of your discussion. If you prepare a submission, ensure that it is concise and clear. In both instances be prepared to send reminders.

General Conditions for Archives

Irrespective of whether your archives is a cupboard, a basement, or an old court house, the priorities are

- to provide a suitable and stable environment
- to make it secure and safe
- to ensure that there is adequate space
- to arrange or allocate the space so that it enhances the work flow.

As the characteristics of suitable space and equipment for each work area are discussed later in the chapter (see Table 2.9), the focus here is the general environment which all archives facilities should try to achieve. Overall, archival facilities should be secure, clean, temperate and protected from violent swings in climate.

Security in an archives facility is a top priority. Because archives are unique, they require more stringent protection than individual published items which may be replaced if they are lost or damaged. Thus, the use of archival records must be confined to the archives itself. It is unwise to permit records to be loaned for use elsewhere, except under very special and controlled circumstances. Areas where archives are stored should be locked and the use of records supervised to avoid loss or, equally bad, misfiling. Access to the stacks should be limited to archives staff only. A record should be made each time material is taken from the shelves for use by researchers or for processing or conservation work as it is easy for material to be mislaid without proper documentation. There should be a supervised place where all persons entering and leaving the archives register their presence, be they staff, researchers or tradespeople. After-hours patrols and alarm systems will help deter intruders.

The general environment within the archives is also vital. Archives must be kept under the best possible conditions in a stable, cool and clean environment. Proper containers, storage equipment and handling procedures are vital and every care must be taken to control levels and changes in temperature and relative humidity. A number of hazards must be avoided or min-

imised throughout the archives, but particularly in storage areas where the archives spend most of their time.

ACT Regional Office, Australian Archives

Environmental Hazards

Temperature and Relative Humidity. The control of temperature and relative humidity is a problem for all archivists seeking to provide a stable and temperate environment for their records. In rooms where the temperature and relative humidity greatly fluctuate between day and night or from season to season, paper is put under considerable strain. This is because paper will absorb moisture at night when the temperature drops and humidity rises and it will release moisture the next day when the temperature rises again. A climate with high humidity and high temperature is very dangerous as mould thrives in such conditions. Where the relative humidity is too low, paper becomes crisp and brittle to the touch.

There are several possible approaches to managing the storage environment. The most comprehensive of these is to install a well-designed air-conditioning system which will control both the levels of temperature and relative humidity and moderate their rates of change.

Air-conditioning can
- heat and cool the air
- humidify and dehumidify the air
- clean pollution from the air.

Once air-conditioning is installed it should run 24 hours a day, seven days a week or its good effects will be undone. To function properly the air-conditioning unit will have to be regularly serviced and the water drawn from the humid air will have to be disposed of carefully.

If you cannot afford to air-condition the entire facility, consider installing it in the storage areas. If even limited use of air-conditioning is beyond your resources, obtain some good quality fans to keep the air moving and, if possible, purchase a humidifer/dehumidifier unit to regulate the relative humidity. With the latter, water will be involved, so plan your installation and maintenance carefully.

Vermin and Insects. It is almost impossible to keep vermin and insects out of a building, particularly in hot and humid climates. Some protection can be incorporated in a purpose-built archives building, but most archives must depend on other measures. Regular inspections of the storage areas and the records themselves, together with regular fumigation of the whole building, are the best safeguards against pests. Commercial pest control companies can fumigate, using the chemical fumigants recommended by the AICCM. Minor outbreaks of mould or mildew may be treated with the advice of a conservator.

Dust should be regularly removed as it carries fungi, mould spores and bacteria that destroy paper. It is unpleasant and even harmful to staff. If the room has a floor made of concrete (which gives off a particularly gritty and alkaline dust), it should be coated. The coating can be brushed or sprayed on to the floor (varnish types of polyvinyl) or applied with a trowel (paste). Linoleum or vinyl carpets can also be used. Fabric carpeting is not recommended in storage areas because it traps dirt and dust in its fibres and produces a lint of its own.

Light should be carefully controlled because of the chemical reactions it encourages in paper and ink. Sunlight should be eliminated because of its intense ultraviolet rays and the heat it generates. West-facing windows, in particular, should be avoided or blocked with panels, shutters or blinds, preferably those with a reflective coating to deflect the heat outwards.

If, for some reason, it is impossible to block the windows entirely, a light filter film can be used on the windows to provide some protection from ultraviolet light. There are, however, pitfalls facing the buyer of film. The market is big and the promises are many. Few of the brands live up to the standards of the glossy brochures. Museums have the same problems as archives in this area, and their advice should be sought. The Museums Association of Australia has published information on this matter.

If sunlight cannot be eliminated from storage areas, shelving should be positioned in such a way that prevents the records being struck. Remember, lighting in storage areas is only needed for retrieving and refiling records and, therefore, should be located to illuminate the aisles between the shelves. Some archives have their storage lights on a timer switch so that they cut off after a set time. Some fluorescent lamps, such as Philips Trucolour, 37 and Softone, give off very small amounts of ultraviolet light. Tungsten incandescent lamps also have low ultraviolet emissions, but as they do produce an amount of heat they are not recommended for storage areas. To compensate for the lower watt lamps recommended for archives, you may wish to use wall paints with higher light-reflecting qualities.

Water Hazards. Water is a major hazard, particularly for records storage areas. Dampness encourages deterioration and the growth of damaging fungi and mould. If possible, records should not be stored below ground level as basement areas are particularly vulnerable to water invasion. Pipes may be located in the ceiling and trays should be fitted underneath these to allow water from leaks to be drained away. Cold water pipes are particularly dangerous to records, as condensation can form on the pipes from contact with the warmer air. Rising damp in the walls can wet the backs of boxes if open shelving is located against walls. The rising damp should be eliminated and the walls coated to seal them against seeping moisture. Shelving should be set away from the walls to encourage air circulation. Be alert to the danger of water from the storeys above, from faulty plumbing, overflowing gutters or a damaged roof. Water can flow down walls, stairs or ramps, through ventilation shafts or holes and seep through the ceiling if the floors above experience a drainage problem. For this reason, it is a good idea not to use the tops of shelving to store records.

Even if all the above measures have been taken to prevent water from entering the archives, it is advisable to install a drain in the floor. Ensure that water flows out and not in from blocked drains outside the building. Regular drain maintenance is advisable.

A very simple early detection system can be installed with the help of a humidity sensor pushed into a hard dry sponge on the floor. The device is connected to an alarm which, when the sponge gets wet, sounds the alarm.

Fire is a major threat which must be minimised. While the next chapter on preservation will discuss the varieties of detection and extinguishing systems in detail, there are a few general points worthy of mention.

First, the fabric of the building should be as fire resistant as possible. The fire rating of walls, floors and doors should be as high as possible. The safest area inside a building should be chosen for the storage area.

Second, preventative measures should be taken so that fire does not break out inside. For example, prohibit smoking in the archives; have the electrical wires insulated from the main structure and locate master switches outside the rooms; isolate areas where flammable chemicals are stored or electrical appliances are used.

If all records are properly boxed and tightly packed on the shelves, fire will not easily get a hold on them. If the ends of the boxes facing the aisle burn away (boxes that stick out slightly over the edge of the shelf will be an easier target), the files or papers in boxes of the kind recommended in this chapter will sit safely on the shelf and not fall off and feed the fire.

Fire detectors and extinguishers are costs that cannot be compromised. A detector attached to an alarm will alert staff before the fire has established itself. Smoke detectors are more suitable for archives than heat or flame sensors because boxes of paper do not burst into flames easily, but rather smoulder and slowly emit smoke. When acquiring fire extinguishers, preference should be given to those utilising carbon dioxide or a fine spray, rather than a jet of water. Chemical extinguishers may be necessary for some types of fires, ie electrical or oil, but may leave a residue on the records. Remember that fire detection equipment and extinguishers should be regularly inspected and serviced.

Sprinkler systems which are automatically activated in the event of fire may be installed. In a properly managed archives the activation of the sprinkler system need not be a catastrophe. All boxes will be well above ground and the shelves will have dustcovers on the top shelf to prevent water dripping from shelf edge to shelf edge. Bound volumes of records will not fare as well; it is therefore essential that, if sprinklers are installed, all archival material including outsized volumes be either wrapped or boxed.

Extinguisher systems with a gas such as halon or carbon dioxide, rather than water, have in the past been used to protect repositories. These gases did not harm the records, they choked the fire by depriving it of oxygen. Unfortunately these systems endangered staff and the environment and are now either illegal or not recommended.

Third, develop and practise emergency procedures. Properly trained staff cannot only prevent fire hazards, they can also fight an existing fire. If fire breaks out during the day, staff are most likely to be the first people to arrive on the scene. If properly trained for fire emergencies, staff can extinguish a limited blaze long before the fire brigade arrives on the scene and salvage operations can begin immediately.

Allocating Space

Having acquired your accommodation and attended to the general environmental requirements, you must decide how to allocate the space. The accepted formula in archives is that 60–70% of space is devoted to storage, 15–20% to processing and the remaining area divided between administration and public areas (see Table 2.9). Depending on the holdings, the clientele, the funding and the archives' standing within its parent organisation, some physical areas of the archives may be emphasised and others kept more low key. For example, a historical society archives may stress the importance of the reference and exhibit facilities, while an in-house business archives may be more concerned with the storage and administrative areas.

The level of your archival activity will also affect how you allocate space. For example, you may have a staff of three, the largest single deposit you receive is five boxes and you rarely have researchers. In this situation you can afford to restrict your processing area (because you never work on large quantities of records) and have a larger administrative area where the occasional researcher may work (as there are three staff members it is likely that there will always be someone to supervise).

Remember to plan ahead for growth. For instance, if you were planning to alter your acquisition policy or raise your profile, you may have realised that there was a need for local business records to be collected and preserved. Business records can be extensive and will require an increase, not only in storage space but also in your processing area.

How you allocate your space also affects the efficiency and speed of your work. For example, if your storage area is distant from your processing and reference areas, there will be a delay in retrieving items. Non-adjacent processing, office and reading areas create difficulties in communication between you and your staff or researchers. Particularly if you work alone, you will need to plan ahead so that you have suitable desk work to do when supervising researchers.

It is advisable to categorise the records in your collection into highly used, frequently used and rarely used. The categories can then be located so that the most highly used are closest to you and the rarely used furthest away from you or on less accessible shelves. If you have several storage areas which are dispersed, this system of ranking records and storing them according can save you precious time.

All archives facilities must plan to accommodate four basic functions: storage, processing, administration and public service; the discussion which follows will treat each in turn.

The Storage Area

Space and Conditions. The storage area, which should comprise 60–70% of total facility space, is the permanent home of the records and its quality and management has an enormous impact on their continued preservation. Traffic and work activities in this

Table 2.9 Space Allocation and Requirements

Allocation of Space Recommended for Archival Facilities

- Records storage/stacks   60–70%
- Archival services and administration   30–40%
- Processing areas (closed to the public)   15–22%
- Reference areas/exhibits and public conveniences   7–10%
- Administrative offices (semi-closed to public)   8%

Absolute Minimum Requirements for Facilities and Equipment

Storage Area
Environment	Clean
	Cold +18–20°C
	Dry (no less than 45–55% relative humidity)
	Dark
Equipment	Shelves
	Fire detectors and extinguishers
	Ladders/step stools
	Trolleys
	Thermohygrograph

Processing Area
Environment	No direct sun
	Free of dust
Equipment	Brush or vacuum cleaner
	Workbench
	Shelves, racks, cupboards
Supplies	Boxes
	Cotton tape
	Wrapping paper
	Folders
	Envelopes
	Plastic clips

Administrative Areas
Environment	Around +22°C
Space	3.3 square metres per member of staff
Equipment	A desk and chair per member of staff
	Bookcase
	Telephone
	Word processing equipment

Public Areas

Reading Room
Environment	Around +22°C

Equipment	A table and chair per researcher
	Bookcases
	Copy machine (share with office)
	Microfilm readers

Exhibition Area

Environment	Low light level if original material exhibited
Equipment	Fire detectors and extinguishers
	Display cabinets
	Screens
	Chairs or lounge

Seminar/Training

Environment	Around +22°C
Equipment	Blinds or heavy curtains to exclude light
	A table and chair/researcher
	Black/white board
	Slide projector
	Screen
	Overhead projector
	Film projector
	Video equipment

area should be kept to a minimum so that the environment is kept stable. Also, the number of people authorised to access the stacks should be limited to minimise misfiling of material. If possible only one person should handle retrieval and refiling to ensure accountability. The only other persons permitted in the stacks should be cleaners operating under stringent guidelines.

The storage area should be clean, cool and free from water hazards. The ideal environment for paper records storage is +15°–20°C and 50% relative humidity. Some lights are needed to access the records, but these should be turned off when not needed for retrieval. A single open space is preferred and it is recommended that unnecessary walls be demolished to utilise the area more efficiently, encourage air circulation and avoid the creation of microclimates. Contrary to the popular conviction that archives are dusty and cramped, modern archivists aim to have storage areas as spacious, clean and uncluttered as possible.

Some non-paper records are very sensitive to dust (paper gives off dust and gases) and should be stored separately. The same records also benefit from lower temperatures and humidity than paper records. Categories of original records that should be considered for special purpose storage are

- photographic negatives
- microfilm negatives
- master magnetic disks, tapes and diskettes.

In an area insulated from the rest of the storage area, these records can enjoy an environment with temperatures as low as +10°C and a relative humidity of 20–30%. Usually these special storage arrangements are beyond the resources of a small archives. However, it may be possible to arrange for use of such storage at a large state or federal archives.

Equipment for Records Storage. In the stack area this is of two kinds: storage for records, and equipment to retrieve and transport records. For storage of records, cardboard boxes are universally accepted as the best and most economical protection for loose papers, files, cards, small volumes, etc. Requirements of a good box are discussed in the segment on equipment for the processing area. Shelving must be of a size and made suitable for the records to be stored. For retrieval of records from high shelves, stepstools and ladders will be necessary and, whenever a number of boxes need to be moved, a trolley will ease and speed up the process.

Shelving for records will be your top purchasing priority. However, the choice and number of shelving units will depend upon your needs and the weight-bearing capacity of the storage area. Costs have to be balanced against factors of space, convenience, safety, ease and speed of access. Most archival shelving is manufactured of steel, treated with an anti-corrosive agent and an enamel coating to prevent rust and scratching. Wooden shelves have to be specially treated and sealed to withstand fire and wood-eating insects and are more expensive than standard steel shelving. Purchasers of steel shelving need to be aware that condensation easily forms on items in a room with excess humidity.

Shelving is made up from standard components of uprights, shelves, cross bars, bases, backs, ends and sides. Shelves are fixed by steel clips or by nuts and bolts which should be zinc plated to resist rusting. Preference is often given to using clips, as shelves can easily be adjusted to accommodate boxes or records of various heights. The distance between each shelf should be the height of the tallest item on the shelf plus an allowance of 20mm to enable items to be placed on the shelf and retrieved without being damaged. The bottom shelf should be at least 10cm above floor level to make it easier to clean the floor and as an extra precaution in case of flooding. As mentioned previously, no records should be stored on top of shelving in case of water damage from above (including sprinklers), and as an added precaution the top of the shelf should be protected by a 'dust cover'.

The standard length of shelves can be either 900 or 1200mm, the standard depth is 400mm. The choice of length can depend on the size of the boxes to be stored, the configuration of the room and the load each shelf is to carry. Shelves and boxes should both conform to metric measurements, although some second-hand shelving will be imperial. In such cases ensure that boxes can be easily accommodated on the shelves and that space is not wasted.

Problems will inevitably result if the floors or the shelves are not made for the loads they are required to take. Before ordering shelving, an average shelf of records should be weighed and the result compared both with the building specifications and those supplied by the shelving manufacturer. To accommodate most archival requirements, the floors should support 1500–2000kg per square metre per storey, rising to a maximum of 80 tonnes per stanchion for certain compactus style systems. A shelf measuring 900mm in length often takes boxed files which weigh about 30kg, with bound volumes being over twice that weight. A range of steel shelving should have the capacity to carry 100kg per shelf, the total weight being calculated by multiplying the total number of shelves.

A major shelving decision is whether to purchase static (or fixed) shelving or mobile (or compactus type) shelving.

Static Shelving. Static or fixed shelving is generally of two types. The most popular consists of rows of free standing shelves erected with aisle space between each row or double row of shelving. Shelving is normally installed back to back, except along walls or other natural boundaries, in which case a single row is installed. If it is a heavy gauge and suitably braced, it is particularly good to accommodate heavier than average records such as bound volumes. It also has the advantage of being able to be dismantled and moved or reconfigured. Some brands can even be converted to mobile shelving if the need arises. The second type of static shelving consists of installing fixed posts from floor to ceiling and attaching shelves between them. Because this type requires more or less permanent placement, it is not recommended for small archives.

Mobile Shelving. Modern or compactus shelving comprises back-to-back shelving mounted on tracks. The shelving moves along the track, generally with a fixed, one-sided bay at each extreme of the shelving. As a row of mobile shelving requires only one aisle, the saving of space is considerable and increases the larger the compactus unit. Movement of the ranges is accomplished by using a manual wheel or handle and can be powered electrically. Because of maintenance expense and the dangers of faulty operation, power-driven units are not recommended for small archives.

Mobile shelving, properly selected and installed, can be an excellent solution for an archives with limited space for storage. However, the construction of the room designated for the stack (see Table 2.10 for definition) may determine that mobile shelving is an impossibility. The load-bearing capacity of the floor requires investigation before any shelving is installed. Fully laden mobile shelving generally requires a greater load-bearing capacity than does static shelving (see above). Other considerations are the need for a level floor and for excellent air circulation as some areas fitted with mobile shelving experience air circulation problems. The air problem can be moderated by providing rubber doorstops at the bottom of shelving to prevent the shelving from closing completely, or by allowing for additional aisle space when ordering the shelving so that the shelving is never closed completely. In a room without air-conditioning, particularly in humid climates, mobile shelving is not recommended for these reasons.

If, in addition, the repository has vertical columns or is of an irregular shape, the advantages of mobile shelving are not great. A floor plan of the area using paper cutouts to represent the shelving according to scale should be used to plan the storage area wisely. Extra-wide shelving can be used for larger items and extra space should be allowed for the area required to open and use horizontal plan cabinets. Aisles between shelving need to be at least 800mm and central aisles at least 900mm.

The central aisle should always lead to the main door to allow maximum ease of access for loaded trolleys and people. From the central aisle, bays of shelving are positioned at right angles. Bays arranged alongside a wall should have an airspace of a couple of centimetres between the wall and the back of the shelf. Tall shelves might need bracing so as not to topple over when loaded. For shelving higher than 2.1 metres, ladders or stools are required, however the use of ladders considerably slows down retrieval and increases the risk of accidents. When configuring the repository you must take into account fire regulations that prescribe width of aisleways, number of exits and so on.

Shelving Layout. Within the stack area, all rows and bays of shelving should be uniquely numbered and identified to enable easy retrieval and to maintain accurate shelf lists. Where there are significant holdings of small accessions or groups of records, it is also useful to number each shelf. A simple system is to give each row of shelving a number from 1 to whatever, to number each bay within each row from 1 (starting always at the left-hand end of the row) and to number each shelf within each bay from 1 (starting at the uppermost shelf but ignoring the top of the shelving, on which you are not going to put records anyway). This will be sufficient for most needs and will also allow shelves to be renumbered easily if additional shelves are added or some are removed when making space for smaller or larger items. Under this system, Location 10/3/5 would mean Row 10, Bay 3, Shelf 5. In some repositories more refined space allocations can indicate

Table 2.10 Vocabulary and Measures

Shelf Vocabulary

Archival Use of Term
Stack	Room, floor or separate area of shelving
Bay	One unit/section of shelving, 2 sides, 1 top, 1 bottom, 1 back (or cross bracing)
Shelf	900–1200mm in length 250–500mm in depth

Shelf Manufacturers' Use of Term
Stack	Row of bays
Bay	One unit/section of shelving, 2 sides, 1 top, 1 bottom, 1 back (or cross bracing)
Shelf	900–1200mm in length 250–500mm in depth

Standard Measures for Areas and Equipment Used in an Archival Context

	Length	Height	Width/Depth
Box	390mm	260mm	175mm
Shelf	900–1200mm	1900–2100mm	250mm
Bay or row length	max. 10m		
Aisle, between rows			min. 800mm
central			min. 900mm
Door			900mm
where trolleys are used			min. 500mm each

the exact position of each shelf of each box. For example, Location 4/6/2/3 would mean Row 4, Bay 6, Shelf 2, Box 3.

Loading the Shelves. Storing a single row of boxes on a shelf provides easy access to all records. If deep shelving is the only shelving available, two rows of boxes, one stored behind the other, will improve space efficiency, but involves double handling. Boxes with minimum retrieval could be stored in the back row. It is undesirable to have boxes stored three deep as the third row could not be reached by a normal reach. To stabilise the range, particularly if the unit is very high, it is advisable to load an empty range from the bottom shelf up.

Bench or Table. The storage area should be provided with a table or bench of the same type as is used in the processing area, so that a number of boxes can be opened and examined as necessary and paperwork to document the files and retrievals can be completed. It may also be useful to fit a retractable shelf within the middle bay of each row to assist rapid retrieval.

Essential Accessories. A constant flow of records will be moving in and out of the stack area and the provision of some mechanical aid for their retrieval and transport might be necessary. To retrieve records from shelving higher than 2.1 metres, most people will need something to step up on. While a sturdy chair may seem sufficient, specially designed stepping stools with a non-slip surface are preferable (these stools are extensively used in libraries and are not expensive). Only step-ladders should be used to retrieve records in archives. Ordinary ladders are difficult to secure on a smooth surface and in narrow aisles the angle of the steps will render the ladder unsafe for climbing. Folding step ladders of aluminium with a flat top on which to place the box while checking the contents are commercially available. Heavier structures on lockable castors will be suitable for very high ranges.

The use of ladders always involves the risk of an accident. That risk can be minimised by wearing sensible footwear (no heels and no thongs) and by working in pairs while using ladders (specially if they are A-frame ladders).

Carting records to and from the stack area will be greatly facilitated by the use of a trolley. The size and type chosen depends basically on the quantity of records to be shifted and the layout of the building.

Handtrucks, with two or six wheels depending on whether there are steps to negotiate or not, carry 4–10 boxes at one time. The six-wheeled handtruck is the only trolley that can negotiate steps and high doorsteps. They do not take up much space in the storeroom, but staff will have to bend and lift while loading and unloading the boxes.

Platform trolleys can be made of steel or plastic and vary in length. Plastic platform trolleys are light, but with only one pair of turnable wheels they can be hard to manoeuvre in winding and narrow aisles.

Bin trolleys and platform trolleys have the load placed at waist level, eliminating unnecessary bending and lifting. With a good-sized load this kind of trolley can be a bit top heavy and may topple over on an uneven surface.

Working in a repository can involve carrying, lifting, climbing, stretching, pulling and pushing. To minimise occupational health and safety risks, it is important that everyone involved in such work understands how best to execute such tasks and what practices to avoid. Safety posters and booklets are essential investments.

Processing Area

Space and Conditions. The processing area is where records are received, accessioned, cleaned, arranged and described for future reference use. This area usually occupies 15–22% of the total archives facility.

As processing activities require materials such as boxes, permanent paper (see Chapter 3) and folders, this area should include space to store such supplies. To minimise the logistics of moving records, the point where materials are delivered or unloaded should be adjacent to the processing area, as should the storage area. If possible, there should be a loading dock which has weather protection so that loading and unloading of vehicles does not expose records to rain and wind.

Space planning should then accommodate the requirements of these separate but interrelated activities:

- Receiving and checking incoming shipments of records.
- Cleaning of dirt and dust from records.
- Sorting, arranging and describing records.
- Temporary holdings of records awaiting processing or transfer to storage.
- Temporary holding of records awaiting destruction.
- Storage of supplies and equipment needed for processing.

The room should have wide doors to enable trolleys to be used to transport material. Because records may be kept here for some months, often without protection while processing is undertaken, the area should be kept scrupulously clean and protected from excess light. Individual worklights are acceptable for close work as no document will be exposed for lengthy periods. Floors should be of material which is easy to clean, vinyl flooring or cork tiles being suitable. Because of light restrictions, the room should be painted in light colours. Since the area will be used by staff, the temperature can be adjusted for human comfort without damaging the records.

Equipment. Workbenches or tables represent the most important pieces of furniture in the processing area. Workbenches can be built with fully lockable castors to enable them to be moved to form long benches in a row or pushed together to form a wide surface, according to the records being processed. These can also double as trolleys if there is not a formal loading dock, and incoming records can be easily placed on top of the benches and wheeled to the area for processing. Care should be taken not to overload them in this use. Workbenches should be about 900mm in height, to be used by staff sitting on stools or standing up. They should be about 800mm wide, with the length to be determined by the number of people using the bench, the type of records processed and the configuration of the processing area.

Shelf space can be built under the workbench. Workbenches are often made of steel crossbars and uprights, with the top made of a hard surface such as pineboard covered in hard laminate for a smooth and clean surface. Shelving manufacturers can make workbenches according to the individual archives' specification and requirements.

When tables are used for processing, the rule is generally the longer the better. Alternatively, use several small tables of the same height to create one long flat surface. One person can comfortably reach over a table area of 2000mm long x 900mm wide while working sitting down.

The height of chairs is dependent on the height of tables and vice versa. Regardless of the height of the table, the distance between the top of the seat and the top of the table should be approximately 30cm for maximum comfort. Benches and tables suitable to work at while standing up (approximately 900mm high) will need to be equipped with special high chairs.

Brush or Vacuum Cleaner. Cleaning surface dirt and dust off records is one of the first tasks the archivist undertakes after records are received. This work should be done in an area separate from the archives proper, as dust and mould spores can get into the air circulation system and cause conservation problems. A library brush or a vacuum cleaner can be used for this task. A tank vacuum cleaner with adjustable suction and changeable nozzles, with or without bristles, is preferred as too much force can damage the records. Nilfisk makes a special attachment for cleaning records and other precious materials.

The processing area needs plenty of storage space, for the records themselves and for materials used in conjunction with these activities. Shelves are necessary for the storage of records before and during processing and records awaiting transfer or destruction (avoid potential problems by storing records awaiting processing and those awaiting destruction in separate and clearly marked shelves). If the archives is receiving records from people and institutions packing records in non-archival boxes, several bays should have wider than normal (300mm) shelves to accommodate oversized parcels and boxes. For the same reason bays with movable shelves should be used in this area.

Materials needed while processing records should be stored in the processing area or adjacent to it. Large cupboards for different sized boxes, folders, wrapping material, rope or tape makes it easy to keep the area tidy and dustfree. Wrapping and packing materials are often sold in massive rolls that are difficult to handle. If the rolls are put on racks, either attached to a wall or freestanding, they are much easier to work with and the material is protected from unnecessary wear and tear.

Fumigation. When consignments of records are arriving from different sources, some are likely to be afflicted with insects or mould or both. These records will have to be treated before they are placed in the stack to prevent the whole collection being affected. As fumigation involves the handling of toxic chemicals it is recommended that the services of commercial companies be utilised. Seek advice from a conservator about the safest and most effective chemicals, the best method of application and so on before contacting commercial fumigators.

Supplies. Records stored in archives should always be protected from the environment by being boxed or wrapped. Inside the box or parcel records are separated by folders, envelopes, jackets or clips.

Boxes of varying shapes and sizes have been tried for archives storage.

A suitable box is
- inexpensive
- made of strong board so that the sides do not cave in while stored
- easy to assemble without tools
- able to accommodate records without force being used in packing
- able to be carried by the weakest member of staff and taken off the top shelf when full
- easily gripped when removing from and replacing on shelves
- capable of fitting the shelves without wasted space (old imperial shelves may not store metric boxes economically).

In Australia most archives have adopted the standard Australian Archives Type 1 box or versions of it. This box is cut in one piece with creases to facilitate folding. Its external dimensions are 39x26x17.5cm and it easily accommodates pages and files of A4 or foolscap sizes. Full of paper it weighs around 5kg, a manageable weight for most people. It has a hole at both ends to facilitate gripping. A boxmaking company can manufacture boxes according to any specifications. It is wise to confer with other archives in the area to see if a box suitable for your needs is already available from a boxmaker or if a coordinated effort can design one.

Outsized material should be wrapped in sturdy paper and tied with cotton tape. If the quantity of outsized material is large and regularly received, it may be more economical to investigate having special containers made. In the same way, quantities of records of smaller dimensions, such as cards, can justify tailor made boxes to accommodate them, particularly if retrieval and usage is high.

Wrappings, boxes and folders can be ordered in permanent materials (ie acid-free and alkaline buffered with a pH of between 8–10, see Chapter 3). Unlike ordinary cardboard boxes and papers, these will not contribute to the general deterioration of records by adding the impurities of their paper to those of the records inside. Records that have been deacidified by a conservator should definitely be housed with and in permanent materials; and, if your budget allows, consider permanent boxes, envelopes and folders for sensitive materials like photographs and films.

When ordering materials, plan to buy sufficient quantities to last a year so that time is not wasted ordering and doing paper-work for small amounts. Maintain a list of all suppliers, put the archives on their mailing list for catalogues and keep these cata-logues in an easily accessible folder.

Administrative Areas

Space and Conditions. In a small archives the reading room and the administrative areas are best kept adjacent. Staff will want to use the reference library or the technical equipment in the reading room and researchers might have to be supervised from the office if a special reading room attendant is not employed. The use of glass wall partitions between the two areas is often a satisfactory solution to the latter problem. For the privacy of the staff, one-way glass is recommended.

Each member of staff will need approximately 3.3 square metres of floor space, but if the office is used for other activities such as interviews with researchers, staff conferences and so on, the space will have to be increased accordingly.

Equipment. The office should accommodate all the records con-trolling the archival holdings and an extensive collection of forms and lists in volumes, binders and folders. To accommodate these and perhaps a reference library, the office will need a filing cab-inet and a large bookcase or two, apart from the indispensable desk and chair. A typewriter or a word processor will be needed if these services cannot be obtained elsewhere.

Public Service Areas

With the increase in family history research and research, for example, into historical buildings and sites, most archives have felt pressure to increase services to the general public. To make records available to researchers in a wider sense of the word, archives have expanded into the realm of user education and public relations. Additional activities such as exhibitions, work-shops and lectures will require additional space.

Reading Room

Space and Conditions. Of the total space allocated, the reading room in a small archives occupies approximately 7–10%.

The organisation may already have an area set apart for servicing information seekers – a library, etc. The facilities of this existing service may be utilised for using original records – but do not forget the need for continuous surveillance by reference staff.

In the reading room researchers should be registered, interviewed and advised on the use and handling of archives before being left to consult reference books, indexes and archival material. To minimise the disturbance to other researchers, these activities could be in an office rather than in the open reading area.

The needs of the users must be incorporated into the planning of this area. Researchers may be elderly, handicapped, have difficulties in reading or in understanding the language. Researchers may want to use the archives as individuals or they may visit as groups. Whether they be staff or the general public, all users require convenient, but controlled, access to the reading room, a logical layout with good signs and an environment which facilitates research work.

Sunlight should be restricted in the reading room as in all areas where original material is used. If the reading room faces due south, light from windows is less damaging, but it is desirable to use curtains or shades to filter or block direct sunlight. To compensate for the loss of daylight, each table may require its own individual reading lamp. General lighting should be kept at a low level.

Equipment. Tables, not desks, are used in reading rooms as no original material should be left in the room after use. To view large-format material without risk of damage, the table has to be big enough for large items to be opened on the tabletop. The minimum table size for a researcher is 1x0.70m. The use of several small lightweight tables that can easily be put together to accommodate different sized material is more economical spacewise than one table. To utilise equipment to a maximum degree, all the tables in the reading room can be of this lightweight type. The tables should have a smooth, washable top to which paper does not stick, and care should be taken when using metal tables as their sharp corners can damage leather and injure researchers.

Shelves in the reading room may need to accommodate a small library of reference books; standard library shelving of 0.25m depth is suitable.

For the finding aids and indexes used by researchers, an area should be provided in the reading room with shelves for binders, books and card drawers for card indexes. Index and reference copies of maps in big binders can be housed on a table nearby.

Microfilm/fiche readers are now almost standard equipment in archives. Reference material acquired from other archives and libraries is often sold in fiche or film format and in-house archives are increasingly faced with records consignments in a micro-format. Many archives are initiating filming of records to facilitate access or for preservation purposes.

Microfilm readers enlarge the micro-image to a readable size. The miniature images generally come on film (in a roll or individual frames on an aperture card) or as a fiche (a flat sheet with several rows of frames) and microfilm readers can be purchased for either film or fiche format or adjustable to read both. To view the reduced image in original scale, the microfilm reader will have to be equipped with a lens that magnifies it at a readable ratio. It is important to choose the appropriate readers for the film or fiche, taking the reduction ratio into consideration as well as purchasing and maintenance costs.

Microfilm reader/printers are bulkier than readers and are more expensive. Like microfilm readers, some reader–printers can be purchased with different lenses making it possible to blow up an image. They can also be supplied with carriers to read several different microfilm formats and reduction ratios and also have the added benefit of producing an acceptable paper copy. Microfilm printers that can use ordinary paper keep the cost of copying down considerably. Second-hand readers and printers are sometimes available. The same warning applies to purchasing these as to any machine with movable parts – cars, washing machines, etc. Investigate the machine's history carefully, consider how often you will use it, and test-drive it ... what seems like a bargain at the time could work out to be a drain on your pocket.

Photocopying machines are generally used to copy paper records. Old or fragile documents should not be exposed to the hazards of photocopying because the heat and light involved in the process will damage the document. A once-off negative taken in an ordinary photographic setting can provide a reference copy for damaged or fragile material.

Complicated machinery always involves maintenance (someone will have to be responsible for the constant supply of bulbs, papers, liquids) and servicing. The latter will be offered by the manufacturer/distributor and should be budgeted for as an ongoing expense in the annual budget.

Before investing in any expensive plant it is sensible to seek advice from other archives or organisations using the equipment and to visit several suppliers to look at the machines in action.

Exhibits

Space and Conditions. A small display area exhibiting some items from the collection in the reading room or outside it will attract attention. Exhibitions displaying original material will of necessity have to be in locked cabinets and under supervision. The range of permissible light levels and the required fire protection measures make it very hard to find suitable areas for display of original material. Copies of archival material magnified to a suitable size with labels and text are often a more satisfactory solution.

Equipment. Because of the risk of theft, vandalism or accidents, archival material should be displayed in special lockable cabinets or not at all. As it is possible to make very good copies of records for a reasonable price (as opposed to copies of most museum items – replicas – which are extremely expensive), such copies of archival material make perfect exhibits. As the copies are conveniently flat, they can easily be displayed on screens.

Other public areas needed/appreciated by researchers are restrooms, an area with secure lockers (for bags, books and coats not allowed in the reading room) and somewhere to have a cup of coffee and a sandwich.

Seminars/Training

Space and Conditions. An in-house archives can often utilise the resources of its parent organisation for seminars or training activities even if the facilities are not adjacent to reading room or offices. For other archives a separate room for these activities may not be feasible, but the exhibition or even the reading room may double as a seminar/training room when closed to researchers.

Equipment. A chair and a table should be provided for each participant. The speaker will need a black/white board and often a slide projector and a screen. Additional equipment – film projectors, overhead projectors and videos can, unless they are extensively used, be borrowed or hired for the occasion.

Other Resources

Small archival institutions with limited resources have a lot to gain by cooperation. Useful equipment not used on a day-to-day basis can be shared, the names of volunteers or potential professional staff can be acquired, and manufacturers can be approached collectively to supply plant and boxes at a discount. Sharing facilities opens up enormous possibilities for archives, especially small archives. Centralised storage for archival records in a limited geographical area, eg the 'Hunter Valley Archival Repository', low temperature storage for master film negatives or regional conservation and microfilming facilities are some areas where cooperation could be invaluable.

If the archives is a part of a larger organisation, there can be valuable resources to be tapped within the organisation. For example, it may be possible to use photocopiers, computers, photographic equipment and human resources (such as word processing operators, marketing advisers, carpenters, labourers) from time to time or on a regular basis. If such facilities and advice cannot be obtained from within, sister organisations or nearby archives may give aid or advice. Disaster planning is one area where the resources of other archives must be investigated. Every archives should have a plan of what to do and where to turn when disaster, natural or human, occurs. For example, which of the archives closest to yours has resources to assist in drying soaked records?

Keeping Things Going

It is never too early to analyse existing practices and subsequently to introduce plans and procedures to improve them. Unfortunately, most organisations only review their practices when compelled to by other circumstances. The most common circumstances are
- when new staff are appointed or positions abolished
- when the organisation is undergoing structural, functional or technological change
- when the organisation is facing scrutiny or
- when things are going wrong.

Whatever the causes, we should all realise that change is a natural and continuous process which we should incorporate rather than try to exclude from our organising process. What we seek to do is to manage the impact of change by having a definite, but flexible, framework of policies and structures within which to operate. Thus, we develop definite limits for our sphere of action within which we can move to adjust priorities and procedures for maximum results.

Measurement and Evaluation

All the preceding paragraphs have concentrated on developing the framework, tools and facilities for your operations. The remaining chapters deal with the technical aspects of archival work. We hope it will be possible to digest and apply the information and strategies discussed. If you do so, how will you know how you are going?

The only objective way of assessing your situation and performance is to set measures of effectiveness. That is, to measure activities. Activities can be measured quantitatively – how often they occurred. They can be measured qualitatively – how good or effective they were. For example, you can measure the number of reference enquiries you received. You can also measure how many you answered, how quickly you were able to answer them and how satisfied the enquirer was.

This information enables you to

- assess and monitor progress and, if necessary, adjust priorities and resources
- predict trends and plan for them and other contingencies in the coming month, quarter, year
- justify requests, analyse and report objectively
- compare your organisation with others
- promote and publicise the program with accuracy and confidence.

Most archival work is susceptible to measurement. Appendix 1 at the end of this chapter lists archival functions and some of the ways they can be measured. To be valid, measures must be accurate; they should be representative and they should be taken for specified periods.

It may not be necessary or useful for you to measure all the activities mentioned in Appendix 1. Conversely, there may be additional statistics you wish to keep. Whatever your decision, it is important to identify what data you need and to plan to capture it in the most efficient way. Attempt to build the collection of data into your daily activities or to have it produced automatically. For example, if you require every researcher to sign the search room register it is very easy to calculate how many people used the search room during the week, month, year. However, if you had to reconstruct this information, it would be time-consuming and probably inaccurate.

If you do invest time and stationery in recording and collecting statistics, do use them. Collate, compare and evaluate them. Having done so, do not keep the findings to yourself. Incorporate them in your annual reports, use them in justifying your budget, and quote them when arguing for additional space or staff.

Advertising Your Achievements

Archives belong to an organisation or community, they rely on that organisation and community for resources and support, and their survival can depend on their visibility. Publicising your achievements is a way of maintaining a profile, attracting interest and support from a wider community and assuring existing sponsors of progress.

Regardless of how you are publicising your achievements, do present the information clearly, concisely, truthfully and attractively. Tailor your presentation for your readers. Plan your publicity so that you will be able to cope with its effects. It is damaging to create a demand that cannot be fulfilled or expectations that are unrealistic.

Be positive about your program. Use every opportunity to keep it visible – mention initiatives, highlight how the existence/use of archives achieved savings or averted disaster, identify fresh uses of archives and publicise significant deposits.

Conclusion

This chapter has focused on establishing the framework for the archives program. Without this structure, professional work, despite its excellence, will founder. The planning, organisation and management of archival resources is a continuous and continuing responsibility. It is a task that requires sensitivity to your immediate surroundings, its staff and clientele, but it also requires an awareness and responsiveness to the wider forces which impact upon our society and its institutions.

Further Reading

Bright, Franklyn F., *Planning for a Movable Compact Shelving System*, Library Administration and Management Association Occasional Paper No. 1, American Library Association, Chicago, 1991.

British Standard 5454:1989, *Storage and Exhibition of Archival Documents*.

Duchein, Michel, *Archive Buildings and Equipment*, 2nd edn, ICA Handbook No. 6, Peter Walne (ed.), trans; David Thomas (trans.), K. G. Saur, Munich, 1988.

Hunt, John, *Managing People at Work: A Manager's Guide to Behaviour in Organisations*, Pan, London, 1981.

MacKenzie, R Alec, *The Time Trap*, Amacom, New York, 1990.

McCarthy, Paul H. (ed.), *Archives Assessment and Planning Workbook*, Society of American Archivists, Chicago, 1989.

Public Record Office of Victoria, *Guidelines for the Storage of Public Records*, PROS82/4, Government Printer, Melbourne, 1982.

Swartzburg, Susan G. and Bussey, Holly, with Garretson, Frank, *Libraries and Archives: Design and Renovation with a Preservation Perspective*, The Scarecrow Press Inc, Metuchen, New Jersey, USA, 1991.

Wilsted, Thomas and Nolte, William, *Managing Archival and Manuscript Repositories*, Society of American Archivists, Chicago, 1991.

Opposite page:
Appendix 2.1
An Overview of the
Archives System

Appendix 2.1   An Overview of the Archives System

Function	Work Activity	Tools for Structure/Control	Measures/Statistics
Total Program	Purpose of program Type holdings, clientele Facility location Administrative context Responsibilities of archivist Components of program from acquisition through PR Facilities and services	Policy document Description of program elements, goals, and functions Organisational chart Functional job descriptions Manual of policies and procedures Budget Annual and long-range plans	Program: short-term objectives for each element and work area

Basic Information for Clients: Information leaflets/brochures describing purpose/functions of the archives, how to obtain user privileges, hours and services available to clients, general types of holdings, location of facility; describing how to prepare to do particular types of research at the archives (family, graduate, historical). General guide to holdings which includes lists of publications and finding aids available for sale.

Appendix 2.1   An Overview of the Archives System

Function	Work Activity	Tools for Structure/Control	Measures/Statistics
Acquisition and Appraisal	Macro-surveying: for identification of potential archives, locations, owners Contacts/negotiation Micro-surveying: for appraisal/disposal scheduling of particular collections and series Disposal scheduling Appraisal Transferring and accessioning	Acquisitions and disposal policy and procedures Prospective acquisition log by donor and by item Survey forms: macro and micro Appraisal/disposal scheduling decision guidelines and criteria Disposal schedules Packing/Transfer box lists Deed of gift Register of accessions Donor card file	Number of: • prospective donors contacted • disposal schedules approved • surveys completed • appraisals made • accessions received

Basic Information for Clients: Importance and process of retention scheduling; how to prepare shipments for transfer to the archives; types of materials sought/not sought by the archives, advantages of making donations, how to begin process of donation, general conditions of donations; reports of new accessions.

Appendix 2.1 An Overview of the Archives System

Function	Work Activity	Tools for Structure/Control	Measures/Statistics
Arrangement/ Description	Close examination of collections to set priorities, levels and recommend sorting, disposal Arrangement: on paper and actual Description Preparation of finding aids	Arrangement/description policy and procedures Worksheet for arrangement and description giving priority level, work to be accomplished, dates began/completed, by whom Separation sheets for non-textual or oversized items List of material recommended for disposal Collection/series level forms for preparing descriptive inventories Finding aids 'linking' collections (ie chronological, subject/function, creator/compiler)	Number of: • series arranged • series described Cost of arrangement and description per series Shelf metres: • arranged • described Cost of arrangement and description per shelf metre

Basic Information for Clients: not relevant.

Appendix 2.1   An Overview of the Archives System

Function	Work Activity	Tools for Structure/Control	Measures/Statistics

Preservation	Preventative: removing clips, refoldering, reboxing
	Managing storage areas
	Preservation services: conservation, restoration, preservation copying
	Environment/container stability monitoring
	Materials testing
		Preservation policy and procedures
		Disaster plans
		Space allocation sheets
		Preservation services worksheets giving priorities, treatments recommended, work to be done
		Stability monitoring report sheets
		Test results sheets
			Number of:
			• collections/series shelved
			• sheets – deacidified
			  – repaired
			  – copied
			• stability tests carried out
			Savings from identifying faulty materials

Basic Information for Clients: how to maintain your family papers and photographs; guidelines for scrapbooks; how to handle records.

Function	Work Activity	Tools for Structure/Control	Measures/Statistics
Reference	On-site: • Admission of users • Reference interview • Information/advice on holdings, use of finding aids General: • Retrievals and refiles • Copying services	Reference policies and procedures Reading room regulations Application for reader's card Reader/visitor register Record request forms Copy order forms Form/guide letters	Number of: • new cards issued • readers/visitors • retrievals/refiles • copies provided • letters sent • publications sent

Remote:
- Research for mail inquiries
- Telephone inquiries
- Distribution of publications

Checklists for research by staff
Publications order forms/inventory control sheets

Basic Information for Clients: Leaflets described above under Total Program and guide sheets for beginning researchers in various popular research specialties, scheduled mini-classes for new researchers.

Function	Work Activity	Tools for Structure/Control	Measures/Statistics
User Education and Public Relations	Information and public relations Public seminars/workshops Publications Exhibits Staff training Technical advisory services Documentation program	Outreach policies and procedures Schedule of outreach activities Planning checklist for press releases, newsletters, seminars/workshops, publications, exhibits, etc Activity evaluation form: staff and participants Participant agreements, deeds, access agreements, request forms	Number of: • events held • participants • hours training/advice provided

Basic Information for Clients: Newsletter, announcements of events, training, exhibits, technical leaflets as needed, media coverage of archives events, activities, accessions.

3 Preservation

Ross Harvey

Chapter 1 notes that 'Archivists transmit knowledge and experience of past and present human interaction to present and future generations. They do this by ... preserving archives'. Preservation is briefly defined as the actions which enable the materials in archives – either the physical media themselves or the information they contain – to be retained for as long as they are needed. This may be for posterity or for a shorter time, say 10 years for some hospital records. This chapter describes current strategies and practices used to preserve archives. It aims

- to provide the reader with an orientation to preservation concepts
- to provide some practical guidance on the preservation of archival materials, in addition to that which is explicit or implicit throughout other chapters
- where necessary, to amplify preservation-related material in other chapters.

Throughout this chapter there is an emphasis on preventive aspects of preservation and also on the need for preservation awareness and active intervention at, or even before, the record creation stage: in other words, the emphasis is on pro-active management.

Defining the Context and Terms

Archivists have long realised that the materials in their custody require physical 'keeping'. This is best exemplified in Sir Hilary Jenkinson's dictum about the moral and physical defence of archives: by 'physical defence' he meant the physical care and security which is required to ensure that archival material is preserved. To ignore preservation is to be professionally negligent. There can be no compromise on this point, and not even a shortage of resources can excuse a lack of concern for preservation. Even the smallest archives must institute preservation practices, many of which can be incorporated into the archivist's daily routines and which need not be costly.

The principle that the archivist must accept responsibility for preservation derives from a cause-and-effect logic which is indisputable. Without properly preserved records, all other archival activities are negated. When the material in one's care is allowed to deteriorate unchecked or become damaged in any way, it is difficult and may be ultimately impossible to make it or the information it embodies available for use.

In addition to stressing preservation as the archivist's responsibility, it is equally important to note that virtually every archival function has a preservation aspect. Other chapters describe preservation concerns when they examine archival functions. Whether one is selecting shelving materials, formulating accessioning processes, or enforcing reading room rules, the immediate and long-term implications for preservation must be at the forefront of the mind.

Although the deterioration of archival materials has been recognised as a problem for many centuries (in 1145 Roger of Sicily decreed that all charters made on paper were to be recopied on to parchment to ensure their longevity), it is particularly acute today. Many factors have combined to cause a current crisis: the age of the materials in our archives, changes in manufacturing processes of these materials with a consequent decline in their chemical stability and physical strength, and a variety of societal influences such as increasing literacy and industrialisation. The major demonstration of this crisis is brittle paper, but the crisis is by no means limited to paper-based archives: it has equal impact on photographs, microfilms, electronic records and all other archival media. The dramatically increasing use of computers and electronic records, with consequent massive changes in recordkeeping practices, is raising a whole new set of preservation concerns. As the vulnerability of our information resources increases, so does the quantity of these resources, and therefore also the preservation problems which they pose.

Definitions

Current use allocates to preservation all of the considerations which seek to ensure accessibility to archival material and to its information content. It is a wide-ranging term which includes managerial and financial considerations such as storage and accommodation, staffing levels and policies. It encompasses physical storage facilities; managerial and administrative procedures and decisions which affect how records are stored and how, and how often, they are used; physical processes of repairing individual records; and information conversion (reformatting) programs such as microfilming, photocopying or digitising. It also includes activities and policies which are directed to the creation of stronger, longer-lasting basic materials such as papers, inks and microfilms. Paul Conway offers a three-part definition which summarises current opinions:

> Archival preservation is the acquisition, organisation, and distribution of resources (human, physical, monetary) to ensure adequate protection of historical and cultural information of enduring value and access for present and future generations.
>
> Archival preservation encompasses planning and implementing policies, procedures, and processes that together prevent further deterioration or renew the usability of selected groups of materials.
>
> Archival preservation, when most effective, requires that planning precede implementation, and that prevention activities have priority over renewal activities.[1]

Conservation is, currently, a more specialised term. It denotes the range of methods and techniques applied to physical artefacts to repair them, make them usable and protect them from further damage. When reading the archival and preservation literature, it is important to note that the terms 'preservation' and 'conservation' were until recent years used interchangeably. The reader must therefore take care to distinguish which usage is being applied.

Responses

Responses to the preservation problem are constantly evolving. There are, currently, two major thrusts. First, there are reactive responses, which encompass conservation as it was previously defined and as it has been practised in archives until the recent past. (For example, all Australian Archives' repositories have conservation laboratory facilities, but in only a few of them are staff being released to operate them; the preservation emphasis now lies elsewhere.) The second are pro-active responses concerned with how to prevent deterioration and limit its occurrence: such responses are often labelled 'preventive preservation'. Whereas in the past the archivist's preservation activities would have been largely concerned with repairing damage to individual items – tears repaired in a map, say – now they will be directed towards ensuring the maintenance of stable low temperature and relative humidity levels in storage areas, or to ensuring that all records in the archive's parent organisation are created on strong, durable paper.

The challenge of preservation is made greater by the sheer quantity of deteriorating or already deteriorated material and by its extent, not only in paper-based records but also in records in all other media. Estimates of the total quantity of records 'unfit for production' are in the region of 6–10% of total archival holdings: in the United States (US) this means that 530 million sheets of paper held by the National Archives and Records Administration are in danger of losing some of the information they contain. It is now recognised that conservation activities carried out in the past were usually not appropriate because they were labour-intensive and orientated towards treating the single artefact: today it is realised that the problem is so immense that methods which deal with material *en masse* are the only possible way in which to proceed. The single artefact-centred methods of the past are particularly ineffectual when applied to electronic media, now an intrinsic part of the future of archives. Traditional conservation solutions offer little of value to their preservation problems, which centre on the volatility and brief archival life of the media. Modern archives preservation has relegated traditional conservation methods to a lesser rank. They are now only one of many possible tools or strategies to be used in the total archives preservation program.

The current approach to archives preservation combines several strategies. Traditional conservation techniques are used to repair limited amounts of material, for example materials for exhibition. Records already present in the archives are appropriately housed and maintained: here such matters as environmental control, security and boxing programs are important. Some records, particularly those which are fragile or in heavy demand, are reformatted; ie their information content is transferred to a more durable physical medium using microfilming, preservation photocopying and other methods. These reformatting techniques, constantly being refined through developments in digital technology, also allow a refocussing away from preserving the original to preservation only of the information content. Another strategy addresses records still in the process of creation by considering preservation implications at the time records of likely archival status are created: an example is encouraging the use of 'permanent' alkaline paper; another is developing procedures for transferring electronic records from one system to another as the record-creating agency updates its computer systems.

Preservation: Who Is Responsible?

Who is responsible for the preservation of archival materials? The answer is, of course, the archivist or records manager, indeed all who work in archives or records repositories; but there are some recognised specialisations. Conservators are the technical experts, to be consulted on specific problems and to carry out repair procedures. They may also advise on and implement macro-level preservation activities such as environmental control, disaster planning, and so on. In larger archives conservation technicians may carry out conservation procedures under the direction of a trained conservator or experienced archivist. The largest institutions may employ scientists who carry out research into preservation, for example into longevity of new media. Repository managers are responsible for macro-level preservation by, for example, ensuring that environmental conditions are appropriate and are maintained at acceptable levels and overseeing pest control and physical security. They are concerned with many aspects of preventive preservation in its widest sense. Repository managers are likely to be found only in the larger archives and records repositories.

Archivists, and indeed all who work in archives or records repositories at all levels, are the most important personnel responsible for preservation, even if their job descriptions do not specify it. Every activity of archives staff should be informed by or directed towards preserving the records: thoughtful handling of records to minimise damage, careful transporting of them, educating users about how to best access and handle them, advising on records creation with an emphasis on their longevity are some examples.

In small archives, one person will combine the specific roles noted above. The single-person archivist or member of the staff of a small archives must therefore be acquainted with a wide range of preservation concerns. Certainly, technical expertise can and should be sought, most likely on a contract or other advisory basis from conservators or experts on climate control or pest control. However, the archivist must know enough about preservation to be aware of when to seek advice: in other words it is important to know your limitations, and the best way to do this is to keep yourself informed. This self-education process can be carried out by reading the professional literature and also the preservation literature, and by attending courses. The bibliography at the end of this chapter provides some starting points.

Nor must we forget the role of users in the preservation of archives. Users are second only to staff working in archives as the group most responsible for preserving the records. Every attempt must be made – and must be carried out as an ongoing process – to inform and educate users about the importance of the records in the archives and the need for careful handling of them.

Knowing Your Holdings

The most sensible approach the archivist can adopt towards the preservation challenge is to calmly begin to prepare plans which will systematically identify and lessen the causes of deterioration. The nature and extent of the problem in the archive must be ascertained. Such information is an essential part of planning for how to allocate financial and personnel resources to achieve the maximum effect. Surveying of records and of the buildings they are housed in provides this information. Surveys assess the nature and extent of deterioration and provide information to enable realistic, appropriate management decisions to be made about preservation; eg areas most in need of attention will be identified and priorities for treatment can be determined. In the longer term, regular surveying provides a way of monitoring the effectiveness of particular preservation strategies. Surveys are of two kinds: environment surveys, which examine the buildings and the physical environment; and condition surveys, which assess the collections.

Environment Surveys

The aim of the environment survey is to evaluate the suitability of the building or buildings for archives storage. It examines all aspects of the physical environment to determine whether the archives building and the environmental conditions within it encourage or obstruct the preservation of collections. Questions are posed in four areas

1 the building itself
2 the environment in the building
3 building security
4 storage areas and workrooms.

Some questions are listed in Table 3.1 to indicate the kind of answers required. Further questions will suggest themselves after a careful reading of Chapter 2.

The answers to these questions can be gathered by visual inspection, by interviewing staff and by monitoring of temperature, relative humidity and light levels. The results of the survey will immediately indicate areas where improvements can be made. Typical responses could be that regular checks of fire extinguishers could be started, and monitoring of temperature and relative humidity could begin.

Condition Surveys

Condition surveys assess the physical condition and state of repair of the archives' holdings and the nature and magnitude of the problems therein. The results will allow the following such matters to be ascertained: What patterns emerge? Do any groups of material, or

Table 3.1 Some Questions in an Environment Survey

The building itself. In what condition are the roof and walls? Do they leak? Are walls and roof insulated? In what condition are the the the attic, basement and storerooms? Are they clean, or cluttered and dirty? Is there any evidence of rodents, insects or mould?

The environment in the building. Can the temperature and relative humidity be maintained at constant levels 24 hours per day, every day of the year? Is the machinery available for this in good condition and well maintained? How are the effects of sunlight minimised? What type of artificial lighting is present? What is its level? Are temperature and relative humidity levels regularly monitored? By what method?

Building security. What type of intruder alarm is fitted? What type of fire alarm is fitted? Is it connected to the local fire brigade headquarters? What kind of fire extinguishing system is fitted? Is it regularly maintained? How many portable fire extinguishers are available? Are staff trained in their use?

Storage areas and workrooms. What is the average temperature and relative humidity? How is it maintained? Is the housekeeping adequate? Is there any evidence of insects, mould or rodents? Where are water and steam pipes located in relation to shelves housing records? Is there any evidence of excess heat? Of excess moisture? Is there any evidence of building leaks on walls or ceilings? Is there any evidence of light damage (fading) on the records? What type of shelving is present? Is there good air circulation around it? Is there a well-planned and supervised housekeeping program?

---

storage areas, or formats of material pose a special problem? They might suggest, for example, that a change from vertical to horizontal shelving would alleviate damage to large items, or that boxing a particular group of records would considerably assist in their retention. Short- and long-term preservation measures can be more realistically addressed using the survey's results.

There are other reasons for conducting a condition survey. These include the need to establish a base for future comparison as a tool to assess the preservation program's progress and effectiveness. Involving many of the staff members of the archives in such surveys will heighten awareness of preservation problems.

Condition surveys can be as detailed or as simple as the archivist thinks fit. They can be carried out in a variety of ways, eg as a special project, perhaps using students or staff hired and trained specifically for this purpose, or can be carried out by regular staff within the normal activites of the archives. Sampling techniques which establish a valid sample of the whole collection are usually applied. The questions asked of the sample are listed in Table 3.2.

Knowing Your Materials

Chapter 1 notes the wide range of media – paper, microform, film, magnetic tape and disk, optical disk, video and audiotapes –

Table 3.2 The Condition Survey: Some data headings

1 Preliminary (date of survey, name of surveyor, etc.)
2 Location of records
3 Type of material present in record group (formats present; date range covered)
4 Condition of records (general appearance, tears, surface dirt, stains, embrittlement, evidence of mould, insect damage, etc.)
5 Storage containers (folders, boxes, pins, paper clips, etc.)
6 Extraneous or interleaved material (staples, tissue paper, loose cuttings, photographs, etc.)
7 Suggested action (rebox, refolder, remove enclosures, withdraw from use, no action, etc.)
8 Priority ranking of records for treatment

and shapes, sizes and formats – letters, paper files, diaries, registers, index cards, maps, plans, microfiche, aperture cards, photographs, videocassettes, computerised databases and electronic mail – found in archives. Some knowledge of the structure and attributes of archival media is a necessary prerequisite for making informed choices about preservation of the media or of the information they contain.

Archival media need to have certain attributes to be 'archival'. Permanence, the ability to last as long as possible, is one; strength is another; durability, or ability to withstand use, another. Archival media deteriorate in two ways: deterioration due to causes intrinsic to the medium because of the way in which it was manufactured, sometimes referred to as 'inherent vice' – acid in paper is the best-known example; and causes which are external to the medium, such as inappropriate levels of temperature, humidity and light, use, and exposure to water, fire, civil insurrections, animal and insect pests.

Paper

Paper (including board and card) is still the most commonly found medium in archives and will continue to be so for the immediate future. Paper products should ideally be strong and durable and should not contain ingredients which degrade into harmful substances such as acid. The reality is that most paper does not meet these requirements, and this is certainly the case for almost all paper manufactured during the nineteenth and twentieth centuries. This period is, of course, the one most heavily represented in archival collections in Australia. Space precludes a detailed description of the reasons why this paper is not long-lived, but a summary is worthwhile here. Increasing demand for paper, as societies became more literate and the structures of society became more formalized and more complex, is the root cause. This increased demand resulted in a shortage of rags, the traditional source of the cellulose fibre from which paper was made, and a search for new fibre sources. Wood became the most commonly used fibre source from the middle of the nineteenth century and forms the basis of most of the paper in our archives. Although paper made from wood pulp has many advantages for paper-making, it also has considerable problems: in particular, the fibres are short and therefore weak, and it contains substances which break down chemically over time to further weaken and discolour the paper. This is exacerbated by additives which are required to make the paper less absorbent so that it can be written or printed on (sizing), or to colour the paper to acceptable levels of whiteness. Readers will be familiar with newspapers which rapidly become brown or yellow and very brittle; and although it is often less obvious, nearly all paper will suffer the same fate.

'Permanent' Paper

Largely for economic reasons, much paper manufactured in the last decade is made by processes which result in a product considerably better for archival storage than that made during the last century and a half. This modern paper is not acidic, often in fact containing a protective alkaline buffer (its pH is $8 - 10$); it also contains lower levels of undesirable substances such as lignin and acidic sizing. If such paper ('permanent' paper) is used to create records, a longer life for the records, measured in centuries rather than in decades, will be assured. Archivists have been increasingly active in encouraging the manufacture of 'permanent' paper and its use for record creation. Recent Australian activity, paralleling that in other countries, has involved awareness campaigns to ensure that this paper is known and used when appropriate, and Australian Archives has been one of several institutions responsible for developing and issuing an interim Australian Standard for 'permanent' paper (AS 4003 (int)) and also in developing and manufacturing such paper. Such paper (Reflex Archival is one example) promises, when more affordable and more widely available, to ensure that today's records – the paper-based archives of the future – will last considerably longer than only a few decades.

In Australia local paper suppliers do not yet stock 'permanent' paper at a realistic price as part of their normal stock. Until such time as they do, the archivist must take other steps. For example, the local supplier could be educated about why 'permanent' paper is desirable; sources of it can be located if it is not available locally; photocopy and other paper used by those who create records could be tested for acidity, for it is entirely feasible that what is sold as 'ordinary' paper is alkaline (although it may not have all the other attributes which distinguish 'permanent' paper). Paper acidity testing is easily carried out using an inexpensive pH pen or pH indicator strips, available from suppliers of conservation materials.

Recycled paper is another concern for the archivist, posing significant problems for records needing to be retained. Much of the fibre source from which recycled paper is made has been through the paper manufacturing process at least once and its already short and weak fibres have been further shortened and weakened by passing once again through the manufacturing process. Caution about its use is urged: it is essential that a distinction is made between records which are not likely to be retained and those which are, and that the appropriate paper types are used when these records are created. Australian Archives was in 1990 recommending that recycled paper and paper which included recycled fibre should not be used for certain categories of records, for example records which were to be kept for more than 10 years, or frequently handled records.

Formats Other Than Paper

Space precludes a description of some of the other materials commonly found in archives, such as ink, leather, cloth and adhesives, but further information about them can be found in some of the works listed at the end of this chapter.

Chapters 12 and 13 provide details of some of the formats other than paper which are represented in archives. Some general points about their preservation are worth reiterating. As a generalisation, the greater the storage density of the medium, the more sophisticated is the equipment needed to access the information stored, and the shorter the life of that medium. The implications for preservation are that either a museum of obsolete equipment in working order needs to be maintained or an ongoing program of data conversion from one medium to a more current medium is required. The first of these solutions is now no longer seriously mooted and attention is being directed towards the latter.

Another point concerns equipment. For preservation reasons it is essential that the equipment used to provide access to these media – microfilm readers, computers, optical disk players, tape recorders and so on – does not damage the fragile media. It is essential to procure equipment of the highest quality that can be afforded, if possible of professional rather than domestic quality, and then to ensure that it is regularly maintained. For example, microfilm reading equipment requires frequent cleaning of the glass plates through which the film passes, and the mechanism which lifts these plates off the film must be carefully adjusted and frequently checked to ensure that it does not scratch the film. Purchase of high-quality equipment and its regular maintenance also have intangible benefits which will benefit the archives: as an example, modern top-of-the-range microfilm reading equipment is less tiring to use than less expensive models, ensuring that the archives user is less likely to complain about having to use microfilm.

The archivist must understand something about the construction of archival media because this knowledge leads to better informed choices about the kind of media which is possible to store, the life expectations of each medium and the implications of different media for managing the archives. The archivist needs to be active, where possible, at the record creation stage in determining which medium is appropriate: recycled paper may be acceptable where records will not be retained beyond, say, 10 years, but 'permanent' paper should be used for records requiring longer life; microfilms needing to be retained as long as possible must be carefully processed to the highest standards and stored appropriately, but those required only for a finite time may need less attention paid to their processing, storage and handling. Attention to these matters at the time of record creation will pay enormous dividends when such records come into the archivist's care for long-term preservation.

Preventive Preservation: Providing Appropriate Housing and Environments

Chapter 2 notes that two of the priorities for an archives building are 'to provide a suitable and stable environment' and 'to make it secure and safe'. It continues: 'Overall, archival facilities should be secure, clean, temperate and protected from violent swings in climate' and provides detailed information about these factors. It notes the vital place of careful handling and appropriate storage equipment. All of these factors are essential to the preservation of archives and Chapter 2 should be studied in detail. Two aspects are noted in more detail here.

Temperature and Relative Humidity

The ideal is to maintain stable levels of temperature and relative humidity in the archives. The primary danger is fluctuation in temperature and relative humidity as rapid rates of change in these ('cycling') cause damage by placing stress on media. For example, mechanical stress is caused by swelling and contracting of paper as water is alternately absorbed and released when humidity levels fluctuate; in similar conditions the binder or adhesive which attaches metal oxide particles to the carrier layer in magnetic tapes weakens and the information-carrying oxide particles are misaligned or drop off. If ideal environmental levels cannot be attained and compromises need to be reached, it is better to aim at controlling the fluctuation of temperature and relative humidity levels rather than to aim at achieving temperature and humidity levels which are unrealistic for the conditions.

As noted in Chapter 2, 'well-designed air-conditioning' is indeed the ideal, but it must be run 24 hours per day every day of the year, otherwise its effectiveness is lost. This clearly has resource implications for managing an archives. For some archives it is possible that the cost of full-time air-conditioning will not be the most effective way of spending the limited preservation dollars. Air-conditioning only a part of the building, for example the area in which microfilm and other non-paper media are stored, may be a good compromise.

If air-conditioning is not possible, other actions can assist considerably in maintaining stable environmental conditions. The essentials are to maintain storage areas as cool as possible, with humidity levels maintained at a stable level, preferably around 50%, with low light levels, and with an airflow through the storage area. There are many ways of achieving this, some involving minimal or no expenditure of money. For example, airflow can be improved by altering the direction in which shelving runs, and temperature and humidity levels in internal rooms change more slowly than in outside areas and so will be better for storage of significant material. Further examples can be found in the preservation literature. As with much else that is effective in preservation, combining common sense, knowledge of the nature of the media and desirable environmental standards, and imaginative thinking will produce effective results.

Regular monitoring of temperature and relative humidity levels is essential to ensure that standards are being maintained. A variety of equipment is available. The most inexpensive is a wet–dry thermometer or sling psychrometer, but although the initial purchase price is low, the need for staff to record and chart readings regularly may mean that this is not, overall, the most cost-effective method. Inexpensive electronic devices, some of which store maximum and minimum levels, can be used in a similar way but have the same drawbacks. A thermohygrograph allows temperature and relative humidity levels to be recorded over longer periods (daily or weekly) and are frequently used in archives. For institutions which can afford them, the best solution is the datalogger, a small electronic device which can be set to record environmental levels over a wide range of time intervals, can store this information for long periods, and when the data is downloaded to a computer (via a modem if necessary) will present the information in a variety of formats. The cost of a datalogger and software is, at the time of writing, about double that of a thermohygrograph, but its increased flexibility and portability

 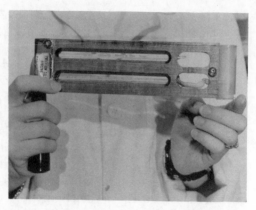

*A thermohygrograph,
sling psychrometer and
(opposite) a datalogger –
equipment for monitor-
ing environmental
conditions*

warrants serious consideration for purchase. Note that all the equipment described requires calibration for accurate results.

The frequently-cited ideal levels of around 20°C and 50% relative humidity are compromises for repositories housing mixed media collections. Other chapters (for example, Chapters 2 and 13) indicate different levels which are desirable for specific media. If the archives has large or especially significant collections of a particular medium, it may consider a special storage area where desirable levels, usually lower than the compromise levels, can be maintained. If this is planned, it will be essential to seek expert advice as recommended levels are often altered in the light of ongoing research.

Cold storage facilities are becoming more widely used for special materials. Considerable expense is involved in their installation, maintenance or lease. Space in cold storage facilities which have high levels of security are available for lease, for example, from a repository established for NSW government records where conditions are maintained at 13°C and 35% relative humidity. The National Library of Australia also leases space in its cold storage facility. Where archival material is stored in areas maintained at lower temperature and relative humidity levels than the area in which they will be consulted, conditioning (allowing the material to adjust slowly to the higher levels before use and to lower levels before being returned to storage) will be required.

Pest Control

Biological pests (vermin, insects, mould) have traditionally been controlled in archives by chemical fumigation. Chemicals used for fumigation are now recognised as harmful to humans and many of them once in regular use are banned in many countries. In their place are being developed other procedures such as the use of low oxygen atmospheres. A policy of 'integrated pest management' using a variety of techniques, only one of which is fumigation, is currently considered most effective for pest control. The main strategies in an integrated pest control program are

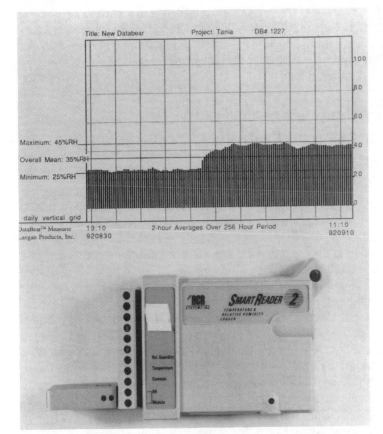

- regular inspections to locate problem areas as early as possible
- environmental control to keep temperature and relative humidity at levels which biological pests do not find attractive
- good housekeeping to remove dust, dead insects and similar food and water sources for biological pests
- alteration of features of the archives building and storage areas which attract insect pests, eg stagnant air pockets or outside lights positioned where they attract insects into the building
- removing affected material from the main storage areas and treating it by such methods as freezing, irradiation or placing it in a low oxygen atmosphere
- chemical fumigation only as a last resort.

Where chemical fumigation is required, it is crucial that expert advice is sought: fumigation is emphatically not a task for archivists.

New material entering the archives may be infected with pests and can have the potential to infect the rest of the collection. Many archives operate a quarantine area for newly accessioned material, in which the material is cleaned if required and assessed for evidence of the presence of pests. If infected, the material will require treatment by freezing, irradiation, being placed in a low oxygen atmosphere, or possibly fumigation. Infected material already in the collection can also be removed to this quarantine area for treatment.

Preventive Preservation: Providing Appropriate Protective Packaging and Enclosures

Storing archival material in enclosures (or 'primary housing') is another important preventive preservation technique available to archivists. Enclosures in common use for paper-based archival materials include encapsulation for single sheet items, folders for unbound documents, boxes of various kinds for larger items and for bound items whose bindings have been damaged, slipcases for bound items, and shrink-wrapping. Non-paper materials can be housed in enclosures, for example, microfilm reels in boxes. The enclosure and the environment it surrounds act as a buffer to slow down the rates of change of temperature and relative humidity levels. Enclosures provide protection from light, dust and airborne pollutants. They also provide protection from water, smoke, heat and other destructive agents present if there is a disaster in the archives.

Material from which enclosures are manufactured needs to be mechanically and chemically stable so that it does not damage the archival materials it houses. Only materials of high quality which are not harmful to the item should be used. Paper and board should ideally be 'permanent' (acid-free, alkaline buffered), although this may not always be possible on financial grounds: it is better to enclose material in boxes made from board which does not meet this standard than not to provide any protection at all. The adhesives used should also be chemically stable.

Sophisticated equipment is not needed to manufacture enclosures. Most can be made using inexpensive equipment such as a bone folder, a cutting mat or board, scissors and a soft brush. For some, more expensive, space-consuming equipment such as a standing press or board shears may be needed.

Some Examples of Enclosures

Encapsulation. Single leaves of paper can be encapsulated between sheets of a chemically inert transparent plastic such as Mylar. Encapsulation is used for fragile items or where heavy use is expected. Items enclosed in this manner can be easily removed from the encapsulation if required. This kind of enclosure is expensive.

Phase Boxes. The term 'phase' refers to the development of this kind of enclosure as an early step or phase in a conservation program at the Library of Congress in which phase boxes provided protection for items and kept together all parts of them (eg detached covers) until such time as further conservation treatment could be carried out. This procedure is now widely used to provide protective enclosures for damaged or fragile bound items. Acid-free, alkaline-buffered card is cut and folded according to a predetermined pattern, and the box is secured by Velcro 'coins' or by cloth ties and washers.

Other Boxes. Many other kinds of boxes can be used as protective enclosures. They include double-tray boxes, boxes made from corrugated card, which are suitable for a wide range of materials, and solander boxes.

Document Folders. Documents, pamphlets and other thin items can be stored in a document folder made from acid-free, alkaline-buffered card cut and folded to a standard pattern.

Slipcases. Slipcases can be constructed to protect bound volumes from abrasion, light and dust.

Wrapping. Wrapping of materials in paper is sometimes used, for instance for outsized material which is not readily accommodated in boxes or folders of standard sizes. If possible and affordable, the wrapping paper should be 'permanent'.

Shrink-wrapping. Shrink-wrapping can be used to enclose low-use material. The equipment used is the same as that employed in manufacturing industries to package material for shipping.

Ready-made boxes are available in standard sizes. The Australian Archives box, made from board and described in Chapter 2, is the most commonly-used example in Australia. Experiments to produce a range of boxes in standard sizes from the inert plastic polypropylene have been carried out (eg by the National Library of Australia and Australian Archives) and offer promising results. Chapter 2 also notes the possibility of cooperating with neighbouring archives: cooperative ventures for purchasing boxes, and indeed most preservation equipment and supplies, enable considerable financial savings to be made.

As noted elsewhere in this chapter, archives preservation is now taking a more pro-active approach. The use of enclosures as a standard procedure for records already in the custody of the archives is a commonly accepted standard technique and has been for many years. It is also now recognised, although not yet widely practised, that more active intervention in the housing of active records is of considerable advantage to their preservation once they have been accessioned as archival material. This applies to their housing in enclosures: wherever possible, then, the archivist must promote and encourage the use of secure primary housing for active records. In this way the archivist's preservation tasks will be lightened considerably in the future.

Preventive Preservation: Precautions in Use, Handling and Display

It is the paradox of preservation that the archives exists to make its holdings available for use, but that such use is probably the major cause of deterioration of archival materials. The archivist must, therefore, take all possible steps to ensure that handling and use of archival material is carried out with care and in a manner which is as nondestructive as possible. Many examples of poor practice readily come to mind: direct harm can be caused to records by smoking (from airborne pollutants or, worse, fire), eating (from grease spots and, less obviously, from food particles which attract vermin and insect pests), drinking (spilling of liquids on to the records). Others are less obvious but no less damaging: using pens which may leak or stacking records high and consequently causing damage to fragile paper when the pile is accidentally knocked over.

Good handling is not merely a set of regulations to be enforced on users of archival material. It is equally applicable to all staff working in archives. There is an analogy here with AIDS: not practising good handling, like safe sex, will have no obvious immediate impact, but the effects will be felt after many years, when it is usually too late to apply a remedy.

Good handling is enhanced by providing appropriate equipment in sufficient quantities and by encouraging or even enforcing its use. For example, providing stable footstools will help staff to reach records on higher shelves without stretching, and so reduce the possibility that boxes are accidentally knocked down with ensuing mechanical damage. Protective supports are another example of equipment which should be provided and used. Most items suffer damage if they lean on the shelves, and supports (such as bookends where appropriate) will assist in preventing such damage by assisting material to remain upright.

Records in transit need special protection to prevent damage to them. Within the archives, items should be transported using a trolley or other equipment designed for the purpose. This equipment must be designed so that the items can be placed on or in it without sliding about. It will have features such as wheels of large diameter to ensure a smooth ride. If more than a small number of items are carried by hand, the ever-present danger is that they will be dropped and damaged.

Education and training of archives staff can be carried out in many ways. The staff member who has undertaken a professional qualification will have been introduced to preservation including, hopefully, an introduction to good handling. Other staff can be introduced to the concepts during induction programs for new staff. Ongoing training – such forums as staff meetings or attending continuing education programs – is essential, if it can be managed. As already noted, it is essential to encourage the use of equipment such as trolleys which promote good handling, even if it sometimes adds to the time needed to complete a task.

Users, too, must be educated and trained, and again this must be ongoing, as new users come to use the archives. One common way of doing this is by using search room regulations: users can be required to read a list of regulations, including some which cover handling and other preservation requirements, and acknowledge them by signing a statement. An initial interview with new users, standard practice in many archives, can be a useful occasion for reinforcing preservation rules. Other methods which have proved their worth include the use of displays and posters and the labelling of fragile material with a message bringing the need for careful handling to the user's attention. One is tempted to suggest that all regular users (and staff) of archives should sit an annual 'warrant of fitness' to ascertain their ability to handle archival material in a careful, non-damaging way.

Archives staff must not be afraid (but often are) of being assertive in drawing examples of incorrect handling to users' attention. This needs to be carried out in a diplomatic manner, but it is an effective way of reinforcing the message.

Exhibitions

Well-designed displays can greatly improve the public's understanding of the archives. They may stimulate donations and are excellent vehicles for explaining aspects of the history of a region, school, company, government or people. Mounting an exhibition is, however, often also the occasion when the archivist breaks all the tenets of preservation.

It must suffice here to emphasise that no items from the archives should be endangered in any way by their display. From the preservation viewpoint, it is preferred that the exhibition of originals be avoided and facsimile copies substituted, with each being clearly identified with captions. If originals must be displayed, the following requirements should be satisfied. Some material will need conservation work carried out on it before it is exhibited: this is often done by contract conservators.

Lighting. Exhibition illumination should be no stronger than 50 lux, be free of ultra-violet rays (definitely not sunlight) and be from a source which does not raise the temperature levels of the

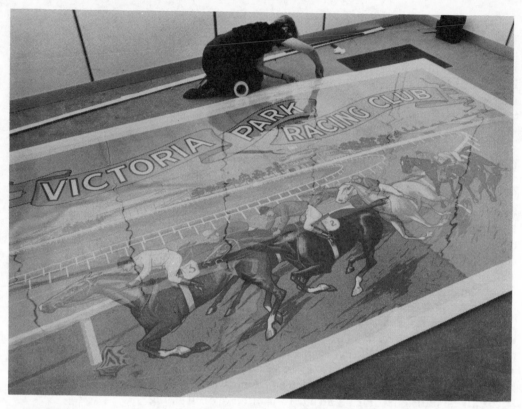

A conservator at Australian Archives ACT Regional Office mounting a large poster for an Archives display on Australia's sporting life, held January 1990. This exhibit had come to Archives in 12 different sections, each folded and stored in an envelope.

display environment. Light levels should be regularly monitored. Never leave an original item on display indefinitely. Fading and yellowing, both caused by incorrect lighting, are irreversible.

Microclimate. The display case, secure from thieves, has its own microclimate, which should be kept at levels equivalent to that in the storage areas. Both the temperature and the relative humidity of the display case's microclimate should be regularly monitored.

Duration of Display. Original items should not be displayed for more than two or three months, regardless of the lighting used in displays. If permanent exhibitions are planned, prepare replacement items and captions; better still, display facsimiles.

Security. To guard against theft, the originals should be laid out in locked display cases and should be placed where they can be overseen by staff. Gallery areas should be supervised by security attendants.

Item Support. All items on display should be supported so that no stress is placed on them. For example, pins should never be used on the item being displayed, and open volumes such as a diary or scrapbook should be supported by a cradle and their

pages turned every two or three months. Simple methods of making display supports are described in the preservation literature.

Conservation Treatment

Although the emphasis of modern archival preservation has moved away from repair of damaged materials to a concentration on strategies which deal with materials *en masse* or which attempt to determine their characteristics at the time of record creation, there is still a place for applying the techniques of conservation to some categories of damaged archival material. Some basic conservation procedures can be carried out without requiring a professionally qualified conservator or special equipment and are appropriate for archives of all sizes. Other procedures require advanced technical skills and are usually carried out in conservation laboratories. These are inappropriate for all but a handful of the largest archives, but it is possible to apply these advanced skills if required (eg for very precious archival material required for display) by contracting the services of specialist conservators.

Other conservation treatments can be applied. These rely on a high degree of technical expertise and very sophisticated equip-

A conservator at Australian Archives ACT Regional Office pasting an Albumen photograph, about 120 years old, onto a new, archival quality backing. This print is from a series of 200 panoramas, many up to 3 metres long, showing early scenes of Sydney and Melbourne.

ment in facilities often costing many hundreds of thousands of dollars to establish. One promising but not yet commercially viable technique is the British Library's process of paper strengthening using gamma irradiation. Mass deacidification is another treatment which has captured the imagination of many archivists, but the reality at the time of writing is that even after many years of development it is still not a viable technique. Its problems include high costs, unsuitability for some kinds of material, and an inability to strengthen already embrittled and weak paper (even though it deacidifies it). Once seen as a panacea, it is now being recognised as only one in the arsenal of hi-tech, expensive conservation treatments. Recent writing, describing the US National Archives and Records Administration's preservation activities and referring to the current lack of viability of mass deacidification, has noted that 'the only safe mass preservation technique for archival records is careful packaging and storage of documents within environmentally controlled storage areas'.[2] The archivist's best course is to read the preservation literature to monitor the development of hi-tech mass treatments, which promise much – but in the future – for preserving archives.

Noted here are some of the simple conservation procedures commonly carried out in archives and which do not require special equipment. This section aims only to describe the kinds of possibilities, not how to apply them. Before deciding to set up an area with equipment and trained staff, it is important to seek up-to-date advice on the procedures from a conservator or experienced archivist. Detailed descriptions of many procedures can be found in the published literature, eg in the books by Helen Price and Mary Lynn Ritzenthaler listed at the end of this chapter.

General Principles

Some general principles apply to all repairs. An important preliminary question is 'Which procedure to apply?' Here, factors should be taken into account such as what is feasible for the archives in technological, financial and practical terms. The value of an item or group of items must also be considered. Guidelines should be developed which allow decisions on individual items or record groups to be made rapidly, eg that all photographs should be enclosed in permanent paper envelopes. To assist decisions, comparative costs of standard repairs, microfilming and preservation photocopying should be known and updated.

Only materials of high quality which do not harm the item should be used in conservation procedures. For example, all paper and board used should be acid-free (with a pH of 7 or above) so as not to chemically damage items; more preferable is alkaline-buffered paper and board which will actively counteract some of the chemical damage that may be occurring. Adhesives, similarly, should be chemically inert and their action should be reversible if required. Advice should be sought from a conservator about local sources of supply for suitable repair materials.

Ethical aspects of archival repair need to be considered. It is generally accepted that all repairs should be reversible, they should not alter the evidential value of the item being repaired, they must not weaken or damage the item, and the minimum amount of action necessary to repair the item should be applied. On occasion the best procedure to follow may be that termed 'benign neglect'; that is, doing nothing active to the item is the best course of action. This may arise when no acceptable repair technique has yet been developed. In such cases careful storage and handling and reducing use of the item while waiting for or developing an acceptable solution is the best course of action.

No matter what the size of archives, advice from a professional conservator or knowledgeable archivist on suitable repair procedures to be implemented is highly desirable. Advice should be sought on such matters as the appropriateness of specific repairs, the best materials to use and local sources of materials. Once under way the program should be regularly reviewed by a conservator or knowledgeable archivist to ensure that standards are being maintained and that advice about any improvements in materials or newly developed techniques is passed on to the personnel carrying out the repair.

Basic Repair Procedures

Simple repairs do not require sophisticated equipment. As for making enclosures, all that is required for most repairs is inexpensive equipment such as a bone folder, a cutting mat or board, scissors and a soft brush. Some – by no means all – simple procedures are noted here.

Dealing with Acid Migration. Acid migration, recognised by staining or browning of paper, is treated by removing and discarding the offending acidic paper where possible or by placing sheets of permanent paper on either side of the acidic paper.

Surface Cleaning of Paper. Dirt on the surface of paper is removed using a soft flat brush, a soft plastic eraser or a document cleaning pad, according to the paper type and its condition.

Relaxing Paper. Paper sheets which have been rolled up or folded need careful unrolling or 'relaxing'. Moisture is reintroduced into the paper by spraying with distilled water, placing the paper between moistened blotters or by using a humidification chamber before the paper is unrolled or unfolded by flattening it under weights and blotting paper.

Removing Adhesives. Pressure-sensitive adhesive tapes are removed from paper by carefully applying small quantities of a solvent and pulling the tape off as the adhesive softens. This process is slow and calls for considerable patience and care.

Removal of Paper Fasteners. Metal fasteners rust, rubber bands become brittle and may discolour paper, string or cloth ties cut into brittle paper and can be highly acidic. These and most other fastening devices can be carefully removed by hand, in some cases using tools such as a spatula to assist.

Mending Tears in Paper. Tears in paper are repaired by patching them with strong acid-free paper as near transparent as possible. Long-fibred handmade Japanese papers which are torn easily to fit the shape of the tear are commonly used, with archival-quality adhesive. Two patches a little larger than the shape of the tear to be mended are cut or torn, adhesive is applied on both sides of the paper being repaired, the patches are stuck on, and the repaired tear dried under weights.

Enclosures; Tipping In. To keep together a bound volume and associated items such as newspaper clippings, the items can be enclosed in an acid-free envelope and kept near the volume, correctly labelled. Some items can be tipped into the volume, ie glued in with a thin strip of adhesive applied down one side of the page.

Leather Cleaning and Dressing. It was formerly considered that leather bindings needed ongoing maintenance to ensure that they did not become dry and brittle. Initial treatment provided a protective coating, then leather dressing was applied regularly, suggestions ranging from every one to every five years. The dressing, usually containing neat's-foot oil and lanolin, is rubbed into the leather, left to dry for about 24 hours, then polished. Recent studies suggest that leather dressing has no preservative effect and may even be harmful.

Preservation Reprography

Copying of material from one medium to another, usually more durable, medium (or reformatting) is a standard preservation procedure. While such reformatting is usually carried out when the original material is too fragile to withstand further use, there are other reasons, such as the need to reduce storage space or a need for duplicate copies, perhaps for security reasons or greater accessibility of the material. Microfilming is currently the major reformatting technique, although it may soon be overtaken by digitising of data. There are important legal and archival factors associated with reformatting: they are discussed in Chapters 4 and 12.

Selection of material to reformat is one important issue. Usually material has been selected as a reactive measure, in response to a specific demand for a copy or because the original material is badly deteriorated. There is considerable room for a more pro-active approach by selecting record groups which will be in heavy demand in the future and reformatting them so that the originals are not subject to major deterioration through excessive use. Material which has no intrinsic value (ie documents in which the information is of value but the nature and form of the document is not) is a good candidate for reformatting.

Another issue is whether to retain or discard the original materials after reformatting. Some badly deteriorated material may be in such poor condition that it cannot be handled further after microfilming because it will disintegrate, and here there would be little point in retaining the originals, legal requirements permitting (see Chapter 4). Storing the originals after reformatting requires expensive storage space. The life of the surrogate needs to be considered: Will it last as long as the original? Will there realistically be a need to go back to the original to make another surrogate copy? Material with no intrinsic value is a likely candidate for destruction after reformatting. Also involved in this question is the matter of standards. Microfilm that has not been developed to the required standards may have a short life; nor may it last if it is not stored to appropriate standards. Some users may have a genuine need to use originals rather than a copy. There will probably be the need to keep the original for at least a short time after reformatting so that the copy can be thoroughly checked to ensure that there are no missing pages or other errors: this happens frequently.

Reformatting offers many advantages. Having more than one copy provides added security against accidental damage, especially if copies are stored at more than one location. Accessibility is enhanced because material can be used by more than a single user at any one time, possibly at more than one site. This is especially true for information in digital data which can, given appropriate equipment and communications links, be used from remote sites.

Standards

All reformatting requires considerable care in preparing the materials, such as checking that files are complete and in correct order. Such checking, while time-consuming, is essential, especially if the original material is to be discarded after copying. It is essential also to be aware of standards and to adhere to them. If they are not followed, then the surrogates will not last as long as they could, and the point of making a surrogate – a copy which is to last longer than the original – will, therefore, be lost. Standards are important in three areas: production of surrogates; testing; and storage. Some examples of standards for microfilming are those which indicate the layout of the image on the film, the desired density of the image, required standards for chemical processing (and, in particular, the amount of residual chemicals which are acceptable after processing), tests for residual chemicals, and storage standards for master microfilms to ensure the longest life of the microfilm. Standards are usually internationally agreed-upon and should be readily accessible through such bodies as the International Standards Organisation, the British Standards Institution, Standards Australia and the American National Standards Institute.

Microfilming

Microfilming is the most commonly used method for reformatting archival material. A considerable amount is known about the longevity of microfilm, and procedures which ensure that the product is of high quality have been developed. Chapter 12 provides more detailed information about microfilming.

Electronic Media

Chapter 12 also provides detailed information about document image processing, ie converting the information content of a document into electronic format. Although electronic versions of archival material are the way forward, it is essential to note that in preservation terms there are still many unknowns. Recent research has investigated the conversion of microfilm to digital data and has concluded that it is feasible on a large scale. Given the many unknowns about the preservation of electronic records and the embryonic state of development of standard procedures and techniques to ensure their preservation, the most responsible technique at present for reformatting paper-based archival material is microfilming.

Preservation Photocopying

Not all archives can command the resources to institute a microfilming or document-imaging program. Preservation photocopying offers a lower-cost alternative for some materials. This process is essentially the same as the normal photocopying process. It is especially suitable for heavily used items in situations where microfilm is less appropriate because it requires reading equipment and may encounter user resistance. It is not appropriate for works with coloured or high quality black-and-white illustrations.

Preservation photocopying is a practical format for smaller- and medium-sized archives which already own or have access to photocopiers. All that is required is a standard photocopier which has been regularly maintained; the higher the quality of the photocopier, the better the result will be. The result is relatively permanent if appropriate ('permanent') paper is used. The copying process may, however, damage fragile items, it does not produce a master copy (although it is of course possible to make a master copy to be stored securely and used to make further copies when needed) and the cost is high for items with a large number of pages, especially if the cost of boxing or binding is added.

Other reformatting methods are sometimes appropriate. Publishing may be either of a facsimile of the item or of the text, usually edited. Transcription of the text by typing or wordprocessing is labour-intensive and expensive and the possibility of transcription errors is high.

Disaster Preparedness and Response

'Disaster planning' refers to a set of rehearsed actions which will minimise the effect of a disaster on the archives and which will assist in restoring the archives building and its contents to a usable condition in the minimum possible time. The term 'disaster' covers a wide range of events, from minor incidents to full-scale emergencies. Disasters in even the best-run archives can and do happen.

The key ingredients of disaster planning are preventive – preventing disasters by planning, reducing hazards, establishing procedures to cope with disasters – and reactive – coping with a disaster by putting into practice procedures which are understood and have been rehearsed. Most disaster plans have four parts: prevention, preparedness, reaction, and recovery.

Table 3.3 General Guidelines for Disaster Planning

Plan in advance
Educate yourself about disaster planning
Adapt advice to local situations
React to a disaster quickly
React according to a plan

Prevention

Prevention refers to actions which minimise the risks posed by unauthorised access, fire and flood and which minimise the damage a disaster will cause. Examples include the use of appropriate storage equipment which offers protection to items, making security copies of important materials, and special arrangements to ensure the safety of the building and its collections during unusual periods of increased risk such as building operations or exhibitions. An essential early step is to carry out a building inspection.

Routine housekeeping and building maintenance plays a vital role in preventing disasters. As one example, regular instruction of staff in fire prevention procedures, combined with regular maintenance of fire extinguishing equipment, lessens the possibility that a fire, if it starts, will spread.

Examples of practical prevention techniques include storing the most valuable materials on upper shelves or upper floors to avoid water damage. If materials must be stored temporarily in basements or lower levels, raising them on bricks and boards or pallets off the floor is a sensible precautionary measure. Fragile items such as phonograph discs may require elastic cords across the fronts of shelves to help prevent damage during earthquake, flood or storms.

Table 3.4 Prevention: Some Points To Consider

History. How old is the building? Has it ever had fire or water damage? If so, were the causes eliminated or only patched up?

Heating plant. Are all openings which connect the building to the heating plant properly protected with fire doors? Is fuel storage safe?

Electricity. Has insulation on wiring become worn or deteriorated?

The roof. When was it constructed? Are there signs of old or new leaks?

Windows. Are they tight? Are they ever left open for ventilation?

Fire protection equipment. Are automatic sprinklers or fire detection devices installed and are they maintained?

Preparedness

The preparedness phase is concerned with producing and documenting the disaster plan and keeping it up-to-date. The first steps are to form a disaster response team whose members are likely to be available at the time of an emergency, to train these personnel and to institute procedures to notify and assemble them rapidly when a disaster occurs. Material for priority salvage should be identified and marked. Documentation needs to be assembled, eg building floor plans and lists of personnel and their addresses and telephone numbers, lists of equipment, and lists of suppliers of items needed during an emergency such as crates, newsprint or generators; it is essential to keep these lists up-to-date. Contact should be established with conservators and facilities in the region who can offer support in a disaster. Equipment required in a disaster needs to be assembled and maintained. Arrangements should be made for access to freezer capacity, and for a mechanism to pay for emergency needs. Measures should be adopted which ensure that damage is minimised if a disaster happens, eg raising materials in the collections off the floor and ensuring that shelving has canopies on top to lessen water damage. Finally, the disaster plan needs to be tested and updated regularly.

Table 3.5   Contents of a Disaster Plan
Summary of emergency procedures
List of people to contact
List of services
Lists of equipment and supplies
Procedures for getting emergency funds
Floor plans of the archive
Summary of insurance arrangements

Reaction

The third phase is concerned with the procedures to follow when a disaster occurs. First steps are to raise the alarm and to assemble personnel. The procedures for this should already be in place and well rehearsed. The next step is to ensure that the disaster site is safe to enter.

The first task after access is gained to a building is to assess the damage. The building must be well ventilated, with heat turned off and everything possible done to reduce temperature and humidity. Exposed materials should be covered if roof areas are missing or if water is draining through the building. Plans to provide temporary protection against the weather should be put into effect. Protection of property may need to be arranged with a security firm or other appropriate personnel.

Next, damaged material needs to be removed. It should first be packed for transporting to a safer place and also recorded. A treatment area needs to be set up, close to the disaster site if possible, to carry out minor treatment such as air-drying slightly wet material. These actions require prior training and preferably also some experience.

With wet paper-based materials there is danger of mould developing after 48 hours if conditions rise above 20°C and 70% relative humidity. Wet material must be removed from the area as soon as possible to facilitate drying.

Recovery

The final phase is that of establishing and carrying out a program to restore to a stable and usable condition both the disaster site and the damaged materials. It includes establishing a conservation program to recover damaged material, cleaning the disaster site, replacing treated material in the refurbished site, and analysing the disaster to improve the disaster plan.

Decisions are required about which material needs to be restored to usable condition first and what the best methods of restoring it are. An assessment of available conservation options and an estimate of costs will need to be made. The disaster site itself needs attention. It must be made habitable again. Steps such as clearing debris, lowering humidity levels and inhibiting mould growth may be necessary. The final step in the recovery process is to assess the actions taken, in order to improve the disaster plan.

Salvage Techniques

There are several ways to dry wet paper material. If the amount is relatively small, and if the exposure to water is slight to moderate, air-drying can be successful. A damp file can be stood up on its end and its pages fanned out, or its pages can be interleaved with absorbent paper. Freeze-drying can be used if freezers are available. Wet items are first prepared for freezing by wrapping them. They are then frozen, preferably in a commercial blast freezer at a temperature of –21°C or lower. They can be kept frozen for long periods, until such time as resources are available for drying them. Frozen items are dried by placing them in a vacuum chamber. Other formats such as microfilm and magnetic disks can be salvaged by applying techniques described in the preservation literature.

Mould control techniques are often required in the aftermath of a disaster. Controlling mould growth without using chemicals is achieved by altering environmental conditions. Any mould present can be cleaned off in an area separate from other materials so that it does not spread. Masks and gloves should be worn. Examples of the kinds of actions which could be taken include improving the air-flow through the room by altering the directions in which the shelves face or by keeping windows partly open, making sure that there are no damp spots in the room. Mould control using fungicides is an area where considerable specialist knowledge is needed. A conservator or a specialist in the use of fungicides should always be consulted. Gamma irradiation is also sometimes used to kill mould.

All archives should have an up-to-date disaster plan. Make sure your institution starts planning for disaster; ensure that the staff are trained in disaster response techniques, and develop cooperative plans with other archives, libraries and museums in your area.

Implementing a Preservation Program

Table 3.6 lists the major elements which can be found in archival preservation programs: they will be no surprise to those who have read the preceding material in this chapter.

The preservation plan of the National Archives and Records Administration of the United States of America contains most of these elements

- environmental control
- holdings maintenance: current materials
- holdings maintenance: at time of accessioning
- interception, assessment and protection: at time of use
- systematic duplication of impermanent documents
- reproduction of frequently used documents
- laboratory treatment of intrinsically valuable documents
- laboratory conservation of treasures
- preservation of non-textual records.

Table 3.6 Elements of a Preservation Plan

Building design: to ensure a stable, secure environment
Environmental control: ensuring appropriate levels of temperature, relative humidity, light; pest control
Holdings maintenance: good housing, cleanliness, storage enclosures such as boxing
Control of handling: security; staff and user education
Reformatting program: copying of information content by microfilming, photo-copying, etc.
Conservation: item treatment, repair
Disaster preparedness and recovery
Public education: general awareness campaigns
Advice at the record creation stage on appropriate materials and procedures

---

Selecting which of these elements to implement first in the archival preservation program is a decision which must be made by the individual archives, depending on its particular situation. For example, if the archives is fortunate enough to be housed in an appropriate building, then the first and second elements (building design and environmental control) will need relatively little attention, whereas for other archives they will need to assume top priority. Surveying the building and holdings, as already noted in more detail above, will be a necessary early step in implementing a preservation program for all archives, for adequate planning cannot proceed far without detailed knowledge about the nature and extent of deterioration.

It could be beneficial for archives in which preservation has not been a priority to implement as initial elements in their preservation plan a survey of the collections and the development of a disaster plan. They can both be carried out in a way which involves a large number of staff. The advantage of this is that a large number of staff at all levels become exposed to preservation concerns, an acquaintance which will be of considerable future benefit when other elements of the preservation plan are implemented. In the one-person archives or archives with only a small number of staff, this benefit will of course be of less importance; nonetheless, there is still considerable merit in surveying the collections as an essential preliminary step to developing a comprehensive preservation plan. Developing and implementing a disaster plan also has the benefit that it is a largely self-contained project, whose finite end may be of advantage in securing and allocating resources for preservation.

Common characteristics of successful archives preservation plans have been identified:

- Develop a written statement which defines the goals of the preservation program, based on a careful study of the archive's preservation problems, an assessment of required resources and of available resources and decisions about what preservation actions are most cost-effective and provide most benefit.
- Develop priorities as an essential initial step.
- Ensure that support for the plan is archives-wide and that staff are knowledgeable.
- Take account of local conditions, eg replacing light sources with low-UV fluorescent tubes has a lower priority if all records are boxed.
- Plan costing and scheduling carefully, taking account of local conditions: eg costings can be derived from local suppliers' catalogues and labour costs from local sources, and scheduling could take account of a local supply of student labour during vacation times to carry out a boxing program spread over several years.
- Translate survey results into a concrete plan with goals, timetable and costings, with the highest priorities allocated to items and procedures costing the least but having the highest impact.
- Employ a conservator or experienced archivist with preservation expertise to assist in developing and implementing the preservation program.

George M. Cunha, doyen of the preservation movement, noted two decades ago the steps to be carried out when starting a preservation program in the small archives (it is still sound advice today):

- Examine the storage environment and evaluate its suitability.
- Determine and implement measures to improve the environment.
- Examine or survey the records.
- Establish a work room or repair area for simple remedial treatment and boxing.
- Establish a relationship with a local conservator for advice and for treatment of artefacts if required.
- Keep informed on new preservation techniques and strategies.

Conclusion

The challenge of preservation must be a central concern of all who work with and use archives. There is a great deal which every archives, no matter how small or how poorly funded, can do to meet this challenge. A systematic and planned approach is essential. The archivist must know what materials constitute the holdings, must learn to recognise the causes and signs of deterioration and must be familiar with the range of procedures and practices which can be applied. Programs should be developed and implemented to stabilise the existing holdings, to prevent future decay and to ensure that new records are created using appropriate materials and procedures for their long-term maintenance. Plans need to be developed to promote preservation awareness and good handling by all staff and users of archives and to anticipate disasters and their effects. Preservation should pervade all activities carried out in archives – it is not a veneer which can be applied over existing routines – and, in addition, it should pervade all activities which effect the longevity of current records. Preservation activities in every archives must be planned and implemented according to a plan, not, as was formerly usually the case, carried out piecemeal in response to arbitrary demands.

Endnotes

1 Conway, Paul, 'Archival Preservation: Definitions for Improving Education and Training', in *Restaurator*, 10, 1989, p. 51.
2 Calmes, Alan, Schofer, Ralph and Eberhardt, Keith R., 'Theory and Practice of Paper Preservation for Archives', in *Restaurator*, 9, 1988, p. 97.

Further Reading

Because preservation techniques and accepted 'best practice' changes rapidly, the reader should read as widely as possible about preservation and should make every attempt to keep up-to-date with recent publications. Reference to the preservation literature should not be limited to only that concerned with archival preservation, for the literature about preservation of library materials is usually also applicable to archives.

Periodicals

Abbey newsletter, Austin, Texas, ISSN 0276–8291.
Conservation Administration News, Tulsa, Oklahoma, ISSN 0912-2912.
Preservation of Library Materials: Newsletter of the Australian Library and Information Association Special Interest Group for the Preservation of Library Materials, Sydney, ISSN 1035–7084 .(previous title: *Conservation of Library Materials)*.

General Texts

American archivist, 53/2, Spring 1990.

Basic Conservation of Archival Materials: A Guide, Canadian Council of Archives, Ottawa, 1990.

Calmes, Alan, Schofer, Ralph and Eberhardt, Keith R., 'Theory and Practice of Paper Preservation for Archives', in *Restaurator,* 9, 1988, pp. 96–111.

Harvey, Ross, *Preservation in Australian and New Zealand libraries: Principles, Strategies and Practices for Librarians*, 2nd edn, Centre for Information Studies, Charles Sturt University, Wagga Wagga, NSW, 1993.

Harvey, Ross, *Preservation in Libraries: A Reader*, Bowker-Saur, London, 1993.

Jones, Norvell M. M. and Ritzenthaler, Mary Lynn, 'Implementing an Archival Preservation Program', in *Managing Archives and Archival Institutions*, James Gregory Bradsher (ed.), Mansell, London, 1988, pp. 185–206.

Kaplan, Hilary A., Holden, Maria and Ludwig, Kathy, 'Archives Preservation Resource Review', in *American Archivist,* 54, 1991, pp. 502–44.

Petherbridge, Guy, 'Environmental and Housing Considerations for the Preservation of Modern Records: A Guide for the Records Manager', in Records Management Association of Australia, 8th National Convention, Darwin, 1991, *The Information Environment: Towards 2000*, RMAA, 1991, pp. 122–73.

Price, Helen, *Stopping the Rot: A Handbook of Preventive Conservation for Local Studies Collections*, 2nd edn, Australian Library and Information Association, New South Wales Branch, Sydney, 1989. An audiovisual kit based on this book, *Preserving Our Heritage: A Paper Conservation Video Kit*, and Bruce Smith's *An Assessment Module to Accompany Preserving Our Heritage* are also available from the Australian Library and Information Association.

Ritzenthaler, Mary Lynn, *Archives and Manuscripts: Conservation: A Manual on Physical Care and Management,* Society of American Archivists, Chicago, 1983.

Ward, Alan, *A Manual of Sound Archive Administration*, Gower, Aldershot, 1990.

Disaster Planning

Anderson, Hazel and McIntyre, John E., *Planning Manual for Disaster Control in Scottish Libraries and Record Offices*, National Library of Scotland, Edinburgh, 1985.

Barton, John P. and Wellheiser, Johanna C. (eds), *An Ounce of Prevention: A Handbook on Disaster Contingency Planning for Archives, Libraries and Record Centres*, Toronto Area Archivists Group, Toronto, 1985.

Buchanan, Sally A., *Disaster Planning, Preparedness and Recovery for Libraries and Archives: A RAMP Study*, Unesco, Paris, 1988.

Environmental Control

'Fumigation', in *Conservation of Library Materials*, 5, Sydney, 1989, pp. 1–4.

Padfield, T., 'Climate Control in Libraries and Archives', in *Preservation of Library Materials*, Merrily Smith (ed.), vol. 2, K. G. Saur, München, 1987, pp. 124–38.

Parker, Thomas A., *Study on Integrated Pest Management for Libraries and Archives: A RAMP Study*, UNESCO, Paris, 1988.

Wood Lee, Mary, *Prevention and Treatment of Mold in Library Collections with an Emphasis on Tropical Climates*, UNESCO, Paris, 1988.

Paper

Market Availability of Papers Suitable for Long-Term Records, Australian Archives, Canberra, 1992.

The Use of Recycled Papers in Records, Australian Archives, Canberra, 1990.

Reformatting

Gwinn, Nancy E. (ed.), *Preservation Microfilming: A Guide for Librarians and Archivists*, American Library Association, Chicago, 1987.

Kenney, Anne R. and Personius, Lynne K., *Joint Study in Digital Preservation I: A Report to the Commission on Preservation and Access*, Commission on Preservation and Access, Washington DC, 1992.

Kormendy, Lajos, (ed.), *Manual of archival repography*, München: K.G. Saur, 1989.

Lesk, Michael, *Preservation of New Technology*, Commission on Preservation and Access, Washington DC, 1992.

Waters, Donald J., *From Microfilm to Digital Imagery*, Commission on Preservation and Access, Washington DC, 1991.

Standards

AS 3674–1989, *Storage of Microfilm*, Standards Association of Australia, North Sydney, 1989.

AS 4003(int), *Permanent Uncoated Paper and Paperboard*, Interim Australian standard, Standards Australia, North Sydney, 1992.

BS5454: 1989, *Recommendations for Storage and Exhibition of Archival Documents*, British Standards Institution, London, 1989.

Surveys

Cunha, George M., *Methods of Evaluation To Determine the Preservation Needs in Libraries and Archives: A RAMP Study with Guidelines*, UNESCO, Paris, 1988.

4 Legal Responsibilities and Issues

Helen Smith

A legal system is a complex paradigm containing many divisions and sub-divisions. It can be broken down into positive law (as set out in various legal sources – legislation, judicial precedent, custom – and literary sources – either authoritative consisting of statutes, law reports, and books of authority, or non-authoritative such as medieval chronicles, periodicals, other books), and all the other conceptions and notions of binding law (natural law, morality, orthodox religious beliefs, mercantile custom, Roman/Canon Law). Because a legal system includes all the rules that are perceived as binding at any time and/or place, no aspect of human life and affairs remains outside a legal system. [1]

Introduction

This chapter is not intended to be a blow-by-blow account of the legislative provisions affecting archival administration and records handling. It does not offer legal advice. Equally, this chapter is not a list of legislation or a citation of legislative provisions, nor does it offer an extensive commentary on specific legislative requirements. Such a document would present several problems. The first would be that, given the rate of legislative amendment (it has been observed that since 1985 some 18,000 pages of legislation and associated documents have been added to the taxation law alone), [2] the list would soon be outdated. A list of legislative provisions would also ignore many other relevant issues such as the increasingly common practice of defining legislation through rules, regulations and determinations. Yet the most compelling reason why this chapter is not a trek through the statutory jungle is that our legal responsibilities are not framed by the statutes or other secondary instruments alone. Our legal responsibilities, obligations and entitlements rely on the context of our actions and activities (and those of others) and that context can be just as crucial as the specific statutory requirements. Most legislation is, therefore, designed to have enough flexibility to allow the judiciary to take account of the circumstances, as well as the law, when determining a solution or making a judgment, and our archival programs should reflect this flexibility.

Awareness of legal requirements and the need to constantly adapt to major and minor regulatory change require a flexible approach to document management and the ability and inclination to enhance or redesign programs or policies as necessary. This chapter seeks to provide a basic explanation of the main legal issues which may affect archival operations. It seeks also to illustrate how events and incidents previously regarded as solely in the realm of the legal profession may impact upon an archivist and how a basic knowledge and understanding of relevant legal principles and issues can support archival administration. Additionally, this chapter attempts to deal with the density of the law and to define the various legislative instruments and their application.

The system of laws will differ, sometimes marginally, sometimes dramatically, from situation to situation. For archivists in government employment, the scope of activities may be structured in accordance with identifiable legislative provisions, whereas a corporate archivist may have less formal operating instructions but may be legally restricted in many other indirect ways through the application of laws to the corporate environment. Archivists in this position may also be confronted with various legal issues arising from local, state, federal or foreign authorities which impose obligations or restrictions on company operations. As many public authorities move towards commercialisation, government archivists may also find themselves contending with the legislative provisions, and competing legal issues, relating to both public and private enterprises. Those employed in the areas of science and technology, education, medicine, religion and other specialist archival services will also be confronted with a range of legal issues, and sometimes, conflicting demands. On top of this are general issues such as privacy and copyright which need to be incorporated into our archival programs. Our legal responsibilities can also be complicated by the fact that we need to address not only current legislation, but also that of the past, while keeping up-to-date with future developments.

In discussing legal issues and responsibilities we need to begin with the basis of the system of rules which makes up the legal system. Much of what is framed by legislation or required by courts and tribunals has its basis in common law. As such it has been developed and refined over many years and defines what are, in essence, practical solutions to situations where disputes arise. In this context the law should not intimidate us, nor should we avoid it because of its perceived mysteries. We should use it in a common sense way and apply it to our advantage. Legal compliance need not imply an onerous duty. It can, and should, provide the impetus for an archives program which is both practical and ethical.

The Legal System

The legal system in Australia is composed of statutory, judicial and administrative law. Statutory law is that which is defined by an Act of Parliament. The Commonwealth and the states and territories are able to pass laws which govern activities within their jurisdictions as specified by the Australian Constitution. Where inconsistencies exist between Commonwealth and state and territory legislation, Commonwealth legislation prevails to the extent of the inconsistency.

Judicial law is that which is determined by a court in the exercise of its function. Commonwealth statutory law is vested in the High Court of Australia and those federal courts which are created by the Commonwealth Parliament. These include the Federal Court of Australia and the Family Court. In addition each state has its own judicial arrangements (refer to Tables 4.1 and 4.2). The definition of judicial law can also be extended to judge-made law and includes precedent and statutory interpretation. Judgments emanating from the Supreme courts, Federal courts and the High Court contribute to the development of the law. In the same way that state law does not cross state boundaries, neither does judicial precedent. However, all state and territory courts are bound by the rulings of the High Court of Australia.

Table 4.1 State and Territory Court Terminology

Summary Courts	• Magistrates' Courts
	• Courts of Petty Sessions
	• Local Courts
	• Courts of Summary Jurisdiction
	• Courts of Requests
Intermediate Courts	• District Courts
	• County Courts
Superior Courts	• Supreme Courts

There is also a range of tribunals and administrative authorities which support the judicial function by dealing with routine or simple disputes. This layer represents part of the spectrum of administrative law and includes entities such as the Small Claims Tribunal. Each organisation, whether it be government or private, will also have its own internal policies and procedures to regulate activities and operations. Such policies and procedures will usually be combinations of the requirements of the organisation, incorporated with interpretations of applicable legislation.

The synthesis of legislative, judicial and administrative law defines the limits of acceptable behaviour by prohibiting or restricting certain actions or activities, prescribing or clarifying expectations, and protecting or conserving rights and entitlements. The formulation of our legal, and the consequent ethical, responsibilities occurs within this framework.

Table 4.2 States and Territories to Which Australian Law Applies

- Mainland states of New South Wales (including Lord Howe Island), Queensland, South Australia, Victoria, Western Australia and their respective off-shore islands
- Mainland territory of the Northern Territory and its off-shore islands
- Mainland territory of the Australian Capital Territory
- Mainland Territory of Jervis Bay
- Island state of Tasmania and its off-shore islands (including Macquarie Island)
- External territories of Australian Antarctic, Ashmore and Cartier Islands, Christmas Islands, Cocos (Keeling) Islands, Coral Sea Islands, Heard and McDonald Islands and Norfolk Island [3]

Identifying and Using Legislation

The law is complex so a complete knowledge of its intricacies is probably impossible. Yet as archivists it is becoming increasingly necessary to acquaint ourselves with some basic legal principles, and to have at least an elementary knowledge of the operation of the legal system generally, and the application of relevant regulatory controls specifically. Across the regulatory landscape we are confronted with prescriptive references to

- time periods and/or actions affecting records retention/disposal
- storage media and the method of transfer from one medium to another
- records handling practices
- reliability of information

- access to information
- security of information
- use of the records
- the form and content of records.

All of the above are specific regulatory mechanisms designed to ensure that particular records are treated in particular ways. They provide the 'letter of the law', yet our legal responsibilities require us to also recognise the 'spirit of the law' and the changing trends in the demands made of our documentation processes.

We have all heard the adage 'ignorance of the law is no excuse', and it is at this point that our main legal responsibility begins. Our first legal responsibility is to know when we are out of our depth and to seek appropriate assistance in those instances, whether that assistance be from legal advisers or from professionals in specific areas such as taxation, treasury dealings, workers' compensation matters or other areas where specialised knowledge is necessary. We should also seek to gain as much of an understanding of the law as we possibly can. This will not only facilitate decisionmaking but will often enable us to phrase questions for our professional advisers in specific rather than general terms, thus increasing our chances of receiving a specific rather than a general response.

Legal Instruments

The most familiar legislative device is the Act or statute, (in some cases referred to as Ordinances). These may be either principal Acts (those which initiate a new law); or amending Acts (those which alter or change an existing Act either wholly or in part). The term 'code' can also be used in reference to principal legislative instruments where the laws of more than one jurisdiction are applied jointly. For example, by virtue of the Victorian *Companies (Application of Laws) Act 1981*, the Commonwealth *Companies Act 1981* operated in Victoria in conjunction with the Victorian *Companies Act 1961*. It was cited as the *Companies (Victoria) Code*.[4]

A principal or an amending Act can also be an 'empowering' Act. Such Acts provide for the issuing of subordinate legislative instruments that allow aspects of the law to be dealt with in more detail, or which provide procedural and/or administrative statements. Subordinate legislation includes statutory regulations or rules, Orders-in-Council, orders and by-laws (see Table 4.3). The definition can also be extended to standards, guidelines and codes of conduct. This form of legal instrument is subject to, or under the authority of, another Act and has legal force through that legislation rather than in its own right. For example, section 45 of the Victorian *Fair Trading Act 1985* allows the Governor-in-

Council to make regulations to facilitate the operation of the Act. Generally, the terms of the principal Act provide for a specific person or body to be delegated with the authority to issue subordinate legislation.[5]

Table 4.3 Types of Subordinate Legislation

Statutory Rules	• Also known as Regulations • Must be tabled in Parliament for approval • Can cover a wide range of issues and are particularly important in determining the full extent of any legislative requirements • The term 'rules' also refers to instruments controlling court practices
Orders and Orders-in-Council	• Must be tabled in Parliament for approval • Orders-in-Council are those referred to the Governor (state) or the Governor-General (Commonwealth) for issue and are made under his or her authority
By-laws or Local Laws	• Made to specifically address a particular geographic area or community and are limited in their scope
Standards, Guidelines and Codes of Conduct	• Usually directed towards the control or operation of particular enterprises or activities

Some types of secondary legislation can be either voluntary or mandatory, depending on the force given to them by principal legislation. For example, under section 12 of the *Public Records Act 1973* the Victorian Keeper of Public Records may issue standards for records management practices for the Victorian public sector. As these are instruments specified by the principal legislation and, as a result, have the force of that Act, they would be regarded as mandatory. Similarly, section 74(1) of the NSW *Fair Trading Act 1987* provides that the Commissioner of Consumer Affairs may prepare a code of practice relating to fair dealing.

The most common form of standards are, however, voluntary and are usually issued by the independent standards authorities such as Standards Australia or the International Standards Organisation or other appropriate industry bodies or associations. Some of these standards, although issued and applied initially as voluntary codes, can become mandatory through reference to them in either principal or secondary legislation. In lieu of the Commissioner of Consumer Affairs prescribing his or her own codes of practices as indicated above, section 92(2) of the Act also provides for the endorsement of voluntary codes by stating that 'a regulation may apply, adopt or incorporate, wholly or in part, and with or without modification, any standard, rule, code or specification of the Standards Association of Australia, the British Standards Institution or any other association or body ...'.

Finding the Law

Acts can be identified initially by title and/or registration number. Each state and territory, as well as the Commonwealth, currently register legislation within their respective jurisdictions using an annual sequential numbering system. Previous arrangements have included numbering within regnal years or continuous sequential numbering across years (eg Victorian statute numbers 1–10262/1857–1985).

Initially all new legislation is released in pamphlet form. At the end of each year all Acts passed during the year, within a particular jurisdiction, are bound together. The legislation is arranged in numeric order according to its registration number. Bound volumes often contain alphabetical or chronological indexes to assist with title identification. Sometimes they also include tables of Acts passed, amended or repealed during the year; tables of Acts that affect any Act passed during the year; or tables of proclamations relating to commencement dates.

To find a particular Act it is therefore useful to know the year of issue, or at least a reasonably narrow time span over which a search could be conducted. A useful hint may be that often the states pass similar laws within a short period. Thus, you may be able to focus your search in a particular jurisdiction if you know of similar legislation in another jurisdiction. For example, state and Northern Territory laws relating to trade practices were all issued between 1985 and 1990 and all except the Northern Territory applied the same title, ie the *Fair Trading Act.* The Northern Territory called its Act the *Consumer Affairs and Fair Trading Act 1990.*

Identifying and locating the principal Act is only part of the story. To appreciate fully and understand the law with which you are dealing, the principal Act must be read in conjunction with any amending Acts, as well as its associated secondary legislation. All amended Acts are registered in the same annual sequential system used for principal Acts and will therefore appear in the yearly bound volumes in numeric sequence. However, they will only contain the text of the amending Act and will not be a consolidation or reprint of the entire Act.[6]

When an Act is amended, a composite version is not automatically issued. Only after several amendments are Acts republished incorporating all amendments into the text. Where an Act has a number of amendments, the consolidated version is issued as a reprint in pamphlet form. Reprints do not form part of the annual numeric sequence and are usually filed in a separate alphabetical arrangement. They are usually not included in annual bound volumes. Universal legislative consolidations, where all Acts are updated to their current version, occur rarely. In Victoria this has occurred twice – 1958 and 1973 (partial).

The difficulty associated with amending legislation is that often the amending Act does not bear the same title as the principal Act. Where the same title is used, the amending Act is identified by using the word Amendment in the title. It is important to remember that even though all Acts bearing similar titles may have been located it is not necessarily safe to assume you have comprehensive coverage of the body of law. Associated legislation which is not connected by title may also be relevant.

Amendments to subordinate legislation operate in much the same way as for both principal and amending legislation. Statutory regulations need to be read in conjunction with any amendments to them. Availability of other types of subordinate legislation is a more difficult question. Often such instruments are only issued by the authority to which they relate. It will often be easiest to contact such bodies directly before engaging in any other searches. Table 4.4 shows the sources for identifying legislation.

Table 4.4 Sources for Identifying Legislation

Principal Acts	• Indexes to Acts (both alphabetical and subject) • Classified Guides • Hansard (the official Parliamentary record) • Government Gazettes • Subscribe to Political or legal monitoring services • Cumulative tables of legislation available from Commonwealth, state and territory bookshops or publication services
Amending Acts (as for Principal Acts)	• Subscribe to an annotation service (such services are available as either annotation volumes or 'pasting' services)
Subordinate Legislation (as for Principal Acts)	• Subscribe to an annotation service (such services are available as either annotation volumes or 'pasting' services) • Contact appropriate government or industry authorities for information about standards and/or codes of conduct

When dealing with multiple amendments, it is often useful to identify whether any consolidations or reprints have been published and use this version as your starting point. The advantage is that the reprint or consolidation incorporates all amendments to the principal Act prior to the release of the reprint. You then need only to work forward from that point and identify subsequent amendments rather than having to track every amendment to the principal Act. This approach should be particularly useful where the principal Act has been issued for a long period of time or if the legislation has been amended many times. A note of caution is probably appropriate here. Consolidated Acts used without reference to the earlier legislation may give a distorted impression of agency establishment dates, amalgamations or name changes. This would then cause inaccuracies in administrative histories or the documentation of provenance.

Interpretation and Application

Once all relevant principal, amending and subordinate legislative instruments have been identified, it is important to establish their parameters. Sections relating to definitions and coverage are indicators of how, and in what circumstances, a piece of legislation can be applied. For example, section 9 of the *Corporations Act 1989* provides a dictionary of relevant terminology. Table 4.5 lists the sources for interpretation and application of legislation.

The section relating to commencement provides an indication of when the Act or other instrument has, or will, become operative. Often sections of the same legislative instrument become operational before others. Some legislation may also have a retrospective application which means it applies to events which occurred prior to the passing of the legislation. The commencement date could be a date specified by the legislation, a date to be announced (usually in the Government Gazette), or when the legislation is assented by the Governor or Governor-General.

Certain legislative instruments also contain provision for automatic repeal or 'sunsetting'. Both the NSW *Subordinate Legislation Act 1989* and the Victorian *Subordinate Legislation (Review and Revocation) Act 1984* introduced a process of staged repeal of regulations. In NSW any regulations passed between 1941 and 1964 ceased to operate after 1 September 1992, and as of July 1992 Victorian regulations over ten years old are automatically repealed. In both cases the regulations would require re-enactment if they were to continue to have effect.[7]

Attention also needs to be given to identifying the commencement or cessation of legislative responsibilities. This involves establishing the limits or time frame of any liability under a piece of legislation. Such time frames may be effectively unlimited or, conversely, may be specified by the legislation. The operation of taxation law in Australia is such that the Commissioner of Taxation is not bound by a period of limitation and may commence actions against taxpayers suspected of tax evasion into an indefinite future. Alternatively, the Commonwealth *Trade Practices (Amendment) Act 1992* contains a sunset period of ten years for product liability claims. This means that any action for compensation sought for injuries caused by defective products must be taken within ten years from the date of supply.

Table 4.5 Sources for Interpretation and Application of Legislation

Commencement	• The section entitled 'Commencement' in Acts and Regulations • Other instruments are generally regarded as coming into operation on the day they are issued • Government Gazettes • Annual bound volumes of Acts/Regulations often provide commencement dates • Legislative provisions which specify when all obligations and/or liabilities commence and/or expire
Interpretation	• Explanatory memorandum that usually accompanies the original Bill • Regulatory impact statements prepared prior to the drafting of both primary and secondary legislation • Reports of Royal Commissions • Reports of the Law Reform Commission • Reports of committees of enquiry laid before Parliament • Reports of parliamentary committees • Treaties • International agreements • Speeches, particularly second reading speeches • Journals of the Senate • Votes and Proceedings of the House of Representatives • Determinations or rulings, eg taxation law • Interpretive statements from responsible authorities
Precedent	• Digests of judgments • Publications providing judicial definitions of words and/or phrases • Professional journals and newsletters[8]

Commencement and/or cessation of legislative responsibilities may also be tied to specified events or actions. This aspect of a piece of legislation would have particular relevance in relation to document retention for evidential purposes. For example, the general requirements for documents used for ascertaining revenue and expenditure, and for the subsequent determination of taxation claims, must be retained for five years *dating from when the documents were prepared*. Capital gains tax legislation also has a retention requirement of five years, but its application is such that the five-year period relates to the *date on which particular assets are sold*.

The extent or consequences of an Act or other regulatory instrument are usually not fully realised until it has been judicially tested. The interpretation applied by courts of law can be just as important as the actual legislation itself. Such interpretation is usually referred to as precedent and includes, or is based upon, court decisions, particularly where a judicial decision has been made with regard to custom or accepted practice. If possible, it is wise to ascertain how any piece of legislation has previously been applied in a litigious situation as this will provide a guide as to how similar situations may be treated by the courts. If you are dealing with a relatively new area of the law, where interpretive decisions have not yet been made, it is possibly safest to take a conservative approach to the requirements of the legislation until judicial precedents indicate a pattern for future judgments.

Inconsistencies across the legal jurisdictions may mean that what is acceptable in one state may not be acceptable in another. Inconsistencies may also exist within the same legal jurisdiction. The Corporations Law requires accounting records to be maintained for periods of seven years and many of the records applicable to taxation claims, and required under that legislation for only five years, would also be included under this broad umbrella. It is important for an archivist confronted by such a situation, particularly when determining questions of retention and disposal, to identify and to isolate those pieces of legislation which have most relevance to their situation, and to ensure that, within the risk parameters defined as acceptable by the organisation, legislative responsibilities have been satisfied.

The interconnectivity of the laws needs to be carefully examined in association with the context of a particular situation. Such questions could be extremely complex and, where necessary, advice should be sought from our legal advisers. The key issue for archivists is that they recognise the potential complexities of the legal sphere and ensure that they do not make hasty or ill-informed decisions. When in doubt consult with your legal representatives.

Access and Disclosure

Appropriate systems and storage methods are essential to facilitate quick retrieval of information from archives, or in the event of a freedom of information request, a subpoena or discovery order, a taxation audit, or merely to meet the public's right of inspection as indicated in a range of legislation. All of these situations involve specific, or implied, time limits for compliance and it is a legal requirement to respond within the set time frame. Inappropriate or inconvenient systems may undermine the retrieval process thus leading to unnecessary burdens as in the case of the Royal Commission into Agent Orange, where records of the Defence Department relating to the Vietnam War had to be identified, located and retrieved. This discovery process used the services of 25–30 people working in shifts 24 hours a day, seven days a week over a 12-week period so that the schedules imposed by the Commission could be satisfied.[9] Inability to produce the required documentation could also have adverse liability implications for our employers, particularly under the recent amendments to the Commonwealth *Trade Practices Act 1974*, where failure to identify manufacturers or suppliers of goods within 30 days could result in our employers being held liable for claims for damages resulting from defective goods – even if they were only the distributor.

Court proceedings to settle disputes usually require all parties to disclose and produce documents which provide evidence of their claim and/or defence. Disclosure requires that the existence of the documents be made known, while production means that the documents are made available for inspection.[10] The existence of relevant documents is required to be disclosed, but the production of documents is not always compulsory. Key exceptions are documents which are privileged or those which are self-incriminating. In litigation proceedings our employers' solicitors will usually be there to advise us of the correct procedures, however an archivist should, as a first reaction, discontinue any routine disposal practices where the documents due for destruction may be relevant to the proceedings.

There are two main ways in which documents are requested by a court or tribunal – discovery orders and subpoenas. Documents are sought under a discovery order if your organisation is a party to a dispute. Documents produced in this manner are generally referred to the other party in the dispute. Subpoenas may be issued to a person or organisation unconnected with a particular litigation proceeding, but whose records may contain relevant information. Documents produced as a result of a subpoena are usually referred direct to the court or tribunal handling the dispute. There are also a number of other types of notices to produce records which may be issued by specific authorities such as the Australian Taxation Office or the Australian Securities Commission. Regulatory authorities may also choose to make use of section 10 of the Commonwealth *Crimes Act 1914* to obtain search warrants. Failure to comply with any order, subpoena, notice or warrant could result in a contempt of court penalty even if the failure was unintentional.[11]

When confronted with an order for the production of documents, the archivist needs to ensure that the request is legitimate and within the scope of the law. In some cases (eg Freedom of Information requests) archivists may be able to rely on their own judgment, or on criteria or rules established for them by specialist advisers. Difficult or complex issues should be referred to legal professionals before proceeding with the request.

Some government agencies may be exempt from compliance, or the production of certain documents may be restricted, by various legislation. For example, the Victorian *Freedom of Information Act 1982* restricts public access to Cabinet documents. It is important, therefore, to determine your legal position in relation to the order before proceeding to honour it. The second requirement is to ensure that the extent of the order is not too broad or too vague, and that the documents required are identified with some degree of precision. Application can be made to a court or tribunal to waive compliance if the order is seen to be vexatious or unclear, or where 'production of the specified documents would require very substantial search and discrete judgement in relation to each document as to whether it touched upon or evidenced the matters specified'. For example, in the case of *Gilligan v Nationwide News Pty Ltd* the ACT Supreme Court ruled that 'the subpoena [was] not a proper use of the process and clearly contravene[d] the rules which govern[ed] subpoenas'. Compliance with the request was, as a result, not required.[12]

Another issue in relation to the provision of information by an order or writ is the need to ensure that the process is undertaken with due consideration of factors such as privacy and confidentiality, national security implications or commercial advantage issues. The concepts of accountability and reasonable care need to be applied to the release of information and, although compliance with an order to produce documents is a legal responsibility, it needs to be resolved against the implications of other relevant issues. There are many situations when compliance with an information request could be interpreted either broadly or narrowly, while still meeting both the explicit and implicit requirements of the request. Again the archivist may be called upon to exercise some discretion and common sense and to bear in mind both the practicalities of compliance and the employers' interests. However, this is not to imply that an archivist should ever act illegally by deliberately concealing information. Yet, where interpretation is possible, it should be applied to the advantage of our employers, or those to whom they extend assurances of protection. For example, on the grounds of customer confidentiality, the National Australia Bank recently sought to limit access of the Taxation Commissioner to documents of the party under investigation rather than opening up the entire records of one of its branches to inspection. The Federal Court refused the injunction, but recognised that the Bank had tried to act in accordance with its duty of care to its customers.[13]

Similar to a bank's duty of customer confidentiality is the principle of legal professional privilege. Under this common law right, legal advisers have been able to provide advice to their clients without fear of disclosure. Again it is the archivist's duty to be aware of the implications of this aspect of document disclosure and to establish, under the guidance of legal counsel, whether certain documents are subject to such privilege before releasing them to other parties. Such documents include all correspondence between a legal adviser and their client provided it was produced for the purpose of obtaining legal assistance. This includes any reports, submissions or other documents prepared for the purpose of obtaining legal advice. The proviso here is that the report is solely directed to the legal adviser and not sent or submitted to other persons. Yet even this age old tradition is no longer straightforward in its application. A majority judgment of the High Court of Australia in 1991 in the case of *Corporate Affairs Commission v Mr Brian Yuill* allowed access to documents which had previously been withheld on the grounds of legal professional privilege. This judgment has been upheld recently in the Federal Court sitting in Perth, where the Australian Securities Commission sought access to documents of Dalleagles Pty Ltd.[14] The rejection of the argument of legal professional privilege exposes a whole new category of documents to possible scrutiny and may make the archivist's job more onerous, especially as it touches on a very sensitive area.

Access to records which are part of a body of evidence being considered by the court may be regarded as being 'sub judice' (in course of trial).[15] Under such circumstances disclosure of the contents of the documents, by either physical release or discussion, could result in the person responsible being in contempt of court. Archivists having access to evidentiary records should always be aware of both the ethical aspects of disclosure and the possible legal sanctions and should not answer specific questions or engage in general discussions without prior authorisation from their employers' legal advisers. This comment extends also to the disclosure of information about our employers' enterprises which is not generally known or publicly available. Such disclosure, regardless of how innocent it may be, could be construed as the provision of inside information and could lead to severe penalties. Archivists owe their employers a duty of confidence and should not use information which comes into their possession for personal profit or other improper means.

This issue highlights the two serious dilemmas facing an archivist when confronted with a legal requirement to identify, retrieve and provide access to documentation, particularly where it may not be in the best interests of their employer to have such information revealed. The first concerns the risk of causing conflict and animosity in such situations. It is therefore absolutely essential, as mentioned previously, to seek advice and assistance from those qualified in the area while always being aware of the penalties under the Commonwealth *Crimes Act 1914* for persons who aid, abet, counsel, procure or are knowingly concerned in offences. The second is the need for archivists to keep themselves well informed of changes in the law, or in its interpretation, particularly in relation to those tangential elements where our legal responsibilities are still evolving.

Privacy and Confidentiality

The subject of access to information necessarily leads to consideration of privacy issues and the juxtaposition of that concern against the issue of disclosure. It was not until several years after the release of the various Commonwealth and state freedom of information acts that the counterpart Commonwealth *Privacy Act 1988* was promulgated. Although both types of legislation apply only to public offices (with the *Privacy Act 1988* applying only at the Commonwealth level), the concepts which it embodies have some degree of universal application. Many archivists also work within archives which have established access provisions which may be statutorily or administratively defined. Whatever the situation, archivists will be confronted with the two (often competing) principles of the public's right to know and the individual's right to privacy. In a business sense this may be defined as an organisation's right to preserve the confidentiality of its commercial information.[16]

Whether requests for information be made under a freedom of information act or other form, the archivist needs to establish some guidelines or criteria for deciding the access conditions of certain records. This will ensure that all relevant issues are addressed in all cases and that a consistent administrative approach is applied. Archivists accepting material from individual donors should ensure that the donor provides written permission for release of personal information and specifies the circumstances of such release.

Speculative research requests may pose problems for archivists where access to records containing personal information is sought. One alternative may be to look for other sources of information. These may be in either summary form where individuals are not specifically identified or existing material available in the public domain. Another avenue could be to remove or in some way obscure the identifying information so that individuals cannot be distinguished. If neither of these options is suitable, then the archivist, in determining a solution, would be wise to adopt the stance of 'an ordinary man [or woman] of reasonable sensibilities' and to consider how such a person would regard the release of similar personal information. Where disclosure would be denied on the grounds of invasion of privacy, the archivist would need to consider whether release of the information would constitute a 'substantial and unreasonable intrusion upon [a person], his home, his relationships or communications with others, his property, or his business affairs'.[17]

In relation to privacy, archivists need to be aware of their statutory responsibilities. There are legislative provisions which impose an obligation to disclose or to provide access to certain information under certain circumstances. There are other legislative provisions which oppose disclosure, particularly in relation to personal and financial information. The archivist needs to be familiar with the legislative framework and to have an understanding of how and under what circumstances the provisions should be applied.

For an archivist the issue of privacy is not confined to a question of whether to release information or to withhold it. Particularly as a result of the *Privacy Act 1988,* the archivist may be confronted with the issue of data integrity and the survival of the archival record. Under the privacy principles enumerated in the Act, people can seek to have documents removed from their personal files or to have personal details amended. In many cases this information may be quite innocuous and may have had no long-term value. The question arises of the manner in which an archivist should deal with the culling of personal information from a possibly permanent-value record, particularly if the culling is performed on the basis of protecting reputations rather than on the removal of inaccurate information.

Accountability and the Document Trail

Increasingly, it appears that the role of the archivist, and of the records manager, is concerned with the maintenance of a document trail, where this trail could be either paper, electronic, digital or a combination. Particularly in the area of disposal, but also in the development of archival and records management programs, legal obligations imposed upon us make the ability to trace and to track records an essential feature of our work.

The requirements of proof and evidence have always confronted us. In a litigious situation such requirements centre on the facts surrounding or accompanying a transaction or action, while from a historic perspective we wish to preserve information that introduces or explains incidents or events with particular emphasis on the continuous or fluid nature of transactions. In recent times, however, the concepts of proof and evidence appear to have become broader.

In the 1980s the introduction of freedom of information legislation heralded the coming of heightened interest in the inner operations and hidden dealings of government. The various Acts provided a right of community access to information in the possession of governments and public authorities. When the concept of freedom of information was proposed for Victoria in 1981, it was done so under the banner of a democracy where 'people are more able to scrutinise what is going on with a government that is open and therefore more accountable'.[18] The inference was that, through access to information, members of the public would be able to expose prejudiced, incompetent or irresponsible actions. Importantly, the legislation had the effect, at least in the short term, of creating an awareness of the need to control information resources with integrity and continuity rather than risk embarrassing revelations of missing or altered documentation. It was not long before the idea of open administration was extended to the workings of the business and financial sectors.

Issues such as fraud, money laundering, tax evasion, negligence and deception coupled with strengthened disclosure laws and the extensive search powers of regulatory authorities means that our document trail extends past the basic ideas of proof and evidence and into such areas as substantiation, authentication, increased accountability and the demonstration of reasonable care. The concept of the document trail flows into all aspects of our professional and private lives and carries with it a more diverse and ambiguous set of legal obligations and responsibilities.

In recent years legislation has been enacted to monitor and control the financial services industry. The two main instruments to achieve this are the *Proceeds of Crime Act 1987* and the *Cash Transactions Reports Act 1988*. Both these Acts provide examples of the requirements of the document trail. By restricting the opening of accounts in false names, the *Cash Transactions Reports Act 1988* attempts to limit the operation of the black economy. It also provides for extensive reporting mechanisms relating to transactions of amounts in excess of $10,000, or to any transactions thought to be suspicious. Thus, an information trail from financial institutions to regulatory agencies such as the Australian Taxation Office and the Australian Federal Police has been established.[19]

Sections 76 and 77 of the *Proceeds of Crime Act 1987* provide for the retention of specific types of documents in original format for seven years dating from events as specified in the Act. In the case of documents relating to the opening of an account, the seven-year period commences from the date on which the account is closed. Of particular importance is the spirit of the law inherent in the definition of a 'financial transaction document as any document whose retention is necessary to *preserve a record of the financial transaction concerned'*.

It appears that our law-makers have recognised that the accuracy of a record may be blurred or its integrity skewed by the absence of contextual information about its creation and use. Records are not created, nor are they used, in a vacuum and the law has broadened its focus to include the manner in which documents accrue in the normal course of business. As archivists working with documentary sources on a day-to-day basis, we need to focus our attention on the record system rather than on just the specific records or record types. Our responsibility is to maintain the document trail in such a way as to allow the passage of a transaction to be identified and analysed at any point in the process.

This need may cause us to reassess our traditional approaches, particularly in relation to document retention and disposal. We perhaps need to concentrate more on the information content of our records rather than on their physical manifestations. We have probably all experienced the changing nature or scope of a record over time and the frustrations caused to researchers when a wealth of detail turns to a trickle of summarised notes or pro formas. The same may also be true of records currently produced and we cannot, therefore, rely on the same degree of information availability from similar documents over an extended period. One tendency may be to continue to collect the records because we have always done so or, as an alternative, we may decide on a cut-off date where we recognise that the information in the record is no longer of sufficient value for retention in our collections. Our legal responsibilities may imply an obligation to ensure continuity of information and not merely the selection of documents because they have traditionally been retained. In terms of the need to maintain an information trail, the question is whether we should not only apply alternative disposal strategies but also be seeking alternative information sources. Some recently developed disposal schedules apply the concept of the 'only record extant' to define a hierarchy of records which can be applied when the preferred record is either lost or inadvertently destroyed. This concept provides us with a method of identifying alternate information sources. It should be a primary concern that the maintenance and currency of our document retention or disposal policies is such that the documentary sources selected for either short- or long-term retention to satisfy information requirements do, in fact, continue to satisfy those requirements.

The area of electronic or digital storage of information is particularly vulnerable to changes in format and data elements. For years archivists and records managers have sought ways to deal with computer-generated records and their maintenance. There is agreement that the data record cannot be maintained as an entity distinct from the system in which it was stored and manipulated. There is also agreement on the need to maintain the program specifications and other associated documentation which provide both access to, and an understanding of, the operating system. As with paper-based systems, the legal focus in relation to electronically-generated and stored information is based on the holistic approach.

In the area of taxation there is a need to retain appropriate documentary evidence to comply with stricter substantiation requirements. Income Tax Ruling 2349 refers to the maintenance of computer records that are required under section 262A of the Commonwealth *Income Tax Assessment Act 1936*. Such records include audit trails that provide a record of the system's activities, including additions, deletions and alterations to both data and software. Record layouts and design specifications for obsolete or modified, as well as current, systems should also be maintained. The object is to provide the means by which a transaction may be traced either forward or backward. Thus, the assessment of taxation claims involves both substantiation from source documentation as well as authentication of the transaction through the audit trail.[20]

Similarly, the issue of authentication and the document trail is of concern in the application of technology to other business processes. The international shipping community is currently moving towards replacement of the paper-based bill of lading (the document that controls transport and disposal of goods) to an electronic format using electronic data interchange (EDI) technology. Of particular concern in the development of the voluntary rules which regulate such transactions is the need for security and certainty of information, hence the inclusion of audit and verification procedures. The guidelines developed for electronic bills of lading also allow for the possibility of non-delivery or mis-delivery of goods, and provide exemptions to the carrier if it can be shown that there was reasonable care taken to determine the correct delivery address. The challenge for archivists and records managers is to identify records that demonstrate reasonable care and to ensure that they are maintained.[21]

The concepts of reasonable care and accountability are essentially the same, however the focus of reasonable care is often less obvious. Rather than maintaining substantive proof of transactions or actions, the demonstration of reasonable care may infer the maintenance of records that also document the process by which the transaction or action was effected. In Victoria the *Health (General Amendment) Act 1988* provides a statutory defence where HIV infection results from the transplantation of cadaveric tissue. It is a defence to show that

- a sample of the donor's blood was tested for the presence of HIV
- the result of the test was negative
- the medical practitioner who transplanted the tissue made or caused to be made reasonable enquiries about the behaviour of the dead person to find out whether that person was at high risk of being infected by HIV.[22]

In the above example the first and second defences would probably be quite easy to prove using case notes. The third defence
may require a demonstration of the nature of the processes that
were undertaken to determine the risk category of the donor and
the extent to which procedures for such investigations may have
been extended or neglected.

If both our primary and secondary levels of statutory authority
are moving towards a systems-based approach to documentary
proof, the judicial system is reinforcing this attitude. As a result
of recent outbreaks of legionnaires disease, and subsequent civil
actions to determine liability, there is sufficient case law to establish that the growth of the bacteria is directly related to the
effects of poor maintenance of air-conditioning facilities. Under
these circumstances the courts will be looking for evidence of
regular and effective cleaning of cooling systems and general
compliance with the codes of conduct relating to legionella as a
defence of liability. In a judicial sense the demonstration of the
processes undertaken, and the extent to which the duty of care
was taken seriously, will be a determining factor. In a recent case
McDonald's Fairfield store in Sydney was a suspected source of
an outbreak of the disease. McDonald's was able to provide evidence to the NSW Department of Health that it had complied
with 'requirements for monthly testing and three monthly cleaning' thus undermining the case against it.[23]

It is no longer appropriate to view records in our custody and
control as single entities – the law does not view them as such.
They are part of a continuum and in dealing with the question of
their management in an administrative or historic context it is
essential to view them *in situ*. The legal and ethical implications
of archival management rest on a question of credibility where
substantive facts may require authentication through the context
of their documentation. We will no longer satisfy our statutory
and judicial authorities by producing our end-of-year balance
sheets as proof of performance, we must now be in a position to
prove how we arrived at the figures.

Copyright

Copyright is the exclusive right to the printing or reproduction of
a work such as a manuscript, photograph, film or letter. It is the
legal right which restricts or prevents unauthorised use or distribution of a work. Copyright exists for published and unpublished
works.[24]

Copyright legislation is a specific area of the law where the
document trail may be of importance. Copyright of a work sub-
sists for at least 50 years and during that time ownership of the
material may have passed into several hands, either by sale or

inheritance or, in the corporate sphere, via subsidiary relation-ships, mergers or company acquisitions. If an infringement of copyright occurs and it is necessary to prove ownership of the copyright, sufficient records which provide evidence of title to the work would be required. This may involve tracing a chain of ownership. As the assignment of copyright is not valid unless it is in writing by the owner of the copyright, documentary evidence of the transfer of copyright should be preserved.

Copyright is also an important consideration when providing access to records in the custody of an archive. This aspect is explored in more detail in Chapter 10.

Evidence

Evidence legislation in Australia, as it relates to the work of archivists, is primarily concerned with the acceptability of docu-mentary sources by a court of law. This extends to defining the scope of a document, the method of duplication and how docu-ments may be introduced into court proceedings.

In Australia the Commonwealth *Judiciary Act 1903* sets the basis for the operation of judicial process. Section 79 provides that 'the laws of each state and territory, including the laws relating to procedures, evidence, and the competency of witnesses, shall, except as otherwise provided by the Constitution or the laws of the Commonwealth, be binding on all Courts exercising federal jurisdiction in that state or territory in all cases to which they are applicable'. As a result evidence law is dealt with at a state or terri-tory level and archivists should seek to gain an understanding of the law as it is applied within their respective jurisdictions. Amendments to the Commonwealth *Evidence Act 1905* are cur-rently before the federal Parliament. When proclaimed, the legis-lation will extend to proceedings in federal courts, Australian Capital Territory courts (until otherwise proclaimed) and external territories. However, section 16 of the *Evidence Bill 1991* pre-serves the operation of state and territory laws where they are not inconsistent with the Commonwealth Act.

The main changes to evidence law in Australia as a result of the proposed legislation relate to the definition of documents and the abolition of the 'original document' rule. These changes are particularly important in terms of authentication and the use of computer or optical disk technology for the storage of informa-tion. The proposed legislation seeks to facilitate the process of authentication by ensuring that documents produced from machines will be acceptable as evidence because of the 'reliability and trustworthiness of the device or process'. This change is based, in part, on the assumption that 'because a business has relied on a device it can be taken to be generally reliable'.[25]

Archives Legislation

Legislation governing the preservation, maintenance and access to public records is, in part, designed to support the process of accountability through the document trail. Eric Ketelaar, in his study of legislation and regulation affecting records and archives management, describes archives legislation as that which 'recognises the fundamental nature of the relationship of government records as instruments of accountability by the government to the people, evidence of public and private rights and obligations, an informational source on matters involving the continuous administration and management of a government; preserves the patrimony of the state as evidenced in its records; and provides exclusive authority to carry out archives and records management functions on a government-wide basis'.[26]

Archives are used in many ways by many people as authoritative evidence of past actions and decisions. They underpin our personal, business and cultural activities by providing a continuous and consistent record. For records to provide such information, archival legislation needs to acknowledge the 'accountability' inherent in the official record of an organisation or enterprise, as well as the cultural significance. Table 4.6 provides a brief summary of the main issues and principles which should be embodied by archival legislation. Further discussion of archival principles and programs can be found in Chapter 1.

Ethics and Risk

The range of regulatory controls that make up the legal system encapsulate our legal responsibilities. However, the system is far from absolute, so that even though we may have a reasonable understanding of our legal responsibilities, the need to interpret their application to a multiplicity of potential situations calls for the introduction of judgment, discretion and the consideration of ethics.

The legal issues of accountability and reasonable care carry with them a subjective assessment of the consequences of non-compliance. From the dual perspectives of ethics and risk we need to define how far we will allow the legislative constraints to regulate our records handling processes. Ethical decisions will be based on a perception of acceptable standards of social, political or industry-based behaviour, while risk management decisions will involve an assessment of our company's or agency's attitudes and the underlying motivations for their varied activities. A single company may occupy several positions in the ethics/risk spectrum depending on the diversity and sensitivity of its operations and the severity of the penalties it is likely to face if non-compliance is detected.

Table 4.6 Archives Legislation – Some Matters for Consideration

Functions of the Authority	• which are defined in sufficiently broad terms to allow the authority to take an active role in the management of records • which are not limited to a list of specific functions • which ensure that the authority contributes to the accountability and efficiency of public administration
Powers	• which allow the authority to receive records into its custody • which require the transfer of records into custody, preferably after a specified period • which prohibit or authorise the destruction of records • which regulate the management of public records, preferably through mandatory standards • which permit or restrict access to records in its custody, through both public enquiry and other means of dissemination • of enforcement and the ability to levy penalties for non-compliance • for the certification of true copies
Legal Title to Records	• which preserves the inalienability of public records • provision for circumstances where sale or transfer of public records may be appropriate, and how this is to be effected • provision for the acquisition of estrays and a right to replevin
Definitions	• as a minimum explanations of the terms 'record' and 'public record' should be included • such terms should be clearly defined to avoid confusion • should be sufficiently broad to allow for changes in technology and formats [27]

For archivists, as for most professionals, ethical principles should underpin all our decisions. These principles are usually shaped by our individual perspectives of what is personally, professionally, socially and morally right, balanced against our business obligations of budget and time constraints and the responsibility we have towards the employers we serve. At times these competing demands may prove difficult to reconcile. There has been much discussion on the subject of corporate ethics in Australia and overseas in recent years and this has resulted in the publication of several codes or guidelines. The archival community both here and internationally has also been concerned with this aspect of professional conduct and has issued or drafted codes of ethics. Regardless of the audience, most of the codes have an underlying principle of elementary fairness which is encapsulated by several key points. These include the following:

• The *recognition of rights* where we should ensure that our actions do not infringe on any just claims or entitlements of our fellow employees, our employers, or those with whom they are associated. The issue of rights extends to both legal and moral entitlements.

- *Honesty* where we should always act with integrity and truthfulness and should never abuse the trust that has been placed in us.
- *Equity* which implies the establishment and application of fair and equal standards in all our activities.
- *Credibility* where any decisions which we make can be justified and explained in terms of acceptable standards of behaviour. Credibility also implies that a balanced and reasonable approach is a feature of our work and that, like the principle of equity, bias or favouritism is eliminated.
- *Sensitivity* where delicate issues are treated with care and compassion and undue harm to individuals is avoided.[28]

The above five elements do not solve the ethical dilemmas which we as archivists will continually face. They are offered as a guide to determining whether our actions and decisions will be acceptable. There will always be a need to balance several competing ideals, yet we should attempt to work within recognised standards of behaviour and to make our decisions, where possible, with due consideration of the elements suggested above. It should also be realised that ethical standards are continually evolving, as are the legal and social principles on which they are based. We should make use of this dynamic environment and attempt to shape some of the standards under which we must work.

One aspect of our work over which we do have some degree of control is that of the formulation of collection policies. Much of what is covered by such policies is of a practical nature, yet there are also ethical principles which need to be acknowledged and this is explored in Chapter 5. There is a significant responsibility which exists in relation to our acquisition or collection policies. It is similar to the legal principle known as 'replevin' which is defined as the process of obtaining redelivery of chattels which have been removed from rightful custody or ownership, rather than the receipt of financial or other such compensation in lieu of the goods.[29] In an archival sense it has specific relevance to the recovery of government records which have been removed from official custody. Mechanisms for such processes are usually defined in the legislation by which the archive has been established. In terms of collection policies replevin is an important ethical consideration as it implies a conscious decision to accept or reject records which are known to have been unlawfully removed from another archive, or which are regarded as being more suitably housed with another collection. This issue will probably be more relevant for collecting or central archives, but it is one which helps to define the ethical aspects of collection policies through a recognition of the concepts of fair-dealing and the common good. Table 4.7 illustrates the way in which ethical principles affect collection management as well as their effects on the other responsiblities associated with archival administration.

The other aspect of our work where ethical considerations will be paramount is that of risk assessment and management, particularly in relation to retention and disposal of records. In order to satisfy our legal obligations, we need to maintain adequate records which document our actions and transactions and which provide evidence of the processes involved. A risk management decision will, however, be made based on how we define 'adequate records'. It is not illegal to dispose of records required by legislation after the statutory period(s) have expired; nor is it illegal to dispose of, at our discretion, records created by our organisations to which no specific retention provision applies. Equally, it is not illegal to maintain records for longer than the statutory requirements. All such decisions require a recognition and an assessment of statutory provisions; liability for actions resulting from product development or delivery, personnel management and occupational safety issues, fidelity in insurance matters, or professional advice; and social and political credibility.

Risk management, by definition, involves the minimisation of potential liabilities which may be present in our records handling

Table 4.7 Archival Ethics – Archival Responsibilities

To archival material	• to ensure the permanent preservation of those records in their care designated as archival • to work for the 'moral and physical defence' of the archives
To our employers	• to abide by an organisation's rules and to not disclose information from records to which there has been privileged access • to disclose any private interest in collecting or trade in archives
To donors/depositors	• to respect the confidentiality of negotiations • to accept material only if it can be properly stored and processed and falls within the collecting interest of the archives
To users	• to treat all users fairly and courteously • to make archival material available equally within the constraints of the access policy and privacy arrangements
To other archival organisations and colleagues	• to cooperate in matters relating to acquisition, organisations and preservation and disposal of records • to exchange information on archival techniques and methods which will benefit archives and their users[30]

systems. To that end we should define which decisions are discretionary and will not expose either ourselves or our employers to adverse situations, and which decisions require a more measured approach, and perhaps, additional advice from relevant professional advisers.

In a risk management situation it is important to realise not only the potential liability of lack of information or documentation but also the possibility that certain information may actually be harmful to our employers. In such situations we need to avoid knee-jerk reactions which may cause us to act hastily. Instead, we need to assess all the pros and cons of retention or disposal. It is quite possible that, although certain documents may be harmful in one situation, they may be absolutely vital in another. The application of risk management to archival processes involves careful assessment of expectations, legal requirements, ethical principles and administrative practicalities in order to achieve a balanced and credible program.

Conclusion

Knowledge and understanding of our legal responsibilities are essential to effective archival and records management practices, but beyond this we must ensure that we have a system in place which will allow us to meet our obligations. We must establish mechanisms whereby we can acquaint ourselves with current and future legislative controls of both a general and specific nature, and we must form relationships with our company's or agency's legal practitioners on whom we can call for advice and interpretive information. We need also to encourage a wide-ranging appreciation of the law within our organisations and to create an environment where compliance is a management expectation. This may involve the assessment of the burden imposed by compliance weighed against the consequences of non-compliance. Perhaps most important is the ability to deal with confusion and ambiguity, as well as the potential costs and difficulties of legislative compliance, while remaining focused on the information needs and budgetary constraints of our organisations.

Archivists should allow themselves to be formed and informed by their experience with the law. The experience will provide an understanding of its meaning, impact and application.

Endnotes

1 Duranti, L., 'Diplomatics: New Uses for an Old Science (Part II)', in *Archivaria*, 29, Winter 1989–90, pp. 4–17.
2 Loton, B., 'The Impact of the Australian Taxation Regime on Australian Business', in *Taxation Institute of Australia 1991 Victorian Convention Papers*, pp. 45–48.

3   *Maritime Law Handbook*, Kluwer Law & Taxation Publishers, Deventer, Boston, 1990 (Australia–1).

4   *Cumulative Supplement to the Victorian Statutes Annotations, October 1991*, Butterworths, Melbourne, 1992, p. 57.

5   Boelens, G. et al., *Finding the Law: Legislation*, Australian Law Librarians' Group (Victorian Division), 1992.

6   Ibid.

7   Morgan, H., 'Liberating Enterprise to Improve Competitiveness, A Three Point Plan to Lift the Burden of Business Regulations', in *Business Council Bulletin*, October 1992, p. 30.

8   *Commonwealth Acts Interpretation Act 1901*, s. 15AB(2).

9   Skimmin, A., 'Legal Aspects of Records Management', in *Longman Professional Conference 1989 Toward Structural Efficiency in Records Management*, Longman Professional, Melbourne, 1989.

10 Saunders, J. B., *Words and Phrases Legally Defined*, 2nd edn, vol. 5, S–Z, Butterworths, London, 1969, p. 82.

11 Roder, M., 'Document Management and the Law', in *The Informaa Quarterly*, 7/1, February 1991, pp. 22–8.

12 *Gilligan v Nationwide News Pty Ltd* (1990) 101 FLR 139 (ACT Supreme Court, Gallop J), in *Australian Legal Monthly Digest*, April 1992, p. 61.

13 Crowe, M., 'Have the Tax Commissioner's Powers Gone too Far?', in *Decisions*, 3/3, National Australia Bank, August 1991, pp. 16–17.

14 Pheasant, Bill, 'Legal Bodies Call for Legislation on Confidentiality', in *Australian Financial Review*, 20 August 1992; 'Balancing Justice Acts' (Editorial), *Australian Financial Review*, 13 July 1992, p. 16.

15 Osborn, P.G., *A Concise Law Dictionary*, 5th edn, Sweet & Maxwell, London, 1964, p. 364.

16 Human Rights & Equal Opportunity Commission, *Guide to the Federal Privacy Act*, January 1990.

17 Hughes, G., *Data Protection in Australia*, The Law Book Company, Sydney, 1991, p. 136.

18 Cain, Hon. J., 'Freedom of Information – The Legislative and Administrative Dilemma', Papers of a seminar conducted by the ASA, Melbourne, 1981, cited in *Public Records Support Group Newsletter*, 2/6, 16 August 1991, p. 2.

19 Coad, B., 'Cash Transactions and Legislation – How Does it Affect Australian Banks?', in *The Australian Banker*, April 1990, pp. 53–7.

20 Australian Taxation Office, *Record Retention Guide for Electronically Stored Information*, 1991.

21 Tulloch, A., 'International Rules for Electronic Bills of Lading', in *Australian Financial Review*, 2 March 1992.

22 National Health & Medical Research Council, *An Australian Code of Practice for Transplantation of Cadaveric Organs & Tissues*, AGPS, Canberra, 1990.

23 *Occupational Health Newsletter*, 272, 1 May 1992, p. 1; 280, 20 August 1992, pp. 1, 4.

24 Saunders, J. B. (ed.), Op. cit., vol. 4, O–R, p. 306.

25 Meibusch, P., 'Legislative Provisions Throughout Australia Concerning the Use of Information Records as Evidence in Courts', in *Storage Media and the Law*, Papers of a seminar conducted by the RMAA, Canberra, 1990; *Evidence Bill 1991* and *Explanatory*

Memorandum, The Parliament of Australia, House of Representatives, 1991.

26 Ketelaar, Eric, *Archival and Records Management Legislation and Regulations: A RAMP Study with Guidelines*, Unesco Press, Paris, 1985.

27 Electoral and Administrative Review Commission (Queensland), *Report on Review of Archives Legislation,* June 1992.

28 Berenbeim, R. E., *Corporate Ethics, A Research Report for the Corporate Board (no. 900)*, The Conference Board, Inc., 1988; SAA, 'Code of Ethics & Commentary', in *SAA Newsletter*, July 1991; ASA, *Draft Code of Ethics*, April 1992.

29 Saunders, J. B., Op. cit., vol. 4, O–R, p. 306.

30 Table reproduced from Schwirtlich, A-M., 'Introducing Archives and the Archival Profession', in *Keeping Archives,* ASA, Sydney, 1987, p. 15.

Further Reading

Argy, P., 'Legal Aspects of Information Technology in Government', in *Computing in Government Conference*, 19 August 1986.

Australian Attorney-General's Department, *Copyright and the Law* (pamphlet).

Australian Current Law: Legislation.

Australian Law Reform Commission, *Privacy Report*, AGPS, Canberra.

Australian Legal Monthly Digest.

ASA, *Privacy Versus Access to Records*, Papers of a seminar conducted by the ACT Branch of the ASA, Canberra, 30 April 1991.

Australian Taxation Office, *Record Retention Guides*, 1991.

Boelens, G. et al., *Finding the Law: Case Law*, Australian Law Librarians' Group (Victorian Division), 1992.

Brown, R. A., *Documentary Evidence in Australia,* Law Book Company, Sydney, 1988.

Campbell, E. et al., *Legal Research: Materials and Methods*, 3rd edn, Law Book Company, Sydney, 1988.

Commonwealth Statutes Annotations, Law Book Company, Sydney.

Electoral and Administrative Review Commission (Queensland), *Record of Proceedings Public Seminar on Archives Legislation*, December 1991.

Farrar, Professor John H., 'Report on Modernising Australian Corporations Law', in *Business Council Bulletin*, August 1992.

Federal Legislation Annotations, Butterworths.

Fong, C. and Ellis, G., *Finding the Law, A Guide to Australian Secondary Sources of Legal Information,* Legal Information Press, Sydney, 1990.

Howe, T., 'Law and Its Effect on Information Management' in *State Seminar Papers*, Records Management Association of Australia Victorian Branch, 24/25 February 1992.

McKemmish, S. and Upward, F., 'The Archival Document: A Submission to the Inquiry into Australia as an Information Society', in *Archives & Manuscripts*, 19/1, 1991, pp. 17–31.

Moore, P., 'Appraisal of Business Archives – Legal and Financial Values', in *Managing Business Archives*, 2nd edn, Fiona Reid and Colleen Pritchard (eds), ASA, 1992, pp. 29–41.

Moore, P., 'Business Archives and the Law: Legislation Relating to the Creation and Retention of Company Records', in *Proceedings of the 5th*

Biennial Conference of the Australian Society of Archivists, Canberra, 1985, pp. 5–39.

Records Management Association of Australia, *Fourth National Convention Papers 1987 State of the Art Workshop on Law and Records*, RMAA, 6–9 September 1987.

Records Management Association of Australia, *Storage Media and the Law*, Papers of a seminar conducted by the RMAA, Canberra, 1990.

Reynolds, P., 'The Legal Risks of Inadequate RM', *Informaa Quarterly*, 8/4, November 1992, pp. 15–18.

Schubert, Dr John, 'Inquiry into Administrative Procedures of the Australian Taxation Office', in *Business Council Bulletin*, June 1992, pp. 34–44.

Skupsky, D., 'Destruction of Records ... Your Legal Obligations', *Records Management Quarterly*, October 1992, pp. 30–4, 56.

'Legal Requirements and Legal Considerations – The Basis for the Legal Records Retention Period', in *Records Management Quarterly*, April 1990, pp. 32–40.

Recordkeeping Requirements, Information Requirements Clearing House, Denver Colorado, 1988.

Smith, C., 'Archives and Copyright', in *Archives and Manuscripts*, 18/2, 1990, pp. 243–257.

Smith, H., 'Legal Obligations and Liabilities for Record Keepers', in *Informaa Quarterly*, 6/1, 1990, pp. 58–63.

State Library of NSW, *Coping with Copyright: A Guide to Using Pictorial and Written Material in Australian Libraries and Archives*, State Library of NSW Press, Sydney, 1991.

Stephens, D. O., 'Making Records Retention Decisions: Practical and Theoretical Considerations', in *Records Management Quarterly*, 22/1, January 1988, pp. 3–7.

Victorian Reports*

Wicks Subject Index to the Acts of the Australian Parliament

Yoxall, H., 'Privacy and Personal Papers', in *Archives & Manuscripts*, 12/1, 1984, pp. 38–44.

*Law Reports are also available for Commonwealth and federal courts as well as other state and territory courts

5 | Managing the Acquisition Process

Anne-Marie Schwirtlich and Barbara Reed

Introduction

Acquisition is the process by which archives add to their holdings by accepting material as a donation, transfer, purchase or loan. The acquisition process involves
- clear assessment of the scope, strengths and weaknesses of existing holdings against the acquisition policy
- identification of potential sources of material that will strengthen or develop the collection
- formation of a strategy to acquire this material
- formally accepting the acquisition.

Acquisition must be undertaken responsibly and in an orderly fashion to avoid uncontrolled and uncontrollable growth in the collection. Every acquisition is a commitment by the archives to the donor or creator, to the researcher and to the item itself. It is a commitment to control and document it; to protect, store and conserve it; and to make it available to interested researchers. It involves, therefore, a commitment of the resources of the archives.

The Purpose of an Acquisition Policy

Chapter 2, Getting Organised, advocates the necessity for an archives policy and outlines what this policy should contain and recommends that a separate and detailed acquisition policy be developed. The acquisition policy defines the nature of the archives. It stipulates what the archives will acquire, what limits it will set on acquisition and what types of material are of particular interest. The acquisition policy is a vital tool for staff responsible for, or involved in, acquisition as it guides their decisionmaking. If the policy is made publicly available, it can be very useful to acquisition staff in other organisations as it can assist them in deciding whether to refer potential donations to you. The policy can also assist donors to determine whether they should approach you about material in their possession.

By defining the proposed scope and content of the collection, the policy should prevent capricious or inconsistent acquisition decisions. It should minimise the extent to which subjective decisions are made. For example, by requiring a decision to be made on the basis of the content and contextual links of the material, it should reduce the possibility of basing the acquisition decision on personal impressions of the donor or personal interest in the material being offered. In addition, a clearly articulated acquisition policy allows the archives a graceful means of refusing material unsuited to its collection.

Decisions which are guided by the acquisition policy should be documented as such. For example, the donation or transfer file should indicate that the acquisition was accepted because it satisfied a particular provision of the policy. The object of this documentation is to demonstrate the rationale and probity of the decision. Acquisition work is guided not only by policy but also by resources. It is possible that, if storage space or finances become straitened in the future, all holdings will be critically assessed to justify their inclusion in the collection. In such a situation it will be much easier to understand whether or why material should be retained if the original decision is explained and supported.

Developing an Acquisition Policy

The acquisition policy must flow from either the legal mandate or the executive decision establishing the archives. These identify the purpose and the functions of the archives which, in turn, shape the acquisition policy.

Chapter 1, Introducing Archives and Archival Programs, outlined the following organisational contexts or institutional settings for archives:
- Large centralised government programs with legislative responsibilities.
- In-house archives.
- Collecting archives.
- Any combination of the above.

There is a slightly greater emphasis in this chapter on the approaches and strategies of collecting archives rather than on centralised government programs or in-house archives. This is because collecting archives tend to have better developed and more innovative approaches to acquisition, which deserve wider application.

Centralised Government and In-House Archives

Centralised government programs and in-house archives acquire and service only the records of their parent or host organisation (and perhaps the records of specified interrelated organisations). For example, the archives of the Rural and Industries Bank of Western Australia Ltd acquires and manages the archives of the R&I Bank but also those of nominated subsidiary companies such as the Agricultural Bank of Western Australia. Similarly, a school archives may care for the archives of the school but may also seek the archives of specified bodies closely associated with the school; eg parents and teachers or citizens' associations, organisations of ex-students and so on.

The purpose of an in-house archives is to document the functions, development, history and contributions of the parent body. The acquisition policy must clarify the responsibility of the archives for

- materials created or used directly in the work of the parent body
- active and semi-current as well as inactive and archival records
- records which, over the life of the organisation, may have been lost or removed from official custody
- records of preceding bodies or closely affiliated organisations (these should be nominated)
- personal papers of individuals closely connected with the work of the parent body (What categories of individuals? To what extent should the records document the connection with the parent body?)
- various formats; eg will the archives acquire only paper- or film-based records; will it also accept objects and memorabilia?

Collecting Archives

Collecting archives acquire records, regardless of their provenance, relating to a particular specialisation. For example, the Noel Butlin Archives Centre collects the records of companies, trade unions, employer bodies and private individuals to document the labour movement in Australia and Australian industry. The National Film and Sound Archive collects films, videos and sound recordings that document the development of the film, sound and television industries in Australia. The Mandurah

Historical Society Incorporated collects material related to the district and the people associated with it from 1829 to 1950.

The purpose of a collecting archives is to document its particular specialisation. The acquisition policy should
- clearly identify and define the specialisation
- nominate the geographic focus (Will it be national, state, regional, local?)
- nominate the temporal focus (1830 to 1970; 1920 onward)
- identify whether the records of institutions, associations, individuals are of interest
- identify the formats to be acquired; eg will only paper-based material be accepted? Will memorabilia and objects be accepted?

Collecting archives devoted to the documentation of subjects, themes or experience will inevitably face problems of definition, questions of what to include and what to exclude and where to draw the line. For example, an archives established to document immigration must define what this constitutes (refugees? displaced persons? illegal immigrants?). It must decide whether it will collect records relating to immigration from all or specific countries, and whether it will document the effect of immigration and to what extent. Will the records of community and ethnic support groups be included? Will the views and activities of those opposed to immigration be documented? Will it document ethnic rivalry in Australia? The wider the collecting ambit the greater the task and the greater the possibility that it may overlap with the acquisition interest of other institutions.

Combined Archives

Combined archives are responsible for acquiring the records of their host or parent organisation and for collecting within a particular specialisation. One such example is the archives of the University of Newcastle, which collects archives of the University, University organisations, staff and students and selected manuscript collections relating specifically to the Hunter Region. The acquisition policies for such archives should cover the points identified in the sections above on in-house archives and collecting archives.

Structuring the Acquisition Policy

An acquisition policy should contain the following elements:
(a) General statement of purpose of institution and/or archives program.
(b) Statement of authority to acquire material:
- nature and basis of authority

- person or body in whom authority to acquire is vested.
(c) Definition of terms:
  - records
  - non-current records
  - archives
  - archivist
  - depositor
  - archival value
  - de-accessioning/disposal.
(d) Explanation of how material is acquired (transfer, purchase, donation, loan).
(e) General description of acquisition focus:
  - official records
  - non-official records
  - reference library material
  - types of materials generally not acquired and why.
(f) Statement of acquisition priorities for the next 5 to 10 years.
(g) General description of conditions which material should meet to be acquired:
  Official
  - that it be covered by disposal schedule
  Non-official
  - that it fall under acquisition responsibility as outlined in e)
  - depositor must be authorised to transfer title to material
  - material must undergo archival appraisal and be recommended for retention (unique, documented authenticity and integrity, demonstrated historical/archival value, reasonable condition, archives must be able to care for it properly)
  - material must be free of legal encumbrances or access restrictions which will diminish its research potential
  - material either become the property of the archives or its responsibility, to be administered as it sees fit
(h) General description of review and de-accessioning of unwanted material:
  - de-accessioning policy, including reasons for it
  - de-accessioning procedure – general
  - disposal options for de-accessioned material, including use of any proceeds from sale of such material.
(i) Information on whom to contact about material for potential acquisition.

In the course of developing or refining your acquisition policy, it is crucial that you take into account the collecting interests and strengths of other institutions. If necessary, discuss your intentions and their ramifications with institutions you believe may be affected, or may think that they are being affected. It is vital that collecting activity be complementary rather than competitive to ensure that our archival heritage survives in an integrated way.

The policy, once finalised, should be officially approved and issued. It should be treated as an authoritative document and should be widely circulated (to other archival institutions, current and potential donors, and researchers). The policy should be evaluated regularly. This process of evaluation should draw on the working experience of all staff involved in its application and on the advice of representative donors and researchers.

Applying the Acquisition Policy

Once the acquisition policy has been officially endorsed every acquisition should be assessed against the criteria outlined in it. However, it is worth emphasising that acquisition does not take place in a policy vacuum. Other considerations may influence the acquisition decision. These considerations may conveniently be categorised as
- general resource issues
- physical format considerations
- issues relating to use
- custody issues.

General Resource Issues

General resource issues frequently impinge on acquisition decisions:
- What are the financial costs of acquiring the material (purchase costs, transport costs)?
- What are the resource implications of acquiring the material (storage, arrangement and description, preservation)?
- What related resources (eg library materials) would have to be acquired to support the acquisition?

Considerations of Physical Format

The physical format of the material, and your ability to manage, preserve and provide access to it, may influence the acquisition decision:
- Is appropriate storage equipment available (for maps, magnetic media, film, photographic negatives)?
- Are suitable environmental conditions available?
- Can adequate maintenance and inspection be carried out (some magnetic media and film need exercising and rewinding; photographic and microfilm negatives require regular inspection)?
- Is the appropriate technology available to provide access to the material (to ensure that you can document and inspect it and to ensure that you can make it available)?

Issues Relating to Use

Identifying who (in terms of categories of researchers rather than individuals) will use the collection and how it will be used can affect your acquisition decision:

- Is there a known demand for the material?
- Will this demand persist or is it temporary?
- Is the demand expected from researchers you identify as your major client group?
- Can the material support a variety of research interests?
- Are researchers likely to be interested in current as well as retrospective material?
- Will researchers need to consult related material held elsewhere?
- Will researchers want to use or gain access to the material in a way that will be expensive or impossible to accommodate?

Custody Issues

It is always worthwhile asking these questions:

- Does any other institution already have custody of material from this provenance? If the response is yes, should the material be in that institution's custody or should custody be shared?
- Would this material better complement, or be more appropriately placed in the holdings of another institution?
- Would researchers consider you the natural custodian of this material? (That is, would they automatically refer to you or would they have to be directed to you after much fruitless initial work?)

Consulting the *Directory of Archives in Australia* (ASA, 1992), which lists over 450 repositories, may assist you to answer these questions.

Developing an Acquisition Strategy

What is an Acquisition Strategy?

An acquisition strategy is a coordinated program of activities designed to deliver a designated set of acquisition results. Once you have formulated an acquisition policy you will need to

- assess your holdings to identify strengths and weaknesses
- obtain an overview of the strengths and weakness of the holdings of institutions in your area, of your type or in your field to identify whether there are areas in which you could acquire material (within the constraints of your legal responsibilities and purpose).

The results of such an assessment will allow you to nominate in what areas you will actively seek material. However, before you embark on your acquisition enterprise you will need to establish certain key matters:

- What resources (time, money, storage, etc) can be made available to acquisition work?
- Can the institution cope with an increase in acquisition? (Is there a capacity to complete arrangement and description or will this increase the backlog?)
- What time is already spent on acquisition work? Is it being effectively used? (For example, you might be spending an hour with each donor who contacts you, whereas by reducing this contact time you could spend it more profitably elsewhere.)

Once you can quantify the resources at your disposal you can formulate your acquisition strategy.

Assessing Your Holdings

The purpose of assessing your holdings is to establish whether and where your holdings are weak and patchy and where they are strong. Using the example of a university archives with responsibility for acquiring the university's official archives as well as those of associations and bodies connected with the university, we can proceed to discuss this in some detail. Assume that the university was established in 1931 and that the archives has custody of the records of all administrative and service departments, minutes of the Senate between 1931 and 1977, but very few faculty records or those of associations or clubs formed on campus.

You would need to assess why your holdings of Senate minutes ceased and why you hold such a paucity of faculty and association records. This would involve examining the administrative files of the archives, understanding the history of faculties and clubs/associations, establishing the quantity of material extant, its value and condition, the extent to which the people controlling it would be susceptible to your approaches, and so on.

Flowing from this exercise you would need to assess which material you would wish to acquire and the priority you would attach to the acquisitions. Then you would proceed to craft your approach to the various bodies.

Obtaining an Overview of the Holdings of Other Institutions

The aim of this exercise is to establish the range and scope of the holdings of other institutions. This is to ascertain whether material in which you have an interest has already been donated or deposited; whether others have developed specialisations which it would be pointless your duplicating and whether there are gaps in the documentation which you could usefully plug.

It would involve consulting the acquisition policies of these institutions, reading articles or leaflets about their holdings, consulting guides and finding aids to their collections.

Developing the Tools to Support the Acquisition Strategy

The range of tools which may be useful in achieving your acquisition strategy are varied. It is important that you select and develop those which will promote your work.

There are two leaflets or brochures which may be useful: one introducing the archives and its acquisition interests; the other explaining the process and benefits of donation or transfer. You may recall earlier in this chapter the recommendation that the acquisition policy be widely disseminated. As policy documents can often be complex and formal documents, it is worthwhile to present the content of the policy in a more accessible and readable format. This leaflet could introduce the archives (its purpose; the range of its activities, services and contributions), outline its holdings and notable use made of them, indicate areas of acquisition interest, solicit donations or transfers, and close with information about whom to contact.

The second leaflet could also introduce the archives (its purpose; the range of its activities, services and contributions), outline its holdings and notable use made of them, explain how material can be placed in the archives and what the legal implications are (donation, transfer, loan, sale), indicate what happens to the material when it arrives in the archives, and why the assistance of the reader would be valued. Chapter 11, User Education and Public Relations, contains useful advice on the preparation of such publicity material.

Consider placing short articles (in appropriate journals, magazines or newsletters) describing your holdings and your acquisition interests or publicising a notable acquisition and at the same time including a plea for other material. Explore the value of producing a short presentation with slides which can be delivered with minimal work and alteration, to a wide variety of groups encouraging the donation or transfer of specified material.

Assess the benefits of training the people in your organisation or in your community who have excellent contacts so that they can act as field officers or 'spotters' for you. Such training would encompass an understanding of the holdings and the areas in which they could be strengthened, a grounding in the acquisition policy and the costs and implications of acquisition, a clear picture of what kind of material is not sought and why, and an explanation of the acquisition process and who to contact. There are benefits to in-house and collecting archives programs in having an informed and articulate network of supporters who can raise the archives profile, answer basic questions and deflect unnecessary contact.

Develop a range of forms to assist in the documentation of the acquisition process. A donor contact form or card is a useful and eminently accessible way of recording information about potential donors and the contact you have had (see Table 5.1). A donor form can be printed on carbonised paper allowing you to file the duplicates and triplicates under different headings. Carefully prepare the text of a standard letter of approach to potential donors (word processors will allow you to customise or personalise the letter, but the bulk of the text can be similar for all such letters) and present it attractively with supporting leaflets.

Develop forms to effect the transfer, loan, purchase or donation of material. These forms should be drafted with care and should, if possible, be assessed and approved by the archives' solicitor.

Table 5.1 Donor Contact Forms

Source of information:	Mrs Margaret Llewellyn
Address:	14 High Street Aberdeen NSW 2701
Telephone:	46 2138
Basis of knowledge of potential donation:	Mrs Llewellyn is writing a history of The Tablelands and was granted access to the records of The Triple X Station by Mrs Short
Possible owner:	Mrs Shirley Short
Address:	12 Blossom Avenue Aberdeen NSW 2701
Telephone:	Not known
Description of material:	Records of the Samson family which owned and managed the Triple X between 1856 and 1935. Existence of personal correspondence, diaries and ledgers mentioned
Information received:	16/4/92
Form filed under:	Llewellyn; Short; Samson; Triple X
Contact information:	23/4/92 – letter to Mrs Short inquiring about papers (file 92/76)

The preparation of a thoughtful letter of thanks is also strongly recommended. Once again the text of such a document (or range of documents) can be standardised. Remember not only to thank the donor or person responsible for the transfer but also any individuals instrumental in bringing about the donation or transfer.

It is worthwhile maintaining a list of donors, or others associated with donations, so that you can include them on invitation lists for functions sponsored by the archives or on your Christmas card list.

A final and vital element of documentation necessary to underpin an acquisition strategy is the creation and maintenance of acquisition files. These files form part of the archives own record-keeping system and contain the comprehensive and consolidated record of contact with potential and actual depositors and donors. Table 5.2 lists the range of documents worth including on the acquisition file for each depositor or donor.

Table 5.2 The Acquisition File

Types of documents appropriate for the file include:
- Records documenting contacts with the depositor or donor (contact forms; correspondence; notes of telephone conversations, reports on visits to examine material and negotiations of terms of transfer, donation or purchase).
- Records documenting the evaluation of the material (valuations for tax incentive schemes; disposal schedules; records appraisal sheets).
- Records documenting the legal and physical transfer of material (records transfer receipt; box lists; transfer proposal or agreement, deed of gift). After the material is transferred and accessioned, further documents may be added to the file to reflect the archival work undertaken to preserve the material and prepare it for research use.
- Records documenting the archival management of the material (worksheets for arrangement and description and/or conservation; applications for access, photocopying or publication).

Methods of Acquisition for an In-House Archives

An in-house archives can be active or passive in its acquisition strategy. Passive collecting involves evaluating material when it is *offered* to the archives. This approach to collecting implies that decisions about what records are of archival value are made by creators before the material is offered to the archives. It also follows that you may not be consulted on the weeding of material by office personnel. An active acquisition policy in an in-house archives involves a very different role. This role demands that archivists identify the strategies that will be employed to appraise functions and/or records and the techniques that will be applied to actually make decisions about what body of records will be selected for preservation. The issues involved in and the implications of this radically different approach are canvassed in detail in Chapter 6, Appraisal and Disposal.

Regardless of whether an institution has a passive or active acquisition strategy, every in-house archives must address the problem of recovering information which has passed outside the control of the institution. This can happen in a variety of ways – employees taking records with them when they resign or retire, records being given to other bodies for some reason or records disappearing to later reappear in the hands of a person or body not related to the institution. Such records are referred to as *estrays*. The archives will need to decide whether it will actively pursue those records known to have gone elsewhere or whether estrays will be accepted and be incorporated into their rightful places as the opportunity arises.

If an estray is discovered in the holdings of another archival institution which does not wish to part with it, the option of copying the material should be considered. In this way, although the original material is not recovered, the information contained in the record is not lost to the archives, and any potential ill-feeling is avoided.

The Process of Acquisition in a Collecting Archives

In the same manner as an in-house archives, a collecting archives must also decide upon its level of collecting activity. Will it actively seek material which fits into its acquisition policy or take the more passive approach of evaluating material as it is offered?

However energetically an archives may try to communicate its needs, it will inevitably be approached with the occasional donation or bequest which does not conform to the acquisition policy. Provided your publicity has been effective, such occurrences will be the exception rather than the rule and, in most cases, such offerings can be politely declined citing the acquisition policy as the basis for doing so.

More frequently, publicity results in indications of where material may be found rather than actual gifts. It is useful to compile the information, perhaps on a form as illustrated above, documenting these leads with any details available on the particular records and on the organisation or individuals who possess them. These records form the basic resource files for organised collecting, and it is important that information about all contacts and potential donors is carefully recorded and maintained.

The information in these files becomes the basis for field-work, which includes the activities of locating and identifying the material to be collected, negotiating for its donation and finally ensuring that the records reach the archives. Fieldwork usually involves visiting the location of the material, which may not be in the immediate vicinity, so budgeting for travelling expenses will need to be considered. In fieldwork one contact often leads to other potential donations and time should be allotted to pursue such unexpected opportunities. Even if a lead proves a dead end, there are public relations advantages to making the existence of the archives collecting interest widely known.

Because many collecting archives have active field programs to locate material, the process of appraising collected materials begins early and continues after the records have been transferred to the archives. A field officer may hear of a possible collection of papers in the possession of an individual. In order to assess whether such material would be worth the time and expense of pursuit, some preliminary work must be done to determine the possible significance of the individual or organisation which created the records and the types of documents most representative of their work. Often by the time the papers are actually seen, the field officer will have a good idea of what archival value the material is likely to have. Table 5.3 provides an indication of the type of information needed to assess potential acquisitions.

All material must be assessed against the acquisition policy. As a start, a quick survey of the material should be carried out. This survey should describe the material accurately, noting the major types of records, the information they contain, their date range and quantity, the order or arrangement of the records, the possibility of future additions to the collection and any problems with the physical condition of the material. A useful companion to the survey is the drawing of a site plan, which documents the location and physical arrangement of the records as they were found at the time of the survey. This plan provides a valuable *aide-mémoire* of the records as they were first seen and may capture clues to their relationships that may be disturbed in packing the records for transfer to the archives. As a result of the information recorded during the survey, sound decisions can be made as to the archival value of the material offered.

Table 5.3 Background Information Required To Assess Potential Donations

1	What relation does the person possessing the records have to the individual or organisation whose records are being discussed?
2	What position did the creator of the records have in relation to the particular field being documented?
3	How long was the person or business active and when did they cease to be active?
4	Are these records unique or were copies distributed to a number of parties?
5	Who has legal title to these records? Were they inherited from a relative? Were they bought? Were they a gift? How is this ownership documented?
6	Are the records likely to contain much published material and is the published material readily available elsewhere?
7	Where are the records of other individuals or businesses relating to this collection held?
8	Are the records offered complete and representative evidence of the work of the creating organisation or individual?

If the material is of sufficient importance to the archives, it is packed, listed and transported to the archives for more extensive assessment.

Collections often contain a proportion of ephemeral material. This material should be appraised in the same way as the remainder of the collection and measured against the dual criteria of the acquisition policy and the appraisal checklist. Ephemera can be of great interest if it has an integral link to the papers being appraised. For example, copies of all of a company's advertisements placed in the national press will be of great value if they are complete and kept with documentation which explains the background to the advertisements. Random copies of unrelated advertising, with no logic, reason for collection or order, will be of little value. Similarly, booklets, social tracts and pamphlets which appear in personal papers have value if written by the creator or consistently collected by him or her. However, random copies of unrelated printed material may be best dealt with by a rare book librarian after a record has been made of the material for the archives.

Means of Documenting the Acquisition

If the material meets all the criteria for acceptance by the archives, you will need to negotiate its acquisition. The most common methods of acquisition are donations, bequests, transfers and purchases. The discussion to follow examines issues in documenting each of these.

The terms of every donation should provide for the transfer both of legal title and of any literary property or copyrights vested in the material. Questions such as 'can the material be made available to researchers?' and 'can copies be made for researchers?' should also be finalised at this time.

A donation to the archives should be documented in a deed of gift. It is best to have a standard deed of gift drawn up or approved by a solicitor to cover the standard clauses. Some of the exact matters a deed should contain are the specific date when the donation is made, a list or a description of the material in sufficient detail to allow future identification, and the signatures of both the donor and a representative of the recipient institution. Where an archives expects further donations from the one donor, a deed may be drafted so as to cover subsequent donations. The agreement then becomes analagous to a disposal schedule, with the donor agreeing to transfer more material from specific series after an agreed lapse of time. In such cases the initial deed may state that subsequent donations will be made in accordance with the provisions established in the initial deed.

Any restrictions on use of the material required by the donor should also be established in the deed of gift. Blanket or unreasonable restrictions on the material, such as 'the papers shall be closed to the public', must be avoided whenever possible. Such restrictions make the material useless for research. Conversely, donors should be advised by the archivist if restrictions are needed for legal reasons or to protect privacy. In such cases advice from the archives' solicitor and from the ASA should be sought.

Similarly, an indefinite requirement that every person wishing access to the material must be referred to the donor for permission should be avoided. Such a provision is often difficult to administer and also raises the question of what happens when the donor dies. Will the papers then be open? If not, who will give permission for access? Donors should look to the archives for advice on the appropriate restrictions. In all cases any restrictions should have a definite time limit and refer to specific documents rather than the entire collection.

The right to dispose of the material, or parts thereof, which fall outside the collecting interests of the archives should also be established in the deed of gift. Such a provision enables the archives to dispose of unwanted material. For example, multiple copies of reference publications such as *Hansard*, textbooks or sets of encyclopaedia are not required by the archives. Such material takes up scarce space, exists in many other places and is inappropriate for a specialist archives collection. At the time of donation you should establish with the donor if he or she prefers

Table 5.4 Deed of Gift

(Please note: All deed forms should be legally approved)

Accession No................

File No..........................

I, *Joan Jenkinson,* of *43 Blight Street, Sydney,* do hereby make a gift of the material specified below to the *Wherever Historical Society* and its successor organisations.

Being the sole owner of the material, I give this material (and any additions which I may make to it) unencumbered to the *Wherever Historical Society* and do declare that I made the gift of my own free will and without influence.

Any copyrights such as I may possess in this material or in any other property in the custody of the *Wherever Historical Society* are hereby assigned to the *Wherever Historical Society.*

The material specified below shall be available to members of public for use from *the date of this deed* with the exception of the items asterisked below which shall be restricted from public use until *1 January 2010.*

Items not retained by the *Wherever Historical Society* shall be returned to me.

Schedule of material donated:
Diaries of John T. Smith, 1932–1945 (5 volumes)
*Diaries of Jonathon A. Jenkinson, 1940–1979 (16 volumes)
Account Books from the business of Jenkinson and Smith, 1930–1950 (20 annual volumes)

In full accord with the provisions of this deed of gift, I hereunto set my hand.

....Date............................
    (Donor)
Signed in the presence of *Jerome N. Wilson*:

....

On behalf of the *Wherever Historical Society,* I, Jennifer Eccles, Archivist, accept this gift.

....Date............................

that such material be returned or whether the archives may dispose of it in any appropriate way, including sale, gift and trade, as well as discard.

Donation of original material does not involve the transfer of copyright unless this is specifically mentioned in the acquisition agreement. In negotiating the transfer of copyright it is important to remember that the donor can only transfer title to the copyright which he or she owns. For example, in a series of correspondence, a potential donor would own the copyright in the letters he or she wrote (both in the original and the copy kept for the record). The copyrights in letters received would normally belong to their writers, not to the recipient. The issues of copyright can be complex, and it is recommended that you approach the Australian Copyright Council to obtain up-to-date advice and copies of its publications.

The Taxation Incentives for the Arts scheme established by the Australian government provides a mechanism whereby material donated to an approved institution can be evaluated by accredited assessors and the value of the material taken as a tax deduction for the donor. The scheme is administered by the Committee on Taxation Incentives for the Arts within the Department of Arts, Sport, Environment and Territories. Archivists should contact the Department for the latest guidelines, and list of approved valuers as they do alter from time to time.

A bequest is a gift of personal possessions, excluding real property and money, made in a will. For archival material to be bequeathed to an archives, it must be specifically mentioned in a will. It is not sufficient to rely on a verbal comment such as 'you may have the papers when I die', as it is too general to be legally enforceable. As with the deed of gift, the bequest should also detail the donor's wishes as to the disposal of unwanted material and the research use of the records. Copyright is always transferred by bequest unless it is specifically excluded by the will. Material may also be donated to an archives by beneficiaries to a will. In these cases the archives must ensure that all the beneficiaries agree to the donation and document the transaction with a deed of gift.

An occasional unwanted bequest may be made to the archives. Such bequests should always be refused by quoting the acquisition policy. However, assistance in recommending a more appropriate repository will be a useful public relations exercise. Bequests can be encouraged within a community by contacting local solicitors and suggesting that they encourage clients to consider the bequest of personal papers in their wills in addition to real property and money.

Transfer is a means of acquisition for in-house archives. As in-house archives acquire material from their parent organisations, the title to the material is not transferred because the parent organisation owns the material regardless of whether it is in the advertising department or the archives. However, it is important to document the transfer of custody to the archives. First, because in some government and in-house archives the provisions of archival legislation or of the archives policy apply only to records in the custody of the archives. Second, it is prudent to ensure that there can be no confusion about whether, and for which material, the archives has accepted responsibility.

It is recommended that the branch, division or unit proposing a transfer do so in writing indicating the area transferring, the officer authorising the transfer, the contact information for the person handling the transfer, and the series being tranferred together with an item-by-item listing of the material. If documentation such as this is provided, the transferring area can retain a copy and check it before seeking access to or the return of items thereby eliminating any false queries.

Purchasing is also a means of acquisition. It is not a common method of acquisition and tends to involve large institutions which have special funds to support such activity. When you are thinking of purchasing material, there are several matters you would be wise to ascertain. Both you and the vendor must be perfectly clear about what material is the subject of the transaction. The material should be listed in sufficient detail to enable clear identification of your title to it in the future. If possible, the vendor's asking price and the amount you agree to pay should be documented via correspondence – especially if through negotiation the asking price has been reduced. There should be documentation to show what the payment covers – eg does it cover packing, freight and insurance costs if the material is to be transported to you? Are you purchasing copyright? If the vendor has any documentation that provides information about the provenance or authenticity of the material, you should try to obtain copies of this documentation. As the buyer, it is your responsibility to satisfy yourself that the material is genuine and is what it purports to be. It is vital that you obtain a receipt documenting your payment for the material. The receipt should name the vendor and the buyer, and nominate the amount paid and the material purchased.

If the purchase is subject to any conditions, these should be stipulated in writing. Depending on the complexity of the conditions, it may be necessary to frame them in the form of a contract or memorandum of understanding. For example, have you agreed that some material will be witheld from public access for a specified period?

Loans are another method of acquiring material. It is a method that may be fraught with potential problems. If material is accepted on loan, the archives will expend staff time and resources on storing, processing and preserving the material. Should the owner later decide to withdraw the material, the archives has no choice but to comply, and the time and effort spent on the material will have been wasted. Should the owner die and the beneficiaries of the estate wish to reclaim the material, the position is identical. In cases where the beneficiaries are remote, unknown or take no action regarding the loan, the legal status of the ownership of the material can remain in doubt for many years. If the archives decides to accept records on loan, you must draw up a loan agreement clearly describing the material on loan and the conditions under which it will be cared for and used. The agreement should set definite time limits on the loan period and make arrangements for the return of the material or conversion to a donation if the time limit is exceeded. It is advisable to have the text of your loan agreement approved by a solicitor.

Conclusion

Acquisition is a crucial activity in the development of an archival collection. It should be carefully documented, not only to provide the archives with guidelines for present activity but also to provide guidance for future generations of archivists to assess the development of the collection. The records documenting acquisition are among the most important part of your own archives' holdings.

The process of acquisition is not static but continuing. Review of acquisitions accepted is becoming more and more important in archival practice, especially as archives must justify their expenditure and holdings.

It is important to publicly report acquisitions as widely as possible. Professional archival journals and those of appropriate disciplines should be informed of new acquisitions on a regular basis, and the archives itself may feature them in a newsletter or issue acquisitions lists. Other archival institutions should be kept informed of the whereabouts of particular records, not only to reinforce collecting interests and areas but, most importantly, to enable reference staff to direct researchers to appropriate records held by other archives.

Sound acquisition policies, well implemented, will form the basis for the continuing good management of any archival collection.

Further Reading

Abraham, Terry, 'Collection Policy or Documentation Strategy: Theory and Practice', in *American Archivist*, 54/1, Winter 1991, pp. 44–52.

Cox, Richard, *Managing Institutional Archives: Foundational Principles and Practices,* Greenwood Press, New York, 1992, ch. 3.

Daniels, Maygene F. and Walch, Timothy (eds), *A Modern Archives Reader: Basic Readings on Archival Theory and Practice,* NARA, Washington DC, 1984, ch. 4.

Duckett, Kenneth W., *Modern Manuscripts: A Practical Manual for Their Management, Care and Use,* AASLH, Nashville, 1975, ch. 3.

Ericson, Tim, 'At the "rim of creative dissatisfaction": Archivists and Acquisition Development', in *Archivaria,* 33/1, Winter 1991–92, pp. 66–77.

Weideman, Christine, 'A New Map for Field Work: Impact of Collections Analysis on the Bentley Historical Library', in *American Archivist,* 54/1, Winter 1991, pp. 54–60.

6 Appraisal and Disposal

Barbara Reed

Archivists are responsible for the identification and care of that small percentage of all records created which are deemed to be of continuing value. Determining which of the records will become archives and which shall be discarded is the archival skill of appraisal. When and how should this skill be applied?

Appraisal decisions are made at different times with different approaches and different emphases depending on the type of archives. The approaches of centralised archival agencies and in-house archives are increasingly concentrating on the identification of the archival record early in its active phase as part of the information strategies employed across the whole organisation. Collecting archives apply appraisal skills in conjunction with acquisition strategies to ensure a cohesive collection.

The relationship between acquisition and appraisal is a close one. Appraisal decisions inform the actual process of acquisition. This relationship has been characterised by the question: 'Why do I retain these records?' The appraisal focus is '*Why* do I retain these records?' and the acquisition focus on the same question is 'Why do *I* retain these records?'[1] How to develop an acquisition policy and manage the acquisition process is covered in Chapter 5.

This chapter first addresses the traditional principles of appraisal and their application in familiar disposal techniques, outlining some of the adaptations which have taken place in practice to cope with problems faced by archivists in applying current techniques. From this accepted practice base, the chapter then addresses some of the challenges to traditional strategies.

An Overview of Appraisal

All archives must be selective in determining what material has continuing value in order to establish a collection which is cohesive, compact and worthy of resources to support it. It is obvious that not all records can be kept indefinitely. Many creators and custodians of records have mechanisms, whether formal or informal, to reduce the bulk of their records during their active use. However, even with such mechanisms, the remaining mass of records cannot be automatically assumed to be of archival value. Whether the creator is an institution or an individual, the proportion of records that are worthy of preservation as archives is currently estimated to be between 1% and 5% of the total records created. Thus, only a very small fraction of records will become archives.

Deciding which records to target for retention as archives is difficult. There is a constant concern that records are inherently unique and that the information that they contain is not recorded elsewhere. If an archivist does not designate such material as archives, they will be lost forever. On the other hand, many records exist in various formats and information is often recorded in many versions in an organisation. Smaller quantities of records containing summarised information may be of much greater research interest than hundreds of metres of records containing diverse information. [2]

Appraisal is concerned with understanding what we are trying to document and balancing sets of conflicting concerns. It aims to reach a set of decisions which can be scrutinised and which will allow the destruction of the majority of records, while identifying, securing and allowing us to justify the preservation of a small proportion of records of continuing value.

Appraisal Principles

Traditional principles of appraisal have been formulated with the needs of in-house (and usually government) archives considered paramount. Despite the fact that these principles are couched in language most common to the in-house context, the basic principles apply to the appraisal of all records.

Records are regarded as having two basic characteristics which determine whether or not they are archives. These are often referred to as the primary, evidential or documentary value and the informational or secondary value. Table 6.1 gives examples of records which may fall within each category.

The *evidential value* of records is based upon the function the records had for the office or person which created and used them. Our interest as archivists lies in their value as evidence of

Table 6.1 Examples of Records According to Appraisal Catalogues

(The listing of records under one particular appraisal category is not meant to be restrictive. Commonly, records fall into more than one appraisal category.)

Appraisal Criteria	Categories of Records	Specific Types of Records
Evidential	*Administrative Records* Without a proportion of records which document the details of administration the creators of the records or their successors could not operate. It would not be possible to plan, organise and make decisions or to ensure consistency or continuity.	• Minutes and agenda of governing body, major administrative committees • Policy and procedure manuals • By-laws, rules and regulations • Annual reports • Reports on major projects • Strategic planning documents • Photographs • Diaries recording contemporary decision making
Evidential	*Records of Legal Value* These records form proof of an event or agreement. Obligations, commitments, rights and delegations of authority fall into this category. Without these records there is no security or foundation for decisionmaking.	• Memos and articles of association • By-laws, rules and regulations • Contracts • Agreements • Statutory reports • Wills • Certificate of title • Registration of patents • Licences to operate • Instruments of appointment • Instruments of delegation of authority
Evidential	*Records of Financial Accountability* These records document the honest and responsible conduct of financial affairs, the financial standing of the organisation and obligations. These records are essential to understand and transact business.	• Financial statements • Financial returns • Audit reports • Statutory reports • Strategic planning documents • Reports on exceptional results
Informational	*Records of Historic Interest for Public Relations and General Interest Purposes* Records of this type allow the context of the records creator to be understood. The social, political, economic, educational and recreational activities and the relations to the wider community are documented through these records.	• All of the above • Promotional videos • Photographs • Advertising copy • Personal diaries • Postcards • Posters • Souvenirs

how that office or individual conducted their business. The three major types of records having evidential value are those that
- have continuing administrative, legal or financial use for the body or individual which created them, or for any subsequent bodies
- record details which may serve to protect the civic, legal, property or other rights of individuals or the community at large
- reflect the development of the creating body, its structures, functions, policies, decisions and significant operations, or which reflect the evolution of the individual's career, interest or activities.

Records having *informational value* are defined as those records which contain information of use not only to the creating person or organisation but also to researchers from a variety of fields of knowledge. Often such records contain information gathered originally for a purpose quite different from the uses to which a later researcher will put them. Examples of records with informational value distinct from their original role include property insurance plans and records which may be used subsequently by persons seeking to restore buildings to their original appearance; census data which is used for family history; or property cards and rate books, originally used to collect taxes and subsequently used to study changes in economic status or ethnicity in various neighbourhoods. The archivist, in consultation with experts from a variety of fields of research, must always be aware of such informational values which enhance or complement the value records may have as evidence of the work of their creators.

These two basic categories are not mutually exclusive. Often, records of primary value are also those rich in information of research interest. The goal of the appraiser is to apply the values carefully and as objectively as possible so that the archives reflect the best and most representative materials of the persons, organisations and events they seek to document.

Appraisal Techniques

Traditional appraisal techniques have evolved over the last 50 years. Before then the impetus to develop strategies to select an archival record was not present. The quantities of records created were manageable and there seemed to be a 'natural' selection which left the archivist free to concentrate more on the documentation and use of the archives.[3] The dramatic escalation of the production of records during the first half of the twentieth century led to the formulation of techniques by which archivists could apply criteria to determine what records should be selected as archives.[4]

These 'bottom-up' appraisal techniques examine physical records and apply a set of values and criteria to those records. What type of value did the records possess – evidential or informational value? Were the records complete, accurate, concise, authorised, arranged for ease of subsequent use and in reasonable condition?

Recent commentators have particulary criticised traditional appraisal strategies which apply such techniques long after the records are no longer in current use and do not take sufficient account of their social and organisational context. Such an approach has been dubbed 'taxonomic'.[5] However, the techniques themselves and the values and criteria they employ still have great validity in many contexts, eg when physically examining older records or when used in conjunction with the top-down approaches to the appraisal of current records discussed later in the chapter.

The most commonly applied appraisal tools are the records survey, the disposal schedule and the appraisal checklist. They are most effective once the context of the records creator is understood.

Understanding the Context of the Organisation

No records can be understood, or appraised with any confidence, until the record creator has been placed in an appropriate framework of interrelationships. As explained in Chapter 1, records are the end result of an activity or transaction and are the tangible form taken by information which circulates within an organisation or society. As such, the records cannot be managed or assessed for continuing value without an understanding of the organisation or social processes which create the records. This concept applies equally to records created by an individual being offered to a collecting archives, to records created by a government agency being appraised by the government archives or to records created by an organisation being appraised by an in-house archives. It is only once this process of 'placement' is complete that the appraisal process can determine which records comply with the acquisition policy.

Data-gathering about the context of the organisation or individual and their relationship to society can be separated into two major areas, each of which needs to be addressed before the records themselves can be addressed. They are
• the social and political context
• the administrative context.

The Social and Political Context

Some of the larger social and political contextual questions are listed in Table 6.2.

Example: A Chemical Manufacturer. To enable an effective appraisal of the records created by a chemical company which manufactures pharmaceutical and agricultural products, the industry, community attitudes to that industry and the organisation itself must be understood.

Such a company will operate within constraints which are established by Commonwealth and state laws. Such laws will include those which dictate the operations of the company itself – through company legislation, taxation and reporting legislation – and laws which regulate the conduct of the company as a corporate citizen – how it deals with its employees and shareholders.

In addition, the industry overall – chemical manufacturing – will need to be addressed. What degree of regulation governs the industry? What is the attitude of the community to such industries? Government regulation in the form of specific pieces of legislation such as poisons acts, dangerous goods acts, transportation of hazardous wastes and environment protection legislation will apply. General community attitudes to the industry need to be assessed. What might be acceptable levels of pollution, for example, will vary with time. In periods of economic recession community opinion has often tolerated higher levels of pollution as a trade off for higher employment. In such an arena, 'green' groups are often active in monitoring standards and applying pressure on a company to ensure compliance with or change established standards. Other government constraints exist in areas such as product liability, national health and safety processes to register drugs and dosages for particular uses. Again, community interaction is not uncommon in these areas to seek either freer access to certain chemicals (eg many of the new drugs yet to be approved in Australia for the treatment of AIDS) or to ban certain chemicals such as 245T.

Local Government regulations will be applied to any manufacturing plant located in a particular area. Municipal regulations will govern land use for a particular area, dictating building and development standards. Appropriate levels of development for the municipality and its capacity to service the required infrastructure requirements will be addressed. Local communities might have concerns which place them at odds with general community standards, preferring local employment over possible environmental problems. However, there may be additional concerns specifically relating to the local community, eg problems with large trucks containing potentially dangerous substances being transported through populous areas.

Table 6.2 Placing the Organisation in Its Social Context

The Organisation Itself

- What are the objectives of the organisation?
- What are the primary functions of the organisation?
- What are the ancillary functions of the organisation?
- What are the programs operating within the organisation?

The Regulatory Environment

- Is the organisation or industry highly regulated by government legislation?
- What formal reporting is required by legislation?
- Are there professional or industry codes of practice by which the organisation or its officers voluntarily or compulsorily comply?

The Social Environment

- What is the prevailing social view of the functions undertaken by the organisation?
- Where are the points of contact between the public and the organisation?
- What public image is projected by the organisation?
- Does the community clash with the organisation or industry in the conduct of its functions and if so where?

The Political Environment

- What degree of lobbying does the organisation undertake and of whom?

The Formal Relationships Between Organisations

- Is the organisation formally or informally part of a larger national body, or an international body?
- Is the organisation networked to other bodies through industry groups?
- Do state or federal counterparts exist?
- Do other organisations perform similar functions?
- What degree of cooperation exists between the organisation and other bodies?

An understanding of the operations of any manufacturing company also involves understanding industrial issues resulting from the company's relationship with its employees. What is the relationship between the company and the employee groups? Is the industry highly unionised? Do state or federal industrial awards and conditions apply, or is the company more involved with enterprise bargaining and individual employee contracts? What is, or was, the company's industrial relations record? Is it known as an harmonious employer or does it have a reputation for confrontation with unions?

The issues and questions raised here in relation to a hypothetical chemical manufacturing company are not comprehensive, but they indicate the breadth of information needed to place an organisation within its appropriate social and political context. Much of this information will be available through company records, however, additional perspectives are needed to round out the perceptions of interrelations between the organisation, the local community and general community values.

The answers to these and similar questions will inform the archivist about the environment in which the organisation creates records. It will also inform the archivist of many of the attitudes to records creation and control within an organisation.

The Administrative Context

Only when a records-creating body has been appropriately placed in its regulatory, industry and social framework can the structures within the organisation itself be appropriately examined.

All organisations and people create records that reflect the structures in which they need to work. Within the organisation it is important to understand the management philosophy adopted and the structures that result from the implementation of that philosophy. Table 6.3 lists some of the considerations that need to be addressed when exploring the administrative structures of an organisation. The variety and diversity of administrative structures is as great as the number of organisations.

Knowledge of administrative structure will inform the archivist of such matters as formal mechanisms for input by external bodies and community representation. Identifying administrative structures of organisations is one of the continuing frustrations of the archivist, for the structure of any organisation is dynamic and subject to change with great frequency. However, without the administrative context, the provenance of records and their status as accountable records cannot be established. These are the cornerstones of our work as archivists. As such, analytical skills in administrative analysis are essential to inform our archival activities.

Monitoring of the Organisation

The information for monitoring of the organisation is not static. By its very nature it involves the interaction of the organisation with bodies and processes outside the organisation. Perceptions, social views and community standards are subject to continual change. These changes must be monitored and recorded. Having undertaken the exercise once, it is not sufficient to assume that the task has been completed. Archivists must not only understand the context in which an organisation or person currently works but also those social and political interactions across the whole span of the record-creating life. Such orientation processes must be undertaken by every archivist who is to be in any way involved with appraisal decisions.

Table 6.3 Exploring the Administrative Context of an Organisation

- Does the organisation favour centralised control with all matters of substance being transmitted to the central decisionmaking structure?
- Does it favour independence of operational units, given a budget and a set of objectives and expected only to report at stated periods or in cases of unexpected results?
- Where is the policy for a particular function made?
- Is it endorsed elsewhere?
- How are policies, procedures and reports communicated through the structure?
- Is the organisation run by a committee?
- How does the committee structure work? Do networks of working parties report to committees which in turn report to standing committees of the organisation's governing body?
- Is the organisation regionalised?
- Does each region have the same structures, functions and delegated authority?
- If one region is examined in detail, will the results of such an examination apply to other regions?
- What degree of independence is delegated to regions or operating divisions?
- Are there branches of the organisation? How do these operate?
- Are support functions centralised and operational functions decentralised?
- What degree of uniformity in processes and activities is required by the organisation?

Information-Gathering about Records

Only when the organisation or individual themselves, their social and political roles and administrative structures have been examined can the records themselves be assessed against the acquisition policy to determine their continuing value to the organisation and to society in general.

Different types of archives approach the task of information-gathering in different ways. An in-house archival program which is closely linked to the organisation's larger information management strategies may automatically become involved in gathering information about record types and procedures undertaken for a variety of other purposes. This strategy will suit such an archives program which will be pro-active, involved in planning systems and determining records of continuing value early in their life cycle.

Other archival programs are not involved in current records policies and are called upon to make decisions on the retention of records only at the end of their active administrative life. In circumstances such as these the data-gathering exercise will be undertaken in response to a specific need. The context of specific records will be required to understand their continuing value and the data-gathering will often be very restricted. In a similar way collecting archives may not be able to gather information about the records in their administrative context until a decision is made to offer the records to the collection.

The Records Survey

The records survey is the traditional archival technique for gathering information about the records in their administrative context. It aims to collect information that describes and identifies the records for a person who has not seen the records and is not familiar with the workings of the organisation or person who creates the records. Appraisal decisions will often need to be discussed widely both within the archives and with the creator. Not all parties to these discussions will necessarily have seen the records. Table 6.4 lists the types of information which should be sought during the survey.

Traditional survey methodology involves the compilation of survey forms (Figure 6.1) and occasionally prose reports on surveys undertaken. The methodology is suited both to records being currently used within a work place and to those which have been determined to be non-current.

To gather detailed information in a systematic and consistent way there is no viable alternative to inspecting records in the surroundings in which they are created. For this reason data-gathering methods such as questionnaires which seek to get the creators to complete information about record series are rarely completely successful, at least in part because it is difficult for users to understand why certain questions are being asked and what level of detail is required.

Disposal Schedules

Once information has been gathered about the records being created and how they relate to the activities and functions of the organisation, the process of developing a disposal schedule can commence.

Disposal schedules are continuing authorities for implementing decisions on the value of records specified in the schedule. Traditionally, disposal schedules list records at series level and, by codifying decisions, avoid the need to make repeated disposal decisions on the same series.

There are a few simple rules which apply when drafting disposal schedules:
• Disposal schedules can only apply to the records created or substantially changed by the organisation. Records created by other institutions should be scheduled for retention as a part of the other institution's records. This simple rule allows materials received for information only to be thrown out as

Figure 6.1 Data-Gathering Form

Department Name: Company Secretary's Department...
Office Address: 4th Floor, 57 Young St, Sydney...
Contact Person, Title and Phone: N. White, Office Manager, Ext 4590.........................

Record Series Title:
.....Minutes of the Board...
Description (what does it do, why – content and purpose):
.....Volumes, bound annually, containing agenda, business papers, minutes of meetings.
.....The Board acts as the major policy body of the company and receives summary
.....reports from all departments at its monthly meetings...
Arrangement (tick one):
    alphabetic.............numeric.........chronological...✓ ...Other (specify) ....
Date Range:
    begins 1910 ends......................still being created?...✓ ....
    annual accumulation...25 ...cm/y r.
Finding Aids?
    Index to Minutes prepared annually, bound with volume
Reference Frequency:
    no of times/week......../month...5..../year........never after...........................
Duplicated? Where?:
    Microfilmed at the end of the calendar year on to 35mm film, stored in fire-
    proof safe
Existing Disposal Procedure:
    Retain in office permanently

Quantity:
.....1.2 metres..
Format:	Manilla folders	Lever arch files
	2 ring binders	bound vols 4
	loose	microfilm
	computer printout	brochures
	other (specify)	

Housings:
Filing cabinets: 2 dr..........3 dr.............4 dr.........✓ ....5 dr.......................
Lateral shelving: width........height........depth......................no of shelves........
compactus: width........height........depth......................no. of shelves.......
                         no. of bays/row..........no. of rows...
bookshelves: width........height........no. of shelves........no. of bays............
printout shelving: no.............width..........no. of openings.....doors....................
tape racking: no.............width..........no. of openings.....doors....................

Prepared by: Janet Smith   **Date:** January 1993

Table 6.4   Information To Be Gathered about Record Series

Information about the Context of the Record
- Which departments or individuals create the records
- Where they are located
- Who should be contacted to check details

Information about the Record Series Itself
- What are the records called
- What does the series do
- What information does it contain
- What is the function which the series supports
- Who uses the records and why
- How is the series arranged Chronologically, alphabetically, numerically
- Is there an index or register to the record series
- How do the creators get access to the information in the systems
- How often is the record series used
- Are the records duplicated or is the information contained in the records to be found anywhere else
- What are the existing disposal arrangements

Physical Characteristics of the Records
- What is the total quantity of the records, in the current offices
- What quantity is stored elsewhere
- What physical form does the record take – files, volumes, computer printout, COM, database

Storage
- Are special housings or environment controls needed to store these records

materials received for information only to be thrown out as soon as the person using it has read the information.

- It is a waste of time to devise disposal classes for ephemeral material. Material falling into this category has been defined by Australian Archives as material which can be destroyed according to 'Normal Administrative Practices' (NAP). NAP is a concept which allows the routine destruction of drafts, duplicates and publications. The test applied by those determining whether to treat material according to this rule is whether it is obvious that no information of continuing value to the organisation will be destroyed.

- Determine the official record. The concept of the official record is used to determine which of the many copies of records that proliferate in modern organisations should be regarded as the authoritative record. Staff newsletters and minutes of committees are duplicated many times over in every organisation and it needs to be clearly established that this material does not need to be kept by every section. The office which creates the record is responsible for determining its disposal status, be it permanent or temporary. This concept is included in one of the elements used to draft a disposal schedule, the office of record.

Components of the Disposal Schedule

The disposal schedule should comprise the following components:

* The Office of Record. The office of record is the office which is responsible for the record during its use for the conduct of business. Any other copies of the record can then be designated as not being the official record and can be destroyed

Figure 6.2 Disposal Schedule

Agency: Zero Company
Date Schedule Issued: 5.12.1986   Date Schedule Expires: 5.12.1996

No.		Disposal Class	Disposal Action
	Series Title/Description of Activity	Office of Record/Retention	All Other Offices/Retention
1	Minutes of the Board: (a) Official set of Board minutes detailing the administration and policy-making of the Zero Co. (b) 35mm security microfilm of minutes produced at the end of every calendar year	Chief Secretary's Office: Retain in office for 10 years then transfer to archives Chief Secretary's Office: Transfer immediately to archives	Retain for 5 years then destroy
2	Correspondence of Mr J. Lyons	Chief Secretary's Office Transfer to archives	
3	'The Nought' Company Newsletter	Employee Relations Department: Retain permanently in office Send two copies of each newsletter to archives at the end of each calendar year	Retain for 2 years then destroy
4	Annual Reports	Public Relations Department: Retain permanently in office Send two copies to archives when issued	Retain for 5 years then destroy

whenever they are no longer required. For example, the office of record for the minutes of a finance committee will be designated to be the secretary of the committee who is responsible for the production and distribution of the minutes. Any other one of the many copies distributed as working papers or for information can then be regarded as ancillary to the official record and need not be kept any longer than required by the recipient.

- Each format of the record should be included. Records can occur in offices in more than one format – in databases and in paper printouts as well as in COM or tape form. Each format of the record should be sentenced and included on the disposal schedule.

- At what point the disposal action specified is to be applied. Each record type has a trigger which indicates that its active life is complete. This needs to be clearly established for each record type on the schedule because disposal action cannot take place while the material is still required for current use. Action on a student record, for example, is complete when the student graduates or leaves the institution. Action on an annual tax file is complete when the taxation return for the year has been filed. Action on an invoice is complete when it has been paid and audited. Until the action is determined to be complete, no disposal action can be applied to the file. Thus, a student file could be active for 15 years in a university provided that the student was continuously enrolled. The notion of a trigger to implement disposal actions is valid in any media.

- How long each part of the record series is to be kept following closure and where it should be kept. Record series do not cease to be current all at one time. Many series are continuing series and, every year, parts of the series can be determined to be of no further value to the immediate functions of the creating office. Invoices, for example, will not need to be kept in the office after audit requirements have been satisfied, but this does not mean that all invoices can be removed from the office at the same time. The disposal schedule should specify for how long records should be stored in the current office, how long in off-site or secondary storage and when the material is to be destroyed or transferred to archives. For example, disposal sentences might read 'Hold in current office for two years, then transfer to storage for five years, then destroy' (see Figure 6.2).

Language to avoid in drafting disposal schedules includes phrases such as 'when action completed' or 'after last reference'. They do not indicate a definite trigger for action and their vagueness encourages people to prevaricate about application of the schedule. Similarly, the concept of 'review' should be avoided in disposal schedules. The 'review' decision is tantamount to saying, after all this effort and work it is still too hard to make a decision on this material; someone else can make the decision later. If the schedule is to have any validity in an organisation, it must make these hard decisions.

Determining the actual disposal sentence involves the application of appraisal criteria (discussed below). The views of the users of the records are of considerable importance in this process. Some records creators are extremely conservative and wish to keep material for lengthy periods of time to cover every possible contingency arising. Other creators are risk-takers and are quite happy to authorise extremely short sentences. The art of determining disposal sentences usually places the archivist between the two extremes.

Determining the disposal sentence can be difficult. The precedents which are available in the form of published disposal schedules should always be used for guidance, although it is necessary to be clear that the disposal decision is different for different types of institution. In business, for example, the concept of risk management becomes far more important than it does in government. Risk management may dictate that while the law states that records shall be kept for five years, the costs to the company to store this information longer than one year would offset the costs of any potential prosecution of the company for having destroyed the records.

When drafting disposal schedules, it is reassuring to reflect that only between 1% and 5% of all records created will ultimately be designated as archives.

Issuing the Disposal Schedule

Once drafted, the disposal schedule should be returned to the creators of the records to ensure that their views are incorporated into the document. The final document reflects consensus between the creators of the record and the archivist. The schedule then needs to be accepted as an official document of the organisation. It should be checked by the auditors to ensure that it meets requirements to keep records for the purposes of audit procedures. It should also be submitted to the legal representative of the organisation (although many lawyers are not as well versed in the legal requirements for recordskeeping as are records managers and archivists). Finally, the document should receive the official imprimatur of the organisation, be that the signature of the Chief Executive, the Department Head or the Chairperson of the Board.

In some organisations there is a reluctance to be very formal about issuing a disposal schedule. Archivists should insist upon this as without the official adoption of the document, the liability for advice on disposal which turns out to be incorrect could rest with the individual archivist.

Since organisations grow and change, disposal schedules must be regularly reviewed to ensure that they are still relevant to the types of records being created in each office. To ensure this process of revision, many disposal schedules are issued with a limited life span, usually a period of five or ten years.

The Appraisal Checklist

Actually determining what to do with records, whether to designate them as having continuing value or determining that they can be destroyed after a specified period, involves the application of appraisal criteria. Appraisal criteria have been developed to assist in determining whether particular records have either evidential or informational value.

Because of the spectre of subjectivity in appraisal decisions, appraisal checklists have been developed to act as a check against which all records are tested. An appraisal checklist is a list of criteria against which every series or collection should be measured. No one appraisal checklist will cover the requirements of different types of archives and such documents tend to be drawn up to suit each particular archival program.

Commonly, such checklists either require specific questions to be answered or require a relative weighting to be completed for each criteria. Of course, every archivist's interpretation of the extent to which a set of records will conform to specific criteria will still be subjective. However, such a document provides concrete categories against which to measure records and as such is infinitely better than an undocumented decision. Argument for or against retention or partial retention can then be based on the appraisal checklist and other background material. A checklist also brings consistency of the appraisal technique from collection to collection. A records appraisal checklist issued by the Public Records Office, Victoria for use by state government departments when proposing records for approval for destruction is attached as Appendix 1 to this chapter.

No appraisal criteria or checklist can be applied to records independently of considerations of context. Those issues discussed above relating to the social and political context of the organisation and its administrative structures should be addressed prior to attempting to apply appraisal criteria.

The elements comprising an appraisal checklist will vary from archives to archives. However, the following matters should be considered for inclusion:

• Do the records conform to the acquisition policy? All records must be measured against the archives' stated acquisition policy. The archivist should resist the temptation to accept material outside the scope of the policy or its logical extension.

- Who created the records? Are the records accountable documents, or drafts, or are they unsourced and of correspondingly diminished evidential value?

- Do the records detail the origins, structure, or policy of the creating body or the evolution of the interests of the individual? Records falling within this broad category would be of evidential value.

- Do the records document the rights of organisations or individuals? Such records may include legal decisions, evidence of property ownership, records of service or records of individual attainment.

- Do the records document the financial responsibilities of the creating body or financial planning? Records which document financial responsibility may often be of continuing administrative use for the creator. Such records are often measured against external criteria, such as audit and legislative requirements.

- Are the records duplicated elsewhere or maintained in another form within the records of the individual or creating body? Identical information may often appear in various documents at differing levels of the creating body. It is necessary to establish which records containing identical information should be kept. As a general rule, if information is reported at more than one level of an hierarchy, the information is kept from the higher administrative level. Records may be summarised into other records, for example, payroll slips usually contain information recorded in identical or greater detail on a computer. The computer itself may hold the information as an active database in digital form and in individual configurations on computer printouts. A further example is the student record card maintained by many individuals and colleges which provide a summarised form of individual student files. All sets of related records in all formats should be appraised together.

- Are the records dependent upon filing codes or plans, indexes or registers? Filing plans, classification schemes, thesauruses, indexes and registers are vital tools for the current and future use of the record series. They provide the key by which the records were originally organised and accessed. Without them the records can be used and understood only with great difficulty, if at all. For this reason, most registers and indexes to record series are regarded as permanent records. Record series accompanied by the original control records (ie indexes, registers, file lists, etc) prove much easier for both archives staff and future researchers to use.

- What is the arrangement of the records? The method of arrangement of the records can either facilitate the extraction of desired information or make such extraction difficult. For example, two sets of identical information may be available – one arranged chronologically and one arranged alphabetically. Which arrangements will facilitate access for the future user?

- Are the records complete? Fragmentary records need to be carefully evaluated. Such records often prove frustrating for the researcher because of the gaps they contain. In general the importance of offering only whole collections, complete series or all the material created to date to the archives should be stressed to office personnel and donors. The opportunity to see the whole range of documentation is vital when the archivist selects which materials to keep.

- What quantity of material is involved? The archives should be characterised by records that are rich, concise and limited in quantity. Neither the archivist nor researchers will want to plough through hundreds of boxes if the same information can be obtained in a more compact form. Record series of large quantity need to be evaluated very carefully.

- Do the records contain confidential information which would require protection for commercial viability or for the privacy of the individual? Records containing information which is potentially sensitive may need to be restricted from public access for a period agreed upon with the creator. The archives will need to determine whether the information recorded will be of sufficient importance to justify the administration of often quite complex access restrictions.

- What are the restrictions required by the donor? Are the access restrictions required by the donor unduly restrictive? Is the material of sufficient long-term value to justify the costs of administration of unwieldy access restrictions?

- What is the physical form of the records? Do the records consist of paper files, computer printout, photographs, microfilm, volumes or machine readable records? If the material exists in more than one format, which will be the most useable and durable?

- What is the physical condition of the material? Is the paper brittle? Has the ink faded? Are the bindings broken or rotten? Has the record been mounted on acidic cardboard? If the condition of the material is doubtful at the time of acquisition, the archives will be obliged to undertake costly conservation work to ensure the preservation of the material.

Once this process has been completed, the material needs to be evaluated within the context of records already designated as archival. Will the material complete gaps or extend coverage in the documentation of an individual, organisation or event? Will the material substantially duplicate material already held? If so, is the new material a better representation than that already held?

Research trends and interests of the using public will also need to be assessed as they relate to the records. *Informational values* of records are often difficult to assess. Anything and everything could be kept on the pretext that someone will want to look at it at some-time in the future. Such an argument does not aid the process of appraisal which, of necessity, is concerned with selecting material as archives. A practical approach to these problems is needed.

The information contained in the records should be evaluated according to the context of its creation. For example, the appraisal statement that student records should be kept for famous people proves administratively and institutionally difficult to implement. Who determines what 'famous' means? Is it local fame, international fame, particular achievements or up to an individual to determine? What period of time should be allowed to elapse before a determination of whether a person is famous or not is made? Ten years or a lifetime?

Rather than enter these subjective and difficult areas, it is better to address the issues within the context of the records' creation. Does the student record of an individual demonstrate any characteristics that distinguish it from its peers? Academic prowess, entry standards, sporting achievements or constant challenge to the rules and regulations resulting in disciplinary action etc, within the educational context can be assessed much more objectively and in a timely manner. It is the educational establishment, its context and the role of the individual within that specific context that is being documented in this example and that should determine the weighting of the appraisal decisions.

No one individual, however well informed in a particular area of interest, can hope to predict research interests of the future. Research trends alter rapidly, particularly with the introduction of computers and techniques of evaluating masses of data. However, it is possible to select material based upon its importance to the organisation and society of *its own time*. The task of constructing a truthful image of society is difficult, but possible, and it is this role which archivists seek to fulfil.

The other major area to be considered is that of the resources of the archives. How much time will it take to process the material? What staff resources will be involved? How much space will the collection occupy? What are the existing commitments on staff time and resources? Where will this material fit into existing priorities for processing?

Other Disposal Strategies

In most circumstances the disposal schedule and the appraisal checklist are adaptable enough to provide appropriate tools to implement appraisal decisions. However, there are some circumstances where, for particular reasons, an archives may determine that these procedures are not appropriate and an alternative disposal strategy is adopted.

Such alternative disposal strategies include the use of the following:

General disposal schedules. Such schedules, while complying with the general format and provisions for drafting, outlined above, are intended to cover functions common to a great many organisations or parts of an organisation. Typically issued by government archival authorities, these schedules cover functional areas such as personnel, finance or stores. Once issued formally through the appropriate mechanisms of the government, these schedules can be applied to a large number of bodies with no further approval of destruction required. General disposal schedules also form a model for developing disposal sentences in these areas in in-house archives.

One-off disposal authorities. For a variety of reasons, archives periodically are called upon to make decisions which are not intended to set a precedent or to be applied other than in a specific set of circumstances. One-off or ad hoc disposal authorities are sometimes issued in these circumstances to cover only the specific records detailed in the authority. This technique allows formal issuing of instructions or authorisation of action, but will not tie the archives to a precedent in the disposal decision taken. Such authorities tend to be restricted to one series of records or the records of one particular part of an agency. They do not constitute a continuing authority for the disposal action nominated, but tend to cover one particular disposal action.

Blanket provisions. In areas of known scarcity, some archives have adopted the strategy that records fitting within particular parameters will be accepted without any further appraisal. Which records, if any, fit into this category will vary from archives to archives. Usually the scarcity of the particular records outside archival custody enable the archives to make these blanket provisions. However, in particular circumstances major social issues can dictate blanket retention. Such is the case in the federal government with material relating to asbestos, which gave rise to a moratorium on destruction of any material on this issue. Examples might be

- all material in the Commonwealth arena which pre-dates Federation
- in an organisation which has suffered a major physical disaster – all records surviving from the time prior to the disaster
- in an organisation – all material from the first ten years of operations

- in a collecting archives – anything to do with women's groups or organisations pre-dating 1940.

Guidelines. Some archival authorities augment their capacity to cover all the records under their jurisdiction by issuing general archival standards or guidelines. These can be applied in general circumstances and do not require further advice from the archives for their application. The Australian Archives guidelines on NAP constitutes an example of this approach.

Records Not Suited to Traditional Appraisal Techniques

Certain types of records have commonly caused problems in appraisal for archivists. For these records, the traditional tools of appraisal checklists and disposal schedules have not worked very well. The most common of these are correspondence or subject files and case files.

Correspondence or Subject Files

Correspondence files are complex sets of records which can cover almost every subject dealt with by an organisation and can be of variable value depending upon who created them. One major characteristic of correspondence files is that no one appraisal decision will cover all the records included in the series. There will be routine administrative material which will not require continuing retention, policy decisions which will be of continuing value and many files which contain a mixture of temporary and continuing value material.

If the filing system has a properly constructed and applied classification scheme, appraisal decisions can initially be broadly made using the categories of the classification scheme. Where there is no comprehensive classification scheme, or where the application of the classification scheme has broken down and 'bag files' have evolved where everything is bundled on to one file with a very general title, there are no short cuts for the appraisal process. File-by-file examination against appraisal criteria is often the only way to deal with these records. In extreme cases where large numbers of 'bag files' exist, often the only way to perform a thorough appraisal is a folio-by-folio examination of each file. The time and resources which must be committed to such an exercise is prohibitive. In many such cases the correspondence files are accepted into archives as a whole, taking the temporary with the continuing value material.

Professional advice on the restructure of such series to permit application of appropriate classification schemes and allow the development of disposal tools to allocate preliminary disposal categories at the time of creation of the records will assist not only the appraisal process but also the capacity to retrieve relevant information while the files are current. Such strategic approaches to managing this type of record will also inform the appropriate management of the electronic office systems if implemented with foresight and consistency.

Case Files

Case files (also known as particular instance papers) are records which usually document the application of a policy or set of policies on a variety of individual sets of circumstances. Often such material contains personally identifiable information, usually of considerable confidentiality. In most instances within each particular set of case files, the same basic activity is being performed, differing with each particular set of facts to be dealt with. Examples of case files include patient case notes in a hospital, student files in a school or university, social security files, and so on.

Such records are usually found in large quantities, traditionally in paper form, and usually require elaborate disposal decisions to be made which aim to preserve a representative sample of the records to demonstrate the processes of the operation, rather than to retain or discard the whole series. Many case file series are now accompanied by extensive data bases which allow agency personnel to call up a plethora of information on a particular case. These databases need to be appraised in conjunction with case files. While masses of data can be maintained in electronic form more easily than in paper, it is unlikely that the expense of such retention will be approved by individual agencies who may be burdened with the costs of ensuring that the records remain readable.

Many such records have informational value for long-term statistical research and have the potential to provide us with one of the best illustrations of the interrelationship between client and organisation and consequently the genuine functioning of an organisation. It has recently been argued that these case files, which document the nexus where the organisation meets its clients, form potentially one of the most valuable concentrations of records through which to document modern society. Further, case files potentially constitute one of the most representative record types in documenting the actual workings and decision-making within an organisation and society as a whole. Case files of particular archival interest will be those in which the expectations or perceptions of service by the client and by the organisation clash. At this point, it is argued, the most accurate reflection of the operations of an organisation and its interreaction with the societal norm and expectations can be gauged.[6]

For these records, archivists have employed a number of strategies:

Dismiss the problem and destroy the files. One typical approach is to dismiss the case file series as too voluminous, with such a small proportion of files which can be justified for retention that the whole exercise is too time-consuming to address properly and the whole set of files is destroyed. While this was never a good response to the problem, in light of Terry Cook's work on the appraisal of personal information, it is no longer tenable.

Sample. The attraction of sampling as a disposal technique in these cases is that it allows destruction of the majority of the voluminous records while still retaining some cases. Determining which cases shall be retained is the nub of the sampling process. This is a complex and very specialised area of archival endeavour. Much more detailed understanding of the problems are needed before an archivist should attempt such a technique.[7]

'Quick and dirty'solutions. Most 'quick and dirty' solutions purport to be sampling. However, very little methodological rigour goes into the development of such solutions and as sampling techniques they have many flaws. Often the implementation of such solutions is delegated to non-archival staff. Such techniques include the retention of all files over a certain thickness (eg 2 cms); or nominating one in every proportion (eg one in every 2,000 files) for retention. The deficiencies of such methods must be fully appreciated before adopting such techniques.

Some Adaptations to Traditional Disposal Practice

Alternatives to the Records Survey

The records survey is undertaken at the series level. It attempts to place each series in its logical place within the administrative context and to document the interrelations between series. As such, it is a very labour intensive procedure which involves an analysis of the records themselves in their work place. In its traditional form, the process of survey has led to archives only being able to provide resources to address a tiny fraction of the material needing to be appraised. In addition, the administrative structures of organisations have been volatile.

Analysis of Functions

A revised methodology for data-gathering is based upon the realisation that functions can be far more stable than administrative structures placed on top of functions. For example, to return to our hypothetical chemical manufacturing company, financial planning remains a stable function within the company from the time of its inception. Without such a function the viability of the company would be under great stress. However, over a period of time, with different individuals steering the company as Chief Executive Officer, the administrative sections responsible for this function are likely to have altered. In its early stages a small manufacturing company is likely to have such a function placed with the senior administrator. As the company grows, it is likely that a financial section will be formalised and a Chief Accountant, or equivalent, be allocated such a function. As the value of strategic planning to an organisation becomes more clearly related to the success and profitability of the operations, this role is likely to be highlighted in a particular position responsible specifically for financial planning. More recently, a department specifically responsible for strategic planning and financial analysis is likely to have been established.

Throughout all these administrative changes, the function of financial planning has remained relatively stable, although certainly becoming more complex.

Data-Gathering

Using the approach that records are a result of activities undertaken within a function, archivists have been developing alternative approaches to gathering information within organisations. The basis of such an approach is to explore the functions within each organisation through a set of interviews. Initially, the head of the department needs to be interviewed. Such senior officers will be able to provide a balanced view of the functions undertaken by the department and to place specific activities within particular functions as well as indicate overlapping functional areas, activities undertaken in common with other parts of the organisation and specific arenas of organisational and legal responsibilities. The types of questions which need to be answered in this interview are listed in Table 6.5.

From the interview with the head of the department, the archivist should then interview the officers specifically charged with undertaking a particular activity. With the broader knowledge of general functions already received, the archivist can focus in on the types of information needed to undertake the activity.

The documentation resulting from this approach can resemble the traditional survey form, or more formal functional analysis can be undertaken resulting in the development of matrices.[8]

Disposal Schedules by Function

From the information gleaned in the interviews, the archivist is able to compile a disposal schedule based on function. Such a disposal schedule is illustrated at Figure 6.3. In it, a section of the

Table 6.5 Analysing Functions

- What are the functions of a particular administrative program?
- Are they conducted independently, or are they responsive to other functions?
- Do other parts of the organisation conduct the same or similar functions?
- Is the function internal or does it involve relationships with bodies outside the organisation?
- Do other organisations undertake the same function?
- Is the function one of the core business functions of the organisation?
- Does the function involve reporting, either within the administrative structure, within the organisation or beyond?
- What activities make up the function?
- Have the activities been separated under different functional umbrellas in the past? How have they related?
- What are the primary records which document each of the activities which contribute to the administration of the function?
- How do the records of the various activities within each function interrelate?

major functional activity Finance is illustrated. From there some of the constituent activities which make up the function are nominated in bold. The office of record - that is, the office held accountable for the documentation of an activity is underlined, and other parts of the organisation creating similar records are indicated.

No attempt is made to break these activities further into series. All records which are created across the organisation related to this activity are to be sentenced according to the provisions included here.

Once drafted, the disposal schedule is negotiated extensively within the organisation. The most effective way to undertake this exercise is to gather the records creators together in functional groups and discuss the provisions of the schedule in detail. Schedules can be drafted for particular functions and the functional areas built onto to form a schedule which operates over the entire organisation.

Compiling schedules in this way is an effective use of archivists' time. The process of interviews is much speedier than physically examining records. An experienced archivist can in this way create functional schedules for entire organisations in six to eight weeks, a time frame unthinkable using traditional methodology. However, there are some risks associated with this function-based approach:

- It is done without detailed examination of the records. It is possible that some records of continuing value may slip through the net. We need to be able defend our methodology and expertise in such an area to the wider community. We need to keep in mind the words of the judgment of Judge

Figure 6.3 Finance (cont.)

Activities	Disposal Sentence	Transfer/Custody
Audit – External		
Arrangements	Destroy 2 yrs after	Destroy from office
Reports	file closed	
Finance	Retain	Transfer to storage 5 yrs after report compiled
Internal Auditor	Destroy 5 yrs after file closed	Destroy from office
Audit - Internal		
Plan and work program		
Internal Auditor	Destroy 10 yrs after file closed	Transfer to storage 2 yrs after file closed
Specific Reports		
Internal Auditor	Retain	Transfer to storage 2 yrs after file closed
Divisions/Sections who are subject of report	Retain	Transfer to storage 2 yrs after file closed
Other copies	Destroy 2 yrs after report compiled	Destroy from office
Quarterly & Annual reports		
Internal Auditor	Retain	Transfer to storage 2 yrs after file closed
Finance	Destroy 5 yrs after file closed	Transfer to storage 2 yrs after file closed
Working Papers	Destroy 5 yrs after file closed	Transfer to storage 2 yrs after file closed
Budgets		
Action Plan review		
Finance	Destroy 5 yrs after file closed	Transfer to storage 2 yrs after file closed
Forward Estimates		
Finance	Destroy 5 yrs after file closed	Transfer to storage 2 yrs after file closed
Divisions	Destroy 2 yrs after file closed	Destroy from office
Expenditure Guidelines		
Finance	Retain	Transfer to storage 2 yrs after file closed
Divisions	Destroy 2 yrs after file closed	Destroy from office
Reallocation of Funds		
Finance	Destroy 2 yrs after file closed	Destroy from office

Fig. 6.3 (cont)

Divisions file closed	Destroy 2 yrs after	Destroy from office

Working Papers		
Finance file closed	Destroy 2 yrs after	Destroy from office
Divisions file closed	Destroy 1 yr after	Destroy from office

[Reproduced with the permission of Records, Archives & Information Management Pty Ltd]

Harold H. Greene in relation to the activities of archivists in the FBI files case:

> Some of the employees of the Archives having responsibility for appraising FBI records retention and destruction plans testified that they were capable of passing on such plans without ever having seen any of the documents involved, whether by category, by type or sample. The court finds those representations to be wholly incredible. The law imposes upon the Archivist and his staff important responsibilities concerning the selection of what among the files of an agency may have permanent or continuing value for historical, research, legal rights and other purposes. It strains the credulity to accept the proposition that such decisions can be made wholly by remote control[9]

- In such approaches we rely greatly on our knowledge of the organisation, its context and the context of both functions and administrative structures. Without this knowledge the methodology will not work.
- There is a reliance placed upon the interpretation of the records creators. If they provide information about activities which is not correct, the archivists work will be flawed. Again, the FBI files case stands as a landmark in this area.[10]
- Functions still need to be tied to administrative structures to ensure that responsibility for the maintenance of the official record is firmly vested with particular offices within the administrative structure. This will involve the archivist in continual monitoring and amendment to issued schedules.

On the other hand, the positive aspects of the function-based approach are that

- it can be undertaken much more quickly
- it concentrates scarce resources on addressing current records
- it can apply to records yet to be created
- it remains valid even after alteration of records format
- it can be linked to classification schemes for current records management

- it forges strong links between the archivist and the records creator
- by focusing on functions, alterations in administrative structures do not invalidate the entire schedule.

While functions are often more stable than the administrative structures which sit above them, they too can be acquired and discarded as perceptions about the organisation's role and responsibilities change. Archivists need to monitor functions in addition to administrative structure. It is the functions themselves, which break down into specific activities geared at getting the function done, which will produce the records we need to appraise.

Problems with the Traditional Appraisal Techniques

Traditional appraisal techniques have been established with the very clear premise that all records must be physically examined before appraisal criteria are brought to bear. During the last decade, complete compliance with this 'bottom-up' approach has been realised to be unachievable and its effectiveness in determining which records are of greatest value has been questioned.

The increase in record production which led to the encapsulation of appraisal methodology has been dwarfed by the explosion of records with which we are now faced. Records are now commonly created in formats other than paper. The legal definitions of record and document are enshrined in national and increasingly in state legislation through evidence Acts or freedom of information legislation, if not in Archives legislation. One such definition, for example, states that record means:

> a document (including any written or printed material) or object (including a sound recording, coded storage device, magnetic tape or disc, microform, photograph, film, map, plan or model or a painting or other pictorial or graphic work) that is, or has been, kept by reason of any information or matter that it contains or can be obtained from it or by reason of its connection with any event, person, circumstance or thing.[11]

As archivists, we are still dealing most commonly with paper-based records. Most electronic systems still have hard copy output, either to comply with aging evidence rules or from administrative convenience. Mechanisms for dealing effectively with non-current records in electronic form have not yet been fully developed. This situation has allowed many practising archivists to follow the 'machine-readable archives' debates with interest, but with little alteration to their practice. However, this comfortable era is ending. Not only is the creation of extensive paper records reflecting electronic systems being resisted by records creators, but the nature of the electronic record is altering. 'Views' of a database reproduced on paper might have been accepted, even while there was recognition that manipulation was lost, but it is now impossible to accurately reflect some electronic documents with embedded links, hypertext connections, etc, in paper format.

In such an environment, even if it were feasible to find resources to address the overwhelming quantity of records produced in modern society, it is increasingly impossible to find a physical record to evaluate and from there to apply measured criteria to authorise their destruction or retention. New strategies for identifying those records of continuing value are required. They are being evolved in practice by all archivists working with the selection of archival records, even if only by recognition that we need to cut corners and can no longer apply the rigorous methodology based on physical inspection and evaluation of each series of records prior to determining its retention period. These tentative developments in technique are gradually gaining support from the evolution of theoretical constructs against which we can better refine the practices we have begun to apply.

Issues Being Explored in the Development of Appraisal Theory

Many of the strategies being explored in revising appraisal methodology are experimental. However, some common elements are recurring in all new writings on appraisal. The extent to which all or some of these elements are suitable for application in each type of archive will vary.

Case Study[12]

'Well done' says the message on an electronic mail system. The electronic mail system is the PROFS electronic mail system used by the National Security Council and the Executive Office of the President of the US. The message is from John Poindexter, in response to an account given to him by his aide Bob Pearson, of Oliver North's false testimony to Congress.[13]

This example allows us to explore a number of complex issues relating to appraisal. Contextual information is shown to be all important. Without the contextual surroundings, the content of the message – 'well done' – is of no significance. Defining
- where the electronic mail system was operating
- who the author and recipients were
- what their functions were
- when the message was sent and received, and
- what the trigger for the message was

enabled this message to be used in testimony before the Congress Committees to show that Oliver North lied to Congress and that John Poindexter knew of it and approved of it.

As well as the specifics surrounding the creation and receipt of the message, we need to have at least a rudimentary idea of the political and social context surrounding the Iran-Contra issue. Here the US Congress had adopted policies and directions which were known to be at odds with some of those held by the US President. At the same time, a small number of officials in the executive government were operating illicitly in total opposition to the policies and direction adopted by Congress. The extent of these operations, who knew of them and who authorised them were the stuff of the congressional hearings in 1987. The political ramifications of these events were still reverberating in December 1992 with the pardon granted by President George Bush to Defence Secretary Casper Weinberger who was about to stand trial on charges of lying to Congress.

How does the society feel about the facts? Moral issues are prominent. The social and political context of the case and its documentary evidence are revealing in relation to the society's attitudes towards questions of accountability, secret undertakings, cover-ups, honesty, responsibility, conflicting loyalties, and so on.

It was revealed in the congressional hearings that Oliver North instructed his secretary to delete all electronic mail messages on the PROFS system dealing with Iran and Contras. His secretary undertook such destruction in line with the instructions on how to delete messages from the electronic mail system. These instructions in fact deleted the index pointers to the information. The actual messages themselves were not deleted. The messages were able to be recovered from backup tapes. So how do we ensure appropriate destruction of information in electronic format? Destroying the index references to information will not be sufficient.

These records exist only in electronic form. The fact that an electronic mail user applied techniques to delete information from the system, yet this information was available in backup version, is a circumstance peculiar to electronic records. As electronic records, the messages cannot be reconstructed without the software shell (the proprietary PROFS system itself) to manipulate, store and retrieve the information. An injunction against the destruction of the National Security Council computer tapes containing messages from the PROFS system was successfully granted. In the resulting legal case – *Armstrong v Executive Office of the President*, it was argued that all historically significant records, with the exception of the Iran-Contra memos, were printed and are in the National Security Council's permanent files.[14]

Is the paper record a true reflection of the computer system? Is the nature of the system such that printing messages without the contextual links - who wrote them, when, in response to what - will render the content meaningless?

Do electronic mail messages constitute records of continuing value? On the face of it, most archivists faced with appraisal of such a system would agree that these systems do not generate significant records. Yet messages from just this system have been used not only in the Iran-Contra hearings but also as an aid in the preparation of the confirmation hearings of Robert Gates as Director of the Central Intelligence Agency and in the investigation of Manual Noriega.[15] This medium seems to encourage spontaneous and uncensored recording of responses to events which allows a genuine reflection rather than an official or tempered view of events. If we appraise totally from a 'top-down' functional analysis, would these records have been identified as having continuing value?

The implication arising from the decision that this electronic mail system contained records of continuing value, not available in other formats, suggests that detailed appraisal of every electronic mail system might be necessary. Such conclusions are daunting. At present, the American National Archives and Records Administration does not consider electronic mail computer tapes to be federal records and thus they are exempt from the disposal schedules which apply to the agency.

This case also involves an archival agency in a potential ethical dilemma about its role in approving destruction of records. From this example it can be seen that in certain circumstances the archivist can become caught in the middle between the people who fund the archival program, who might like particular information destroyed, and an archivist's own opinion of 'the greater public good'.

Social Context of Appraisal Decisions

The essentially subjective nature of the process of appraisal - the identification of some records as being of continuing value over others - has always been recognised, but was hedged by the development of appraisal criteria and checklists which attempt to construct a set of questions to be applied to all material subject to appraisal. This application of standard questions for each set of records examined provided some semblance of objectivity to the process of appraisal.

The work of appraisal is the cornerstone of all archives work. Selecting what shall constitute the documentation of our time to remain accessible to future generations is arguably the most important archival task. From that flows all other archival work. Only after records have been identified as archives can the other archival processes be applied – arrangement and description, provision of access to the archives and retrieval from the archives. As we look back on several decades of deliberate appraisal decisions as reflected in our archives, we are aware that with today's perspective on social circumstances and issues we may have made different choices in what material to designate as archives. If the process of appraisal was truly an objective process, such reassessment of our collections would not be necessary. Such evaluations lead us inevitably to question what social perspectives are different for us than for those who went before. The fact that we are unavoidably influenced by our cultural and social biases is revealed. Rather than shy away from such realisations, archivists are now working to make the cultural assumptions explicit and incorporate the documentation of those assumptions in the decisionmaking which results in the selection of archives.[16]

We need to be sensitive to the fact that we bring our own perspectives to bear on the records of the past. The records of environmental monitoring will be appraised very differently in the 1990s than they would have been in the 1950s. Our sensitivity to such issues as ozone depletion, global warming and climatic patterns is much greater as a community, and as members of that community, archivists making appraisal decisions will reflect that community attitude.

We also need to accept that these attitudes alter over time. Society places different importance on different things at different times and issues such as sensitivity or confidentiality will alter over time. The documentation relating to the incidence of venereal disease among serving troops in the Middle East in World War I is now of interest to us, not a matter of overwhelming embarrassment as it was even only one generation ago. Convict ancestry is now a status symbol in certain quarters, whereas in the early part of this century records were destroyed, hidden and falsified to hide such stains from family names.

How then does this affect archivists appraising records of previous decades? Do we attempt to reconstruct valiantly the mind set and societal preoccupations of the time as advocated by Hans Booms:

> archivists have no other choice than to conduct their appraisal according to the emphasis and weight placed on events of the time by contemporaries. Only in this way can they free themselves from the social value of their own time, to which they are unconsciously subject.[17]

Or do we accept our cultural and social bias, but ensure that the issues and concerns of the time when the records were created are acknowledged?

One strategy for ensuring that appropriate attention is paid to retrospective sensitivity to the concerns contemporary to the record is to construct a continuing set of data, documenting changes to the operations and activities of the entity which created the records. This type of data-gathering catches contemporary changes in structures of organisations which are indirect reflections of the sensitivity of certain social issues in the community. Within an organisation, for example, the creation of Equal Employment Opportunity Coordinators in the workplace reflects a growing concern about discrimination in employment practices in the workforce. The creation of Freedom of Information Officers reflects a greater emphasis on the appropriate and accountable nature of information-gathering in institutions.

Archivists thus need to be actively informed about the activities and operations of their universe, not waiting until the products of the activities (the records) come to their attention.

Appraisal as an Integrated Part of Record Creation

Recreating the circumstances surrounding records creation, the social mores, organisational context and culture, once society and the organisation has moved in other directions can be a daunting task. Our organisations are no longer the stable entities they once were. Administrative change and reorganisation, the addition and shedding of functions, redistribution and altering of relationships between parts of an organisation or between organisations is now the norm.

Similarly, the methods of producing and recording our information are altering at a staggering rate. It is difficult now to think of the average desk top without thinking of a computer. Yet this has really only become a fact over the last decade. The methods of undertaking work have changed.

Record creation and storage formats are being altered and updated with increasingly short life spans. Hard disks, floppy disks, tapes and optical disks are media which are assured by manufacturers to be durable. Such assertions are usually taken at face value by the records creators who work on an administrative imperative to be able to retrieve information only for about two years. The administrative concept of long-term retention of records is, when teased out, usually no longer than 10 years and, at the most, one person's working life. Archival considerations of continuing accessibility are not even thought about, yet alone included in technology planning in most organisations when considering implementation of new technology.

These issues, combined with the archival imperative to capture an appropriate record of our society, have progressively pushed the need to appraise records further and further forward. The traditional appraisal approach, to wait until the administrative needs of records are passed, leaves records too vulnerable. We are increasingly aware of the need to manage records of continuing value for the whole of their life span, from creation to destruction. In the environment of the modern bureaucracy or business enterprise, this involves the identification, at least at a preliminary level, of records of continuing value as soon as possible to the time of their creation and in some cases even before the record exists.

Appraisal of electronic systems is now being advocated as a part of system design. The requirement to tag sets of data as being of long-term importance should be being built into the programming constructs. Strategies to migrate data identified as having continuing value into new software and hardware platforms should be regarded as an integral part of good systems maintenance.

Continuing Value and Reappraisal

Traditional archival practice, particularly in the arena of appraisal, has designated archives as being of permanent value. What this label implied was that the records so designated were to be preserved for ever more. In our own uncertain times, with 'info-glut', media of untested durability and constant resource cuts, emphasis has changed from the notion of 'permanent' to that of 'continuing value'.

With such an alteration of emphasis, archivists can side step some of the problems inherent in designating material as permanent. Where we can justify the continued expense of ensuring that information remains readable and accessible, material will be protected to the best of our archival capacity. However, certain material in our archives never quite reaches that degree of importance to be placed on the constantly growing list of records requiring painstaking conservation services. In other cases conservation priorities for collections alter. In these circumstances archivists are no longer in the contradictory position of determining that they cannot justify resources or staff to keep in perpetuity records designated as permanent.[18]

The notion of continuing value accepts also that there are cultural shifts between generations. Particularly in the environment of electronically created and stored records, information must be demonstrated to have a continuing value to the next generation before adequate resources can be justified to keep the records readable.

The issue of reappraisal has been an issue of contention in the archival community for the past decade.[19] While accepting that in the past some selection decisions may have been uncoordinated or unfocused and consequently in need of rationalisation, it is important not to apply reappraisal of archival collections to reflect only narrow concerns of one particular set of archivists or generation of archivists. Reappraisal of material on the basis of its research use is hotly contested as a methodology. However, it remains a fact that many archives do from time to time undertake focusing exercises which de-accession material, often to more appropriate repositories.

Risk Management

The 'values' base of traditional appraisal decisions, with its implicit cost-benefit analysis is being questioned. That is, the implicit equation of the institutional costs to retain records is weighed against the social benefit of having the records retained. One side of this equation – social benefit – cannot be convincingly argued within an institution whose primary activities are not aimed at a vague social good.

In place of this cost-benefit analysis, perhaps appraisers should look to apply the concept of risk management. In the risk management environment the key question becomes: What damage will occur to the institution or society if particular records are not maintained? What records are necessary to protect the institution from exposure to litigation or allegation? The thrust of the appraisal process becomes more closely linked to the continuing work of an institution, which is not then expected to bear a burden of 'public good'.[20]

We have altered the focus of the archivist from the Jenkinsonian view that we should justify what we destroy [21] to the position that we should justify what we retain.

Accountability

Within public institutions greater emphasis is being placed on accountability as a major criteria for creating and, subsequently, retaining records. In 1989, in the government context, Chris Hurley, then Keeper of the Public Record Office, Victoria, expressed it thus:

> It is a question ultimately of accountability. The statutory regulation of the disposal and treatment of government records is the foundation, in a democratic society, upon which all other measures of public and internal scrutiny of the affairs of government rest; of discharging the audit and efficiency review functions, of review by the Ombudsman and administrative review tribunals, of guaranteeing public rights of access to information, of preventing falsification and misrepresentation. It is the keystone for all the rest.[22]

Accountability in recordkeeping is increasingly influencing all aspects of recordkeeping. Legislation such as freedom of information Acts, judicial review Acts and administrative appeals tribunals Acts all embody the need for managers to accept responsibility for decisionmaking and to be able to demonstrate appropriate bases for their decisions. In effect, the recordkeeping structures are being altered by the need to trace accountability. For example, the electronic mail systems are having to provide frameworks for recording contextual information, for as we see in the case study, the records do not make sense and accountability cannot be traced without them.

Questions of accountability bring the importance of record-keeping and issues of identification, authentication and responsibility for records to the forefront of public attention. Recent Australian cases of notoriety include the loss and subsequent finding of registers recording details of correspondence between the NSW Police Commissioner and the NSW Minister for Police in relation to deaths in police custody; the alleged non-receipt, and subsequent production from within the Bank, of a damning report on management of overseas loans in the Westpac Letters case; and, alleged destruction of government records and their substitution with photocopied look-alikes (minus the handwritten annotations) revealed in evidence to the WA Inc Royal Commission in July 1991.

An approach to determining what information should be retained when evaluating current records systems is to clearly place the burden of the decision on to the responsible administrator who then becomes explicitly accountable for the maintenance of the records and for any shortfalls revealed in the recordkeeping processes.

Accountability is becoming increasingly important in determining not only what documents should be created but also which documents should be retained, an ironic return to the Jenkinsonian concept of the administrator determining which records should be regarded as archives.[23]

Pre-eminence of the Documentation of Provenance

The significance of archives and their capacity to continue to be relevant as records of evidence to organisations and future users depends on being able to maintain the context of the records. In this chapter the importance of provenance and context has been stated and restated. It cannot be overemphasised. Time and time again, in all manner of situations and circumstances embracing all records-creating functions from private enterprise to government to individuals, the necessity of this concept has been proven.

The context in which records are created is arguably more important than the contents of the records, a fact which significantly differentiates the archives/records discipline from that of librarianship. This concept of provenance has always been primary in the management of archives. It is increasingly of relevance in the management of current records, a fact underlined by the evolution of electronic information systems and data exchange. For example, the information content of the case study – 'well done' – has no significance without its context being understood.

Gathering information about systems as they are created – how they work, what activities they support and the related outputs of the system – is a further example of data-gathering as a precondition to appropriate appraisal decisions. This type of data-gathering is an extension of the archival information-gathering about contexts and administrative structures which has been used for descriptive practices for many years.

The gathering of contextual data about organisations, their structures and their functioning is relatively painless if gathered when the information is contemporary. Australia has long been accustomed to a high rate of administrative change. Between 1971 and 1975, 90 changes to administrative structures of the Commonwealth government were made at an average rate of 18 changes of departments of state in each year.[24] Exposure to such administrative change has not led to the abandonment of administrative structure as a concept for archival control; rather, it resulted in the development and refinement of the elegant Commonwealth Record Series system, designed with its emphasis on series, specifically to accept the reality of administrative change and allow archival documentation to remain anchored in its appropriate contextual framework.

The concept of responsibility and accountability are linked to roles allocated or delegated to people within an organisation's structure. Without a knowledge of that structure, we are unable to determine who has the specific carriage of a particular function. The notion of 'office of record', the 'provenance' of the particular record under scrutiny, remains of primary value in archival work. Without knowledge of provenance, we risk making appraisal decisions based on content rather than context. If that methodology is followed, we risk failing to discriminate between the various layers of an administration which may conduct the same function or maintain records on a particular function, but which are not held responsible or accountable for the particular function. The Librarian's 'Finance – Statements' records become of equal status with the Accountants records also named 'Finance – Statements' if we do not record the 'competence' of certain administrative positions and designate the responsibility for maintaining the accountable record as a part of the administrative structure.

Appraisal of Functions Not Records

As indicated in Chapter 1, records are increasingly being defined as by-products of transactions. Records are only created as they are required to document some transaction or activity. This conceptualisation of records allows appraisers an alternative approach to their work. Instead of appraising the record as the first line of approach, we should first look to appraising the function and then look at what is being recorded as a result of undertaking that function. In this way, functions known to be potential creators of large proportions of archival records can be targeted in appraisal strategies for more detailed examination of the records created in the administration of the function. However, if the function can be defined as one which will produce little in the way of archival records, it can be placed well down the priority list in targeting more intensive work on the records themselves.

In keeping with the broadening of our understanding of our record-creating universe, we need to look in more detail at the functions which are common functions shared by records creators. This may result in the compilation of function-based disposal schedules. These functions may not be appropriate to all records creators, but are shared by more than one records creator. For example, all licensing functions might be considered together, or perhaps all examinations functions might be considered together as has been attempted in the Public Record Office of Victoria's General Records Disposal Schedule for Examination and Assessment Records.[25]

We also need to investigate those areas where the functions of organisations or agencies overlap and interrelate. The records in different agencies which deal with different aspects of the same function should be considered together. Thus, the relationship between the police, the Director of Public Prosecutions, the courts and the Corrective Services Department should be analysed as a part of a consideration of the function of administering justice. Appraisal decisions made in one area should inform appraisal decisions made on records created in the administration of other aspects of the larger function of administering justice.

By such organisational and functional analysis, archivists can be seen to be actively placing scarce resources in areas where they will best produce results. Function-based appraisal and disposal documentation will, if constructed carefully, remain intact for the duration of the function.

Non-Custodial Archives

Traditional approaches to archival collections have, very properly, stressed the capacity of archival repositories to manage the records and the format of the records prior to accepting responsibility for custody. This area, too, has been rethought.

In some circumstances perhaps it is no longer necessary to have the physical records within the archives itself. In some cases physical custody is no longer technically possible. Such realisations of the limitations of archival organisations to store records or make them accessible, according to archival mandate, seems to be a response forced in times of radical reduction in resourcing. In such circumstances archival institutions are looking for alternative strategies. One of these resembles the 'distributed collection' notion of our librarianship colleagues where cooperative strategies are put into place following conceptual agreement about which body will assume responsibility for what part of the collection. Archives have begun to stress the primacy of maintaining intellectual control or the ability to be able to locate and retrieve material designated as archival, rather than having to physically store archives in the one location.

One practical example of the concepts of non-custodial archives is the management approach being explored by Australian Archives to deal with the problems presented to them by electronic records. Electronic records are created within a bewildering array of technical environments, often using proprietary software and hardware. One approach in dealing with electronic archives has been to require the deposit of such material of continuing value in 'neutral' formats such as ASCII flat files which are capable of being read into a variety of machinery. Unfortunately this rendering of records 'machine-independent' involves losing much of the original context of the records and their capacity to be manipulated dictated by the specific hardware and software which created it. The Australian Archives is developing an appraisal strategy which concentrates on the identification of electronic records of continuing importance and working with agencies responsible for the records to ensure that those agencies undertake the responsibility of maintaining those records in formats which continue to be readable within their own operating environment. In such a model the Australian Archives undertakes the traditional role of appraisal, continues to maintain finding aid documentation, however does not accept physical custody of the records which remains the responsibility of the agency creating the records.

A further example of a non-custodial archives is the Australian Science Archives Project (ASAP) which acts as a 'clearing-house' for records relating to the history and philosophy of science in Australia. Operating from a base in the Department of History and Philosophy of Science at the University of Melbourne, the ASAP itself has no collection. Instead its mandate is to locate collections of records relating to Australian science, to identify archives, to document those collections and then to locate those archives within an appropriate custodial institution. In some cases the collections remain in private hands. The ASAP, however, undertakes the additional role of compiling discipline-based finding aids across all the disparate collecting institutions. The

ASAP itself is a non-custodial institution, concentrating on the appropriate documentation and placement of collections and creating appropriate finding aids to allow access to a distributed set of collections located in many different archival repositories or private hands.

This notion of non-custodial archives is relatively recent in the development of archives in Australia. It opens the possibility of designating records as being of continuing value where the archives itself cannot feasibly undertake the preservation of the record or guarantee access to the record. Traditionally, such limitations would have resulted in material being identified as having no continuing value as archives.

Uncharted Territory

Many of these issues are challenging traditional appraisal approaches. Some of them will, in time, be integrated into mainstream archival appraisal theory and practice. Others may well be abandoned or further refined. Some will present as yet unresolved conflicts, such as using concepts of accountability and risk management in appraisal, or issues relating to the determination of disposal guidelines for records not yet in existence. In most of these cases, where appraisal difficulties arise, appraisers need to be actively involved in the creation of the records. Potential ethical conflicts can, and do, arise where an organisation determines that its imperative is not to retain potentially damaging documentation, although that documentation may clearly be of continuing social value. In some cases this may lead the archivist into treacherous ethical shoals where the priorities of the institution to retain or destroy records may be at odds with the archival assessment of the societal benefits of retention or destruction of the records.

New Appraisal Strategies

As indicated in Chapter 1, there are broadly four categories of archival institution – large centralised government programs, in-house archives, collecting archives, and combinations of the above. In each of these categories new strategic approaches to appraisal are emerging which seek to address the issues raised above. Many of these strategies are in emergent forms and are being subject to scrutiny and testing in a variety of archival programs.

Functional Analysis

The inclusion of functional analysis in the appraisal process has already been adopted as a strategy in some archival institutions. In some cases it has been brought about by the necessity of dealing with increased records with limited resources. Targeting those areas of an organisation which create potentially archival records over those areas known, or assumed, not to do so is the first step in the adoption of such a strategy.

Two articulations of a more formal theoretical construct for appraisal decisions based on functional analysis have recently been developed. In the first, the archival institution has undertaken, both by direct research and based on cumulative experience, an analysis of those parts of their archival domain whose functions have traditionally resulted in the creation of a high proportion of records of continuing value. In the second, a wider ambit has been determined, identifying first what it is that the archival profession wishes to document and then the parts of the institution or institutions where those records are created.

The first approach has been referred to as 'records acquisition strategy' and is being developed by the National Archives of Canada.[26] This approach envisages three complex stages:

- To identify primary locations and generic sources of potentially significant archival records – or setting of acquisition targets.
- An ordering of these targets into an intellectual order of collecting priority and an analysis of their internal administrative components.
- An evaluation and ranking of records at the series level – the development of a *records disposition plan.*

This strategy begins with macro-appraisal, or top-down analysis of the record creator, rather than the records.

The second approach has been proposed for institutions and has evolved from the thinking on documentation strategies. In this approach generic studies of certain types of institutions are proposed. From these generic studies, broad definitions of the functions undertaken by specific types of organisations, such as hospitals or universities, are advanced. For example, one of the functions of a university is defined as being 'to convey knowledge'. Once the functions are defined the records typically created by institutions involved in those fields are examined to determine their potential archival significance. Specific types of records are then targeted for further identification and further, more traditional appraisal evaluation. The first such study of universities has been issued by Helen Samuels, the developer and proponent of the notion of both this approach and that of documentation strategy.[27]

In both intellectual constructs for functional analysis, the context of organisations is evaluated as the issue of first importance. This applies at various levels depending on the type of archival mandate an institution has. If a central government archives is undertaking such a study, a thorough knowledge and analysis of the functions, activities and interrelationships within the

government needs to be established. From there, an appreciation of the role of each level of the hierarchy needs to be undertaken – ministry, government department, statutory authority, and so on –
- in traditional hierarchical terms
- laterally to identify where the functions of government overlap, intersect and inform each other
- by function within each component of the structure identified.

The alignment of the functions and the parts of the hierarchy which administer the functions and any existing knowledge about the record types or series created by these functions needs then to be listed in order of importance for allocation of the next level of archival endeavour, the physical documentation and examination of the records.

Collecting Projects

Collecting projects result from an initial realisation that a certain event or issue has not been appropriately documented. Such projects are most often to be found within collecting archives, rather than in in-house or government archives.

Defining collecting projects involves the formulation of a plan to ensure that documentation of the issue is targeted for acquisition. The material targeted may be housed in one or more repositories. Usually the collecting project involves events which are reasonably easy to define and are finite. An example of a collecting project involving one archives is the Rainbow Archives Project in the Mitchell Library of the State Library of NSW in which the alternative lifestyle communities established on the north coast of NSW were identified as being undocumented in the archival records of the state. A collecting project has now been in operation for some five years with all records acquired being deposited with the Mitchell Library.

Another example is the National AIDS Archive Collection funded by the Commonwealth Department of Health and organised and administered by the Noel Butlin Archives Centre at the Australian National University. This project is to create a public resource of AIDS educational materials developed and used in Australia during the 1980s. It includes material produced by federal, state/territory and local government, a wide variety of non-government organisations and individuals. The project was proposed through the Commonwealth Department of Health, Housing and Community Services to ensure that material, known to be difficult to capture, would not be lost.

Such projects are one-off events to complete the historical record for a discrete issue or happening.

Documentation Strategies

In the late 1980s the documentation strategy model was proposed to further the concepts of cooperative acquisition strategies. The model focuses on documenting an ongoing activity, issue or geographical area and involves creating a continuing mechanism involving records creators, administrators, historians and archivists to determine which records should be kept as archives and to ensure that such documentation is identified, created if necessary and transferred to an appropriate institution. The documentation strategy focuses less on what records do exist than on what records should exist. The functional analysis again takes precedence over the physical examination of records as a strategic approach to appraisal.

At present the documentation strategy is still being developed, the theoretical models being supported with some American case studies. The strategy will suit topics of great complexity, particularly technically specialised areas where records are often being created and maintained in non-traditional, often non-paper, format.

A potential documentation strategy might be the development of in-vitro fertilisation technology, developed across many institutions and involving a complex web of relationships between individual scientists, hospitals, research institutions, government departments and community groups. The range of any such project would involve issues from newly developing scientific and medical techniques, bureaucratic regulation, legislative enquiries as well as complex and challenging moral and ethical issues. Any documentation project in this area would involve many technical specialists, administrators and policy-makers of many institutions in addition to archivists.

Documentation of the Kakadu National Park might be another such appropriate target concerning complex and emotional issues and involving the whole of society in areas much broader than the ostensible subject area. Many organisations and businesses would be involved, including federal and territory governments, mining companies, peak employer bodies, industry lobby groups, many environmental groups and the park's traditional owners and managers.

The development of techniques to improve acquisition strategies emphasise cooperation rather than competition is an on-going process. The technical archival literature will provide all practising archivists with up-to-date information on the latest developments.

Conclusion

Appraisal is one of the most intellectually exciting fields of archival endeavour. The role of appraisal in the archival processes is of crucial importance. Decisions about what to document determine not only the nature of our collections but also the nature of the record we leave for the future. The development of appraisal practices has been relatively recent. However, in times of resource restraint and information explosion, they are unable to meet the task of defining the records of continuing value. New approaches and strategic thinking is required to allow us to be conscious of the decisions we take in selecting records. The need to be more involved in our contemporary society and implement appraisal processes either before or at the time of the creation of records challenges many of our theoretical bases. To use such approaches which remove archives from the scholarly and leisurely application of selection criteria once the records are non-current, appraisers need to understand and apply organisational theory and social theory. Many of these departures are only now beginning to be discussed in our professional literature.

Endnotes

1 Based on Ericson, Timothy L., 'Creative Dissatisfaction', in *Archivaria*, 33, Winter 1991–92, p. 68.
2 This comfortable assumption has been challenged through the FBI files case in the US, however, as a general proposition, it remains valid. Steinwall, Susan D., 'Appraisal and the FBI Files Case: For Whom Do Archivists Retain Records?, in *American Archivist*, 49, No. 1, Winter 1986.
3 Jenkinson, Hilary, *A Manual of Archive Administration*, 2nd edn, Percy Lund, Humphries & Co, London, 1966, Part III.
4 Schellenberg, Theodore, *Modern Archives: Principles and Techniques*, University of Chicago Press, 1956 (reprint 1975), Chicago/London, Ch 12.
5 Cook, Terry, 'Documentation Strategy', in *Archivaria*, 34, Summer 1992.
6 Cook, Terry, 'Mind over Matter: Towards a New Theory of Archival Appraisal', in *The Archival Imagination: Essays in Honor of Hugh A Taylor*, B. L. Craig (ed.), Association of Canadian Archivists, Ottawa, 1992.
7 See, for example, Hull, Felix, *The Use of Sampling Techniques in the Retention of Records: A RAMP Study with Guidelines* (PGI/81/110), Paris, Unesco, 1981; or Cook, Terry, 'Many are called but few are chosen: Appraisal Guidelines for Sampling and Selecting Case Files' in *Archivaria*, 32, Summer 1991.
8 Saul, Lindy, 'Disposal Methodologies: A Private Industry Approach', in *Keeping Data: Papers from a Workshop on Appraising Computer-Based Records*, B. Reed and D. Roberts (eds), Australian Council of Archives and Australian Society of Archivists, Dickson, ACT, 1991.
9 Steinwall, Susan D, op cit., p. 60.
10 Ibid.
11 *Archives Act* 1983.

12 Example courtesy of David Bearman, Archives and Museum Informatics.

13 100th Congress 1st session. Joint Hearings before the House Select Committee to Investigate Covert Arms Transactions with Iran and Senate Select Committee on Secret Military Assistance to Iran and the Nicaraguan Opposition. 11, 12, 13, 14 and 19 May 1987, Exhibit 69, p. 751.

14 Ibid.

15 Putnam Miller, Page, 'Washington Beat – Investigation in PROFS Case Produces Significant Findings', *SAA Newsletter*, Society of American Archivists, May 1992, Chicago, p. 9.

16 Booms, Hans, 'Uberlieferungsbildung: Keeping Archives as a Social and Political Activity' in *Archivaria*, 33, Winter 1991–92.
Brown, Richard, 'Records Acquisition Strategy and Its Theoretical Foundation: The Case for a Concept of Archival Hermeneutics' in *Archivaria*, 33, Winter 1991–92.
Cook, Terry, 'Mind over Matter', Ibid.
Eastwood, Terry, 'Towards a Social Theory of Appraisal', in *The Archival Imagination*, op.cit.

17 Booms, Hans, op.cit., p. 31.

18 O'Toole, James 'On the Idea of Permanence' in *American Archivist*, 52/1, Winter 1989.
Bearman, David. *Archival Methods*, Archives and Museum Informatics Technical Report, 3/1, Spring 1989.

19 Rapport, Leonard, 'No Grandfather Clause: Reappraising Accessioned Records' in *American Archivist* 44, Spring 1981, and ensuing debate.

20 Bearman, David, *Archival Methods*, op.cit.

21 Jenkinson, Hilary, op.cit., p. 142.

22 Hurley, Chris, quoted by Spencer Zifcak, 'On the Record: Government Accountability and Access to Public Records', in *Public Records Support Group Newsletter*, 2/7, September 1991.

23 Jenkinson, Hilary, op.cit., p. 149.

24 Scott, Peter and Finlay, Gail, 'Archives and Administrative Change: Some Methods and Approaches. Part One', in *Archives and Manuscripts*, 7/3, August 1973, p. 116.

25 PROS 87/10.

26 Brown, Richard, Ibid.

27 Samuels, Helen, *Varsity Letters: Documenting Modern Colleges and Universities*, The Society of American Archivists and Scarecrow Press, Methuen NJ, 1992; Samuels, Helen, 'Improving Our Disposition: Documentation Strategy', in *Archivaria*, 33, Winter 1991–92.

Further Reading

Brown, Richard, 'Records Acquisition Strategy and Its Theoretical Foundation: The Case for a Concept of Archival Hermeneutics', in *Archivaria*, 33, Winter 1991–92.

Bearman, David, *Archival Methods*, Archive and Museum Informatics Technical Report, 3/1 Spring 1989.

Booms, Hans, 'Uberlieferungsbildung: Keeping Archives as a Social and Political Activity', in *Archivaria*, 33, Winter 1991–92.

Cook, Terry, 'Documentation Strategy', in *Archivaria*, 34, Summer 1992.

Cook, Terry, 'Mind over Matter: Towards a New Theory of Archival Appraisal', in *The Archival Imagination: Essays in Honour of Hugh A. Taylor,* B. L. Craig (ed.), Association of Canadian Archivists, Ottawa, 1992.

Eastwood, Terry, 'Towards a Social Theory of Appraisal', in *The Archival Imagination: Essays in Honour of Hugh A. Taylor*, B. L. Craig (ed.), Association of Canadian Archivists, Ottawa, 1992.

Hurley, Chris and McKemmish, Sue, 'First Write Your Disposal Schedule', in *Archives and Manuscripts,* 18/2, Nov 1990, pp. 191–203.

Picot, Anne, 'Techniques for Information Gathering/Planning', in *Keeping Data: Papers from a Workshop on Appraising Computer-Based Records*, B. Reed and D. Roberts (eds), Australian Council of Archives and Australian Society of Archivists, Sydney, 1991.

Samuels, Helen, *Varsity Letters: Documenting Modern Colleges and Universities,* The Society of American Archivists and Scarecrow Press, Metuchen, NJ, 1992.

Saul, Lindy, 'Disposal Methodologies: A Private Industry Approach', in *Keeping Data: Papers from a Workshop on Appraising Computer-Based Records*, B. Reed and D. Roberts (eds), Australian Council of Archives and Australian Society of Archivists, Sydney, 1991

Opposite page:
Appendix 6.1
Records Appraisal
Checklist

Reproduced with the
permission of the
Keeper of Public
Records

PRO
11B

Public Record Office, Victoria
Records Appraisal Checklist
Public Record Office, Victoria

Complete this form for each group of records listed on the accompanying Destruction Authority (form PRO 11A) not covered by a Disposal Schedule.

> **Are you eligible to use this form? See instructions on back of form**

1. Records Description:

What is the purpose and format of the records? . . . .
. . . .
. . . .
. . . .

What information do the records contain? . . . .
. . . .
. . . .
. . . .

Are the records controlled by an alphabetical or numerical system? If so, describe (e.g. 81/1 to
84/306 or Adams to Young). . . . .
. . . .
. . . .
. . . .

What is the date range of the records? . . . . . / . . . . . / . . . . . to . . . . . / . . . . . / . . . . .
Are similar records still being created? If so, describe. . . . .
. . . .
. . . .
. . . .

What is the quantity of the records proposed for destruction? . . . . shelf metres
Where are the records located? . . . .
. . . .
. . . .

At what age do the records become inactive? . . . .
. . . .
. . . .

Are the records created because of a legislative requirement or are the records mentioned in any
legislation or regulation? If so, describe. . . . .
. . . .
. . . .
. . . .

Appendix 6.1 (cont.)

2. Primary Values:

	Yes	No	Retention Period/Custody Requirement
Statutory:			
Is there a statutory requirement relating to retention or custody?	☐	☐	. . . .
Name of Act/Regulations/Ordinance:			
. . . .			
. . . .			
Fiscal/Audit:			
Are records financially accountable?	☐	☐	. . . .
Could records be used as evidence in cases of fraud?	☐	☐	. . . .
Legal/Constitutional:			
Do records relate to legal/constitutional basis of State?	☐	☐	. . . .
Do records provide evidence of rights, obligations or entitlements of the State, individuals, organisations, etc.?	☐	☐	. . . .
Do records provide legal basis for administrative action?	☐	☐	. . . .
Administrative:			
Are records required for agency/government to carry out current function?	☐	☐	. . . .
Do records provide evidence of origins, structure, policies, functions, activities and procedures of agency/government?	☐	☐	. . . .

3. Secondary Values:

	Yes	No	Retention Period/Custody Requirement
Research:			
Do records provide significant source for research?	☐	☐	. . . .
Field of potential research:			
. . . .			
. . . .			
. . . .			
. . . .			
. . . .			

Appendix 6.1 (cont.)

4. Other Factors:

	Yes	No
Duplication:		
Is information duplicated elsewhere?	☐	☐
Is information summarised elsewhere?	☐	☐
Do records summarise information elsewhere?	☐	☐
Related Records:		
. . . .		

Cost Factors:

What type of storage is used? . . . .

. . . .

. . . .

What type of equipment is used? . . . .

. . . .

. . . .

What type of maintenance is required? . . . .

. . . .

. . . .

Sampling:

Is sampling a possibility? . . . .

. . . .

. . . .

F.O.I.:

Have records been subject of F.O.I. requests? . . . .

. . . .

Contact Officer: **Phone number:**		
Title:		
Signature:	**Date prepared:**	/ /

Appendix 6.1 (cont.)

Instructions for Use of Form PRO 11B

Are you eligible to use this form?

To establish your eligibility to use this form please answer the questions below and follow instructions provided.

1. Are the records listed on form PRO 11A covered by a Disposal Schedule approved by the Public Record Office?
    YES Go to question 2.
    NO   Complete a separate form PRO 11B for each group of records listed on PRO 11A.

2. Does the approved Disposal Schedule require authorisation for each destruction by the Keeper of Public Records or, where applicable, by the Auditor-General?
    NO   It is not necessary to obtain authorisation to destroy these records. Do not use forms PRO 11A or 11B. Instead, use form PRO 29 to notify the Public Record Office of the destruction.

    YES It is necessary to obtain authorisation to destroy these records but it is not necessary to describe the records proposed for destruction on Form 11B. Do not use form PRO 11B; only complete form PRO 11A.

How to complete the form

Step 1:   **Prior to destruction,** complete this form in **duplicate** for each group of records listed on form PRO 11A by:
    (a) describing the records (1)
    (b) indicating the primary and secondary value of the records (2 & 3)
    (c) providing information about record duplication, costing, sampling and F.O.I. (4)

Step 2:   **Forward both** copies of the form for each record group together with both copies of form PRO 11A to the Public Record Office for authorisation of destruction. If necessary the Public Record Office will liaise with the Auditor-General to seek his authorisation.

Step 3:   **Following return** of copies of the form together with a copy of form PRO 11A signed by the Keeper of Public Records and, where applicable, by the Auditor-General proceed with destruction.

See PROS 82/5, Supplement to Procedures for Disposition of Public Records, Appendix M for further information on primary and secondary record values.

7 Accessioning

Paul Brunton and Tim Robinson

Accessioning provides basic physical and intellectual control over material coming into an archives. The process can begin before or during the transfer of records and must be completed as soon as possible after receipt. At its minimum level, it should provide information about the creator, contents, format, extent and repository location in such a way that documents cannot become intermingled with other material held by the archives and receipt documents can be provided to the source of the records transfer.

Documents prepared during accessioning should, as far as possible, be integrated with other documents prepared to use and manage the record, including those which record their context. For many archives, however, documentation prior to transfer may be scant, while more detailed work will have to be undertaken according to internal priorities. This gives the accessioning documents particular importance, as they may be all that exist for some time. If you are the first archivist in an organisation, it is possible that for some time all you will be able to do will be to accession material. There will be many other demands on your time and you will be expected to be able to locate quickly everything that has come into the archives. To be unable to do this will do little for the image of your archives or for your self-esteem.

While there are essential elements to be included in all accessioning procedures, you should make sure that the system you develop is appropriate to the scale of your operation and will meet your present and expected demands for further physical and intellectual control. Do not develop over-elaborate, cumbersome forms or systems no matter how theoretically desirable they may be. Archivists at all levels find that resources do not expand to meet needs and you may have created a burden for yourself. It would be undesirable to have to refuse to accept material into the archives because you have too great an accessioning backlog already.

In some circumstances to have material controlled only at accession level may be acceptable for a considerable time. This is particularly the case in in-house archives if the records held in the archives have been created within large coherent series, the contents of which will often be self-explanatory. As a general rule, records which have been kept as part of an organisation's system tend to need less processing than items such as personal papers, which may well require intensive work to make them accessible to users.

Accessioning consists of a sequence of different activities. These include preliminary sorting of the accession, recording the essential identifying information about the material and its creator in the accession register and providing suitable storage for the material. Some of these activities may be slightly different in in-house and collecting archives. However, their purpose – to gain basic control – is the same and the documentation produced is very similar.

Most records being transferred will not be in a physical state where they can be placed straight onto shelves. The variety of formats found among archives may also mean that the one accession cannot be stored on the same shelf. Conservation requirements may also mean that different records media such as photographic negatives, photographic prints or magnetic tapes should be stored in special conditions, although not all archives can afford such facilities (see Chapter 3, Preservation).

Physical Transfer of the Material

Archivists should be involved in boxing of the records following formal completion of the donation, bequest, transfer, purchase or loan. This involvement may mean being on-site, may be carried out through the issue of clear procedures, or may have to occur on the archives' own premises. Whenever possible, the records should be placed in standard archives boxes to minimise the need for reboxing once the material is in custody. A list of the contents including date ranges of every box should be made. The boxes should be clearly numbered and labelled with the name of the donor, creator, bequeather or loaner. A sample of a container list is shown in Table 7.1. At this stage it is essential that no attempt be made to sort or reorganise the material as valuable evidence inherent in the undisturbed order may be destroyed. A copy of the list should be placed in each box and the original

Table 7.1 Container List

Diocesan Archives Box List
Received from: St Jude's Parish Church

Address: Hardy Vale, NSW
Telephone: (056) 245 6324
Contact Person: The Reverend Robert Spanish

Box No. Contents (Series Title, inclusive dates of first and last folder title/numbers)	Archives Only

1 Church Registers (5 volumes) 1859–1980
    Volume 1: 1859–1889
    Volume 2: 1889–1915
    Volume 3: 1915–1939
    Volume 4: 1939–1959
    Volume 5: 1959–1980
	(This area is often used for assigning shelf numbers once the records enter the archives)

2 Correspondence, 1957–1970	
3 Correspondence, 1970–1980	

4 Fund Raising Committee
    Minutes, 1945–1979
    Ladies Auxiliary Minutes, 1950–1967
    Youth Activities Committee Minutes, 1959–1975	

Note: An accurate box list for each accession is vital as it often serves as the basic documentation to control the acquisition until it can be completely arranged and described. In many cases the box list contains sufficient information to be incorporated immediately into the archives' system of finding aids.

---

stored with the related accessioning documentation, which is discussed later in this chapter.

In every case material received by the archives from each source should immediately be acknowledged with a receipt. The receipt should clearly state, where appropriate, that the material will need to be examined and appraised in detail before any final decisions are made on whether all or part of the material will be accepted for permanent deposit.

Analysing Material To Determine Provenance

The single most important step in accessioning material is the determining in terms of its provenance or the origin of the records, ie the organisation, office or person that created, received, accumulated or used the records in the conduct of business or life. This relationship to the records differs from that of other offices or persons which may have stored or owned the records at a later time. The latter refers to the sequence or chain of custody which is a part of the history of the material, but does not determine its provenance in the archival sense. The central place of the principle of provenance in archival theory and practice is explained in more detail in Chapter 8, Arrangement and Description.

For an in-house archives, it is not usually too difficult to work out the provenance of a body of records if the material has been received as part of a regular transfer program. However, it is important that the person or office transferring the records is not confused with provenance. For example, a batch of student files may be received from the school caretaker. The provenance of these records is not the caretaker as he or she did not create, receive or use them in the course of business. The caretaker merely provided temporary storage for the student files, and their correct provenance is the Registrar's Office. The former location and provenance of records are both important pieces of information. Most often they will be the same person or office, but they need not be.

In a collecting archives a single acquisition might contain material created, received or used by several different people and/or organisations. During the process of acquisition, it may have become clear that the material to be accessioned, although received from a single location or person, has in fact two or more provenances. If two or more parts of the material obviously have no relationship, and could only have come together by accident, they may be separated. Each should then be accessioned separately according to its provenance.

Sometimes it will not be possible to identify easily the different provenances of various parts of the one acquisition. In such cases it is preferable not to attempt to separate the material until a very detailed investigation of the records can be carried out. How this is done will be explained in Chapter 8, Arrangement and Description. Often the relationships between records are subtle. The temptation to sort new acquisitions too hurriedly must be resisted to prevent permanent damage being done to the integrity of the records through an inexact understanding of the relationship between various items.

Where there is reason to question the exact provenance of all the records in the one acquisition, it is best to accession it all as a single unit according to the provenance of the majority of the material. The aim of accessioning is to gain speedy basic control of the material. If subsequent examination reveals more than one provenance in a single accession, it is often a simple matter to accession the unrelated records again under their correct provenance.

Accessioning in an In-House Archives

An in-house archives provides a service to the various units of its parent organisation (whether they are called divisions, departments, branches, offices, or parishes, etc). In trying to make that service as efficient as possible, the archives requires the active cooperation of the units transferring the material to its custody. When an office or other records-creating unit wants to transfer records to the archives, it should first contact the archivist to arrange a convenient time for the transfer and to ensure that the records are in fact eligible for transfer. (See Chapter 5, Managing the Acquisition Process, for information on the decisions to be made before records are accepted into the archives.) If the records are accepted, then the office should prepare them for transfer according to the guidelines developed by the archives. This involves boxing the records in standard boxes and listing them so that they are securely housed and it is clear exactly which records are being sent.

Transfer Procedures

To assist the archives' clients, the archivist should produce procedures for the transfer of records which set out the steps to be followed when preparing the material for transfer. For example, the procedures should include instructions on how to complete the form used for the records transfer list and how to box the records correctly.

The importance of establishing and maintaining proper procedures for this activity cannot be overstated. The instructions should ensure that material received from different offices is identified and packed in a standard way. This helps the archivist manage the holdings more efficiently, both in terms of storage and of retrieval. For example, when an office requests records from the repository for further administrative use, the archivist should be able to locate them quickly and accurately using the transfer list. The procedures are also useful in lieu of training programs for archives whose offices are spread widely geographically and/or who rely on the efforts of people who have many duties apart from transferring records (for example, a central church archives receiving records from many different parishes).

Although time-consuming, there are some advantages in the archivist being active within administrative departments. The presence of the archivist in the departments raises the profile of the archives' operations and often provides the only opportunity that some staff will have of meeting and talking to the archivist.

Being present during the packing means that the archivist can ensure that only the records he or she has selected for transfer to the archives will actually be sent. It will also mean that the records are packed correctly. Those inexperienced in packing records often attempt to cram too much into a box, being concerned about wasting space. This prevents the boxes from sitting properly on the shelves, damages the records and makes retrieval difficult.

There is often a temptation in offices pressed for storage space to send anything and everything to the archives. Treating the archives as a dumping ground for records which should more properly be scheduled for destruction or semi-current storage is common. In the absence of proper disposal schedules many officers are unwilling to make the decision to destroy records and are only too happy to put off having to decide what to do by sending the records to the archives.

Some archives, from very small to extremely large government operations, also operate semi-current records storage for their organisation. In such cases there will be a larger quantity of material being regularly transferred to the archives, although it will not all be for permanent storage. In a smaller archives the sheer quantity of material may prevent the archives staff from being involved in all transfers. Here there will be really no option but to have the unit (or department) creating or transferring the records pack and list them. To maximise the efficient use of the archives staff time, it may be necessary to be very strict on the terms on which records are transferred. It may be necessary to return to the unit or department records which have not been packed or listed correctly. It should not be necessary to do this more than once with any unit or department.

Having received the material, the archivist must carefully check the transfer list against the actual records received to make sure that everything is accounted for.

The archivist should then prepare an accession sheet for the records, one copy of which will be returned as a receipt to the office which sent them. After this, the archivist must arrange for the proper storage of the records in the repository, taking care to place any records which need special storage, such as films, into the correct storage environment if it is available. The archivist must record the location(s) of the records on the master copy of the accession sheet and on any other location control he or she maintains. All the steps in accessioning for an in-house archives can be achieved in a fairly streamlined way when the organisation's records are covered by disposal schedules. This enables the archivist to work out a program for the orderly transfer of records from the different offices, so that he or she can expect to receive transfers from a particular office at the same time each year.

Accessioning in a Collecting Archives

A collecting archives, sometimes called a manuscript library or historical records repository, collects the records of a variety of organisations, individuals and families. In such institutions records created, received or maintained by a single organisation, individual or family and received in one transfer by the archives must be accessioned as a single unit as they share the same provenance.

However, collecting institutions, especially those that acquire organisational records, may receive several transfers of material of the same provenance over a period of time. As with an in-house archives, it is often necessary for the archivist to be present at the stage of packing and listing prior to transfer. Donors giving manuscript material to the archives will not react well to being asked to complete a long form or to obeying particular packing instructions. Such requirements may result in bad publicity for the archives and may result in the loss of potential donors. It is also the case that many manuscript collections are being transferred at a time of some significant event in the life of the donor, such as a death or move. Such circumstances are not conducive to the completion of forms.

Often the archivist in a collecting archives will not have such a close relationship with the creators of the records as the archivist working in an in-house archives does with the various offices of the parent organisation. The work of accessioning will usually all be done by the archivist once the material has arrived in the archives, although if the archives has a field officer he or she may be able to list and box the records before they are sent to the archives.

The following case studies illustrate some of the issues and questions involved with accessioning in a collecting archives.

Case Study 1

The papers of a local identity contain the official minute books and financial records of the local Progress Association for the time that the person was secretary of the Association. If it is possible to separate these minute books and financial records from the rest of the material as separate series (see Chapter 8 for an explanation of identifying series) without the loss of information gained through context, this should be done and then both groups of material should be accessioned separately as each group has a different provenance. It is most important that you refer to the other accession in your documentation for each of the groups of material, otherwise the information about the context in which they were received could be lost.

You may find that other records of the Progress Association have come to your archives from another official. Accessioning by provenance will enable you to provide initial access to all the records of the Association, even though they have been brought into the archives by different people at different times.

It is often thought that it would be easier for users if all material produced by the same person, or all material relating to the same subject, is brought together. However, to remove an item from the context in which it was created, received or maintained (ie its provenance) is to destroy much of the meaning of the item.

Case Study 2

A number of photographs by a particular photographer are received by the archiver from the photographer. As these share the same provenance, since they were all created and retained by that photographer, they should be accessioned as a unit. Even though other examples of that photographer's work are already held by the archives, having been received from another source, for example, from a client of the photographer, the new material should be accessioned separately because it has a different provenance.

The difference is that the photographs were commissioned by the client and draw their meaning as part of the client's family records rather than as work of the photographer. Retrieval of all the photographs by a particular photographer can be achieved by means of an index or other finding aid produced later. (See Chapter 9, Finding Aids, for more details.) Although it may seem that observing the principle of provenance in accessioning is time-consuming, it is time well spent. The determination and recording of provenance provides as much valuable information about the photographs as the recording of the photographer or subject alone.

Case Study 3

An archives is presented with some family papers. Among the papers are found a number of unidentified and undated portrait photographs. The knowledge of their provenance and their relationship with the other material may be used to deduce their approximate dates of creation. One of the letters sent to the family makes mention of enclosing a photograph. A diary, when examined in detail, refers to the visit of an itinerant photographer to the town. These clues, when used in conjunction with further research, may eventually provide identification of the portraits.

If the photographs had been placed in a group of unidentified portraits, without the proper recording of their provenance, there would be little likelihood of any further information ever being discovered about them.

Accessioning Documentation

The recording of information about each new accession is important to the running of the archives. Being the first level of control over new material, it must be done in a standardised manner. While the formats and media of records may determine how they will be stored, they will not have any influence on accessioning procedures. That is, the archival theories behind accessioning apply equally to all types of material. Whether the records are photographs, magnetic tape or paper, they will be accessioned in the same way, despite the later differences in storage and handling.

The Accession Register

The most important source of documentation for basic control information is the accession register. The register can come in several formats. The format outlined here consists of a loose-leaf folder of individual accession sheets, with one completed for each accession. This format has some flexibility as copies of the sheets can be made and filed in several different sequences, as explained below. Many archives now use computers to capture accessioning details. (See Chapter 12, Using Computers and Document Imaging.) Backup records must be kept, and printouts onto archival quality paper are necessary in most instances. This is because the accession register is a vital record for the archives, ie a record without which the archives cannot perform its basic functions. The accession register is the basic document for all subsequent control and processing of the collection.

An explanation of what information to include under each heading on the following example forms is given below.

Accession Number. It is easiest simply to make this an annual number, ie the first accession of 1995 would be 1995/1. This is the unique number which identifies each accession until further work is done during the arrangement and description stages.

Provenance. In most cases this will be the full name of the organisation or person, or agency within an organisation, that created, received or accumulated and used the records in the conduct of business or life. A standard format for the recording of these names should be adopted for ease of filing.

Description. This should briefly record the types of record, eg files, correspondence, ledgers, photographs, magnetic tapes and any unexpected material noticed during appraisal.

Date Range. This is the inclusive dates of the creation of the material, not the dates of its subject matter. It can, however, distinguish between creation dates and content dates for cases where older material has been brought forward into the record – see Table 7.2 for an example.

Quantity. This is the shelf metres occupied by the accession. The number and type of containers may also be useful.

Location. In some archives it has been found useful to maintain a location index, either manual or automated. This is particularly useful where there is likely to be some degree of movement of the archives.

Access Conditions. Access to records held in archives may be determined by a number of factors. With donated material, often the donor will have imposed particular restrictions, either a fixed period of closure or the requirement that potential researchers apply to the donor in writing for access. This last restriction should be discouraged as over time it becomes increasingly difficult to administer. Other forms of restriction of access are mostly legislative. Various Acts such as those relating to freedom of information, privacy or defamation may be applicable depending on the nature of the archives and the records themselves.

Copyright. Copyright legislation varies and is also subject to amendment, but the basic principles remain. Copyright is a type of intellectual property which can be owned independent of the objects to which it refers. The ownership of copyright in a document means the ability to control how and when it is reproduced or copied, within particular legislative limits. Copyright can be sold or transferred or licensed independently of ownership of the documents, as stated above. For an archives, this means that while the physical documents may be the legal property of the archives, the copyright in those documents is not. The archives cannot then permit reproduction without the permission of the copyright owner. It is common practice to attempt to the obtain copyright to manuscript material donated to an archives, but often this is not possible either because the donor does not wish to give the archives copyright or is unable to do so because he or she does not own the copyright.

Physical Condition. Many archives record brief notes about the physical condition of material as it is accessioned. This alerts the archives to particular conservation problems and the general overall condition of the archive's holdings. It is better to have such information recorded on a form than to attempt to rely on memory of which records need attention since the period of time between accessioning and further description may be considerable.

Box List. In larger and varied accessions it is good practice to compile a more detailed box list for each accession. This simply records the contents of each container. Having given each container a number which is linked to the accession number, the nature of the records is briefly described along with their approximate date range. Each separate item in the accession will have a number, not only boxes. Some items such as large framed objects will not fit in a box, but they must still be included in the listing. The box list is often only a temporary document, which will become redundant following full arrangement of the records. Should a decision be made later that some of the material in the accession is not to be retained by the archives, the appropriate annotation should be made to the box list.

Notes. This includes information about the physical condition of the material, whether or not a box list exists and any other information which may be of later use.

Donor/Previous Custodian. In the case of a collecting archives, the donor is the person, family or organisation who signed the donation form. If there was an intermediary who brought the material to the archives, his or her name should be also recorded. For an in-house archives, the previous custodian will be the transferring office. Remember to record the name of a contact officer in the office.

Acquisition File Number. Record the number of the file which has the information relating to the accession. A copy of the completed accession sheet should be placed on the file.

Acknowledgment Date. Record here the date on which formal written acknowledgment of the records was made.

Compiler. Record the name of the archivist who accessioned the material.

Date. Record the date the accessioning was completed. Tables 7.2 and 7.3 present examples of completed accession sheets.

Other Documentation

The advantage of having the archives accession sheet divided in half (see Tables 7.2 and 7.3, where confidential details are on the bottom half of the form) is that copies can be made of either the top or bottom sections to create various finding aids to the records.

The top half of the accession sheet can be copied and the copies filed alphabetically by provenance. This provides one basic level of entry to the archives' holdings, ie by name of the creating organisation or person.

Table 7.2 Archives Accession Sheet Example – In-House Archives

Provenance: Headmaster's Office	Accession Number: 1995/1
Description: Correspondence Files	

Date Range: 1 August 1948 – 4 July 1960 (Contents 1928–1960)	
Quantity: 4 metres (22 boxes)	Location: 1995/1/1–10: Bay 20 Shelves 1,2 1995/1/11–22: Bay 40 Shelves 8–10

Accession Conditions/Copyright:

Access only with written permission of Headmaster

Notes:
Arranged by annual single number system. See Index, Accession Number 1995/2. 1948–1949 files are water damaged. Includes some published documents from 1928. Box list available. Previous accession: 1979/4.

Confidential Details:

Donor/Previous Custodian: Mr Fraser, the Caretaker	Accession Number: 1995/1
Address: Room 22	
Telephone: (H) (W) x95	

Intermediary/Contact Officer: Mr Kerr, Assistant to the Caretaker	Telephone:
Acquisition File Number: A.F. 103	Acknowledgment Date: 23 Feb. 1995
Compiled by: Anne York	Date: 25 Feb. 1995

Table 7.3   Archives Accession Sheet – Collecting Archives

Provenance: Benlith Potteries Pty Ltd	Accession Number: 1995/15
Description: Records, including minutes, financial records, building plans and photographs	
Date Range: 1883–1958	
Quantity: 17 metres (100 boxes)	**Location:** Bay 10 Shelves 1–25
Accession Conditions/Copyright: Open access, copyright not held by archives	
Notes: Box list available. The donors are unrelated to Benlith, but purchased the building and offered the records they found.	
Confidential Details:	
Donor/Previous Custodian: Development Inc.	Accession Number: 1995/15
Address: C/- Benlith House George Street Benlith, NSW 2999	
Telephone: (H) (W) 937 7624	
Intermediary/Contact Officer: Mr Andrew Hewson – Manager, Human Resource Relations	Telephone: x 92
Acquisition File Number: A.F. 401	Acknowledgment Date: 1 Apr. 1995
Compiled by: L. Blunt	Date: 10 Apr. 1995

Another copy of the top half of the accession sheet can be made and filed according to selected record types from information given under the Description heading in the form. This finding aid would provide a quick guide to all accessions of, for example, photographs or microforms or magnetic tapes or maps held in the archives. Because the information on the top half of the sheet is not confidential, these copies in various configurations can be readily used by researchers.

In a collecting archives it is very important to have an alphabetical index to the donor of each accession. This is because people will invariably remember that one of their family or friends presented a collection to the archives, but they will not remember precisely when or what it was. An index to donors may be constructed quite easily by copying the lower half of the accession sheet and filing it alphabetically by the name of the person or group of people who presented the collection. However, because donors' names and addresses are confidential, these files should be accessible only to authorised archives staff.

To be able to retrieve material quickly from its shelf or shelves in the repository, it is necessary to create an index to holdings by location number. This could be done by copying the top half of the accession sheet, although it is more practical to extract the location and accession numbers and record them on cards if more sophisticated systems are not available. A separate location index has the advantage of being easily updated when further work is done on the records and locations of individual containers change. It is also the best way of keeping track of different formats of material from the one accession which may be stored in different locations.

Preparing a Box or Container List

Earlier in this chapter the importance of listing the records prior to transfer was stressed. For a collecting archives, this will often not be possible as the archivist may not have enough time to list the material adequately before it arrives at the archives. If this is the case, preparing a box list becomes one of the steps in the accessioning process subsequent to transfer.

The main point of the box list is to provide physical control of the records at a container level – ie to indicate what material is in each box or container in a collection. Each container must have a distinguishing number that includes the accession number. Adding another number to the accession number will help identify the components of each accession. For example, 1995/1/10 represents the 10th container of the first accession of 1995.

Conclusion

The process of accessioning will provide a basic level of control over the records entrusted to your archives. It is a most important process in archival work. Accessioning needs to be completed as soon as possible after the receipt of records and is the foundation upon which all further archival work is based.

The completed accessions sheet, when copied, will provide several basic finding aids to the records. If time is limited, it is far better to have accessioned all your archives and so have a basic level of control over them all, than to have completely processed only a small part of your holdings while the bulk of the records remain unaccessioned.

Further Reading

See Chapter 8, Arrangement and Description.

8 | Arrangement and Description

Paul Brunton and Tim Robinson

An archives must have control over its holdings both for its own internal good management and so that the records will be available for use. The accessioning methodology described in Chapter 7 gives initial but limited control. It clearly defines the extent of a collection of records on the basis of its provenance and ensures that the collection does not become intermingled with other holdings. However, before records can be fully used for research they need to be identified and placed in context.

After accessioning, the sequence of steps by which the necessary degree of control is effected and recorded is known as arrangement and description. This chapter provides advice on how to identify records creators and establish series of records, with some emphasis on the processing of disordered material. It also gives advice on identifying, and, if necessary, restoring original order. It explains the notions of series, of records creators (the structural aspects of provenance) and of original order, concepts which are at the heart of traditional arrangement and description work. Often this work is rather like doing a jigsaw puzzle because the archivist is trying to fit all the different pieces together. He or she may have to return to the same place several times, each time gathering more clues as to how the different pieces fit into the overall pattern.

Arrangement is the process of physically organising records in accordance with the accepted archival principles of provenance and original order. Behind this physical process are a number of documentation processes which record the context of the records. Examining the records to determine their original order is the first phase of arrangement. The second phase is the physical reorganisation into that order, which may involve reboxing, labelling and shelving the records.

Description is the process of recording standardised information about the arrangement, contents and formats of the records so that persons reading the descriptions will be able to determine whether or not the records are relevant to their research (see also Chapter 9, Finding Aids).

Arrangement and description are interdependent activities and are normally undertaken together. The documentation processes involved in arrangement and based on provenance and original order are of great importance because archives, unlike books, draw much of their meaning from their context. Books, being discrete items, complete in themselves, can be catalogued and used and understood individually. However, archives, being the organic products of continuing work or life activities, can only be fully understood through a knowledge of why and how they were created and used over time. As one's life or business changes, these new directions are reflected in the records and provide important evidence for the researcher. Each collection of records is different and the amount of arrangement that is necessary will vary. Some collections may still be in their original order, while others will need extensive reorganisation either to restore the order in which they were created and used or to impose a new order if none previously existed.

Arrangement involves sequential activities. First, the archivist surveys the whole collection to discern whether or not the material, during its active life, was kept in any identifiable way. If so, the archivist records the method of arrangement and, if necessary, restores to its original arrangement any material that might have been disturbed or disordered.

In the process of arrangement the archivist will discover much about the creation of the material and the relationships between its various parts which, if not fully explained, will soon be forgotten. Users cannot be expected to examine the whole collection to determine how and why individual parts were created and what functions of the organisation or activities of the individual or family the constituent parts record. This information is vital if the records are to be fully understood.

Setting Priorities for Arrangement and Description

Arrangement and description, like all other archival functions, must be properly planned and made to fit in with an archives' other responsibilities. Whether the archives is in-house or collects material from a wide variety of organisations and individuals, the

archivist will need to set priorities for arrangement and description. The key questions to be answered in setting priorities are:
- Which collections to do first?
- What level of detail is required?
- How much time to spend on each collection?

Some collections will have a high priority because there is a known research demand for them, while others will have a lower priority because the basic control established during accessioning is sufficient for the time being. In an in-house archives priority may need to be given to the records of greatest significance to the functioning of the organisation, such as those of the board of directors or governing council.

Often it will be difficult to forecast how long the arrangement and description of a collection is likely to take, especially if the archivist's time is divided between several tasks. However, targets should be set and progress reviewed at regular intervals. It is helpful to remember that arrangement and descriptions are activities which reinforce archival control; they are not intended to provide an exhaustive interpretation of the records.

The Principles Governing Arrangement

The arrangement of a collection involves the identification and organisation of its various parts according to accepted archival principles.

Two basic principles of arrangement are followed worldwide and have developed over a long period: the principle of provenance and the principle of original order.

There have been many unsuccessful attempts to arrange archives in ways other than by following these principles. These other systems have generally tried to classify archives as if they were books in a library. On the surface they may offer a useful system for retrieval purposes, but they are actually a disservice to the material because they obscure much of its meaning. For example, any attempt to place archives into arbitrary subject classifications would involve the archivist in a great deal of unnecessary work, which would actually make the material harder to use. Information on the context of the records and their relationships with each other would be lost forever. Difficulties would be encountered in trying to determine in which category to place documents, as very few documents have only one subject. It would also be extremely difficult to predict the uses to which the documents would be put in the future and therefore to which subject classifications they should be assigned.

The Principle of Provenance

The term provenance in its structural aspects refers to the place of origin of the records, ie the organisation, office or person that created, received or accumulated and used the records in the conduct of business or personal life (see Chapter 1 for a fuller discussion of provenance).

As mentioned earlier, archives should not be intermingled with those of different provenances. Material created and/or received by a single individual or organisation or office within that organisation must be treated as a single collection and items should not be mixed either physically or intellectually with material of a different provenance. The following are some examples illustrating the importance of observing the principle of provenance.

Case Study 1

The widow of David Reid donates the papers and research material accumulated by her late husband to your archives. Included in the collection are letters addressed to David Reid, a number being from John Armstrong, a well-known local history teacher. The other letters are from members of significant and long-established families in the district. Before his death, David Reid had been preparing for the centenary of the history of the district's settlement and had been collecting information for use in celebration activities. Your archives already has a large volume of papers donated by John Armstrong and a great deal of other material relating to the families of the district.

It may be tempting to divide the letters from the David Reid collection on the basis of their authorship and to place them with other records by the same writers. However, to do this would be to ignore the principle of provenance. Even though the letters are written by various people, they were all sent to, and retained by, one person – David Reid. By separating them, you would be destroying the evidence of Reid's activity in preparing for the centenary celebrations. The information contained in the letters is not lost because they are not being placed with other material on similar subjects by the same authors. Good description and finding aids will clearly show where information on a particular subject may be found. What the finding aids cannot show is the information about David Reid's activity, work methods and the development of his research. These can only be gained by seeing his papers as he used them himself.

Case Study 2

The papers of Desmond Michael were deposited with an archives, however at the time little was known of his life or work. Included in the papers was a bundle of photographs of late nineteenth-century buildings with cast iron decoration. It was only discovered years later that Michael was interested in architectural history and was researching the history of a particular architectural iron foundry. If the provenance of the photographs had been ignored and they had been arranged on the basis of the building in each photograph on the assumption that this was the only information the photographs conveyed, important information would have been lost. First, the results and methods of the collector's research would have been destroyed. Second, the fact that the iron decoration on the buildings in the photographs was made by the foundry Michael was researching would be obscured. This was the reason the photographs were kept together originally, a fact, however, unknown at the time the photographs were received.

The Principle of Original Order

This principle states that records should be maintained in the order in which they were originally kept when in active use. It is not the order imposed on the material by someone who was not involved with the records while they were in active use (see Chapter 1).

This principle must be followed, ie the original order must be preserved unless it is absolutely clear that there was no original order and the material has been assembled haphazardly.

The original order does not have to be neat, easily understandable or obviously meaningful to be retained. If an order has been imposed on the papers by the original owner, this must be retained, for to do otherwise will destroy meaning in the material which may not be readily apparent or which needs special expertise to understand.

Reassembling original order has been compared with the restoration of a building, where the aim is to preserve all evidence of the various stages of the building's life. The aim is not to restore it to its condition when built, as this obliterates the historical development of the building by its owners and users. Likewise, reassembling the original order of records involves respecting the various changes made to the ordering of those records by their legitimate owners and users.

The original order of records is evidence of the way in which a particular activity was performed by an agency or person. It is evidence that individual documents alone cannot give. Papers on a file build up a record of the performance of some transaction, their order reflecting the order in which parts of the function were fulfilled. The total picture is revealed only by the totality of the individual documents in their original order, an example of the whole being greater than its parts. The understanding of provenance is related to original order, and in original order is part of the provenance of a record. Beyond knowing the name of a creating agency, an archivist must know what functions it performed and how these functions gave rise to the records, features which are often captured by the order of the records.

Case Study 3

You have just been appointed the first archivist for a small company which has been in business for 60 years. Your first job is to clear out a basement storeroom where all the old correspondence files for the last 50 years have been stored. Initially, the old files were stored on open shelving, then in boxes, and later it appears that staff just opened the door and threw the old files into the room. To complicate matters further, the boxes have broken and many files have fallen on to the floor.

On closer examination, things are not as bad as they first appeared. Although the files are scattered, they are still individually intact and all have covers with numbers or other annotations on them. The earliest files were arranged by subject, then an annual single number system was introduced. The last system used was a classified number system, ie one where the number denotes the function of the file (policy, personnel, legal, etc). Because of the filing system markings, putting the files back into order is quite straightforward, except for one portion. For the two years prior to a change in filing system, the old files have two sets of numbers: the old system and the one which replaced it. Renumbering files with new numbers is known as 'top numbering' and often leads to this sort of confusion. It would be incorrect to place these renumbered files with the older system. The top numbered files should be kept with the newer system as this represents a further stage in the active life of the records and so constitutes the original order. The later system has been imposed by those responsible for the papers during their active life and the subsequent change does not represent a disturbance but rather a continuity that should be respected and retained.

A system or order imposed on the material by someone not concerned with the active life of the records does not need to be respected as it does not reveal anything meaningful about the original use of the records. Therefore, this artificial arrangement will need to be examined to see if any clues to the original order remain. If so, material should, if possible, be rearranged to reflect the original scheme.

A particular case of the importance of original order can be found in Victorian family photograph albums. It is relatively easy to remove the images from the pages, because they are usually slipped rather than glued into place. However, photograph albums usually have some pattern or plan. In family albums, the photographs were often arranged by family hierarchy, ie father and mother followed by children then other relatives and their families. Even if no other information is known about the people in the photographs, their relationships to each other may be tentatively deduced from their arrangement in the album. This information would be lost if the original order were not maintained or recorded.

Preparing for Arrangement and Description

At the time of accessioning, the archivist will have given the collection an overall identifying Accession Number. This will serve to control the material intellectually and physically as the process of arrangement and description evolves.

Before attempting any work on an accession, the archivist should assemble source material which will reveal as much as possible about the organisation, individual or family who created, received or used the material. This will help the archivist to understand the background of the records and provide information useful later in the compilation of an administrative history or biographical note. The sort of information that the source material should record includes the following:

- For an organisation: the date of its establishment; its functions at that time and thereafter; the names of the various sub-units and their functions; names of principal officers; and any significant events or changes and their dates.
- For units within an organisation: title, allocated functions, activities and its relationship to the organisation as a whole.
- For an individual: dates of birth, marriage and death; changes of address; names of employers and types of work; special interests and significant activities; membership of associations, and offices held, with relevant dates.

The archivist should then examine the whole accession without disturbing the order or disorder of individual items. This initial inspection should be carried out in a large work area where there is no possibility of the material under inspection being moved, disturbed or intermingled by accident with other material held by the archives. A large desk with sorting shelves nearby is most suitable for this work. The archivist should have a pencil and notepad ready on which to record information about the types of material found and the rough dates.

Archives by definition are unique; they are also often fragile and usually contain within them the seeds of their own physical destruction. For all these reasons, archivists must take great care when handling records during arrangement and description. Always clean your hands before beginning any work which requires you to touch records, keep work surfaces clean and do not handle the records more than necessary. Very simple conservation measures such as removing pins, clips, staples and other fasteners can be undertaken.

However, measures should be taken to indicate the fact that certain items were previously fastened or pinned together, eg by placing those items in folders. Anything more complicated should not be attempted, and any damage to the records should be noted for the attention of a conservator.

This initial examination may also reveal desirable background information which has not been found elsewhere. For example, there may be an unpublished history of the organisation or biography of the person or there may be newspaper cuttings or other material which gives this information. Your notes should be kept in such a way that the collection can be reorganised and arranged on paper first before any physical rearrangement takes place.

During the examination of the records, you may discover confidential, sensitive or potentially embarrassing information. The archivist has privileged access to information and should not reveal it to unauthorised persons. It is part of the ethics of the archival profession that the archivist respects the confidentiality of the records entrusted to his or her care.

When processing a large collection, it might be found to be easier, and more productive of consistent results, if two people work on the entire collection together. One person can record the information, while the other examines the records. If your archives does not have enough staff available to do this, there are several other ways of organising arrangement and description work. One is to set aside a morning or afternoon when the archives is closed to outside researchers to work solely on sorting a large collection.

In examining a collection the archivist should ask the following questions about the material and record the resulting information in a systematic fashion. The information thus gained and recorded will be further refined to provide the final description. As you become more expert, you will find that you can quickly and accurately ascertain the following in many instances:

- Who created, or received, or compiled and maintained the record during its active life? For an organisation, which department or office created it and for what purpose? For an individual, in what capacity and for what purpose did he or she create the record? In the case of letters received, it is not the writer (ie the creator) of the original letter who is important in this context but the recipient. Copies of letters sent, retained by the writer for his or her own record, remain part of the writer's records, not part of those of the person who received the original letter.
- What is the type of record: diary, minute book, ledger, correspondence, publication, photograph or newscutting?
- What type of information does it record?

- What is the range of dates over which the material was created? These are the dates of the actual writing of the record, not the dates mentioned in the contents of the record.
- What is the arrangement of the material? Is it in some order? If so, what is the basis of the organisation? For example, is it alphabetical or chronological or arranged by some other system?
- In the case of volumes, is the whole volume used for the same purpose? For example, if it is a diary is all the volume used for that purpose, or does a section of it record financial transactions or the minutes of a meeting?

Archives, unlike books, do not set out to tell the user what they are. Therefore, do not automatically believe any title or description on a volume or bundle of papers. The archivist must look through the material to determine at first hand what it is. Before any physical rearrangement is undertaken, it may be necessary to examine the whole accession in this fashion a number of times. With each examination the archivist will become more familiar with the nature of the material and so will be in a better position to identify individual items and place them in their original relationship with other items. Arrangement and description are in fact one process. However, for ease of explanation, this chapter treats each process in turn.

Arrangement

First the archivist should ensure that the material of the same provenance has been identified. You will have attempted to have done this at the time of accessioning, but now you have the opportunity to review the earlier work in the light of your research into the creator of the records. You must ensure that only items of the same provenance have been brought together, as the arrangement of individual series items will now be determined.

To identify correctly the provenance of the records, it is necessary to know which person or office created, received and/or used the material. For this purpose, an organisational chart or family tree will be of great assistance. The archivist may need to compile this chart from the information obtained from the background research into the records. Information useful for this purpose may also be obtained during the initial inspection of the records themselves.

Identifying Series

The next step is to identify the component series. A series consists of records which have been brought together in the course of their active life to form a discrete sequence. This sequence may be a discernible filing system (classified, alphabetical, numerical, chronological or a combination of these) or it may simply be a grouping of records on the basis of similar function, content or format. The important factor is that the grouping was made during the records' active life. This applies to both organisational and personal records.

In an in-house archives the identification of series will often be quite simple as records transferred to the archives are likely to still be in the same order as when they were created and used. Most organisations arrange their records according to some identifiable system of filing so they can be easily retrieved and used. Each file or part of the series usually has an identifying number or symbol which clearly locates it within the series.

Particular attention should be paid to identifying those series that have begun their active life as the responsibility of one creator and have subsequently become the responsibility of another or of a succession of further offices. The series should be recorded under the provenance of the last office, but each of the preceding offices (provenances) should be noted for the period of its responsibility.

For example, the function of awarding and paying war pensions might first be undertaken by a department of veterans' affairs, the function may then be taken over by a department of social security and then it might become the function of a department of the aged. A series of records used to transact this business might be client files. It is necessary to identify the provenance of this series at each period of its history.

The following are some examples of series:

- Items arranged in accordance with a filing system. For example, this would include correspondence which has been arranged using an annual single number system, ie where each file has a distinguishing number consisting of the year and a sequential number; this would mean that the first file of 1956 would be number 56/1. Another example would be files which are arranged alphabetically by the title of the file.

- Items grouped together because of a similar function. Most items grouped together because of a similar function, such as a run of cash books, will also come into the category of items arranged in accordance with a filing system, even if this is simply placing the books on the shelf in chronological order.

- Items grouped together because of similar content. An example is a collection of papers kept together because they relate to a particular subject, such as a court case.

- Items grouped together because of similar format (eg photographs or sound recordings). It should be remembered, though, that it is not the form which determines whether a collection of items constitutes a series. In fact, the form of items within one series may change. A series is only determined by form when items of the same form have been kept together as a result of their creation, receipt or use. For example, photographs of students at a school would be a different series to photographs of building projects if the photographic records were created to perform different functions and were maintained by different offices, but would be considered the same series if they were part of a single documentation project.

In identifying series, the principle of original order must be applied. The archivist should determine what records have been brought together during their active life to form a single sequence.

A useful tool in identifying series and their original order is any contemporary finding aid to the records. For example, registers or indexes to correspondence can be of great assistance if a number of series have become confused. A register of letters received will provide the period of time the series was maintained, the order in which the letters were received, a summary of their content and details of how the letters were numbered on receipt. Indexes will not necessarily show the original order of the series they control, but they will give an indication of the filing system used and the scope of the records. The importance of these registers and indexes and other similar records is dealt with in Chapter 9, Finding Aids.

Often the archivist will be presented with donations of small quantities of material. These will have been accessioned on the basis of provenance. When only a folder or small bundle of individual documents is involved, the reconstruction of series may not be relevant. In this case a chronological arrangement, if feasible, based on the date of creation is probably the most advisable. However, this only applies to very small quantities of material and should be regarded as a last resort.

It will sometimes happen that an item is not related to any other item. In this case it is correct to leave it as a single item series and not attempt to force it into another series of which it is not naturally a part. There is no minimum size for a series. Obvious examples of single item series are a diary or a single photograph album.

Artificial Series

Where there is no discernible original order, then artificial series may need to be created. However, one must first be certain that there is in fact no order and that the material has been brought together haphazardly. Order in this context is not the same as orderliness. Just because a collection of papers looks messy does not mean that the person who used the papers during their active life did not have some order in the way individual documents were placed with other documents. The significance of this positioning of documents may not be immediately apparent to the archivist. Also, before imposing an artificial order, one should be absolutely certain that the chaos is not the result of subsequent disturbances of the collection, in which case the archivist must try to re-establish the order in which the papers were kept during their active life. If order is imposed, it should be clearly noted that the order of the collection is artificial and imposed by the archivist.

In establishing artificial series from material which shares the same provenance, items which record the same function should be brought together. The form of these items may change over time, but the form is not the only criterion for the series. For example, a series of ledgers may begin with bound volumes, change to loose leaf volumes and then become computer printouts. Despite the physical changes, the activity recorded remains unchanged, and so all these items may be looked on as part of the one series.

Decisions concerning the formation of artificial series often face the archivist when arranging collections of personal papers that contain letters. Letters received and copies of letters sent can be brought together to form series. Each of these series can be arranged chronologically or alphabetically by the name of the writer or the addressee. The method chosen by the archivist in establishing artificial series for letters will depend upon a number of factors. If the letters are undated, or inexact in dating, it will be better to arrange them alphabetically than to try to establish dates. If it is clear from examining the letters that they are more meaningful if grouped by writer or addressee than if arranged chronologically, this method should be adopted. It may be found, on examination of the letters, that a chronological arrangement will better reflect the 'flow of events' recorded by the letters. If so, they should be ordered chronologically. Similarly, it might sometimes be possible to form one series comprising both letters received and copies of letters sent. Once again, the determination as to whether this arrangement should be chosen will depend on it being of value in making the letters more meaningful.

It is emphasised that this discussion is only concerned with letters for which there is no original order to be maintained. It is a situation which is more likely to occur with personal papers than with organisational records.

The format of the records may be a useful key to establishing artificial series. Photographs are often kept together and so may constitute a series. However, in the absence of any information about the original arrangement of the material, function is a more important basis for creating artificial series, just as it is for identifying existing series. Photographs found included in files of correspondence would not be made a separate series just because they are photographs. Their function and meaning are dependent on their remaining a part of the correspondence series, although they might be stored separately.

In the papers of a real estate agent, for example, where there were family photographs and photographs of sale properties in no order, it would be better to form two series. Family photographs would become one series and photographs of sale properties another. This would better reflect the function of the records.

Determining function should result from a thorough examination of the records. Do not accept at face value what is written on spines or labels. For example, a collection of volumes labelled 'Finance Minute Books' when examined could be found to contain also the minutes of the security committee of the same organisation. Each of these sets of minutes forms a separate series because it records separate functions. Each set of minutes would be described as a separate series, although, of course, physically the two sets coexist within the same volumes.

The archivist will often find newscuttings clipped together or placed loosely in volumes. These should not be placed with other newscuttings to form a single series until a thorough examination has been undertaken to find out why particular newscuttings were kept together. Usually there is a reason, and separate series can be created on the basis of material that has been brought together to fulfil some function or because it relates to a particular subject or activity. Examples could be newscuttings relating to a court case or newscuttings written by or about a single individual which may have been kept together for these reasons. Remember, though, that newscuttings are not unique and that newsprint is of poor quality. The newscuttings must be judged to be very important to be retained in an archives.

In any archives there is likely to be large numbers of photographs. Often photographs are wrongly thought of as museum objects and not as archives. By now it should be clear that the format of the record is not relevant in deciding how it should be treated. What is important is that the provenance of a record be determined and recorded and that the original order of the records be respected and preserved. Photographs are therefore the same as any other record, and in order that their maximum informational value be preserved they must be accessioned, arranged and described like other records.

It might often seem the best solution to bring together all the photographs in a collection to form an artificial series. If there is no original order and photographs can be brought together by function, this is to be preferred. It is the function of a record which is more important than its form. For example, a series of photographs may have been taken by a local council specifically to document the demolition of buildings in its area. These photographs should be kept together and recorded as a series, just as other photographs produced for other purposes by the council should be kept as separate series reflecting the way they were created and used.

Often a series will not have a title of its own and the archivist will have to assign a title which accurately reflects the function and content of the records. In assigning titles it is of particular importance that terms are used consistently.

Description

Description is sometimes defined as the process of establishing intellectual control over the holdings through the preparation of finding aids. This chapter deals mainly with description of context. Chapter 9 deals with finding aids more generally.

The basic description document used in most repositories is the series description sheet. The purpose of this is to record a detailed description of the nature, contents and format of each series and relate it to its provenance. Examples of completed series description sheets follow (Tables 8.4, 8.5 and 8.6). The layout of the sheet may be adapted for individual needs providing the essential information is included.

In arranging an accession a great deal of information about each item will have been discovered, such as why it was created, by whom and its informational content. Each series must be described and an account given which places each series in its context in the whole accession. For records of organisations, this account is called an administrative history. For personal papers, a biographical note fulfils the same purpose.

Administrative History, Agency Description, Biographical Note

The organic nature of archives means that a description of each separate series alone will not adequately convey the full meaning and context of the records. Each collection needs to be seen as a whole with each of its constituent series placed in context. This is often done by means of an administrative history or biographical note. In addition, agency descriptions may also be completed (see Chapter 9). Whereas administrative histories usually relate to the entire organisation, agency descriptions detail individual units within the organisation.

In isolation an individual series may not provide information on its links with the rest of the collection or the reasons for its creation and demise. The reasons for changes (of form or function)

Table 8.1 Checklist of Sources

For the Administrative History of Organisations

The following is a guide to sources which should be consulted for background information about an organisation. Some may be obtained in libraries prior to the examination of the records, others will be found among the records of the organisation itself, usually in files categorised as policy, administration or history. The organisation may also have produced procedure manuals, handbooks or organisational charts which should also be consulted.

1 Legal instruments of creation, eg certificates of incorporation, articles of association, registration of company documents.
2 Constitutions, rules or by-laws.
3 Annual reports, published or unpublished.
4 Company records kept by various governmental authorities, eg bankruptcy records and those kept by the registrar of companies.
5 Histories of the organisation, either published or unpublished.
6 Published company and/or business directories.
7 Newspaper or journal articles or notices.
8 Interviews with present or former members of staff.

For Biographical Notes on Individuals and Families

As with organisations, the records of the individual or family itself should not be overlooked as a source of biographical information. Other sources include the following:

1 Records kept by government authorities, such as birth, death and marriage records, wills, bankruptcy records, immigration records, land records, musters and censuses, electoral rolls and cemetery records.
2 Records of organisations with which the individual or family may have been associated, eg educational institutions, churches, banks, clubs and societies or employers.
3 Biographies, autobiographies or family histories, either published or unpublished, and general histories which may include biographical detail.
4 Biographical dictionaries, both general and specific, eg those devoted to a particular trade or profession.
5 Directories, telephone books and gazetteers.
6 Newspapers and journals; articles and notices.
7 Interviews with the individual or family.

within a series need to be explained because it will not be self-evident. The reason for the very existence of some series may not be apparent without an overall history of the organisation or individual being given.

In writing an administrative history or biographical note, much information will be derived from the records themselves. However, it will be necessary to consult other sources to complete the details (see Table 8.1, Checklist of Sources). Tables 8.2 and 8.3 give examples of an administrative history and a biographical note.

Table 8.2 Administrative History

1	Name of Creator: Benlith Potteries Pty Ltd	2	Date Range: 1883–1958

3   Administrative History:

Benlith Potteries was founded by Irving Smith in 1883. It began manufacturing earthenware pipes and sanitary fittings and by 1895 also produced domestic china ware following the discovery of a deposit of high quality clay. Irving Smith died in 1893 and his business was bought by Seymour Wheeler. In May 1901 Benlith Potteries became a public company. Seymour Wheeler became Managing Director and his son, Josiah, became General Manager. He remained General Manager until 14 August 1919 when he was succeeded by Cedric Ives. Ives was General Manager from 1919 to 31 March 1930. He was succeeded by Colin Pitts who remained General Manager until the company's dissolution on 31 March 1958.

4   References:

Wells Industrial Gazetteer, 1885–1913.

Peterson, A., *An Informative Treatise on the History and Development of Sanitary Ware in the Colonies*, Atlanta, 1899.

Boyd, R. (ed.) *Biographical Dictionary of Plumbing*, Wagga, Vic., 1978.

5	Name of Preparer: C. Conway	6	Date of Completion: 23 Dec. 1986

Series Description Sheet

A series description sheet should include the following information. The headings Related Series and Notes will not always be used, but entries should be made under the other headings. When abbreviations are used in the series description sheet, or in any other documentation, care must be taken to ensure that these abbreviations are standardised throughout the archives. Examples of series description sheets are shown in Tables 8.4, 8.5, and 8.6. (Points 1-14 below correspond to each table.)

1   **Provenance.** This records the organisation, agency of that organisation, person or family that created, received or accumulated and used the records in the conduct of business or personal life. This links the series with other series with the same provenance.

2   **Series Number.** This is a discrete number allocated to each series from the series register (further discussed later).

3   **Series Title.** This names the series. The series title should be succinct and incorporate the type of record and reflect the function it performs, eg Applications for Registration of Motor Vehicles. If the creator of the records has assigned a name to the series this must be used though it may sometimes need amplification. If there is no assigned title, the archivist will need to assign one. It should be noted if this is done.

Table 8.3 Biographical Note

1	Name of Creator: Phillip Hall	2	Date Range 1 Apr 1930-

3 Biographical Note:

Journalist. Born in Blackwell. Hall began work as a copy boy with the Blackwell Gazette after leaving Blackwell High in 1945. He became a journalist in 1950 and took a special responsibility for the history of the Blackwell area. He was a founding member of the Blackwell Historical Society in 1949 and became President in 1956, an office he held continuously except from 1964 to 1969 when he was overseas. In 1955 he married Annabelle Roberts. He served on the Blackwell Council from 1960 to 1963, the final year as Mayor. He has published three books: *Blackwell Municipal Council: A Centennial History*, 1956; *The Roberts Family and Their Circle*, 1970; and *History of Blackwell*, 1976.

4 References:

Who's Who in Blackwell, Camford Press, Blackwell, 1974. Hall, Emilia, *The Halls of Blackwell*, Oxbridge Press, Blackwell, 1972.

5	Name of Preparer: C. Conway	6	Date of Completion 8 June 1980

4 **Date Range.** This should show the earliest and latest date of the material, any significant gaps or concentrations. For this purpose, the date is the date when an item was created not the date of its subject. For example, the date range of the correspondence of a historian of medieval times which discusses medieval history is the dates during which the correspondence was written, not the dates of its subject. The date of a copy of an item, either a photocopy or a typescript copy, is the date when the original was created, not the date when the photocopy or typescript was made, although contents' date ranges may sometimes be given separately.

5 **Quantity.** Use a consistent standard of measurement. The accepted standard of measurement is to record the shelf space occupied by a series in metres. If the series has only a small quantity of material, the number and type of containers may also be recorded.

6 **Physical Characteristics/Condition.** This is a description of the physical characteristics of the items in the series. For example, are the items handwritten, typescript, a combination of both, reproduced in some way, newscuttings, or printed? Are they bound volumes, loose sheets, or files? Are they photographic prints, photographic negatives, or sound recordings?

7 **Content Description.** The important things to be mentioned in this section are: the relationship of the records to the work of the creating office or person, the types of records and the types of information contained therein, and representative or exceptional matters or transactions conducted.

8   **Arrangement.** This is the manner in which the records are arranged, ie chronologically, alphabetically, according to a classified system. If the arrangement has been imposed by the archivist this must be recorded.
9   **Related Series.** Series which have a direct and significant connection to this series, eg file control records such as indexes or registers and, in the case of copies of letters sent, letters received, would be mentioned under this entry.
10 **Access Conditions.** This documents the existence of any restrictions on access and the conditions affecting the supply of copies of items or information from the records, including copyright information.
11 **Notes.** This records anything the archivist feels should be recorded about the series that has not been recorded elsewhere and may be of use to persons using the records.
12 **Shelf List** (including contents note). A shelf list is a listing by identifying number of the contents of each container or freestanding item such as a volume. The contents note should clearly establish what is contained in each box so that researchers may choose appropriate records with precision. Usually, the information presented will identify the first and last unit of material in the box. This is basic for physical control of the holdings. The location of each container should be given. To simplify the location of containers, each shelf in the repository should be numbered.
13, 14 **Name of Preparer and Date Completed.** For future reference it is important to know who prepared the description and the date it was completed.

Additions to Series

In an in-house archives it will often occur that regular additions to series are transferred to the archives as the material becomes non-current. Often this can be planned for as the material will be transferred under a records disposal schedule. For example, correspondence files more than ten years old may be transferred every ten years. Similarly, in a collecting archives, additions to series may arrive as further material is unearthed or becomes non-current. Once material has been assessed as truly part of a series already held by the archives, it will be necessary to revise the series description sheet to incorporate the additional material. The Date Range and Quantity will need to be changed and perhaps additional information will need to be supplied under Physical Characteristics, Description and Notes. The Shelf List will need to be adjusted and the Series Register annotated to indicate the additional material.

Table 8.4 Series Description Sheet

1 Provenance: Phillip Hall	2 Series Number: 41

3 Series Title: Research Papers for the *History of Blackwell*

4 Date Range: Mar. 1959–Aug. 1963, Jan. 1970–Nov. 1975	5 Quantity: 1m

6 Physical Characteristics/Condition:
Manuscript, typescript, carbon typescript with manuscript corrections. Notebooks, loose sheets, correspondence, newscuttings. The notebooks show water damage.

7 Content Description: (Relationship to work of office/creator, types of information contained therein, representative/exceptional matters mentioned):
The material consists of notebooks kept by Hall during his reading of original sources, newscuttings from local papers, correspondence with various libraries and archives and local families. Includes three letters, 1962, from William Davis, novelist and former resident of Blackwell, concerning his childhood there. Some of the bundles include various drafts for Hall's *History of Blackwell*, published in 1976. The records end in 1963 and begin again in 1970 because during the intervening period Hall was overseas.

8 Arrangement:
Twenty bundles, each referring to a particular subject or person. Filed alphabetically by title.

9 Related Series:

10 Access Conditions:
Available for consultation. Permission to copy must be obtained from Mr Hall.

11 Notes:

12 Shelf List:

Container No.	Brief Contents Note	Location
41/1	Aborigines Blackwell Council Blackwell Family Blackwell Gazette Blackwell Lodge Court House Dairy Cooperative	Shelf 29/1
41/2	Davis Family First Settlement Gold Rush Hotels Land Scandal Majestic Picture Palace Moss Family	Shelf 29/2
41/3	Piper Family Roberts Family School Trade Transport War Memorial Women	Shelf 29/3

13 Prepared By: C. Conway	14 Date Completed: 6 Aug. 1980

Table 8.5 Series Description Sheet

1 Provenance: Benlith Potteries Pty Ltd	2 Series Number: 56

3 Series Title:
General Manager – Copies of Letters Sent

4 Date Range: May 1901 – Mar. 1958	5 Shelf Quantity: 5m

6 Physical Characteristics/Condition:
Press-copy letterbooks, carbon typescript volumes and loose bundles. From 20 May 1901 to 31 December 1910 copies of letters were kept in press-copy books. Five volumes each with index at front. From 2 January 1911 to 31 December 1935 copies were kept on carbon typescripts which were pasted into volumes. Twenty-five volumes, each with an index. From 2 January 1936 to 13 March 1958, copies were kept on carbon typescripts which were kept in loose bundles one bundle for each year. Twenty-three bundles with one index kept on cards files at 58/1.

7 Content Description:
(Relationship to work of office/creator, types of information contained therein, representative/exceptional matters mentioned):
Series comprises copies of business letters sent to clients and suppliers of Benlith Potteries Pty Ltd. Major matters of business discussed include purchases of chemicals for glazes, additives for producing various grades of pottery, prospective orders for customers wishing unique items, marketing strategies and conditions. Also included are a few letters (20 August 1915 to 1 February 1917) written by Mr Josiah Wheeler in his capacity as Secretary of the Patriotic Fund in the Benlith area.

8 Arrangement:
Chronological. Each volume contains index, card index exists for loose bundles.

9 Related Series:
Series 55, General Manager – Letters Received. Series 57, Register of Letters Received. Series 58, Index to Letters Sent.

10 Access Conditions:
Open

11 Notes:
Originals fragile. Issue microfilm (Microfilm 34).

12 Shelf List:

Container No.	Brief Contents Note	Location
56/1	May 1901–Dec. 1902	Shelf 1
56/2	Jan. 1903–Dec. 1904	Shelf 1
56/3	Jan. 1905–Dec. 1906	Shelf 1
56/4	Jan. 1907–Dec. 1908	Shelf 2
56/5	Jan. 1909–Dec. 1910	Shelf 2

(series continues on additional sheets)

13 Prepared By: P. Foster	14 Date Completed: 19 Nov. 1968

Table 8.6 Series Description Sheet

1 Provenance: Jonathan Williams	2 Series Number: 28

3 Series Title:
Williams Family Portraits

4 Date Range: *c.* 1846–1956	5 Quantity: 0.34m

6 Physical Characteristics/Condition:
1 sixth plate daguerreotype; 2 half-plate ambrotypes; 3 100x60mm tintypes; 25 cartes-de-visite in one album, 10 cabinet portraits, 1 framed black and white photograph with hand colouring 700x500mm; 1 octavo album with twenty silver gelatine photographs. The daguerreotype is tarnished.

7 Content Description: (Relationship to work of office/creator, types of information contained therein, representative/exceptional matters mentioned):
Portrait photographs of members of the Williams Family. The photographs were collected by Jonathan Williams in the course of his family research. They cover three generations of the Williams Family. Most are identified and dated except for some of the cartes-de-visite. The daguerreotype of Edward Williams c. 1846 is by Freeman Bros. of Sydney, NSW and the ambrotypes are by T. S. Glaister also of Sydney. The twentieth century photographs were all taken by members of the family.

8 Arrangement:
Chronological (order imposed by archives).

9 Related Series:
Series 29 Williams Family Research Papers; Series 30 Williams Family Correspondence.

10 Access Conditions:
Available for research use. 28/1–28/3 and 28/15 may only be viewed under supervision. Copying permitted by donor, subject to Copyright Act.

11 Notes:

12 Shelf List:

Container No.	Brief Contents Note	Location
28/1	Edward Williams, daguerreotype, *c.*1846	Safe 1
28/2	Josephine Williams, ambrotype, *c.*1860	Safe 1
28/3	Maybelle Williams, ambrotype, *c.*1860	Safe 1
28/4	Williams family album, cartes-de-visite *c.*1865–1878	Shelf 18
28/5–14	Williams Family members, cabinet portraits *c.*1880-1890	Shelf 18
	Edward Williams Jr	
	Josie Williams	
	Belle Williams Jones	
	Fred Williams	
	Thomas Williams	
	Mary Williams Brown	
	Frank Jones	
	Bill Brown	
	Frank Jones Jr	
	unidentified infant	
28/15	Moses Williams family album, 20 silver gelatine prints, *c.*1950–1956	Shelf 18
28/16	Josiah Williams framed portrait,*c.* 1915	Framed Storage

13 Prepared By: M. Griffith	14 Date Completed: 20 July 1962

A Note about the Description of Photographs

Particular features of photographs should be borne in mind when describing them. Photography is a relatively recent phenomenon, 1839 usually being accepted as its beginning date. During the nineteenth century, photography went through a number of significant developments which people unfamiliar with the history of this record medium sometimes find intimidating.

The changes are quite simple to understand when set in their historical context, and the identification of the different processes becomes straightforward. All archivists have the responsibility to be knowledgeable about the records in their care. Just as an archivist who deals with early twentieth-century paper records should know the difference between a press copy and a carbon copy, an archivist should be able to tell a daguerreotype from an ambrotype if he or she deals with early photographic records.

In describing photographs it is essential to be able to identify the process used to produce the record. This information is of great importance for the conservation of the records and is also of great value in determining their date range.

Some processes are also rare and so have their own intrinsic value as examples of the process which is important in the history of photography.

As with the creator of any record, the photographer's name is a vital piece of information in the description of any photographic record, and it must be recorded on the series description sheet if it can be discovered.

No attempt will be made here to provide an account of the various processes or of the history of photography. It is recommended that any archives which includes photographs, and it would be an unusual collection that did not, should acquire some standard texts on the history of photography. The archivists should become familiar with the different processes.

For conservation and storage requirements, it is often decided to remove photographic records from textual records and store them separately. This is acceptable, but where it is done the accession register, series description sheet and other finding aids must have the location annotated accordingly. It is also good practice to include a separation sheet (such as used for museum objects) when photographs are removed from a collection. An example of a separation sheet is given in Table 8.7. Photographs, like any segment of a collection, have strong ties to the records surrounding them, and often only their context reveals their true significance. It is therefore important that a user of a particular collection be aware that photographs form an integral part of it and that they have been stored apart from the papers. A particular example of the links between records of different media may be a photograph enclosed with a letter or a diary accompanied by travel photographs.

Table 8.7 Separation Sheet

Series:	Series Number:
Item(s) removed by:	Date:
Description of material separated:	Action taken:
(Give original container number and type of material, eg photograph, map, drawing, printed material, medal)	(Give details of recipient, new storage locations as appropriate)

Table 8.6 provides an example of a completed series description sheet for photographic records. Further information on the management of photographic records can be found in Chapter 13, Managing Records in Special Formats.

Shelving the Records

Once the intellectual arrangement of the records has been determined, the records themselves may have to be reordered. The material should be physically arranged into the various series which have been determined, and individual items can be numbered to reflect this arrangement if there are no existing control symbols to do the job for you. This is important when some items may need to be separated for conservation or storage reasons, and it also helps to control the issue of items to researchers. Just as the intellectual control of a collection has been refined in the description process, its physical control is refined at this stage of the arrangement process.

The next step is the final boxing of the material for placement on the shelves. Boxing should be done by series, making an effort not to put more than one series in a container unless too much space would be wasted. Conservation is a major consideration here since the records will remain in storage for most of their lives. Oversized materials and some media may require special boxes or storage locations which should be noted on the series description sheet under shelf list.

As all material may not be able to be stored together, the numbering system is the link between the individual items and the intellectual arrangement of the material which has been determined on paper. Any imposed numbering system is only a device for locating or issuing items and, unlike library classifications, does not have any intrinsic significance. It should be as simple as possible. The essential element of a numbering system is that each container or freestanding item, such as a volume, must have a unique number.

Each series is given a number, beginning at 1 and having no upper limit. All series in the archives, no matter what their format, whether paper documents, photographs or magnetic tape, are numbered from the same sequence. For this purpose, a series register which records what numbers have been assigned to which series must be maintained (see Table 8.8 for an example).

Not all the parts of a single series may be received in the one accession. Therefore, a single series may be formed from two, three or more separate accessions as illustrated by Series 45 in Table 8.8. A series register may also record other details, such as cumulative date range, quantity and location of the records, particularly if it can be easily updated.

Having prepared the boxes and listed their numbers and contents under 12) Shelf List on the appropriate series description sheets, it now remains to assign them a shelf location within the storage area. Most archives have a numerical system for designating spaces on shelves. For a discussion of these, see Chapter 2, Getting Organised. A quick check of the master space allocation sheet should reveal available spaces for new material in the storage area. Do not worry about keeping all the boxes of one series together if it is not possible. Archives systems are designed to allow random shelving. All that is important for future access is for each container to have a unique number and a unique 'address' in the storage area. When the material is placed on the shelf, the shelf number should be recorded on the outside of the container or unboxed item as well as entered on the appropriate series description sheet under item 12 Shelf List: Location.

The Final Steps

Now all the series description sheets and administrative histories or biographical notes for the one collection can be placed together in a folder, if your system is still paper-based. At this point,

Table 8.8 Series Register

Series Number	Provenance	Series Title	Accession Numbers
41	Phillip Hall	Research Papers for *History of Blackwell*	1980/13
42	Blackwell Sports Club	Minute Books	1980/14, 1984/29
43	Blackwell Sports Club	Correspondence Files	1980/14, 1984/29
44	Mavis McIntyre	Group Portraits	1980/15
45	Stephen Jones with C. Smith	Taped Interviews	1980/17, 1980/22, 1990/11

attention is paid to the sequence of the individual series description sheets, as their order should reflect the structure of the collection. For example, in the case of records of an organisation the folder would represent the overall administrative history, then move through each creating office as through an organisational chart. The individual series description sheets would be placed under each creating office in a sequence that reflected their importance for that office's work.

A title page might be added to the folder indicating the name of the collection of records, followed by a table of contents. Altogether, the folder with its label, the title/contents page, the administrative history/biographical note and the individual series description sheets comprise the descriptive inventory or collection guide, which are described in more detail in Chapter 9, Finding Aids.

The final step is to recheck all the documentation in the folder to ensure that the notes and numbers are all correct before the production of the final version. When the polished description is completed, it can be photocopied and placed in the reading room as a preliminary descriptive inventory of the collection which is now fully ready for research use.

Conclusion

The methodology suggested above is one which has proved useful in a number of Australian contexts. It is offered as a basic framework for thought about records creators, series and original order. With the advent of computerised systems (discussed elsewhere in this book), standardisation (a relatively new prospect in Australia) and expanded concepts of provenance, the arrangement and description process seems poised to enter a new phase. Within this new dynamism, however, there will remain the stimulation of tackling archival jigsaws – of teasing out the creator of records, the series within which the records were ordered and the relationship of the items to the whole. The importance of this activity to the use of records also will remain, along with the stimulation such activities provide for archivists themselves.

Further Reading

Bearman, David A. and Lytle, Richard H., 'The Power of the Principle of Provenance', in *Archivaria,* 21, Winter 1985–86, pp. 14–27.

Berner, Richard C., 'Arrangement and Description of Manuscripts', in Richard J. Lytle (ed.), *Management of Archives and Manuscript Collections for Librarians*, Society of American Archivists, Chicago, 1980.

Collings, T. J., *Archival Care of Still Photographs*, Information Leaflet No. 2, Society of Archivists, Sheffield UK, 1984.

Cox, Richard J., *Managing Institutional Archives*, Greenwood Press, Westport, 1992, ch. 5.

Gracy II, David B., *Archives and Manuscripts: Arrangement and Description*, Society of American Archivists, Chicago, 1977.

Hensen, Steven L., *Archives, Personal Papers and Manuscripts: A Cataloguing Manual for Archival Repositories, Historical Societies and Manuscript Libraries*, 2nd edn, Society of American Archivists, Chicago, 1989.

Hill, Edward E., 'The Preparation of Inventories at the National Archives', in Maygene Daniels and Timothy Walch (eds), *A Modern Archives Reader: Basic Readings on Archival Theory and Practice*, National Archives and Records Service, Washington DC, 1984, pp. 211–35 [also readings in Parts 5 and 6 of this book].

Hurley, Christopher, 'Personal Papers and the Treatment of Archival Principles', in *Archives and Manuscripts,* 6/8 February, 1977, pp. 351–65.

Macneil, Heather, 'Weaving Provenancial and Documentary Relations', *Archivaria,* 34, Summer 1992, pp. 192–97.

Miller, Frederic M., *Arranging and Describing Archives and Manuscripts*, Society of American Archivists, Chicago, 1990.

Ritzenthaler, Mary Lynn, Munoff, Gerald J. and Long, Margery S., *Archives and Manuscripts: Administration of Photographic Collections*, Society of American Archivists, Chicago, 1984.

Thibodeau, Sharon G. 'Archival Arrangement and Description', in J. G. Bradsher (ed), *Managing Archives and Archival Institutions*, Mansell Publishing, London, 1988.

9 | Finding Aids

Jennifer Edgecombe

What Are Finding Aids?

Finding aids lead researchers to the information they are seeking from or about archives. They may be generally defined as the descriptive media (such as registers, guides, inventories and indexes) that establish physical and intellectual control over the holdings of an archives and make it possible to retrieve particular records or information from these archives.

The arrangement and description processes discussed in Chapter 8 produce descriptions of the records, arranged according to provenance, providing a structural view of the records. The finding aids present this information in a variety of ways, supplementing it with additional information and indexes to help users find their way into the records. The purpose of this chapter is to outline the main elements of finding aids and to highlight the principal issues involved in producing them.

Traditionally, the recording of information about archives has been broken into discrete activities, with each activity having its own form of documentation. This has resulted in some of the same information about records being recorded a number of times during appraisal, accessioning, arrangement and description, and the production of finding aids. Agency and collection names, series titles, date ranges, quantities and information about records creators have often been recorded repeatedly. The increasing automation of archival control systems means that it should be possible to record this type of information in a computer system just once. The relevant elements can be extracted when a particular aspect of the documentation is required.

This integration of the documentation process should lead to greater flexibility for finding aids. A wide variety of different finding aids can be generated from the one set of information. The archivist is not limited to particular content and formats. The scope of these finding aids may range from a general overview of the archives' entire holdings to descriptions of individual series and to specific items of interest within series. They may feed into networked systems or be entirely local in purpose and distribution or access.

Physically, the system of finding aids for an archival institution can consist of a variety of formats including pamphlets, books, looseleaf folders, optical disks, microfilms, card indexes and computer databases. If the finding aids are effective, they assist in the preservation of material by reducing the handling of archives needed to locate information.

The information about the records and their creators produced earlier in the documentation process forms the core of the finding aids system. It shows the original context of the records – the major creating agencies, the series they recorded, the relationships between series with recordkeeping systems and detailed listings of the series. This information shows how and why the records were created and how they are related to other records produced by that administration or individual. It is important to convey information about the purposes, functions or activities which gave rise to the records as well as details of the physical records themselves.

The archivist has an obligation to maintain a view of the records in the context in which they were created. Apart from the moral defence of the archives, this is necessary because the demands which will be made on the records for information cannot be predicted. For example, a corporation might use its archives to check on previous policy, to provide evidence for a court case or to produce an advertising campaign. Outside researchers might require information about the corporation's history, its buildings, an uncle who worked there, or its relations with employees. Finding aids which reveal the original structure and function of the records aim to ensure maximum flexibility for future users through their reconstruction of the original recordkeeping systems, rather than by presenting the archivist's interpretation of the records.

Researchers often do not find it easy to relate their enquiries directly to finding aids based on provenance. Most enquiries refer to the name of a person or organisation, to a particular date, to a geographical area, to a particular format (photograph, map, plan, diary), to a building, to an event, or to a combination of these, rather than to the administrative framework of the records. The archivist should be sensitive to this gap between the researcher's information needs and the structure of traditional finding aids.

For this reason, archivists prepare ancillary aids such as indexes, special lists and source analyses to help the researcher to link a subject query to the creating agencies whose functions might relate to that subject. It becomes possible to retrieve particular records or information by using a range of reference points, such as format, date, function, name and subject.

It is important that the system of finding aids is user-friendly. Inadequate finding aids can undermine all the effort expended on arrangement and description. Users may be deterred by a disjointed collection of lists and descriptions. They may tire of waiting for assistance, because they need intensive help from the reference archivist. If they persist alone, they may simply fail to locate information which is actually there.

A clear, well-planned system of finding aids which helps users to progress independently alleviates these problems. Users need less assistance from the reference archivist, although they may still need assistance to infer the functions which might involve a particular topic and the agencies which carry out these functions.

Institutions everywhere are under pressure to justify their existence by showing that they are performing well. Improved finding aids lead to a more efficient use of resources. The needs of more clients can be better served. What better performance indicators could we offer?

The Variety of Finding Aids

There is no mandatory list of finding aids which every archival institution must produce. An appropriate system of aids should be developed for each one. For example, while most archives using the Australian Archives CRS system would create an inventory of record-creating agencies and an inventory of series, each institution may produce additional indexes, special listings and supplementary finding aids specific to its own holdings. For example, a local government archives might add a list of past mayors and an index for the council minutes.

Rigidly prescribing the elements and format of specific finding aids is pointless, particularly in view of the impact of automation. However, if their purpose, scope and major elements are considered, most finding aids fall into one of seven major types. The finding aids created by an institution should form a network, with common elements such as series titles or record-creating agency titles to link them. Remember that there is no hard and fast rule about which elements are contained in each type. The distinctions will frequently be blurred, but most archival institutions produce finding aids in each of the following types:

General Guides. These include summary information about the holdings of a number of archival institutions. Each institution contributes its own information.

Guide to the Finding Aids. This gives a brief overview of the system of finding aids for an institution, showing how they are related and how to use the system.

Summary Guides. This structural finding aid provides a contextual summary of all the record-creating agencies or individuals whose records are held in the archives and brief details of the series they created. It shows the relationships between the records.

Inventories of Agencies, Series or Items. These lists show the provenance and original order of records, and are accompanied by context information and indexes. This is the central part of the finding aids system.

Control Records Produced by the Creators of Records. These include indexes, registers, computerised information, computer-assisted paper-based recording systems, and metadata for electronic information systems.

Indexes and Special Lists. These give access to the other categories through various reference points such as function, date,

A selection of finding aids from an archives using a variation of the CRS system: (clockwise from bottom left) General Guide to Holdings, volume of Agency and Series Registrations, volume of Series Records and Consignments and Item Lists, Index to Agencies, and a Guide to the Finding Aids.

subject and format. They are sometimes known as subject finding aids.

Supplementary Finding Aids. These are collections of background information, special subject guides for popular research topics and source analyses prepared when handling reference requests.

Table 9.1 summarises the scope and content generally associated with each of these categories.

Major Categories of Finding Aids

This section deals with each of the seven major categories of finding aids in more detail, indicating the different features of each category and the purposes for which they are used.

General Guides to Holdings

The purpose of these guides, which include directories of archives and reports of holdings, is to publicise summary information about different archives and their holdings. They can be assembled at an international, national, state or regional level. Some give an overview of holdings and services, as in *The Directory of Archives in Australia*, published by the ASA; some are topic-based, like directories of material relating to lighthouses or to immigration. Others report information on individual collections held by contributing institutions. This last kind, formerly published in hard copy or microfilm, is now usually accessed through national or international networked databases.

Common Elements of Directories

The entry supplied by each institution generally contains
- basic contact information for the institution's address, phone number and opening hours
- a brief description of the holdings, ranging from a statement of collecting areas to the names of major creating agencies or individuals and the titles of selected significant and/or frequently used series
- access conditions – reader's ticket, restrictions on particular records, where applicable.

General guides to holdings are usually encountered outside an institution and they will often be the first point of contact with a researcher. Their purpose is to publicise and provide information about holdings (and, in the case of directories, services) to both the research and archival communities.

Table 9.1 Major Categories of Finding Aids: Types, Scope and Content

Type	Scope	Content
General Guides	Many institutions in an area, state, country or internationally	Standardised summary of information about holdings of each, plus index; sometimes based on a specific subject
Guide to Finding Aids	A single institution	List of finding aids and how to progress through them
Summary Guides	Holdings of a single institution	Overview of the holdings – administrative history, agencies and series
Inventories	Part of the holdings of a single institution; sometimes a single agency within the institution	Descriptions of record-producing agencies, series and items, plus background indexes, lists and supplementary finding aids
Control Records Produced by Creating Agencies	A record-creating agency or individual	Registers, indexes and other retrieval aids for the creators
Indexes and Special Lists	Ancillary aids to any of the other categories or to selected records	Subject, title, function, format, medium and date entries with references leading to specific aids or records
Supplementary Finding Aids	Subject areas for which there is a high demand	Subject guides and back ground information compiled from source analyses, secondary sources and reference enquiries

Guide to the Finding Aids

This guide introduces the reader to the particular institution and its finding aids. It is intended as an on-site orientation to the archives. This guide lists the finding aids and shows the user how to progress from one to another within the system. It often outlines the nature of the holdings and the system of arrange-ment and description. In some institutions this introduction is provided on videotape, while in others it may be provided as a pamphlet, wall posters or tape/slide presentations.

This guide is especially important for the novice researcher and should be set out as clearly and simply as possible.

Summary Guides

A summary guide as a finding aid is often produced when the collection has grown in size and complexity. A need then emerges for an overview of the collection. Cambridge University Archives, for example, has produced such a guide. Specialised guides existed for various parts of the collection, but there was nothing to show the overall context of the records and the relationships between them.

The summary guide introduces the reader to the holdings of an institution – acquisition policy, scope of the holdings or how the whole collection came about, inventories of creating agencies and usually series titles and date ranges, how to use the records and what finding aids exist. It illustrates not only the creating agencies or individuals but also any connections between them and the record series attached to each. Connections between series are shown. The guide also gives an overall map of the collection.

The *Guide to the Archives of the Legislative Assembly of New South Wales* (Part 2, 1988) illustrates some of the characteristic features of summary guides. An introduction gives the administrative history of the lower house of the NSW Parliament and the history of its records. A section gives advice on citation of the records. The main part of the guide contains sections on each of the major groups of series within the collection, accompanied by explanations of the parliamentary process as it relates to these.

The *Guide to Records of the United States Senate at the National Archives, 1789–1989* is another published guide to an institutions records. In addition to the features already mentioned, it discusses the most common research uses of the material. It contains a comprehensive index and references to noteworthy individual items. It highlights related sources throughout and contains bibliographies, details of microfilm and other National Archives finding aids, plus table summaries and timelines tables.

In its summary guide an institution includes the elements useful for approaching its particular holdings, taking into account the other finding aids which have been prepared.

Inventories

Inventories built around series descriptions form an excellent basis for an institution's in-house finding aids system. Much of the initial work on descriptive standards involved analysis of the existing finding aids prepared by archival institutions. Finding aids based on series descriptions are the most common and the most consistent, probably because they provide for both management and retrieval purposes. Inventories present series descriptions in the context of the agencies or individuals which produced them.

Supplementary aids are added, including explanatory and background notes, control records produced by the records creators, and some of the indexes and special lists described in later sections to give researchers a range of access points.

It is important to note that these inventories consist of networks of interrelated aids, and they will not necessarily be contained in a single volume or computer database – they could be a combination of card indexes, looseleaf folders, published volumes and computer records. For some institutions, inventories are very closely associated with a summary guide.

The following sections describe two popular methods of presenting inventories.

Descriptive Inventories

The components of a descriptive inventory include the following:

Title Page. This contains the title of the finding aid, incorporating the proper name and citation of the collection or group of archives, the name of the individual or office responsible for producing the finding aid, the name of the archival repository and the date of completion of the aid.

Table of Contents.

Preparer's Notes. This sets out the major decisions made in producing the finding aid, including the influence of original classification systems and recordkeeping systems. There are instructions for using the inventory, lists of symbols or abbreviations, an explanation of control symbols used, the proper form for citations, and any acknowledgments.

Introduction to the Records. This contains the history of the records, why they are important (in their own time and in retrospect) and how they came to the archives. Gaps are explained where appropriate. Anything unusual about how the records were created or accumulated is explained, particularly for personal records.

Administrative History. This gives brief highlights (1500 words or less) of the individual's career and life or the organisation's foundation, development and major programs. Special lists and supplementary finding aids such as organisation charts, timelines and lists of chief officials can be included here.

Series Descriptions. The series descriptions should be presented in context to show their relationships. If the inventory is for a record group, the series descriptions will be grouped in categories which usually reflect provenance, ie the hierarchy of an organisation, the key divisions in an individual's work or life or the functions the records supported (eg accounting, policy or teaching). Arrangement of categories usually follows a hierarchy of importance or date. For each category there will be

- information about the particular activities of the office or individual(s) who created the records.
- the series descriptions for that category. This might simply consist of abbreviated series registrations, omitting such information as donors' personal details which would be inappropriate on a public finding aid. There should also be information about relevant control records prepared by the records creators, item lists, conditions of use and other related finding aids and records.

Indexes and Other Listings. There might be separate indexes of series titles, subjects and names, or any of these might be combined. If the inventory is for an organisation, the functions performed by various sub-sections of the organisation might be included.

Bibliography. The published and unpublished works used to prepare the inventory will assist researchers who require further background.

Interconnected Inventories of Agencies, Series and Items

Interconnected inventories are prepared by institutions using the Australian Archives CRS System. This system of arrangement and description lends itself to the preparation of finding aids which link information about the creators of records to information about the records themselves. Series usually form the link between these inventories, through series identification numbers. Appendix 1 outlines the inventory system developed by the Public Record Office, Victoria based on CRS system principles.

The common components of an interconnected inventory system include the following:

Inventory of Agencies. This inventory is based on the documentation of the record-creating agencies or individuals. For each agency, an administrative history is produced, indicating related, predecessor and successor agencies. Biographical notes are produced for an individual. A list of the series created by that agency accompanies each agency registration, with appropriate titles and control numbers for locating the series descriptions.

Functions Index to Agencies. This is one of the most important aids to linking the usual subject-based query to the records of a person or body which might be relevant. It presents an alphabetical list of the basic categories of political, social and economic activities or functions, linked with the names of the agencies or persons involved in or responsible for each. This gives access to the inventory of agency registrations.

Inventory of Series. This consists of abbreviated versions of the series description (some information, such as donor's personal information, is not appropriate in a public finding aid). Information about relevant control records produced by the records creators is also included. Each series description is accompanied by any relevant folder or item level lists, or lists which indicate their location.

Students visiting Australian Archives for a demonstration of RINSE (Records Information Service) and Functions Thesaurus, October 1990.

Inventory of Items. Inventories of items are prepared when the series description is inadequate for access. An inventory of items would be needed for a series of general correspondence files if no box lists of file titles accompany the records when they are transferred or if the listings are inadequate for retrieval. Each entry consists of

- a control symbol, taken from the original control system where possible
- item title
- date range of the item, and
- dates of the earliest and latest documents.

Background Information. The same types of introductory and background information, such as preparer's Notes, introduction to the records, special lists and bibliography, as prepared for the descriptive inventory described earlier.

Control records produced by the creators of records can be micro-filmed to prevent damage to the originals.

Format

The series descriptions might be kept in looseleaf folders for a paper-based system. In an automated system both agency and series descriptions are held on computer, able to be searched on such access points as title, subject descriptor and date. Alternatively, the index and inventories of agencies and series might be printed out at regular intervals on paper or microfiche.

An archives based on the CRS system might still prepare a descriptive inventory for the records of a particular agency. The State Archives of Western Australia, whose documentation is based on the CRS system, has produced *Order in the Court*, a descriptive inventory for the records of the Supreme Court of Western Australia.

Control Records Produced by the Creators of Records

In addition to the finding aids produced by archivists, there are control records produced by the creating institution during the earlier, active life of the records. These can be incorporated into archival finding aids systems.

They include indexes and registers created to assist in the control and retrieval of records. When the records are transferred to archives, wherever possible these aids should accompany them. The creating agency often prepares useful documentation when transferring records to archives or relocating records. These control records can save a great deal of processing time and help to show how the creator used the records. They are themselves

Table 9.2

Control Records Prepared by Records Creators

Registers are used to record information about documents or files received or dispatched by an office, or created in an office. For correspondence, this would include date, author, summary of contents and a file reference, arranged chronologically. If the register was for controlling files created in an office, it would record the date, file number and title. Information is arranged chronologically and numerically.

Indexes also control documents and files, but do so by creating another point of access to the system. The file titles and contents of the documents are arranged alphabetically by name or subject. They are sometimes in the form of card files.

Filing system descriptions supply filing classification lists and key codes and outlines of filing systems, explaining the alphabetical, numerical or other codes and symbols used. These indicate how a filing system operated when it was in current use in a business or office.

Procedures manuals for accounting systems can reveal the original structure of the records and assist in retrieval in the same way as filing system descriptions.

Lists of authorised terms describe terms used to classify file titles in filing systems. They are sometimes called thesauruses when highly structured.

Computer-assisted records management systems track files or correspondence. They are usually a combination of filing system and index.

Metadata are the data elements which define the structure of a database. They describe how data is stored, including the records, fields, access paths and coding schemes.

archival records, but they will also be used as finding aids. If this means that they will be heavily used, it would be wise to consider having them copied into another format, such as microform, to reduce wear and tear on the originals.

Control records will probably not stand alone as aids to the user. The archivist may need to produce contextual notes to show how these records formed part of a recordkeeping system, which can be used to gain access to other records created within the system. This will all be incorporated into the finding aid system, possibly as part of a descriptive inventory or in the series description of the control record or by links to related series.

Some commonly produced control records which researchers will encounter in an archives are listed in Table 9.2.

It is important to acquire these aids, or copies of them. An in-house archivist should cooperate with the records manager to encourage staff members to retain these records. It is not very useful to microfilm all of the accounting department's ledger cards, unless a manual is kept or filmed to explain the abbreviations and conventions used. Retiring staff members frequently

Copies of an agency's control records are transferred to the archives in the form of an automated keyword listing of file titles supplied as Computer Output Microfiche.

have old manuals, indexes and lists tucked away in cupboards, so be alert.

The archivist can also work with records management and information technology specialists in the area of electronic records to ensure that material potentially useful for finding aids is retained. This can be as early as the design stage. Electronic records contain a good deal of information about themselves. For example, an electronic mail system could be structured to record information about each document: identification of the originator and recipient, size of the document, and the place and time of its creation, and if and when alterations were made. Descriptions of the data structure are known as metadata. The system could be designed to incorporate its own finding aids. Some external documentation with instructions for use might be needed, but the potential access would already be there. In fact, more contextual information might be available than on a manual, paper-based system. However, the archivist must make the system designers aware of the desirability of retaining this information in an accessible form.

Indexes and Special Lists

Indexes and special lists are the elements of the system which help the researcher to match up a subject inquiry with the structurally-based inventories produced by archivists when arranging and describing archives. The main types are

- subject and title indexes
- function indexes
- chronological listings
- media guides.

The agency and series descriptions in inventories can be used for information retrieval. Collection titles and series titles can be scanned for general information. However, in many cases these will not yield the information which reference enquiries require. For example, a structural finding aid gives an overview of a particular corporation's sections and their functions over time. It would be quite simple to locate the records relating to a particular building because the corporation would probably have had a property section. It might be much harder to find records on the treatment of women in the corporation's workforce. It is unlikely that this area would have been handled by a special officer or department until fairly recent times, so that earlier relevant material would be widely scattered.

Indexes can indicate the content of the various record series much better than just the titles would do, by providing extra access points such as subject, name, medium and form.

Indexes

Indexes are created most often for inventories, guides to high-use collections and guides to holdings. Indexing the finding aids is much less resource-intensive than indexing the content of the archival material itself, and is still extremely useful. Indexes can be in the form of card files, printed lists, printouts or computer output microform, or simply held on computer.

Entries are taken from the names of the records creators, the titles of collections, series and items, the series descriptions, the administrative histories and biographies. Sometimes subject descriptors are added. The entries are usually arranged alphabetically, with references to their occurrences in the larger work. If possible, the index entries should refer researchers to the pages of a structural finding aid, such as a descriptive inventory, rather than directly to the item required. This ensures that the items are seen in context in the series or collection, which may enhance interpretation of this item or lead to further relevant items.

Sometimes an archivist will decide that it is necessary to index the content of a particular series. This is especially useful for personal papers and general correspondence when other finding aids simply do not provide sufficient access. It might be done for a series which is often requested but frustrating for researchers, or for series which are currently under-utilised.

Automated and Computer-Assisted Retrieval

If inventories have been created on computer, several kinds of retrieval are possible.

For on-line finding aids, researchers would not be aware of a separate item called the 'index'. They would simply be requesting entries containing certain words or date ranges, perhaps in certain fields, such as series titles or dates.

Some systems use free text searching, where all entries are searched for a particular word or string of letters. Other systems just search an inverted file, which is an index created using selected terms from the computer entries. Computer retrieval will only bring up records containing the exact terms searched, and not synonyms. Problems can be minimised by the use of lists of authorised terms or thesauruses.

Remember that, as with all computer-assisted control systems, automated indexing is subject to the 'garbage in: garbage out' syndrome. The more accurate and consistent the input, the better the result. Consider the possible standardisation of titles and the compilation of a list of stop words to ensure that only meaningful terms are indexed by the computer.

Computers can assist in indexing and retrieval without elaborate programs and databases. The most basic word processing programs for personal computers contain some facilities for indexing and putting lists into alphabetical order. A small archives might also find that a listing of series titles, descriptors and dates in a word processor file with a limited word-searching facility can be a useful addition to the finding aids.

When designing an automated system, make sure that the data fields used in computerised series descriptions will be useful in generating the required indexes. For example, family names should be entered before initials so that a useful alphabetical list can be generated from that field. Perhaps towns and states should go into separate fields so that entries could be listed by state, ie geographical area.

Manual Indexing

There are nearly as many sets of rules for compiling an index as there are indexes. These rules cover things like alphabetical order, word-by-word or letter-by-letter; the treatment of apostrophes and abbreviations; the order of dates and other numerical items; the format of personal and institutional names and the structure and type of cross references.

Since indexing the content of the actual records generally has a low priority for the archivist, and because it is time-consuming, this is the sort of project which is often given to volunteers. The management of volunteer labour is covered in Chapter 11, User Education and Public Relations. However, it must be stressed that the apparently straightforward task of indexing can be disastrous unless house rules are carefully laid down and maintained.

Indexing names in correspondence series is a relatively routine task which illustrates the need for these house rules. Typical questions which need to be considered include the following:

- Are family name and initials to be used, or full given names?
- Which names are the family names (ie when the countries of origin are unfamiliar to the indexer)?
- Are nicknames and familiar names to be indexed as main entries or cross-referenced?
- Are all names to be indexed, however brief the reference, or only important ones? Which ones are important?
- Will the index distinguish between the names of those who have letters addressed to them and those who are just mentioned in the course of a letter?

It is not the intention of this section to elaborate on indexing rules. Some titles are suggested in the Further Reading section at the end of this chapter. Be prepared to spend time on establishing conventions, standardising terminology and assisting the indexers with these.

Using Optical Disk

A technique which is growing in popularity for large photograph and document collections is to transfer images onto optical disk. The researcher can retrieve images quickly and a working copy of the chosen document can be printed. Careful indexing is vital because the indexing is the computer's only access point for retrieval – it cannot read what is contained in the image. As with all new technology, it is wise to become familiar with the terminology and archival implications before committing your institution. What is the expected life of the disk? How easy is it to index? What problems will there be in migrating the information to a new format when the old one is outdated?

Using Optical Character Recognition.

Some archives have begun to utilise the capacity to write heavily used records into a computer format by scanning. There is less need to index the content as it is possible to carry out free text searching on scanned items for retrieval of information. It is still necessary to record carefully which records are contained on, for example, a particular disk. The finding aid consists of a reproduction of the whole document.

Functions Index

The functions index was discussed in the section Interconnected Inventories of Agencies, Series and Items. A variation of this aid for an in-house archives would list the functions or types of business conducted by the host organisation with the names of the responsible sub-units under each.

Chronological List

Since many researchers limit their research to a particular time frame, a useful aid is a time line organised by five- or 10-year date segments listing alphabetically the names of creators active within each segment. It ties the names of creating bodies or individuals to the dates of their operation.

Media Guides

Frequently, records in a particular medium such as photographs, plans, maps, magnetic tapes and gramophone records make up a significant proportion of the holdings or are very heavily used. Special media guides are useful for these. Researchers might be looking for records in a particular medium, for example, if they were researching movies or photographic techniques.

If the system is automated, no separate guide is needed. Users might ask the system for, 'all entries before 1930 which contain "photograph" and "automobile"'. Other automated systems might simply produce a hardcopy printout of the titles of series containing cassette tapes or plans.

The context of the items should be retained in the same way as for written records. This will depend on the type of aid being produced. If it is simply an index which leads the researcher to the series descriptions, then context information will be available in those descriptions. If the guide is more detailed, some context information should be provided. The entries should also lead researchers to related and background material in other formats. These items rarely exist in isolation.

Supplementary Finding Aids

These finding aids are usually created to cover popular research topics in a particular institution. They include special lists of background information, subject files and source analyses. Some of these aids supply information which does not require reference to the archival documents. Supplementary finding aids are compiled from the existing finding aids system and from secondary source material. Selected secondary sources are sometimes made available as well, alongside the archival finding aids.

Special Lists of Background Information

These lists contain quickly retrievable summaries of important facts about an organisation, locality or individual. Such lists are often prepared as an aid to writing administrative history and can be appendices to relevant descriptive inventories. Some examples include lists of chief executive officers, mayors, school principals, committees, public buildings or churches together with relevant dates. They are often arranged chronologically.

A timetable of key events may be prepared. Do not include too many items, but restrict its subject area or compile several different lists on different subjects. Otherwise, too much time will be spent searching for the relevant event.

Source Analyses

A file of research enquiries can be useful for producing subject guides to popular topics, which then saves the reference archivist time in assisting researchers. Australian Archives plans to produce sample searches for popular research areas, drawing upon the source analyses they have prepared over many years when attending to research enquiries. Guides are often prepared for particular types of users such as family historians.

Discretion is required in distributing information about previous searches. There is no problem with making available the lists of records which have been found useful for common inquiries. However, ethical problems arise when considering how much detail should be revealed about an individual researcher's discoveries. Generally speaking, all researchers should have equal access to records which are open, but should this extend to the handing over of all references on a new subject area, which a Ph D candidate has laboriously collected from the files, to an Honours candidate who then publishes a quick summary before the original researcher?

Planning Finding Aids

Planning of finding aids is not done in isolation from planning for other archival functions. The archives' overall priorities must be taken into account when goals for the finding aids program are set. Since a major aim of the whole process of gaining control of archives is effective retrieval of information, obviously this should be considered at every stage of processing records. All stages should contribute to an integrated approach to retrieval.

The service philosophy of the institution should be considered. If you want to promote self-help, then you must create the conditions where self-help is possible. The necessary time and money must be spent on creating finding aids which facilitate this. Better finding aids should produce greater user autonomy, and this will reduce the demand on reference assistance, freeing archivists to work in other areas. The production of finding aids should not be regarded as a luxury.

Several key areas which must be considered when the archivist is planning finding aids are outlined below.

Who Are the Users?

In-house archives will mainly be used by administrators and public relations departments. The user group for public archives is ever-changing. Public archives were once only used extensively by academic historians, but now there are many other users. Genealogists and family historians form a large user group, and there are academics from many disciplines other than history. People of vastly differing social, educational and ethnic backgrounds are using archives.

It is important to take into account the educational level, research experience and interest of your major user groups in designing supplementary finding aids and deciding which types of index will be useful. If your holdings consist mainly of scientific research records and the users are generally other scientists, this should shape your finding aids. You would then concentrate resources on the access requirements of the scientists rather than on those of the lay user.

Resources

Some important factors to consider are
- numbers and skills of the staff
- financial resources available
- the time available for production of finding aids
- the cost of production.

These considerations will influence the types and also the depth of finding aids produced. Less detailed finding aids might be chosen because of lack of time, similarity of item content, cost and expectation of limited use. In other cases, item-by-item description in finding aids might be justified to provide access where none exists, produce an inventory as security against theft, prevent unnecessary handling and compensate for the limited skills of untrained assistants.

Privacy and Organisational Confidentiality

Occasionally, it might not be possible to include some materials in public finding aids to respect privacy or confidentiality, particularly within a system where the document is also present for access, as with some modern information systems. An obvious example would be the inclusion of photographs of certain secret Aboriginal ceremonies on an optical disk. For an in-house archives, there might be descriptions of material relating to business dealings and commercial trade secrets which the management does not want made public, but which the series description has to make explicit. Remember, however, that there is still a difference between a description of the document contents and the actual documents.

Standardisation

There are two aspects to standardisation which relate to finding aids. One is the international pressure to exchange information about holdings electronically in a standardised form. The other is the benefit to be gained from standardising procedures within an institution.

International Moves Towards Standardisation

Considerable work has been taking place on descriptive standards in North America and Europe. Approaches have been hampered by the changing possibilities provided by information technologies. There has also been a divergence in the emphasis adopted by different groups. Some have tackled the problem through the context of records, while others have been more concerned with standardising the actual description of records. To complicate the issues further, electronic recordkeeping perspectives have forced us to consider whether standardisation of documentation at the front end is as pressing an issue as standardising approaches to records in custody, which comes back to how we visualise our future. Is it as part of a network of custodial institutions sharing access to the records we hold, or will we add to this the maintenance of access to records not in custody? These issues will take some time for archivists to work out, and they remain one of the greatest professional challenges we face.

A section of the reading list at the end of this chapter provides further reading on the development of work on descriptive standards. Appendix 2 sets out the USMARC AMC format as the user sees it. This format is widely used in the US for the exchange of detailed information about holdings in a standardised form.

Standardisation within the Institution

It is useful to standardise data elements and terminology within an institution in the areas of function, form and authorised terms. Archival processing is made easier and researchers are helped by knowing what to expect when certain terms are used. This has already been mentioned in relation to the functions of agencies and the preparation of indexes.

In fact, most of this standardisation should already have taken place, before the finding aids are produced, at the arrangement and description stage. The ultimate production of finding aids must be considered during all stages of the documentation process.

Format of Finding Aids

If you have a manual system, the format must be considered in terms of binders, pamphlets, volumes, cards and microform. Make sure the aids are set out attractively and take care that they are easy for users to follow. Looseleaf format is ideal for anything likely to be updated, such as series sheets with accompanying item lists, when new consignments arrive.

Some institutions publish finding aids. As it is an expensive undertaking, it would be wise to consider the following points before proceeding:

- Is your aim to produce up-to-date information or publicity? Publishing promotes the collection in a way that is impossible for in-house card catalogues and inventories, and increases the collection's potential for users. It reaches people the archives might not otherwise reach.
- It is useful for people to have something they can take away to plan research and annotate.
- The information is inevitably superseded due to new acquisitions. It can only be a snapshot in time. Reviews invariably criticise this aspect of archives' published information.
- It is difficult to add new material. This problem could be avoided if the work was produced using a word-processing or desktop publishing package and regularly updated.

If the archives control system is automated or there are plans for computerisation, consider whether the users actually need on-line access. It is expensive to provide a user-friendly computer interface, and this may limit your system unduly. The Public Record Office, Victoria decided not to provide this, for example, because it would have been too expensive to obtain the storage capacity needed to hold or generate data in a form which was readily comprehensible to public users. Instead, they decided on regular issues of a complete, updated summary guide in computer output microform.

Such decisions rest on factors like the state of your archives' information technology, the size of the institution, the nature of the collection, the volume of storage required, the number of regular users, the size of the budget and the amount of development required to provide a user-friendly interface to the system.

Conclusion

The creation of a well-planned system of finding aids which is straightforward to use should be an important objective for any archival institution. There is little point in carefully preserving the records physically, then meticulously arranging and describing them, if the finding aids produced are not adequate for a user to identify the records which are likely to relate to a particular enquiry.

Once a system of finding aids has been set up and is being used, it should be reviewed periodically to ensure that it is achieving the goals of control and retrieval.

The impact of computer technology and automated techniques of information retrieval on the production of finding aids for archives has already been considerable. And there should be fur-

Appendix 9.1   Extract from the Summary Guide of the Public Record Office, Victoria

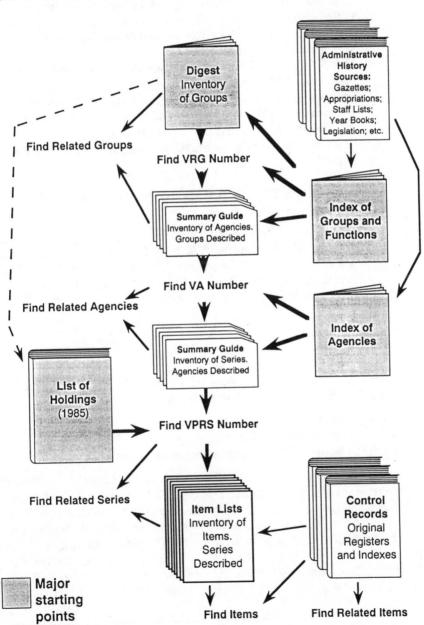

Summary Guide to the Public Records of Victoria   21

Figure 11 - How to Use the PRO's Finding Aids
For more information see pages 5 - 9.

ther benefits for the archivist and researcher from current developments in this area. Despite changes in the format and potential coverage of finding aids, their role of providing the link between the records and their users remains a crucial one for the success of every archives program.

Appendix 9.1 Extract from the Summary Guide of the Public Record Office, Victoria

This Appendix (see p. 269), Figure 11 from the Public Record Office's Summary Guide, shows the interrelationship of components of its system. The Public Record Office, Victoria operates a series-based methodology (VPRS Number) linked to agencies (VA Number), and brought together within a method of agency grouping (VRG Number). The system is explained in Helen Smith and Chris Hurley, 'Developments in Computerized Documentation Systems at the Public Record Office, Victoria', in *Archives and Manuscripts,* 17/2, November 1989.

Reprinted with the permission of the Keeper of the Public Records.

Appendix 9.2 USMARC AMC Format as seen by a Researcher

This appendix consists of a possible users' view of a collection description using the USMARC AMC format. A fuller representation of the format can be seen in the original, Miller, Frederic M, *Arranging and Describing Archives and Manuscripts,* Society of American Archivists, Chicago 1990.

The following is one example of how the Bailey record could be made to appear to users of the Saratoga Historical Society's on-line public catalog.

Bailey, George Rogers, 1911–1987
  Family Papers, 1789–1986, 1919–1982 (bulk)
  35 cubic feet (archives boxes), 150 individual autographed manuscripts

George Bailey was born in 1911 in Bedford Falls, SA, where his father, Peter Bailey (1879–1934) was President of the Savings and Loan. Upon his father's death George took over the Savings and Loan. He served as President until the bank closed in 1970. He then served until 1981 as Vice President of the First National Bank of Middletown. Among his many local activities, most prominent were his service as Chairman of the Board, Southside Community Center, 1961–1966 and member of the Chamber of Commerce Executive Committee, 1971–1976. He was also a Delegate to the 1956 and 1960 Republican National Conventions. He married Mary Hatch (1913–) in 1932 and they had four children. Mrs. Bailey was active in the Middletown Museum of Art and served as Chair of the Women's Committee, 1965–1973.

Organized into 6 subgroups: I. Business Activities, 1928–1986; II. Civic Activities, 1936–1986; III. Political Activities, 1940–1982; IV. Personal Files, 1911–1986; V. Mary Hatch Bailey Papers, 1915–1986; VI. Autograph Collection, c.1789–1978

Access unrestricted.

Summary: Papers include business records relating to Bedford Falls Savings and Loan Association, First National Bank of Middletown and local banking activities; civic activities, especially involving the Southside Settlement and Community Center; political activities, especially involving the Republican Party; various personal files; a collection of autographs of famous Saratogans and U.S. Presidents; and diaries, papers and correspondence of Mary Hatch Bailey (Mrs. George Bailey).

Cite as: George Bailey, Family papers, Saratoga Historical Society

Autograph collection: Photocopying prohibited except with permission of Mrs. Bailey or the estate. Associated material: Peter Bailey Papers (MS90–067)

Finding Aids: Entire collection, Inventory and folder listing; Autograph collection, Item listing. Gift of Mary Hatch Bailey, 1989

Location: Department of Manuscripts, Saratoga Historical Society, 200 West High Street, Middletown SA

1. Averington, Clifford, 1885–1963. 2. Ellis, William, Governor, 1878–1949. 3. Sherman, Joseph, 1912– . 4. Lindquist, George, 1909–1967. 5. Hetherington, Winston, Mrs., 1914–1988. 6. Middletown Museum of Art. 7. Republican Party of Saratoga. 8. Southside Settlement. 9. Southside Community Center. 10. Banker's Roundtable (Middletown, SA). 11. Bedford Falls Savings and Loan. 12. Businessmen's Club of Middletown. 13. First National Bank of Middletown. 14. Middletown (SA.) Chamber of Commerce. 15. United Fund of Saratoga. 16. Banks and banking — Saratoga. 17. Charities — Middletown, SA. 18. Political parties 2 – Saratoga. 19. Bedford Falls, SA. 20. Middletown, SA. 21. South Middletown (Middletown, SA). 22. Autographs. 23. Bankers. I. Bailey, Mary Hatch, 1913–

Further Reading

Aitcheson, J. and Gilchrist, A., *Thesaurus Construction: A Practical Manual*, 2nd edn, Aslib, London, 1987.

Bearman, David, 'Documenting Documentation', in *Archivaria*, 34, Summer 1992, pp. 33–49.

Bearman, David A. and Lytle, Richard H., 'The Power of the Principle of Provenance', in *Archivaria*, 21, Winter 1985–86, pp. 14–27.

Berner, Richard, and Haller, Uli, 'Principles of Archival Inventory Construction', in *American Archivist*, 47/2, Spring 1984, pp. 134–55.

Cleveland, D. B. and Cleveland, A. D., *Introduction to Indexing and Abstracting*, 2nd edn, Libs Unlimited Inc, Englewood Colorado, 1990.

Flint, John and Berry, Anne, *Local Studies Collections: Guidelines and Subject Headings for Organising and Indexing Resources*, 2nd edn, Library Association of Australia (NSW Branch), Sydney, 1985.

Gilliland, A. J. (ed.), 'Automating Intellectual Access to Archives', in *Library Trends*, Winter 1988, whole vol.

Roe, Kathleen D., 'From Archival Gothic to MARC Modern: Building Common Data Structures', in *American Archivist*, 53/1, pp. 56–66.

Salton, Gerald, *Introduction to Modern Information Retrieval*, McGraw-Hill, New York, 1983.

Smith, H. and Hurley, C., 'Developments in Computerised Documentation Systems at the Public Record Office, Victoria', in *Archives and Manuscripts*, 17/2, November 1989, pp. 165–82.

Lucas, Lydia, 'Efficient Finding Aids: Developing a System for Control of Archives and Manuscripts', in Maygene F. Daniels and Timothy Walch (eds), *A Modern Archives Reader: Basic Readings on Archival Theory and Practice*, National Archives and Records Service, Washington DC, 1984.

Walch, V. I. (ed.), 'Report of the Working Group on Standards for Archival Description', in *American Archivist*, 52/4, Fall 1989, pp. 440–61.

Standardisation

Archives and Museum Informatics Newsletter, Pittsburgh USA.

Cook, Michael and Procter, Margaret, *Manual of Archival Description*, 2nd edn, Gower Publishing, Aldershot England, 1989.

Hensen, Steven L., *Archives, Personal Papers and Manuscripts: A Cataloging Manual for Archival Repositories, Historical Societies, and Manuscript Libraries*, 2nd edn, Society of American Archivists, Chicago, 1989.

International Council on Archives, Commission on Descriptive Standards, *Draft ISAD(G), General International Standard Archival Description*, The Secretariat of the ICA Commission on Descriptive Standards, Ottawa, 1992.

Miller, Frederic M., *Arranging and Describing Archives and Manuscripts*, Society of American Archivists, Chicago, 1990.

Planning Committee on Descriptive Standards, Bureau of Canadian Archivists, *Rules for Archival Description*, Bureau of Canadian Archivists, Ottawa, 1990–.

Sahli, Nancy, *MARC for Archives and Manuscripts: The AMC format*, Society of American Archivists, Chicago, 1985.

10 Access and Reference Services

Sigrid McCausland

Introduction

In earlier chapters we have looked at the activities which involve archivists in the acquisition and control of their holdings. However, archives are not kept merely for their own sake; they are also to be used.

This chapter covers the range of activities involved in making the use of archives by researchers possible. These activities are central to the operations of the archives as a whole and they intersect with many other major archival operations, such as appraisal, creating finding aids, preservation and providing public programs. The role of the reference archivist is a crucial one: enabling members of the public to use unique materials and supervising that use, ensuring that policies and legislative provisions are administered fairly and providing the archives' public face.

Access refers to the terms and conditions of availability of records or information maintained by an archives for examination and consultation by researchers. Administering access to archives involves establishing procedures which will ensure that legislative requirements and donor agreements are upheld, and that the records are protected from theft, damage or rearrangement.

Reference Services is the general name given to the facilities and services that enable the researcher to use the archives and its records once access to them is approved. Enabling that use involves the archivist not only in helping researchers to identify, select, and read records but also in such activities as providing a suitable environment for research, answering mail and telephone enquiries and providing reprographic services to assist researchers to obtain copies of records.

The types of access and kinds and extent of reference services will vary from archives to archives, depending upon the purpose of each operation and the nature of the records held.

Before an archives embarks on providing reference services, it must decide on the framework under which those services can operate. This means addressing several basic questions, such as which records are available for research, under which conditions and who may see them (everyone, only approved researchers, only staff of the organisation that the archives serves, etc). Rule-making and careful administrative planning are necessary preludes to assisting people to locate information about the archives and to offering effective services to people who wish to use original archival materials. The access policy document must first be developed and approved, and then regulations and guidelines drawn up to support the broad intent of the policy.

Access

Access is regulated in many different ways. In some cases the framework for providing access to the archives' holdings is embodied in specific archives legislation, for example Section 33 of the *Archives Act* 1983 indicates that Commonwealth records are generally available for use by the public 30 years after the year of their creation. It also spells out the grounds on which some categories of documents may be withheld from the public after 30 years. For some government archives, the decision to release information must be referred to the department or authority currently responsible for the function involved. Legislation may sometimes specify that some records, such as the minutes of meetings, should be available immediately, without setting down a general access period, as is the case with the NSW *Local Government Act*.

For many archives in both the corporate and public environments, the determination of access policy to archival holdings will be linked to the organisation's internal policies and regulations on access to current records, such as confidential trading information or student files. Most organisations will have guidelines for the release of personal information on their own staff, even when these records are no longer current.

In collecting archives the policy on access to holdings will usually be on a collection-by-collection basis: ie availability of a collection for research will depend on the agreement made between the donor or depositor and the archives at the time of transfer of the collection to archival custody. In some instances each researcher may require the permission of the depositor, such as a business or community organisation, to gain access to the organisation's records held by the archives. Here, granting

Paul Lawson-Brown, officer in charge of the Access Subsection of Australian Archives, ACT Regional Office (second from right), outlines the access examination process carried out on records over 30 years old to members of the Joint Statutory Committee on the Australian Security Intelligence Organisation, 1990. The Committee's task was to investigate the impact of the coverage of ASIO by the Archives Act.

access involves a vetting process by the records creators, where the archives is the service provider but not the decisionmaker.

Each archives should have a written access policy which takes into account the nature of the information contained within the collection and the purpose and resources of the archives' program. Policies establish the framework within which the archivist can administer access to records so that they can be used by researchers. The access policy should be drafted to suit the special requirements of each archives and the authorities governing the archives should approve and issue the policy with a full understanding of the resources required to administer it properly.

In in-house archives, where there are no or few legislative provisions affecting access such as business archives, the archivist needs to consult within the organisation in drafting the access policy if it is to become an effective instrument of authority for the archives. It does not help to adapt a 'model' policy for adoption if it uses terms and concepts more appropriate to other contexts or if it does not address particular issues of importance, eg confidentiality of commercial information within the business context.

Developing an Access Policy

To design an access policy to suit the needs of the organisation, one must consider a range of factors, some of which will be more significant than others depending on the context in which the archives is operating. Archives whose access provisions are laid down by statute may need to develop specific procedures to support the general principles of the legislation. Other archives will need to draft their access policy statements by considering the following principles.

Relevant Legislation. Organisations attached to federal, state or local government departments should be aware of all Acts, ordinances and regulations applying to the records they create and maintain. Access to some of the records held by government-funded archives may be affected by freedom of information legislation.

Sensitivity or Confidentiality of Records. Organisations and individuals create records that contain information relating to their personal or business affairs which could cause embarrassment or financial loss if made available for examination by researchers. Records of this nature include agreements made by an organisation or individual with other bodies, information provided in confidence, personal and health records of staff or family members, and information relating to fraud or security procedures and systems that might hamper business operations if access to them were not restricted or monitored. Collecting archives may have to restrict access to records they have received which contain defamatory, libellous or personal information about a person other than the depositor.

Protection of Individual Privacy. Personal details about a living individual should not be released to researchers unless the individual's permission has been obtained. Information supplied by individuals for the purposes of obtaining a particular benefit or to fulfil a requirement stipulated by law should not be made available to researchers. However, information from these records may be able to be used for statistical purposes providing no specific names or identifiable information is recorded that would reveal the identities of particular individuals. Legislation and the organisation's policies relating to privacy of personally identifiable details must be respected, for example policies on the protection of details of a bank's clients' accounts and credit ratings.

Restrictions Placed upon Records by Depositors. When an archivist in a collecting archives is offered records by depositors, access restrictions relating to them should be clarified. The archivist must consider the implications of restrictions placed upon records prior to accepting and accessioning them into the collection (see Chapter 5, Managing the Acquisition Process, and Chapter 7, Accessioning). If there are restrictions on major collections or if the archives has a policy of referring most requests for access to depositors before researchers can use them, then this should be indicated in the archives' access policy and publicity information. Information on restrictions should also be indicated in finding aids available in published form or on-line, as they can have a significant effect on both the researcher's expectations and their preparation time before the visit. Details of restrictions of any kind should be clearly mentioned in all forms of publicity about the archives and its services.

Clientele. The policy document should define the clientele or community of users that the archives program will serve. This decision will largely be determined by the purpose of the archives, the composition of its holdings and the resources at its command. In the case of public archives, the clientele may be prescribed by legislation and will usually include government bodies and members of the public within an area of political authority. Some in-house archives, such as those caring for the records of businesses or private institutions, may usually provide access only to employees of, or persons under contract to, the parent organisation. Further limits based upon age, membership, affiliation or research interest may also be imposed. For example, readers' or search tickets may not be issued to children or to persons engaged in casual research. Persons living outside the area of service, ie out of the state or country, may also be excluded from service or be required to pay a special fee. Some archives, such as the Council of the City of Sydney Archives, charge a higher fee to professional researchers than to ordinary members of the public.

Equality of Access to Records. This is an important principle, which is intended to ensure that the archives provides reference services without favour or prejudice to its defined clientele and does not grant privileged or exclusive use of material unless required to do so by law, depositor or purchase conditions.

Levels of Access. As well as determining the clientele, the archivist must decide the level of access a researcher is to have to and within the archives. Access is usually granted in levels ranging from receiving general admission to the reading or search room to obtaining permission to reproduce or publish specific documents. The access policy statement must therefore cover conditions of access for
• the reading or search room and finding aids
• inspection of particular collections or categories of archives
• examination of individual series or documents within a series
• copying of individual documents or photographs for private study
• quotation of portions of documents
• further reproduction or publication of documents, photographs or other archival materials.

Degree of Control over Holdings. The possibility of archival materials being physically available for research depends upon their being located and described so that appropriate documents may be requested and retrieved. Some types of records require more extensive controls than others. For example, a box of loose documents may require control numbers for each, while pages in a bound volume may not. Most archives' finding aids indicate what types of records are housed in a particular box, but not what specific documents or information might be present. Researchers unfamiliar with archival materials may be disappointed that the archivist cannot offer instant access to a particular document or that they must examine several boxes of material under supervision with no guarantee that they will find what they seek. It is useful, then, for the access policy to explain that researchers will be provided with finding aids and instructions for using them, but must select their own records and do their own research work. The policy should also state that records which have not been brought under control through arrangement and description will not be available for use.

Physical Condition of the Records. If the records are in a poor condition or have been physically damaged, the archivist should consider restricting access to them until they can be restored by a conservator. An alternative to denying access to badly damaged records is to provide a duplicate copy of the record to researchers (ie photocopy or microfilm copy). This alternative can be employed very effectively for highly used records, where closure would cause considerable inconvenience to a large number of researchers. If the majority of the records in a collection are in poor physical condition, access to the whole collection might be restricted until arrangements can be made for its repair or reproduction. Records should not be made available to researchers if continued handling is likely to hasten their deterioration.

Security of Records. Archival materials are unique and many archival records have importance as legal or financial evidence. Access provisions, therefore, must protect them against loss, damage, misfile or tampering while they are in storage as well as during research use. Researchers, whether from the parent organisation or members of the public, should not have access to records storage areas. Retrieval and return of material should be limited to one or a few authorised staff members. This practice minimises the risk of misfiles and pinpoints accountability for any loss or damage. Records required for research should be requested on a standard form and a copy of the request retained until the material has been returned, checked and refiled in its proper location. Staff must also be allocated to supervise records during use and security measures instituted to protect the materials, to detect breaches and to apprehend the persons responsible. See Table 10.1, Security Measures for a checklist of recommended precautions.

Fees. The access policy document should include a statement of the archives' policies and practices concerning fees for the use of facilities or services and for the provision of copies. It should indicate the basis of any fees, for example, whether these are set by administrative regulation or by institutional cost recovery objectives. If fees change annually, it is advisable to publish a separate list of fees which can be inserted into the archives general policy leaflet or access leaflet as required.

Consideration of the above criteria will assist the archivist in planning and designing an access policy specifically tailored to the needs and requirements of the parent or funding organisation. The archives should be aware of the repercussions of providing an access service to the public and the effect it will have on the parent or funding organisation and the allocation of archival resources especially as regards staff, time and money.

Administering Access to Archives

Once the access policy has been set out and approved, the next step is to prepare the administrative procedures which support the policy. The design of an access application form is the key activity here. The form is signed by both the researcher and the archivist to indicate that both parties are aware of their responsibilities in having archival material made available. It records basic details concerning the researcher and his or her research interests. The form must be clearly designed and not cluttered. It can be divided into three parts: information provided to the applicant relating to the conditions of access, information supplied by the applicant concerning his or her research work, and information supplied by the archivist concerning the outcome of the application. The access form makes the applicant aware of conditions regarding the use and handling of archival record (see Table 10.2, Access Application Form).

The applicant should be asked to provide personal details, including name, address and telephone number, so that he or she can be contacted in the future. Acceptable proof of identity and address should be provided by the applicant. The applicant should be required to date and sign the access application form to signify his or her compliance with the conditions outlined.

The access application form is a necessary document which should be used by every archives, for without this form applicants are not held accountable for what they do to the records or publish from them. Formalising access to the archives means that the archives can take action against researchers if they violate the access conditions. The information provided by the researcher on the access application form may also be used by

Table 10.1 Security Measures

Security Requirement	Method of Implementation
Restrict Entry	Limit access of staff, visitors and tradespeople to the building or archives area and use specifically designated doors and entrance ways.
Identification	All visitors, including staff, should be required to show identification before being admitted to the archives and its search room.
Registration	All visitors should be required to register their name, address, nature of business and the time of entry each day upon arrival. When visitors leave the archives, staff should record their time of departure in the same register.
Non-Public Areas	Issue all visitors who will be frequenting non-public areas of the archives with visitors' badges or identification cards which should be worn or carried conspicuously. Visitors should be accompanied by a staff member at all times while in restricted areas. The identification card or badge should be returned upon departure.
No Baggage	Do not permit researchers to take coats, brief cases, bags or enclosed containers into the search room. Provide a cloak room or area where these items can be stored until researchers have completed their work for the day. As researchers leave the search room, their research materials should be inspected.
Requests	Record request forms should be completed for all original records. Users should not be permitted to order more than three containers or the equivalent in unboxed materials (volumes, folders, bundles) at any one time. Only one volume or folder should be examined by a researcher at a time. Original records must be used under direct supervision.
Reshelving/Refiling	Researchers should not be allowed to reshelve or refile records. Archives staff should be responsible for this function so as to reduce the dangers of mishandling and misfiling.
Copying	Copying should be done by staff members in order to ensure careful handling of the records.
Written Rules	Provide a concise but complete set of written regulations to each researcher and ensure that these are understood and respected by researchers.
Emergency Procedures	Develop clear, legally sound procedures for handling physically and emotionally ill or suspicious persons and be sure that all staff abide by them. Also establish procedures for the orderly evacuation of the building in case of disaster, emergency or threat and be sure all staff are aware of and abide by them.
Storage Areas	Limit access to storage areas to staff and keep the number of staff involved in retrieving original records to a minimum.

the archivist as a source for defining trends concerning the use of the archives and for planning other programs such as the microfilming of potentially high-usage records. The archives should decide whether access forms are to be completed by applicants for a stated period of time, for example one or three years, or for a specific research project.

In addition to setting out the general conditions of access on the access application form, the archivist should spell out specific rules governing the behaviour of researchers in the search room (See Table 10.3, Regulations for the Use of the Search Room). For convenience, the rules can be printed on the reverse side of the access application form.

The procedure for obtaining access to original records in an archives may also include the issue of an annual reader's or search ticket or some other form of written permission to each approved applicant. If this is the case, the archivist should maintain such records carefully, whether on card or file or in a database, so that there is an orderly system to refer to if information concerning an applicant has to be checked.

Another matter to be included in the framework of rules for the use of archives is citation practice. All references to archival materials should carry an approved form of citation properly identifying the records and acknowledging the archives. The citation should include the name of the organisation holding the record, the creator of the record, information relating to the record's specific reference or archives number and title, date of the item and/or unique identification of the entry within the item. It is useful to have a simple handout containing examples of the archives' preferred method of recording references to its holdings, including full and brief citations. Some major archives, such as Australian Archives and the National Archives of Canada, have specific brochures on citation of their records.

There are two other major areas of responsibility to be considered when the archives is drawing up its policies and rules for users: copyright and reproduction of records. These are dealt with at some length below as they are complex and can contribute significantly to the workload of reference staff, whether in a small archives or in a large institution offering a full range of reference services.

Copyright

Copyright is the exclusive right, granted by law, to make and dispose of copies of and otherwise to control a literary, musical, dramatic or artistic work. Copyright belongs to the creator of a work and passes to his or her heirs, unless it is sold or transferred to another party. Copyright is a very complex area, and

Table 10.2 Access Application Form

Conditions of Access to the Archives

1   That all research conducted in the archives be carried out under the direct control and supervision of the archivist and his or her staff.
2   That records made available to the researchers will not be marked or interfered with in any way and will be returned upon completion of use in their original order and condition to the archivist.
3   That no copies of records will be made without the specific permission of the archivist. Any copying will be subject to the physical condition of the records and to copyright legislation.
4   That no publication of material from the archives will be undertaken without the written permission of the archives. If publication of material from the archives is approved, then its source must be acknowledged.

Name of Applicant...
Address ....
....
Tel. No..
Nature of Research ....
....

I agree to comply in all respects with the above conditions.
Date...
Signature ....

OFFICE USE ONLY

Recommendation (Archivist)
....
Date ....
Signature ....
Approved by..
Date..

archivists are advised that virtually all of the holdings of an archives, in Australia, are subject to copyright under the provision of the Commonwealth *Copyright Act 1968*.

If the material in question is in the form of a written record and is unpublished, as are most archives, copyright is perpetual. Once the record is published, the copyright has a fixed time limit, after which it may be copied without restriction. To make the matter more complicated, graphic materials such as photographs and maps are also subject to copyright, but for a stated period of time.

Determining whether or not material is out of copyright and, therefore, able to be copied without consent is time-consuming, but necessary. Likewise, the effort to trace the owners of copy-

Table 10.3 Regulations for the Use of the Search Room

1   Researchers may use the search room only after they have completed the access
    application form and the archivist has authorised the form.
2   Access to records is governed by the archives' access policy, and material is issued to
    researchers subject to any specific conditions relating to individual collections.
3   No bags, briefcases, coats or enclosed containers are to be taken into the search
    room.
4   No smoking, eating or drinking are permitted in the search room.
5   *Pencils only* are to be used for writing. Biros, fountain pens, felt tips and other pens
    and correction fluid are not permitted in the search room as they contain substances
    which can cause serious damage to records.
6   Researchers must handle all records carefully and must not mark, fold, tear or other-
    wise harm the records in any way. Any damage found in material issued should be
    reported to staff immediately.
7   Researchers must not rearrange or interfere in any way with the order of archival
    material.
8   Usually only one volume or folder at a time will be issued to each researcher.
    Researchers must return materials to the issue desk as soon as they have finished
    using them.
9   No archival material is to be removed from the search room by researchers.
10 Material from the Archives' collections will be copied if the conditions of the archives'
    reproduction policy are met, and if the proposed copying does not breach the provi-
    sions of the *Copyright Act 1968*.
11 Researchers must respect Search Room conventions of courtesy and, where possible,
    silence. Equipment such as typewriters, laptop computers and tape recorders may be
    used only with the express permission of the archivist.

right for material created decades earlier can be demanding, but permissions are required if researchers contemplate further copying or publication of the material.

Since most archives consist of original unpublished works subject to copyright, the archivist's first step is to identify the copyright owner(s). Copyright is owned by the person who actually wrote the material unless the work was produced in a situation of employment. In the case of in-house archives, the host organisation would hold the copyright on records or publications produced in the course of its work. However, the institution does not hold copyright in documents sent to it by other persons or bodies. The ownership of copyright in material produced in the workplace or under contract or commission will depend upon copyright ownership still being addressed in a specific agreement. If it is not, then it is very likely that the employer or contractor will be the owner.

Since most of the records and publications in collecting archives are produced by outside persons or organisations, the copyrights belong to them, not the archives. Ownership of copyright does not pass with ownership or custody of the material. It must be transferred separately and in writing. The only exception to this is a bequest. Material bequeathed always includes transfer to the beneficiary of any copyrights held by the testator.

Under the fair dealing provisions of the copyright legislation, researchers may make their own copies (including hand written or typed transcriptions, tape recordings or photocopies) of 'reasonable' portions of material for the purpose of research or study. Generally speaking, however, archives and libraries are not permitted to make copies of unpublished written material for researchers unless the author has been dead for over 50 years and more than 75 years have elapsed since the material was produced. Because of these copyright restrictions and the need to protect original records from damage, archives do not permit researchers to make their own photocopies.

For more information on copyright, consult the publications listed at the end of this chapter, or contact the Australian Copyright Council at Suite 3, 245 Chalmers Street, Redfern NSW 2016; Toll Free Number (008) 22 6103.

Reproduction of Records

An archival institution should consider very carefully the question of reproducing its records for the benefit of researchers. For example, conservation problems can arise from the frequent handling of original material for copying purposes. Also, the clerical work associated with the receipt, checking, recording and dispatch of requests for copying makes significant demands on staff time. As discussed above, reproductions cannot be provided to researchers without first ensuring that the provisions of the *Copyright Act* have not been infringed.

An archives should require researchers to submit an application in writing for permission to make a reproduction of any item from its holdings. The archivist should ensure that each application includes sufficient detail about each item so that it can be identified and its copyright status determined prior to copying. Specific information should also be supplied concerning the form in which the item is to be reproduced or published, eg photocopy or photographic print.

The reproduction of records will be facilitated by a form requesting information on the records to be copied and stating the conditions that must be complied with in order to obtain copies from the archives. Examples of such conditions are as follows:

- The right of the archives to refuse permission to copy if any damage is likely to result to the record.

- A reminder to the researcher that sale of a copy does not involve sale of the copyright and no further reproduction of the work may take place without permission of the copyright owner.
- That any reproduction made cannot be sold or given away without the permission of the archives.

The applicant should be required to sign the reproduction form, signifying his or her compliance with the conditions outlined (see Table 10.4, Reproduction Application Form). For the archivist's use, a section might also be included at the bottom of the form for recording information concerning the copying of records, such as the number of copies made, method of reproduction (photocopy or photographic print), name of the photographer (if applicable), fee to be charged, receipt number (if one is issued) and the recommendation of the archivist. This information could also be used to provide statistics for quarterly or annual reports, to record use of the reproduction service by researchers and to justify the appointment of extra staff.

Copying can sometimes be a strain on the resources of the archives. It may be necessary in some cases to restrict the number of copies per week per researcher so that the archives is able to maintain a balance in the services offered to all researchers. Also, copying of large items in full should be discouraged unless the archives or its parent organisation is able to include such material in its own copying program. Copying of archives should not become a substitute for note-taking by researchers.

In general an archives does not make copies from copies (microforms, photocopies) of archival materials which have been obtained from other archives and libraries unless the other institution has given permission to do so. Copies of such materials should be ordered from the repositories which hold the originals.

Most archives charge for making copies. Government archives may find that fees for reproduction are regulated by legislation, and, if so, the scale of fees should be incorporated into the reproduction policy statement of the archives concerned. Other archives will need to fix a scale of fees, given the likelihood that different types of copying will be offered, for example photocopies of paper records and photographic prints.

Fees levied for copies are of two types: those to recover the cost of producing the copy and royalty charges for further reproduction or publication of the material supplied. Charges to recover the cost of producing copies should at least equal the expense of all materials and of the staff time expended in making them and in processing the orders. Fees which are royalties for the use of archival material in media programs or publications are less common, though some larger research institutions with rich collections of prints and photographs do have them. The main

Table 10.4 Reproduction Application Form

Conditions of Reproduction of Archives

Conditions regarding the obtaining of photocopies, microforms and prints from the archives.

1 The archives may refuse to approve any copying likely to damage the records.
2 Copies of records are provided under this agreement for the purpose of private research and study only. A separate application must be made for permission to reproduce further or publish material.
3 Where the archives owns the copyright in any record reproduced, it shall not by reason of the delivery of such reproduction at the request of the applicant be deemed to have assigned or otherwise transferred the copyright thereto.
4 No copies of the archives are to be sold or in any way further reproduced or published without prior written consent of the archives.

Description of records to be copied ....
....
....
....
....
....
I...of...
do hereby apply for approval to obtain copies of the above records from the Archives. I have read the conditions set out above and agree to abide by them in full.
Date.............................Signature..

OFFICE USE ONLY
No. of copies: ....
Cost: ....
Receipt No.:...
Method of reproduction: ....
Name of photographer (if applicable):...
Approved by:...
....
Date: ....

motivation behind publication fees is the need for extra funds for conservation, rather than the desire to make money. The problem with royalties is that they usually cost more to collect than they bring in, and they do pose a hardship for many small or specialty publishers and documentary filmmakers.

An archives with a large clientele, or a collection used and copied regularly, may consider designing a policy similar to that of the Mitchell Library in the State Library of NSW or the Council of the City of Sydney Archives. Both these organisations charge fees according to the use to which the reproduction is to be put, eg motion picture film, commercial television program, advertising, decoration, exhibition or for private research purposes. The fee is based on the monetary profit to be gained from the use of the material.

Although it should not be a requirement for the granting of permission to publish, publishers and authors should be encouraged to deposit a copy of works based upon or using the archives' holdings in the archives' reference library.

Designing Reference Services

The provision of reference services can be one of the most rewarding aspects of archival work. The archivist can experience much satisfaction in giving direct assistance to people using archival material for research purposes, and the image of the archives may be enhanced by favourable reports of its service from grateful users. Careful planning is an essential ingredient for the success of any reference program, for without it chaos and frustration for both archivist and user can result.

The design of the reference program will depend upon the availability of funds; legal or administrative controls that could affect reference services; the clients the archives is servicing; the records held by the archives; the requirements for making them safely accessible to users; and the priority given by the organisation to reference services as opposed to other archival functions such as arrangement and description, and preservation. The implementation of the reference program will depend on the available resources, including space, equipment, staff and funding as well as that vital commodity for all archives – time.

Assistance to researchers should actually precede their arrival in the archives in the form of brochures or letters explaining the archives' access policies, services, general holdings and regulations governing research use as well as any logistical details such as location, hours of operation, public transport and parking. Chapter 11 provides information on how to prepare brochures on services and similar publications. Researchers should be encouraged to contact the archives well in advance of their visit so that the documentation necessary to secure access to the search room or to a particular collection can be prepared, eliminating delays which eat into all-too-valuable research time.

All researchers should be advised that archives, unlike libraries, are not self-service. Researchers cannot be permitted in the stacks to browse and select material. Rather, they must use the finding aids provided and request records which will be retrieved by archives staff. In a large archives this process can take half a day or longer, and researchers must understand this from the outset. Reference assistance may be divided into four categories:

- providing a suitable environment for research
- providing information and advice
- providing support services to facilitate research
- documenting reference services.

Providing a Suitable Environment for Research

A separate, purpose-designed search room should be provided for researchers using archival materials. This space should have well-signposted links to the other public use areas within the archives building. It should be truly user-friendly, to welcome regular users and encourage people new to archives. It is probably a good idea to put yourself in the place of the first-time visitor when designing a new reference facility, whether you are adapting an existing space or planning a new building.

Even in the smallest archives, it is desirable to set aside a special area for research which involves original material as opposed to books, other printed material and microfilm. Because these materials are unique and irreplaceable, they must be used under close supervision. If it is not possible to devote a whole room to this purpose, then perhaps part of a large room can be sectioned off. At the very least, a table or tables should be reserved exclusively for researchers using original material. If researchers are to use large-sized records such as maps and architectural drawings, then surfaces suitable for consulting these records must be provided. The researcher must always have enough space for consulting the records and for note-taking. The archivist, or other staff members, should be located nearby to answer questions, retrieve records and provide effective supervision.

The search room should create an environment conducive to concentrated research work: it should be properly lit, away from noise and passers-by and have adequate heating, cooling and ventilation. Other considerations here include the placement of computerised finding aids and the allocation of space for equipment such as microfilm readers and tape recorders. Physical access to the search room should be designed with the needs of wheelchair users in mind (see Managing Facilities, Equipment and Stores in Chapter 2, Getting Organised, for a list of the requirements for public areas in an archives).

As well as facilities for the use of the archives themselves, enough space and appropriate shelving is needed for the archives' reference library. The archives own finding aids, generous supplies of all the forms to be completed by researchers and copies of any brochures and other publicity material should be kept as close as possible to the researchers' work area. This is most important as a well-designed research area, with an attractive appearance and layout, should also fulfil the goal of facilitating self-help by users.

Dr Jurgen Real, visiting archivist from the Bundesarchiv in Koblenz, Germany, spent three months at Australian Archives, ACT Regional Office in 1991 doing archival work on the former German colony New Guinea.

Sometimes archives' reference facilities will be shared with the Australiana section of a combined library/archives service or may for convenience be located in the same building as related services, as in the case of municipal archives and local studies centres. These joint public service areas should be developed cooperatively so that researchers' differing needs are remembered and that archives and library staff benefit from each others' strengths and experience.

The Reference Interview

The reference interview provides the researcher with essential information relating to the archives, for example, access to the archives' facilities and collections, opening hours, rules for the use of archives, the arrangement of finding aids, other archival collections that may be of assistance, and guidelines for citations and reproduction of records. Likewise, the interview provides the archivist with information about the researcher, ie his or her research topic; the purpose of the research (eg whether for publication or a thesis); the material he or she expects to see, any deadlines for the research; and possible copying requirements. It is an important step in providing effective reference services: it establishes the relationship between the archivist and the researcher.

In conducting a reference interview the archivist is beginning the task of assessing the individual researcher's needs and matching them to the holdings and services offered by the archives. There is an important inferential process at work in the interview: the archivist is matching their knowledge of the records and the agencies which created them with the researcher's questions which are usually expressed in terms of subject/person/place. The archivist's questioning, listening and negotiating skills are used to assist the researcher in the quest for information from the archives' holdings.

During the reference interview, the archivist has to respond to the researcher's questions about specific records or about the likelihood of finding material on their topic. The archivist must also use presentation skills as each new researcher potentially has different needs and expectations. For example, the archivist will need to gauge the level of interest and usefulness of the finding aids: a once-only visitor with specific information needs does not require the full tour of the finding aids system. A failure to communicate at this time may lead to the researcher not understanding that there is a standard twice-daily delivery of records from the off-site repository, and thus experiencing unexpected delays. The end result might be a frustrated research trip for the researcher and poorer relations between the archivist and the researcher.

Large archives may have the resources to produce an orientation video introducing their basic services and/or explaining their finding aids. The idea here is that the most common initial questions are covered in the video, leaving visitors to begin their research as soon as they arrive, thus saving the archivist's time in repeating the same information over and over again to each new first-time researcher. The advice given in Chapter 14 should assist the archivist in the production and use of video. The video is not intended to replace the archivist who can provide more detailed assistance to researchers once their research is underway: this often happens in any case as the experience of archival discovery is shared by the researcher and the archivist.

Providing Information and Advice

Assistance to Researchers. Having persons come to the archives to use the records is desirable because it enables the archivist to give them direct assistance. However, some archives may not be able to allow personal access due to legal or administrative regulations or lack of space. Consequently, these archives may provide their reference services via mail or telephone. Most archives will provide all three types of service.

Persons who have taken the time and trouble to come to the archives to use the records should be greeted and treated with courteous enthusiasm. In addition to information on access to the archives, its finding aids and holdings, reference archivists will often have to provide a range of advice to researchers on other matters. This includes supplying the names of qualified persons who can undertake research for a fee; advising on the correct citation of archival sources, especially when their work is to be published and could lead to requests for the same material by other researchers, and advising of other repositories with similar or related holdings.

Archivists responsible for reference services are advised to plan the search room hours and services to allow time for the staff on duty to prepare the room for each day's work, ie replenish forms, check microfilm readers and put finding aids back in order. If staff and/or equipment are limited, then it is advisable to have a formal booking system for researchers. Likewise, there should be time at the end of the day to check and refile materials. The following are some guidelines to follow in setting up hours of service:

(a) Search room hours should be one hour shorter than the archives working hours, ie search room 9.30am to 4.30pm when working hours are 9am to 5pm.

(b) Search room services:

- New requests for records received less than 45 minutes before closing will usually be held over until the next day.
- Photocopy orders will be processed twice daily; orders for same day delivery must be received by noon.

The archives should produce a brochure containing basic information on its holdings and services. The brochure is useful for first-time researchers and also as advance information for researchers who write before making a visit. You can exchange copies of information of this kind with other organisations as a further service to the researcher. The brochure can be used to promote the archives and its services. Larger archives with more complex holdings and a greater variety of services often produce a 'family' of related brochures for this purpose (see Table 10.5, Content of Archives Brochure).

This brochure can be designed as a four-page pamphlet with the name and logo of the organisation recorded on the front cover and the above information contained on the centre double page.

The information contained in the brochure is intended as an introduction to the archives and its services and does not replace the statements and forms associated with the different activities involved in providing access and reference services.

Mail Enquiries. This method of providing access to archival information may be preferred by some archives more than others due to their large and geographically scattered clientele or lack of space and resources to accommodate researchers. People requesting information should include basic facts concerning their requirements, for without specific information the archives may provide responses of limited value to the enquirer. All mail reference enquiries to the archives should clearly specify the topic and include

Table 10.5   Content of Archives Brochure

Location	The Archives and Its holdings
Address with Map Showing Location	History of the Establishment of the Archives
Mail Address	Scope of Holdings/Focus of
Telephone Number	Collecting Interests
	Records Held by the Organisation
	• main types
Opening Hours	• important collections

Access	Services
Access Policy	Finding Aids
• summary	
• types	
• availability	
Procedures for Obtaining Access	Reproduction of Archives
	• summary of policy and services
Special Requirements	Equipment available
• eg search ticket	• eg microform readers, tape recorders
	Citation Guidelines
	• include example of a correct citation
	Published Information
	• eg guides to major collections

- name of person/place/event
- approximate dates
- location of place/event/person
- type of transaction or document required, eg will, rate assessment valuation or notice.

In dealing with mail enquiries, the archivist will usually need to set some kind of limit on the time spent researching and composing responses. It is very easy to spend hours trying to answer one letter, while other work mounts up. Alternatively, limits can be placed on the number and type of questions per letter, for example, no more than three requests per letter, all of which must relate to the same name or topic. Form letters, designed to suit the most frequently asked questions, are used successfully by many archives to reply to mail enquiries. You may develop a general list of sources to be checked; these should be developed for popular types of request, beginning with the general and moving to the more specific. These lists save time for the archivist and can be very useful to researchers.

Often researchers will want to order copies of documents the archivist has found, so it may be advisable to send out a reproduction request form along with the response. All copies and postage charges should be paid for in advance to avoid the time-consuming task of chasing bad debts.

Answering mail inquiries can be facilitated through the use of a mail enquiry worksheet on which you record the request number, name of the enquirer, the sources consulted, results of the search, explanatory notes, copy order forms prepared, draft response, amount of time spent and names of staff members. Such a worksheet not only provides the information needed to respond to the request, but also is invaluable for answering future requests on the same or closely related topics.

Telephone Enquiries. All archives should be prepared to give out basic information about their services, hours of operation, general holdings and finding aids over the phone. The provision of detailed information by telephone is more difficult. In an in-house archives, answering telephone queries from users within the organisation will often be a feature of the archivist's day-to-day work. If these queries become fairly complex or require lengthy research, then it would be preferable for the enquirer to do the research (or to arrange for someone else to do it). Similarly, if a member of the public requests detailed information by telephone and that person is able to come in to use your research facilities, it is quite reasonable to suggest politely that they do so.

However, this is an area where it is difficult to make rules, as a friendly, efficient telephone service can be a very good advertisement for the archives. On the other hand, archival materials are often more complex and difficult to search than books and so are not suitable for quick reference services. A small archives in particular may not be able to cope with a steady flow of telephone enquiries while trying to maintain an adequate search room service and carry out other archival functions at the same time. Careful monitoring of the volume and type of enquiries received, an awareness of the archives' overall priorities and resources and common sense all need to be used when deciding on the standard of telephone service to be offered.

Research Services

For Members of the Public. In most cases the archivist will need to set limits on the amount of research undertaken by staff on behalf of researchers. This is not because of any apathy towards clients and their needs, but rather because detailed, lengthy research is outside the archivist's usual role of supporting the research efforts of other people. The reference archivist's job is to guide researchers to the records, but not to interpret their contents. However, special circumstances, such as a major commemorative project for the parent organisation, might require the limits to be lifted temporarily. In such cases it is essential that the work be well defined and limited in time and that extra funding be provided for its accomplishment.

One solution to the problem of providing research services, especially for distant users, is to refer the researcher to an individual who will do the work for a fee. Most archives maintain lists which include the names, addresses and specialities of contract researchers. The archives will supply the list to an enquirer, but further arrangements, including charges, are left to be agreed upon by the enquirer and the researcher. The list should carry an introductory sentence or two from the archives explaining that the list is provided as a convenience to persons unable to conduct their own research and should not be construed as a recommendation or endorsement by the archives of any of the contract researchers listed.

General guidelines for staff setting out the type and level of assistance to be provided to researchers should be compiled. Such guidelines should emphasise that the role of the archives staff is to support and assist rather than to do research. Giving tours of the archives, explaining how to use the finding aids, ensuring fair and equal treatment for all researchers, and referring people to other repositories with relevant holdings are examples of supporting work by staff.

For an In-House Archives. The archivist may be required to provide detailed information to the organisation that the archives serves as a condition of its establishment and primary reason for existence. Some archives of an organisation may only be available to officers of a particular department for business or confidential reasons, and therefore the archivist should ensure that strict security procedures are followed so that only those officers designated can obtain access to specific records. For example, most organisations will only allow particular officers in the personnel or industrial relations department to view individual staff records. The problem of administrative change and recording the ownership of records and the creator or successor owners will need to be addressed. Access to records by creators and owners can be very complex and requires written guidelines which should be determined at the time of accession and strictly followed.

Employees of the organisation should be encouraged to examine records whenever possible in the archives search room so as to ensure that they are handled correctly. The archivist may also be required to conduct searches on particular subjects for officers of the organisation. The archivist should not neglect this type of reference service since, first and foremost, the archives should be of service to the organisation funding and supporting its existence.

Another factor affecting the allocation of priorities for reference services in collecting archives is the provision of services to donors.

Providing Support Services to Facilitate Research

Finding Aids. Archival records are virtually useless to 1researchers unless finding aids or published guides are available or have been developed by the archives to lead researchers into the records. The more comprehensive the finding aids, the easier researchers will find the task of locating the correct records for their research and the less time the archivist will need to allocate to their assistance. However, it should be remembered that researchers should not expect either the finding aids or the archivist to locate very detailed information as this is the task of their own research. Finding aids should note any limitations placed upon access to records by the organisation or depositors. For more information on the different types of finding aids see Chapter 9, Finding Aids.

Reference Library. A specialist reference library should be established to allow researchers to refer to general information on a specific subject from secondary source material. The reference library should be designed to supplement the archival collections. It would usually include copies of official or statistical information relating to the organisation, such as annual reports of the company, department or authority as appropriate and historical information relating to the collection such as a history of the organisation or surrounding community or state. Universities and other educational institutions publish annual calendars which are useful summary sources for their archives. The reference library may also include finding aids from other archives with holdings of a similar or related nature and copies of published works based on the archives' own holdings. This library should not be a circulating library, rather it should be purely an in-house resource for the use of researchers and the archives' staff.

Retrieval/Replacement of Records. This is a basic reference service, but one which must be well organised, no matter what the size of the archives' holdings or the extent of its storage areas. If records are stored in an off-site repository removed from the immediate vicinity of the search room, a system of retrieval and replacement of records will need to be developed to ensure that this activity is carried out with as little disruption and harm occurring to the records as possible. Researchers will need to be informed of time delays that result from the retrieval of records from an off-site repository. Provision will also have to be made for the temporary storage of retrieved records in or near the search room until they have been examined fully by researchers.

Records should only be retrieved from and replaced in the repository by archives staff. An archives cannot afford to misplace or misfile records so the replacing of records should be supervised and monitored to make sure that records are returned to their correct locations in the repository.

A method of ensuring that this is accomplished efficiently is to introduce a record request system which records not only the name of the person requiring the record but also the location from which it was retrieved and to which it should be returned after use. A sample record request form is shown in Table 10.6. The record request system usually includes a triplicate record request form which is used to control the whereabouts of all records. The original part of the form is retained by the archivist, the duplicate copy can be used as a loan marker and the triplicate copy is attached to the record and handed to the researcher requesting the record. In archives where requests are recorded in a computerised system, it is still necessary to use markers to replace files or other materials retrieved at their shelf location. Most systems can print labels to do this, thus saving time and reducing clerical work.

Upon retrieval of the record from the repository a copy of the duplicate record request form should be placed in the exact location of the record as an indication of its removal. The archivist can use a 'Record out' card if preferred, but the same information concerning the researcher's name and the location of the record should be noted.

Reproduction. Most archives offer some kind of service for reproducing small quantities of material from their holdings. Photocopying is the cheapest and quickest method, but photographic prints and copies from microfilm reader/printers are also frequently supplied. Copies should be paid for in advance by researchers. The archivist should set scheduled times for researchers' copying to be done so that this work is balanced with other reference tasks and researchers do not come to expect or demand service every time they want copies made. Researchers may want to copy the records themselves for a specific purpose, such as for the production of a video or film clip or because the copying service they require is not supplied by the archives. In this case you will have to provide someone, perhaps a volunteer, to supervise the researcher's photography session. It is a good idea to keep a special appointments book for this work if you have frequent requests from researchers to do their own photography.

Documenting Reference Services

These activities are important as they provide the archivist with the data to plan effectively, to allocate resources and to report

Table 10.6 Record Request Form

Somewhere City Archives	Record Request Form
1 Identifying Number............................	2 Name...
3 Date...	4 Signature...
5 Search Ticket Number........................	6 Description of Material Requested .....
7 Date Range	

Archives' Use Only	
8 Authorised by and Date.......................	9 Comments ....
10 Issued by and Date...............................	11 Returned by and Date...........................

Notes

1 Identifying Number: Records all numbers needed to retrieve material, ie accession, series, box and shelf as appropriate.
2 Name: Full name of person requesting records (in block letters).
3 Date: Enter day, month, year.
4 Signature: All requests must be signed.
5 Search Ticket Number: As required.
6 Description of Material Requested: Give full and proper citation of material, ie collection or agency, series, document or volume as appropriate.
7 Date Range: Record date range of requested material.
8 Authorised by and Date: Record the signature of the archivist responsible and the date to indicate approval of access.
9 Comments: Enter any special provisions or conditions governing use or note if records are unavailable, eg if receiving conservation treatment or issued to another researcher.
10 Issued by and Date: Initials of person retrieving the material and date of retrieval.
11 Returned by and Date: Initials of person refiling the material and date of refile.

accurately to management on the work of the archives. Guidelines and procedures for the following activities are recommended to maintain a consistent and systematic approach which can be communicated to archival staff, researchers and the parent organisation.

Documenting Research Use. The following procedures may assist the archivist in administering reference services and recording information concerning the archives' clientele:

- Registration of Researchers and Topics. As a security measure and to ensure that the volume and type of research use of the archives are properly documented, the archivist should record researchers' visits and may request researchers to sign a register for each visit, giving their names, search ticket numbers and times of entry and departure.

Search ticket application forms are good sources of information about current clientele, research topics and types of research (thesis, publication, personal) underway. The archivist needs this information to set priorities for future acquisitions and for the processing of new material. Researchers should be assured that the information provided in both documents is used for statistical and planning purposes and is not for public use.

Researchers can also benefit if information about existing research work is shared. Persons working on the same families or on related topics may be brought into contact with each other by voluntarily registering their research topics or interests. The key word here is voluntarily as not all researchers will wish to share their work with others. Those who are willing may complete a card recording their topic and information on how they may be contacted by others or the archives may invite its users to publish brief details of their research interests in the archives' newsletter.

- Record Activity and Condition. As part of the archives' preservation program, the archivist should review the record request forms to identify high-use material which may require conservation or benefit from microfilming to reduce wear and tear. Records awaiting return to the shelves should also be checked to detect any conservation problems.
- Responses to Mail/Telephone Enquiries. Reference requests should be numbered and coded by type of request (family history, administrative) on receipt so that this information can be easily compiled for statistical purposes. Along with the original request, this record should contain the research worksheet which includes information on sources and their locations and is invaluable for handling follow-on or similar requests. The archivist may wish to create an index, arranged alphabetically by research topic, to be used to record the reference request and worksheet numbers so that these documents may be easily retrieved.

Research Aids. Special finding aids may be produced for highly used records on a given subject or in a particular medium, such as sources relating to a particular geographical area or oral history tapes held by the organisation. The most common examples of these aids are publications devoted to records useful for genealogical research, such as Australian Archives' *Relations in Records*. Research aids can be developed by the organisation as part of its finding aids program, or from the work of researchers using the records, or as part of a special project funded by the organisation or by outside grants. The production of supplementary finding aids is one area where the work of properly trained and supervised volunteers can make a valuable contribution to the archives' operations (see Chapter 11, User Education and Public Relations, for further information on volunteer labour).

Exit Interviews. Where possible the archivist should interview researchers who have completed their work in the archives. Discussion will produce feedback about the facilities provided and perhaps information about related collections and sources that the researcher has used elsewhere. If holding an exit interview is not feasible, a simple questionnaire might be drawn up for researchers to complete and a suggestion box provided so that researchers are able to express their opinions on the services available. The purpose of seeking all or some of these forms of feedback is to ensure that the researcher's reactions and preferences are documented and can be used in future planning for the archives.

The archivist also needs to remember that researchers belong to other networks in society and that their impressions and experiences of archival institutions may be important for future planning of reference services.

Improving Reference Services

The archivist who assists researchers in using archives has a responsible and rewarding job. However, as in any service provider–client relationship, problems may arise simply because we are dealing with people. Some potential problems can be identified, while others require on-the-spot solutions involving the archivist's reserves of patience, tact and fairness.

You can start by putting yourself in the researcher's shoes: this person may be in a new environment trying to cope with unfamiliar concepts. This is why it is important to have brochures and posters explaining the archives' services, and that the finding aids are logically arranged, well signposted and physically easy to consult. This is also why the reference interview is such an important mechanism for breaking the ice and establishing rapport between the archivist and the researcher. In general the more 'take-away' information you have explaining your policies and services, the better you will be able to prepare researchers in advance of their visits.

There are some simple ways to reduce potential problems in the search room. For example, your finding aids should clearly indicate when a copy rather than the original will be issued to the researcher. Always tell researchers how long they are likely to have to wait for their material to be retrieved, especially if it is stored off-site. Any changes to services, such as variations in opening hours, new scales of charges for copying, and especially relocation of the archives, should be publicised as widely as possible.

Researchers themselves are very important sources of contact between the archivist and the community. Their experiences of using archives can help to spread the word about the information contained in the records and the value of archives to society as a whole. Their contributions to any efforts to improve the type and level of service offered should be sought by reference archivists.

Archivists usually find that the vast majority of researchers are very grateful for the assistance they receive and that, in turn, they feel encouraged to continue to provide a fair and willing service. Occasionally disagreements or misunderstandings can occur in the search room. In such cases it is desirable to take the persons involved to a private setting where the matter can be sorted out without disturbing others. It is also a good idea to have a colleague, preferably a senior person, present during the discussion.

Health crises and other emergencies can also cause problems, and the archives should have effective, well-rehearsed procedures for handling them. Regular training of staff in first aid and emergency treatments is advisable.

During the last few years there has been a great increase in the use of archives in Australia, particularly by genealogists and people interested in local history. However, this has sometimes been a problem for archives which have had to cope with increased demand without a corresponding increase in staff, facilities and equipment. There is no easy solution here as resources invariably lag behind demand. However, you can anticipate some periods of peak interest. For example, you can note any centenaries and other anniversaries of local or general significance which are coming up, and remember these when you are working out priorities for finding aids.

For some archives, the only way to cope with a rising tide of enquiries and to maintain other archival services at a reasonable level will be to re-examine services to researchers. This decision should be based on a thorough study of the level and efficiency of your current services, for example can more form letters be used? Can researchers be made more self-sufficient using small group rather than individual orientation? Can the search room hours be reduced based on a study of use patterns? Any reduction in services will usually be unpopular with your researchers. Once again, it is important to give people plenty of warning of the nature of any changes and the reasons for them.

Planning your reference services carefully and monitoring their effectiveness will help to minimise problems which arise in providing those services. Add to this a welcoming and professional approach to dealing with people who need your assistance, and you will be well-equipped to deal with the demands of your clientele.

Issues in Reference Services

Developing Reference and Management Skills

Dealing with researchers who may come from many different backgrounds and whose experience in using original materials often varies widely is not always an easy task for the archivist. As for other areas of archives management, reference work requires training. Archivists need to know how to deal with people as well as to understand their technical responsibilities to the materials in their custody. Some of the body of knowledge used in archives reference work is included in formal coursework for trainee archivists. There should ideally be cross-training for archivists and public historians in the concepts and skills of each other's professions.

Where the archivist works alone, dealing with telephone and in-person requests for assistance must be balanced with all the other daily tasks such as appraisal and producing finding aids. It may often be difficult to set aside time for developing and improving reference services, but taking a measured approach will prove helpful to the lone archivist. The archivist should ensure that opening hours leave sufficient time for other tasks. Likewise, planning and adapting the search room to allow for maximum self-direction by researchers is a priority. Leaflets and posters explaining how to use the archives are essential for the lone archivist in managing reference services.

Many sole archivists may learn most of their 'trade' on the job, but they should always be aware of training opportunities which offer support to their work as information service providers. Sometimes these opportunities will be offered by archival institutions or professional organisations; on other occasions, general courses on communications and public relations may prove valuable in suggesting techniques for responding to face-to-face requests.

In larger archives where specialisation or rotation of different professional duties exists, training for reference work should be part of an overall program for new staff. All areas of access and reference services should be covered to ensure that the new archivist can quickly become confident in explaining services and guiding researchers. Procedures for answering letters, for processing requests for copies, in recording telephone requests and so on should be updated regularly to reflect any changes in practice. Studying procedures should be reinforced by observation of the search room in action and by following experienced colleagues through all the stages of answering mail and in-person requests.

In an in-house archives, reference staff should always become familiar with the functions and organisational structure of the parent institution. Without this background they will be unprepared to answer enquiries about the organisation, whether they come from inside the organisation or from the public. Similarly, it is crucial for reference staff in a collecting archives to know the institution's acquisition or collecting policy so that they can respond to requests for assistance and direct possible donors to specialist acquisition staff.

Stress

Archivists, in common with many other people in 'helping' professions, sometimes find it very difficult to cope with constantly having to deal with the public. It has been recognised relatively recently that the stress of providing assistance to a large number of people with a considerable range of information needs can adversely affect the archivist's ability to provide the information and other services required. Stress may not merely a passing phase or a response to peaks in workload. It can be a debilitating, long-term condition with physical and psychological effects. It can lead to 'burnout'.

In archives reference work, stress can be experienced by archivists in large archives whose major daily duty is to serve on the reference desk. Equally, it can be the fate of the sole archivist or the archivist working in a small archives which has a high rate of use and where other responsibilities have to be fitted into a busy day. In the latter situation answering telephone calls and dealing with casual 'off-the-street' researchers can seem to be irritating interruptions to other planned activities such as appraisal and arrangement and description.

Yet how does the archivist balance the competing responsibilities which form part of his or her job? How does the reference archivist keep up enthusiasm for a job which often consists of answering routine and repetitive questions? One of the most important ways of dealing with stress is to recognise the symptoms and then to admit that there could be a problem. Symptoms of stress can include fatigue, irritability, inability to concentrate or to make decisions, unwillingness to accept change, officiousness in handling familiar requests and a general feeling of inability to cope.

Stress is usually a collective rather than an individual problem in the workplace – if it affects one person, then it is likely to affect others. The working environment and common problems of heavy workloads need to be discussed and tackled by the whole group to find acceptable solutions for all concerned. Analysing work patterns and reducing low-level repetitive tasks where possible is one place to start. Recognising those minor calls and visits as valid intrusions into the daily schedule and striving always to answer them carefully and cheerfully can help. Questions which at first seem trivial or misdirected can lead to new discoveries for the archivist as well as satisfying the need of the enquirer.

Often, simple changes in routine, such as new rosters or new ways of sharing mechanical tasks, can improve the archivist's ability to handle the whole program in front of them. Allocating and frequently revising priorities in response to new demands can help control workloads and meet deadlines. If the problem stems from inadequate resources or insufficient staff, then it may be necessary to review the reference service as a whole. If a case for additional resources or staff cannot be mounted or is unsuccessful, then some services may have to be reduced. Such measures should be seen as a temporary solution, allowing for a return to previous levels of service at a later date. It may be better to reduce search room hours than to continue to offer services which the people providing them find increasingly difficult to deliver.

Electronic Records

An increasingly important issue for the management of reference services in archives is the provision of access to electronic records. As more records in electronic media are retired from active use and transferred to archival custody, they become the responsibility of the archivist. Much of the literature has concentrated on appraisal, description and preservation of electronic records. But ensuring that researchers can use electronically stored archival information is equally important for the future of archives as service-providing institutions.

In some ways the archivist's role with electronic records is much the same as with traditional paper-based records: to provide access in accordance with general policy and particular restrictions, and to explain finding aids and to make sure that the correct records are delivered in response to the researcher's request. However, electronic records pose a challenge to the established notion of a reference service located in a single location.

Electronic records do not need to be retrieved and refiled for use by the researcher on the archives' premises. Nor does the archivist necessarily have to be in the same physical location as the records to administer their reference use. A researcher working from office or home may access and download electronic information from archives. As more archives have finding aids which can be viewed from afar via communications technology and electronic databases, research use of archives has the potential to become quite a different process from the existing range of activities described in this chapter.

It is not yet possible to predict all the ramifications of this shift away from a service centred on paper records, paper or microform finding aids and personal service from the reference archivist. As research methods and researchers' expectations become more sophisticated, archivists need to be prepared to meet this new challenge. Procedures for the use and protection of electronic records need to be formulated, with particular care being taken to safeguard any privacy provisions regarding personal details about individuals. Reference archivists will still be required to advise about the context of the creation of these records, but they may have less control over the research process given the researchers' ability to manipulate and reformulate the data as it suits them. The equivalent of exit interviews will be essential if the reference archivist is to keep pace with the research process and to maintain an involvement in assisting other potential users of the same and related electronic sources held by the archives.

Studying the Use of Archives

Most archives maintain statistics about their users and about the types and frequency of records requested. These statistics are regularly reported in annual reports or special submissions arguing for an increase in budget or staff or for new buildings for the archives. However, it is often acknowledged that not enough use is made of information gathered and collated about reference services. Still many archives bemoan the underuse of their materials and the lowliness of their public profiles. It is also often argued that archivists are ineffectual in selling their services and their value to their masters. Archivists are, therefore, now focusing their attention on ways of reminding decisionmakers of their importance to the organisation and the community.

Conclusion

The fundamental reason for keeping archives is to enable them to be used. To this end, each archives must design policies and procedures which cater for research, while at the same time ensuring the physical protection of the records it holds. The access policy should be clearly explained and properly regulated. Similarly, reference services which support the archives' overall goals must be designed, taking into account both the archives' resources and researchers' needs. Reference is very much part of the public face of archives – the archivist should always strive to deliver appropriate assistance fairly and efficiently to all his or her researchers. Patterns in the use of archives vary over time, and the archivist has to be prepared to respond to changing types of enquiries and to changing levels of reading room demand. Documenting reference services well, evaluating them regularly and adjusting them when necessary will enable the archivist to carry out this important archival function in a truly professional way.

Further Reading

Australian Copyright Council, *Copyright in Australia*, Australian Copyright Council, Sydney, 1992.

Dowler, Lawrence, 'The Role of Use in Defining Archival Practice and Principles: A Research Agenda for the Availability and Use of Records', in *American Archivist,* 51, Winter and Spring 1988, pp. 74–86.

'Facing Up, Facing Out: Reference, Access and Public Programming', in *Archivaria,* 31, Winter 1990–91, pp. 90–141.

Kepley, David R., 'Reference Service and Access', in James Gregory Bradsher (ed.), *Managing Archives and Archival Institutions,* Mansell Publishing, London, 1988, pp. 228–40.

Pugh, Mary Jo, *Archival Fundamentals: Providing Reference Services,* Society of American Archivists, Chicago, 1992.

Ruth, Janice E., 'Educating the Reference Archivist', in *American Archivist,* 51, Summer 1988, pp. 266–76.

Smith, Clive, 'Archives and Copyright', in *Archives and Manuscripts,* 18/2, November 1990, pp. 243–57.

Whalen, Lucille (ed.), *Reference Services in Archives,* The Haworth Press, New York, 1986.

11 User Education and Public Relations

Ann Pederson

All of us who keep archives and other historical materials have two equally important responsibilities. The first is to identify, acquire and preserve records of lasting value. The second is to make these materials, and the information they contain, available for use. It is primarily in fulfilling this second mission that we undertake educational programs – a planned sequence of projects and activities which inform the wider community about our holdings and services and involve its members directly with their documentary heritage.

This second task is especially challenging and important for archivists because, unlike libraries and museums, visits to archives are not a feature of one's early life or education. Most people do not come into contact with original records until university and, even then, not unless they are doing research degrees. The result is that few people know what an archives is, what sort of work goes on there and why that work is invaluable. This lack of general knowledge and understanding about archives is sufficient reason for archivists to undertake active programs aimed at the public. It is vital that archival work be understood and appreciated by the wider community, not just an educated few. Otherwise, archivists will reap the fruits of their own indifference: inadequate facilities, diminished funding, reduced services or, at worst, closure. History abounds with the losses of those who smugly catered to an elite. The treasures of the ancient world destroyed by uninformed hordes and the works of the Italian Renaissance burned by Savonarola come immediately to mind. While these are dramatic examples, we must all be reminded that the neglect can destroy just as effectively as violence.

Educational activities provide occasions for the public to view rare or unique works.

Given resources and imagination, there is a smorgasbord of educational activities and projects which may be offered. Some of the better known include publications, workshops and seminars, exhibits and special events such as open days or commemorative celebrations. However, it is essential to select from this banquet with care, choosing projects which complement and strengthen the archives effort overall, rather than those which, though exciting, actually divert staff energies and resources for little lasting benefit.

The Benefits of Well-Planned Educational Programs

The key concept in describing the value of educational programs is involvement. Educational activities attract and involve people with the archives and its work and, in so doing, transform those faceless members of the general public or of our own higher administration into personal clients of our services – into researchers, donors, volunteers and active supporters of the archival enterprise. Educational programs are engaging vehicles which bring people face-to-face with archival materials, generating an initial interest and enthusiasm which, properly nurtured, will develop into a continuing relationship of mutual appreciation.

For instance, in one notable case the patriarch of an influential family was invited to lend some photographs to an exhibit for the town centenary. This man had never entered the doors of the local historical society until the day he came in to discuss the loan, but became so interested that he not only came to the exhibit opening, but subsequently joined the society and donated his family papers to its archives. Furthermore, through his influence, several leading businesses made donations of money and services to the society. Examples of such conversions abound ranging from the workshop attendee who becomes a committed volunteer to a philanthropist like David Scott Mitchell whose bequest established the superb research library of Australiana that bears his name.

Educational programs, then, must be developed as tools which naturally extend from and enhance other archival work such as research, preservation, and collecting. They can be very rewarding, both for planners and participants.

Many of the products of educational activities serve a dual purpose. Designed to inform and instruct the clients of the archives, they are equally useful for orienting and educating new members of staff and prospective volunteers. In addition the research and analysis involved in developing educational aids often improves the overall standard of archival services. In a material sense they foster appreciation for the value of historical records and help ensure support for those who care for them.

Perhaps, most important of all, they encourage greater communication between the keepers of archives and the various institutional, social, and professional communities to which they belong. Archivists who plan and take part in educational activities develop perceptions which help them to do a better job of serving the needs of their clients. Correspondingly, members of the community who are introduced to archival work through educational projects may come to appreciate the legal and financial as well as cultural benefits of well-managed modern record services and use these insights to economic advantage in their personal and business enterprises.

A Planning Approach to Educational Programs

Educational programs come in such variety of type and scope that careful planning is needed to select those which best suit the purpose, resources and clientele of your institution as a whole. Most people underestimate the amount of work and coordination required in undertaking educational projects. Involving the wider community in activities at the archives or using archival materials requires special care. Public interest, enthusiasm and contact with original sources is to be encouraged, but not at the peril of the records. For example, you must ensure the safety of the archival items in the exhibit without making those who view them feel uncomfortable. All users and visitors should be courteously informed, preferably in advance, of the security measures which must be followed in the archives to eliminate the possibility of misunderstandings. Likewise, archivists must accept that they will sometimes make mistakes with educational activities.

One cannot absolutely predict public response to a workshop or publication; they can love it or leave it for a dozen reasons that have little to do with the project's worthiness. One can only research the undertaking well, seek and accept professional advice, plan for reasonable contingencies, and go. Above all, keep good records (you are keeping your own archives too, remember!) and evaluate the project thoughtfully. Thorough documentation of all phases of work will be invaluable in planning future activities.

At this point the need to plan is clear, but what exactly should one consider in developing a program of appropriate and beneficial educational projects? To create an effective education portfolio, archivists should follow four basic steps. First, define the goals of your institution. Second, determine the nature and needs of your audience. Third, locate and obtain the necessary resources. Fourth, select and plan an appropriate program to suit them. All activities must harmonise with the purpose and responsibility of your institution. Study the documents which established your archives and any subsequent records modifying them. Acts of Parliament, corporate charters and archives policy statements are records which determine the scope and focus of your work. These documents will also help you identify your audiences.

Finding out who your clients are and what they need to know and do to make the best use of the archives is a critical second step. Some of these clients may not be obvious because you know them in another capacity and may not think of the importance of their active support for your operation. They may be the managers or advisory Board of your own host organisation or they may be current users of your services as either researchers or

*A panel display demon-
strates the types of copies
available and their cost.*

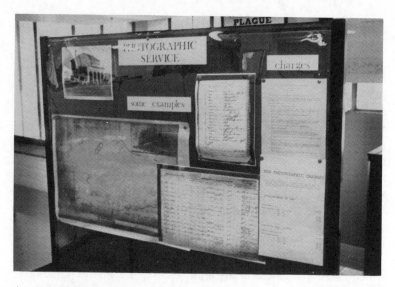

donors. They may be potential users, ie people for whom you are
there to serve, but who have never made contact with you.

Identifying client groups is a simple matter of knowing where
to look. The most obvious user group is the archives' present
researchers. There are records readily at hand which provide
information about who they are and their interests. The most
important of these records is the reader's ticket application form,
but other documents such as daily registrations of visitors/
researchers and lists of participants in workshops are also
valuable. People, offices or organisations who deposit their
records with the archives comprise another important client
group, one that uses the archives' storage, conservation and reference facilities and services as extensions of their own information systems. Acquisition and accession records and record
request forms (call slips) will reflect who they are and their patterns of use. The administrators, managers, and advisers of the
host organisation are particularly important clients for an in-
house archives as the effectiveness of their work may depend
upon the archives' care of vital organisational records.
Furthermore, their decisions in allocating funds are so crucial to
the archives operation that the needs and interests of this group
should receive top priority. In-house correspondence, reports and
budget papers provide important sources of information about
management concerns.

Another important group, often overlooked until their services
are needed, is that comprised of information officers and media
representatives. These professionals should be sent, at least
selectively, special event invitations and externally focused
communications such as calendars and newsletters. Maintaining
regular contact and encouraging involvement with archives

activities is a long-term investment that will yield dividends, including that all-important media coverage when the archives really needs it.

Knowing the groups and the information sources about them enables the archives to establish a regular program of user documentation. One of the first things you will want to do is create a mailing list enable you to communicate easily with your clients and with other individuals and organisations of importance to the archives. This aspect will be discussed in more detail later in the chapter. Abstracting information from the records provides a base of statistical data which will be invaluable in justifying expenditure and forward planning. Usage statistics may include

- number of contacts made with prospective depositors (individual and offices)
- number of accessions
- number of visitors/researchers
- number of readers tickets issued
- list of research topics
- number of records retrieved/refiled
- list of record services used and frequency of use
- number of copies provided
- number of letters sent
- number of publications sent
- number of events/workshops held
- number of participants in events/workshops
- number of hours of training and advice provided.

Obviously, each archives must select the level and range of statistics it keeps on client use according to its own resources and needs. Over-documentation is almost as bad as no documentation, and unused statistics are a waste of valuable time.

In setting priorities for reaching client groups, a suggested rule of thumb is to begin your efforts by making the delivery of existing services to established client groups more effective. For example, new researchers visit the archives daily. All first-timers, regardless of their previous experience with archives, will require orientation and they usually ask the same basic questions as they try to learn their way around. What educational tools could be provided to facilitate this process? A basic leaflet about the archives, its location, its holdings and services could be sent to enquirers in advance of their visit. Attractive, welcoming and easy-to-read signs can orientate newcomers quickly to the facilities. A simple plan of the public areas showing major features and explaining rules for using them could be distributed to visitors on arrival. A self-service library of brief video presentations on selected topics may ease researchers into their work with more confidence. Any or all of these suggestions could streamline the transformation of a new client into a productive researcher and make reference services more effective for all.

After you have improved the delivery of existing services to established clients, efforts may be made towards attracting or impressing the groups that can help your institution most, with the aim of building up additional resources. The point is that you now have a base from which to extend your reach to new activities and/or to contact new groups of potential users.

No educational activity can function without a commitment of resources of various kinds. The category that comes most easily to mind is that of facilities, equipment, and supplies, but it need not be the first to be considered as often such items can be hired, borrowed or donated. Your most important resource will be the time and talents of your staff, their knowledge of the archives and their continuing involvement and commitment before, during and after the project.

Bring your staff together and ask what kinds of projects would interest them and find out as much as possible about their skills and hobbies. You may have a good photographer, writer, designer or speaker among the crew. Others may have special subject knowledge that could be used in creating exhibits or publications. When considering a new idea, ask the staff from a variety of work areas for their views before plans advance too far, and give all interested staff an opportunity to be involved in all stages of the project, especially in the evaluation of its success.

In deciding where to start with the planning of educational programs, begin with what you know best. Choose projects that will enhance the services, collections and audiences most important to your archives. Ask staff members for suggestions of educational aids that would make work in their areas of responsibility easier. For example, a one-page handout could explain how to fill out a request for documents from the collections or how to order a copy. Frequently asked questions provide clues to areas where such aids or special small group training sessions could streamline reference service. Likewise, persons contacting the archives by mail often have similar questions, presenting the opportunity to design special information sheets or brochures to satisfy common types of requests.

While these ideas focus upon improving reference services, similar measures are helpful in other areas of archival work. Table 11.1 summarises ideas for educational aids which facilitate a number of archival functions.

Whatever types of educational aids you choose, whether designed for individual, group or community use, keep in mind that your aim is to have a coordinated and complementary program, rather than a disparate array of bits and pieces pulling in different directions. One effort should lead or extend logically to another, either in content or scope or both.

Table 11.1   Overview of Education Aids for Archives Work

Archival Function	Audiences		
	Individuals	Small Groups	Wider Community
Access and Reference	Orientation interview. Basic brochure on holdings, facilities and terms of access. Simple handouts (reading room rules, how to request records, obtain copies, special access).	Letter inviting use (universities, genealogical societies, etc). Mini classes for beginning researchers. Slide-tape show about using the archives or starting research. Training for volunteer reading room assistants.	Slide-tape or video encouraging use of the archives. Loan/sales of microforms of selected records. Seminars on popular research topics.
Finding Aids	Leaflet guide to major holdings. In-house finding aids.	Comprehensive guide to holdings. Training for volunteer indexers.	Individual guides to records of particular creators (Colonial Secretary) or on special subjects (gold, convicts). Reports on national or international guides or databases. Sale of microfilms of finding aids or indexes.
Acquisition and Appraisal	Personal contacts with prospective depositors (persons, organisations). Leaflet on donating material to archives. Rotating exhibitions of new acquisitions.	Slide-tape show on identifying archival materials. Slide talks on donating to archives. Workshop on identifying materials of historic value or disposal scheduling training for volunteer fieldworkers.	Field projects to survey and record potential acquisitions or to copy records in private custody. Video or slide-tape about archives field work. Conference on appraisal.
Arrangement and Description		Slide-tape or video on arrangement and description. Training for volunteers.	Work placements or intensive courses for students, volunteers or other professions.
Conservation	Leaflet on handling of various record media. Simple exhibitions (before and after types of damage, particular problems).	Slide talks on damaging agents, preventative measures, disaster minimisation. Work-shops on basic preventative and restorative techniques. Training for volunteers.	Slide-tape show or video on various aspects of conservation. Conferences on conservation issues.
User Education and Publications	Tours of the archives. Feature articles and news releases on major holdings, collecting efforts, new acquisitions, research projects. Simple displays on facets of archives work or background of the archives program.	Tours of the archives. Seminars on archival work or research methods for students. Slide talks about various aspects of archives work or research projects undertaken at the archives by staff or researchers.	Newsletter Open Days Conferences Major Exhibitions Friends of Archives events

Look into ways that the effort and expense of one project can be used to advantage in related or spin-off activities. Design your basic slide talk with sections that can be tailored to different audiences or edit your basic brochure information into a script for a video about the archives.[1] Similarly, the visuals and text information for an exhibit might be turned into a slide show which can be shown to audiences long after the original exhibit has been dismantled.

There is also an advantage in clustering activities around a major event or point in time. A local centenary, holiday or festival presents a good opportunity for the archives to attract wider publicity and a larger audience than usual for tours, workshops or exhibits featuring the special theme. Some institutions which sponsor conferences plan exhibits to complement them or vice versa so that the interest generated by one activity encourages participation in the other. Such an approach is useful because it gives participants an opportunity to explore more facets of a subject once their interest has been captured.

Take advantage of the experience and resources of other institutions. Many archives, libraries, museums and historical societies will have undertaken similar projects and may be willing to share their experiences. Collect copies of brochures and signs; solicit slide shows, workshop and exhibit ideas; and ask for planning reports and documentation. Consider joint ventures with neighbouring institutions. The benefits of shared projects are numerous. Pooled resources can lead to larger and more professional activities as well as to improved relations with colleagues in related professions.

User Education and Public Relations: Selected Programs

Potential user education and public relations programs are as numerous and varied as the archival institutions that sponsor them. However, all successful ones are characterised by the following qualities: a clear purpose, well-defined scope and content, and appealing presentation. Materials and projects for clients, whether internal or public, must be attractive and evoke interest and participation.

The following text focuses upon selected types of activities and is intended to provide general guidelines for development rather than explicit how-to instructions. (For more detailed information, consult the works cited under Further Reading or explore the extensive literature available on individual types of programs.) Educational activities will be discussed in the following sequence: Exhibitions; Public Relations; Publications; Classes, Seminars and Workshops; and Special Events.

Exhibitions

Exhibitions for archives may be described as the use of archival material to present ideas which inform or educate the viewer. Exhibitions provide a vehicle for the archives to show off its collections and help fulfil the archives wider mission of encouraging public respect and appreciation for past achievements. Although difficult to measure, the effects of a well-designed exhibition program are undeniably beneficial. Exhibitions inspire interest and involvement which can result in donations of records, funds, services or personal time to the archives. An archives need not be large or wealthy to mount a good exhibition program. Since most archives have very modest facilities and resources, archivists will be relieved to know that research on exhibition effectiveness affirms that viewers respond best to small, well-presented exhibitions. It is the subject matter of the exhibition, its placement and its design, rather than its size or complexity, that determine its appeal.

All exhibitions, however small, require commitments of money and of that even scarcer commodity – staff time and skill. They also present conservation and security problems and are, by nature, temporary in duration. For these reasons and in light of other priorities and commitments, archivists must not embark on a series of exhibitions simply because it is expected or because other institutions have done so. Rather, the decision to exhibit should be a positive and considered one, made to achieve genuine benefits for the archives.

Planning an Exhibit

Once the archives has committed itself to an exhibition program, the first step is to decide the focus the exhibition will have. Below are some questions that will facilitate this process. Is the aim mainly

*   to show off materials from the collection?
*   to inform viewers about the nature of archival materials, archival work and/or your archives?
*   to educate them on a point of history?
*   to interest, intrigue or inspire them?

Ideally the exhibition program will be structured to accomplish all four of these purposes, either simultaneously or sequentially.

After the exhibition goals have been identified, planners must then determine the location, structure and audience for the exhibition. Decisions here are more difficult because they must be reached by weighing many variables, such as resources, facilities, available equipment and existing work commitments, to come up with a workable plan. Sometimes key factors like conservation and security will limit possibilities for the location

This exhibit case would be more suitable if it had a solid pedestal base and more depth to allow materials to be seen from all sides.

and presentation of the exhibition. Some venues, though popular, are not sufficiently secure. For example, it would be unwise to place an exhibit case of original archival treasures in the central railway station or a very busy shopping mall.

Many archives must mount their exhibitions in donated cases, often obtained from shops which have closed down. While these gifts are most welcome, they were not designed for the display of irreplaceable documents and impose limits on the kinds of records that may be displayed to maximum advantage. Exhibition planners then must determine which of the variables affecting the exhibition are most critical and adjust their choices accordingly to come up with a workable compromise.

If conservation and security considerations seem to be cramping your plans for exhibits, consider using skilful facsimiles or duplicates of printed items instead of unique originals. Reasonable facsimile reproductions can be made by photocopying the originals on to paper of the same age taken from the blank pages of an old non-archival volume; even better results can be obtained by a skilled photographer. It can often be more appealing to copy and enlarge only the key passage in a document since viewers are not likely to be enthused enough to read many lines of difficult handwriting. The selective use of photographic panels or murals is also effective. All copies of documents and photographs should clearly be labelled as such and identified by the full citation and size of the original.

Once the logistical factors of the exhibition have been defined, planners can turn their attention to content. Choices here revolve around three factors: appropriateness for the proposed audience; the availability of suitable records, photographs and objects; and the exhibitor's knowledge, skill and imagination. Some ideas for exhibition topics or themes are listed in Table 11.2.

Identifying material suitable for exhibition can be facilitated by keeping exhibition potential in mind as records are appraised, arranged and described or used in the reading room. Staff with these archival responsibilities are often a fruitful source of ideas and knowledge, and exhibition planners in search of ideas and material should make a beeline for them. In fact, it is highly desirable for archives staff to work closely with public information officers and exhibit designers as a team to produce educational materials and exhibitions. In this way the expert knowledge of all is pooled and the resulting project will generate internal enthusiasm and pride.

Correspondingly, the occasion of an exhibition can provide opportunities for direct communication between the archives and the managers and administrators of its host organisation. Often the direction to prepare an exhibition for an important anniversary or event comes from above. The easiest course is to rush

Table 11.2 Some Ideas for Archival Exhibitions

About Archives Work:

General	• Archival activities from acquisition to research use • What are archives?
Achievements	• Ways in which archives sources or staff saved money and time for host organisation or community • New facilities, programs, equipment, publications • Anniversaries and commemorations
Acquisitions	• Recent acquisitions (after processing) • Depositing papers (what is involved) • Types of records sought (documents, photographs, ephemera)
Arrangement and Description	• Detective work identifying forgeries, estrays, unsigned materials, facsimiles • Sources and process of research on provenance and administrative history • Unusual records
Conservation	• A document before, during and after conservation • Hazards of metal fasteners, sticky tape • Types of damage and their causes • Preservation microfilming • How to handle various types of records
Reference	• Copyright in archives (manuscripts, artworks, photographs) • Protecting confidentiality and privacy • We'd like to know ... (examples of research enquiries) • Effects of theft/vandalism • Sources or how-to's on popular research topics (tracing your family, dating your home, railways, gold, convicts) • We helped ... (books, theses, TV programs produced from records in the archives)
About the Community	• Yesterday and today (photos, problems of life or business, events in the news) • Holidays (records describing or depicting) • Commemorations (royal visits, jubilees, centenaries) • Local firsts • Landmarks and localities • Leading businesses, industries, public or charitable agencies • Pioneers and their families • Local personalities

A staff team works to mount a major exhibition.

around, prepare the exhibition and present the finished product for applause. But, in so doing, the archivist has missed a valuable chance to acquaint his or her supervisors with the work and resources of the archives. Build upon the initial interest which inspired the directive by discussing exhibition ideas and content with management representatives at key points. Better yet, encourage management to assign a staff member to work with the exhibition team. The exposure to archives resources and the communication developed during the project is an investment that will yield long-term benefits.

Exhibition Guidelines

Exhibition planning and design is a specialised field with a rich literature of its own which archivists are urged to consult. The sources recommended in Further Reading are a good starting point. A detailed explanation of the steps and considerations required for planning an exhibition is well beyond the scope of this chapter, but it is possible to suggest a concise list of guidelines and insights which may be useful in the development of exhibitions for archives. A selection of these tips are embodied in Table 11.3.

Exhibition layout can be a challenging and exacting task. Supplies for constructing exhibits are expensive, and it is important to measure dimensions and arrange materials accurately to minimise wasteful errors. Be sure to allow space for labels, text blocks and the supports or case furniture that will hold the records safely in position. Many designers prefer to do an inexpensive paper and cardboard model of the exhibition, using copies of the records pasted on sheets cut to size. Mounting the test exhibitions into the case allows the preparer to assess the overall effect and recheck all measurements before cutting into the expensive matte board, fabric or perspex.

Exhibit planning also includes accessories such as slide shows, videos, posters, or catalogues that extend the impact of the exhibit over a longer term. For small exhibits, only a simple

Table 11.3 Tips for Exhibition Planners

Overall	• Exhibition area should be supervised and secure • Base tone and contents of exhibitionson your own institution and holdings. • Do a limited number of exhibitions well; change them every few months • Use few, but a variety of, record types and objects per exhibit • Do plan activities such as lectures and workshops to promote or complement the exhibit • Design to achieve general impact of message on viewer within 45 seconds • Plan height limits within comfortable viewing range (1.1–1.7m)
Conservation	• Do not leave originals on exhibit longer than one month • Keep lights separate from display case interior • Use low ultraviolet fluorescent lamps or special bulb shields • Monitor humidity inside cases and correct as needed • Provide suitable acid-free mountings and supports for records and volumes • Use facsimile copies if conservation or security is in doubt
Display Techniques	• Exhibits should be three dimensional; avoid the printed page look • Keep the exhibition simple and uncluttered • Group material in some order with a feature or focus • Use colour and texture to enhance, not overwhelm • Place materials on different levels and planes within the case • Use mounts to group small items so they do not get lost • Use coloured film overlays to point out key passages of text • Seek design help from museums, galleries and design professionals
Equipment	• Cases must be secure, ie have sturdy, unusual fastenings • Use a few cases of varied, but related, style • Cases should provide easy access for changing exhibits • Choose cases that are versatile or permit viewing from all sides
Labels and Text	• Labels and text should encourage viewers to study materials • Language should be clear, simple and brief • Do not over label; this can detract from the overall effect • Identify items on exhibit with proper citations • Use appropriate type styles and sizes for easy reading • Display transcripts with manuscript items
Materials	• If possible, select records with graphic appeal and that are easy to understand; single-sided, one-page pieces are ideal • Borrow appropriate objects or costumes, rather than acquire them • Be sure all reproductions are top quality and labelled as such

publicity poster is really worthwhile. Catalogues, in particular, are companions to an exhibit, but cannot substitute for it. Their main value lies in allowing the exhibit preparers room for more explanation and scholarly discussion than the exhibit panels permit. Videos and coffee table publications are generally reserved for more complex exhibits with substantial funding, as high quality productions can be quite expensive. Slide shows are within reach of most archives and provide a means of sharing the exhibit with wider and more dispersed audiences. Producing a synchronised cassette with music and narrative to accompany well-composed slides adds a professional touch.

As the exhibit nears the final stages of preparation, arrangements for its promotion should be well underway. All new exhibits, however modest, should be announced in appropriate media outlets. The types and extent of publicity will naturally reflect the magnitude and importance of the exhibit and its proposed audience. A single case exhibit in the reading room might be announced with a poster in the foyer and a short piece in the archives newsletter. Having an opening for the exhibit provides an occasion to invite persons to the archives. Even the small exhibit mentioned above could be opened with tea and biscuits on a day when the reading room is likely to be crowded.

Whatever the scope of your exhibit program, the archives and its staff will benefit most from a balanced approach that is thoroughly in tune with the institution's aims and resources. The community, too, will be enriched from the additional opportunity to explore the archival sources of its heritage and grow in its appreciation of the valuable and important work of archives.

Public Relations

Designing a program of archival services without paying specific attention to public relations is like planning a party without inviting the guests. Regular communication with client groups is as important as any of the purely archival activities, maybe even more so since our work is so heavily dependent upon the cooperation of depositors and users. Certainly, effective communication of the nature and value of archival work to our constituent host organisations and larger communities is *critical* if we are to obtain necessary resources to carry out our increasing responsibilities. Client relations, public relations or publicity, as this work is variously termed, is a positive consciousness that should initially infuse one's work and then later be formalised into publicity, interviews, speeches and other outreach activities. It is important to build client-centred thinking into archival work with policies and procedures. A checklist of steps to complete during acquisition should include acknowledging each gift and placing the donor's name on the archives' mailing list. The reference staff could give departing researchers a self-mailing form soliciting their ideas for improvement. Visitors and researchers should be included when invitations are sent out for workshops or exhibits. Staff members, whether speaking to groups or meeting individuals, should always have a supply of basic brochures about the archives. While it is not appropriate to hand out leaflets in the street, one never knows when a casual contact might spark genuine interest which should be followed up.

Managing the Mailing List

The heart of any program of client relations is a well-managed mailing list. Direct communication with client groups, including the media, through the mail is a capability all archives must have; however, it is one that can lead to wasteful expense if it is not carefully monitored. Developing a mailing list begins by identifying those individuals and groups with whom the archives has a need to communicate. A comprehensive list might include the following recipients:

- Government officials and agencies responsible for or interested in heritage.
- Members of the governing or advisory board.
- Depositors, actual and potential.
- Managers and administrators of other branches of the host organisation.
- Volunteers.
- Members of your organisation or associated Friends groups.
- Media representatives or personalities.
- Recent visitors, researchers and participants in archives workshops or functions.
- Professional associations of archivists, historians, museum curators, conservators, librarians and records managers.
- Appropriate groups such as libraries, historical societies, history teachers, university schools or departments of history.
- Sponsors, actual and potential, including corporations, businesses, charitable trusts, granting bodies.

Occasionally there may be a special promotion, such as the sale of a publication, where a more general audience is sought. Rather than inflate the mailing for this occasion, consider using a marketing service that specialises in direct mail or approaching a publications distribution company.

Since postage can be a considerable expense, organise the mailing list to permit access to selected categories of addresses. This can be done manually by creating separate sets of master labels or colour-coded cards. A computer system can be invaluable because of its capacity to select, retrieve and print out the desired addresses on labels. For example, in advertising a local workshop, it might be useful to organise the system to select only those addresses with postcodes within reasonable travelling distance of the archives. The expense of large mailings can also be reduced by presorting for bulk mail handling. Consult the post office for advice and incorporate their requirements into the planning of promotional material.

Once the list has been established, it must be maintained accurately. The culling and updating should be done regularly by archives staff or volunteers. If the list is large, it may pay to employ a firm which manages all aspects of mailing services.

Publicity

Publicity is getting a message across to an audience in an accurate, well-presented and timely manner. There are two basic ways of communicating with an audience: the direct method, which utilises the mail or a specialised distribution system; and the indirect approach, which works through an intermediary, usually a radio, television or newspaper journalist.

With the direct approach, the archivist, singly or working with an in-house publicist, prepares and packages the message which is then sent directly to known recipients. This method has several advantages. The archivist knows that the message sent is exactly what has been designed and that the timing suits the programs' needs. The archivist has also selected the recipients as persons or agencies worth cultivating.

However, there are also disadvantages to direct contact. The archives may not have the resources to produce materials to a professional standard or to bear the expense of regular mailing to a wide audience. Errors in timing can also result from lack of marketing experience or knowledge of competing activities.

Working through the media, the archivist is able to minimise costs, obtain wider coverage and deliver more professionally packaged messages, but not without certain risks. The message and the timing may undergo changes to meet media programming demands. Each media team attempts to package and present the best material from what is available at any given time. The competition among news and feature items for space or air time is heightened by the additional pressures of deadlines, audience ratings and those all-important sponsorship dollars. Thus, working within the dynamic environment of media requires archival publicists to be both flexible and persistent in their efforts to exploit media resources.

Perhaps the best idea is to plan publicity efforts that combine self-distributed information with selected media exposure, relying more on the former than the latter. Using this approach, one can always be assured that the message will reach a primary audience and may be magnified and multiplied if media coverage is obtained.

Whatever approach used, one of the best ways to increase the chances of success in obtaining appropriate publicity is to cultivate good relationships with writers, editors and program-makers, both in-house and outside, who work in the field. Journalists are greedy for interesting material and most archives hold plenty of it. It is a matter of matching these interests and people on a regular basis. Including appropriate media representatives and publicists in the archives' mailing list will ensure that they are reliably informed of approaching activities and invited to special events. In addition, ideas and visual materials for feature stories about the archives and its collections should be provided to reporters with cultural or historical interests and responsibilities. Researchers, volunteers and staff members may also be canvassed for ideas and encouraged to give interviews regarding their work or knowledge. Earlier in this chapter, ideas for exhibitions were discussed, many of which will provide suitable topics for news items, feature articles or documentaries.

Whatever the topic, care should be taken to ensure that all materials provided to journalists and editors, are accurate, concise, well written and presented in an interesting way. Beginning the piece with an arresting opener, closely followed by the who, what, where, why and when information is a well-accepted formula. Be sure to include a name and telephone number of the person to contact for more information.

Help with publicity initiatives may be more available and forthcoming than you think. Many people with publicity skills and experience are willing to help a worthy cause. Retired members of the media and public relations community have a wealth of experience and contacts and may welcome the opportunity to use them on your behalf. Keep in mind, however, that help is just that. The archives must always accept its responsibility to provide the resources to get the work done.

Publicity is an art which calls for several levels of effort. All archives, large and small, must keep their clients informed about the archives' work and activities. This basic effort involves placing 'publicity' on the agenda for major planning meetings. Staff can then identify recent accomplishments that should be reported and develop a calendar of coming events. Responsibility for preparing these items and the dates of completion should also be established and monitored. Initially, these reports may be placed in the reading room and sent to selected archival and historical journals quarterly or half-yearly. This information forms a base which the archivist can use to prepare and distribute an authoritative annual report to the archives' primary clientele. As the publicity program grows, archives staff or volunteers can expand on the core material by preparing brief articles describing research projects, notable visitors, accomplishments or materials from the collections for inclusion in a newsletter.

The second level of publicity involves designing special publicity for specific activities or events sponsored by the archives. Although these are also announced and reported as part of the basic publicity program, they usually require specialised promotion tailored to the needs of each occasion. The effort required to produce customised publicity can be minimised by including the category 'publicity' in a checklist for planning special programs and activities. Attention can then be given in a systematic way to designing the message to be delivered, defining the audience to receive it, identifying the methods most appropriate and to establishing the time frames, personnel and services needed.

Up to this point, the emphasis has been on preparing publicity materials for distribution, either directly or indirectly through the media, and on establishing and maintaining a good rapport with professional communicators. But do not overlook the most important public relations assets of all – you and your staff. Opportunities to promote the archives present themselves many times daily in formal and informal ways, within and outside of the workplace. The key to success in this area is to exhibit a genuinely helpful and positive attitude in all interpersonal dealings, be they with staff, clients or the public. Professional expertise, shared with courtesy and good humour, contributes to a pleasant working environment and clearly conveys the message that archives are rewarding as well as worthwhile enterprises.

As a natural extension of this outward-looking mentality, set aside time in the working week to call on or meet with persons or groups whose interest you wish to cultivate. There is a danger here, particularly if you have an outgoing personality, of spending too much time on outreach to the detriment of less exciting but equally important archival tasks. Your time and energy, like your collections, must be preserved as well as made available for access and use.

Inevitably, and delightfully, these contacts will lead to invitations to speak before groups or be interviewed on radio or television programs. Anticipating such eventualities, you would be wise to learn a bit about public speaking. Take some slides of the archives and select materials from the collections to accompany your talk; these will add dimensions and increase the impact of your enthusiastic words. It is also useful to look to your staff and to long-time researchers and volunteers for candidates with the potential to share the limelight.

Publicity for the archives is a challenging task requiring flexibility, tact, persistence and a sense of humour. The archival publicist must temper his or her enthusiasm and skills for promotion with the knowledge that creating too much demand without the resources to handle the response can overwhelm or threaten the existence of the very materials and programs he or she hopes to strengthen. However, properly managed, a regular and balanced program of publicity can be an invaluable asset for any archives.

Publications

Publications are among the best known and most popular user education programs and are valuable tools for communicating information about the archives, its holdings and services. Also their impact is longer term and more easily measured than other forms of user education. However, publications also represent a considerable investment of resources. Much time and energy, usually of senior staff, go into their preparation, and production costs can be substantial, particularly if multiple colours and illustrations are used. The advice is the same as with other user education efforts – proceed with caution and build on established strengths. This message cannot be over emphasised because unsuccessful publications are an expensive embarrassment which will occupy the shelves for a long, long time.

The term 'publication' can be used to describe a wide variety of productions, ranging from a single A4 page to an elaborately illustrated book. The characteristic common to all is that they convey information to users of archival records and services in a consistent form that can be kept and referred to as needed.

Basic Publishing

Every archives will find it needs publications to help it accomplish its work in three major areas: repository services, reference, and educational activities. Repository services such as depositing or transferring records into the archives can be facilitated by developing manual-style booklets for clients which explain the procedures and documents needed to accomplish these tasks. Such publications, used in conjunction with personal contact and special training programs, foster good working relationships with donors and depositors who regularly transfer their modern records to the archives under a disposal schedule or continuing agreement.

In reference work, publications can make existing services more effective in a number of ways. For example, a free brochure providing brief answers to those frequently asked questions about the archives' purpose, location, holdings, services, hours and conditions of access can be distributed widely. Table 10.5 in Chapter 10, Access and Reference Services, gives details of the points to cover in a basic brochure. Similarly, how-to information sheets on using the finding aids, requesting records or ordering copies can help researchers learn procedures more quickly and confidently. Descriptive inventories to individual collections can be produced in multiple copies and distributed to libraries and other archives with related research interests. This practice helps to promote the use of the archives collections more widely and enables out-of-area researchers to determine whether or not a research trip will be fruitful and make better informed requests through the mail.

Checklists outlining the steps and sources for popular research topics such as family or local history are also valuable, as are sheets referring researchers to other institutions whose holdings complement those of the archives. All of these publications are simple and effective ways to inform users and help to minimise the strain on resources caused by having to prepare individual responses to repetitive inquiries.

Additional Publications

It is through regular and selective publishing that the archives establishes its wider reputation as a research institution. New additions to the publications family should reflect and reinforce the natural growth of the archives program, rather than be products of momentary inspiration. The archives may begin by publishing an overall guide to its holdings which abstracts basic information from the descriptive inventories of individual collections and presents it in a summarised form. A basis for the guide may be established by compiling the individual collection reports which the archives may have submitted to journals or to national guides such as the *Guide to Collections of Manuscript Relating to Australia*. Such comprehensive work may be further complemented by developing guides to sources suitable for major types of research such as family, local or business history. However, specialised guides should be undertaken with caution as records are often useful for a number of fields and a good index to the comprehensive guide can serve these research interests just as well at less expense.

Many archives find it beneficial to combine their publicity and publishing initiatives in a newsletter announcing and reporting archives activities to the community. The newsletter need not be elaborate – a single typed sheet with a distinctive heading will serve. It is more important to concentrate on producing accurate, well-written articles and to distribute the newsletter at regular quarterly or half-yearly intervals. Categories for articles may include newly processed collections, program achievements, interesting documents or photographs, a calendar of coming events, special projects and activities, research in progress, notable visitors and staff news.

The archives will also produce occasional publications encouraging clients and members of the community to become involved

Well-designed news-letters attract readers and reflect well upon the archives.

in educational activities sponsored by the archives. Individual brochures and leaflets are issued to promote exhibits, work-shops, classes and special events such as open days. These pieces serve both as announcements and as invitations to prospective participants to preregister for the occasion.

The need for a basic or additional publication is easy to identify. Staff liaising with depositors can report issues or problems that occur in the course of their work. Reference staff can keep track of frequently asked questions and of common research problems and topics. A list of these can then become the basis for ideas for training sessions and workshops as well as for publications.

*Reproductions of posters,
maps and photographs
make interesting
souvenirs and generate
income and publicity.*

ARCHIVES OFFICE POSTCARDS 10¢

Having selected those questions and problems which would be effectively handled with a publication, the archivist can then concentrate on the specific information to be conveyed and the best way to present it. To save effort and money, related issues or topics may be grouped into a single publication, provided that the proposed combinations are compatible and the information will not require frequent changes. It is wasteful to put volatile information into a publication which might otherwise have a long life. All publications should be assigned a unique number which embodies their date of production. This number should be altered when the piece is revised, but not if it is simply reprinted. Two copies of each publication should be set aside as part of your own program's archives.

Good Design: A Wise Investment

Each publication, regardless of how modest, should be designed to attract readers. Appropriate, readable typefaces combined with simple graphics and a pleasing balance between text and white space will enhance the message to be conveyed. Coloured inks and papers can also be effective, but these should be used selectively with the advice of an experienced designer to avoid aesthetic blunders and/or costly mistakes. It is a good idea to think of each of your published pieces, including your letterhead, as family members which share a visual identity. Standard page sizes, typefaces and cover formats will help establish continuity of image and still allow each item to have individual distinction. Having a person with professional design credentials or experience create an overall graphic image and standard framework for your program is a worthwhile investment.

Souvenir Publishing

Many cultural institutions, archives among them, offer a selection of souvenir items for sale to researchers and visitors to promote the institution and raise funds. Souvenir publications include postal and greeting cards, notepaper, and frameable prints and posters reproducing graphic items from the collections. More complex examples are diaries or calendars, exhibit catalogues and sets of facsimile documents. Souvenir objects such as carry bags, tea towels, ties, scarves and insignia jewellery are less common in archives than in museums, but some larger institutions do have shops, often operated by volunteers or members of a Friends group, offering a range of such items. This type of publishing is truly an option rather than a necessity. It is expensive because many items fail to meet costs, and it can expose the archives' program to criticism from those who view souvenir items as trivial gimmicks. Opportunities for the production of souvenir items are frequent, but all should be scrutinised carefully to identify pitfalls and unfavourable consequences. As a general rule, such projects should be undertaken and financed by sources outside the archives and should not be endorsed or condoned by the archives unless they meet stringent quality standards. This policy avoids most of the problems, such as high expense and unsold stock, which can accompany souvenir publishing.

Large-Scale Publishing

Publications in this category are usually undertaken by archives with comprehensive, well-established programs or by a group of cooperating institutions often working in conjunction with a professional publisher. Examples include publishing the full text of collections of diaries, letters, literary manuscripts or other personal papers; publishing business/corporate records; or republishing runs of rare journals, gazettes and newspapers. Other prospects in this category include illustrated publications such as exhibit catalogues and those featuring collections of historic photographs or documentary art.

A number of questions must be answered before undertaking such projects:

- What is the need for the publication? Is it compelling intellectually and economically?
- Will all the records be published or only a selection? If the latter, what criteria will be used to select those to be included? Who will make those judgments?
- Will the publication be hard copy, microform or CD technology?
- Who will have the copyright in the publication?
- What is the anticipated market for the publication? By whom and how will the publication be marketed and distributed? Is the market large, eager and easily reached?

- What staff, equipment and supplies are needed to prepare the records, the text and the illustrations for publication? By whom and how will these expenses be met?
- Does the archives have the resources, both financial and human, to self-publish and market a quality product?

Unfortunately, the answers to these questions are usually discouraging to self-publishers, but worthwhile projects may still be realised. The answer lies in shifting the initiative and the financial burden of producing the publication to resources outside the archives. Two main possibilities should be investigated. First, the material the archives seeks to publish may be part of a larger body of documentation held by several institutions. This is particularly true with collections of rare journals, gazettes and newspapers. By joining forces with other libraries and archives, the project may be able to attract special funding and produce a more authoritative and significant work than if it were undertaken by a single institution.

Second, the archives should approach established scholars and publishers who specialise in documentary works. These experienced professionals will investigate the proposed project and make recommendations regarding its feasibility. Keep in mind that working with professional publishers requires flexibility and an understanding of the realities of a competitive trade. These outsiders are, in essence, no different from other researchers working on publication projects. The archives is only the source of the raw material; and, beyond the normal obligations to protect materials from loss, damage or legal infringement, it will have no control or responsibility for the quality of the product.

An exception to this situation is one in which the archives develops a formal partnership with a publisher to jointly produce a work. In such cases the archives staff may be responsible for most or all of the work of preparing the records for publication. The publisher usually assigns his or her own editor, designer and publicist to work with the archives to maximise the prospects of marketing success, but will still expect the archives to provide mailing lists and strategies for reaching non-commercial purchasers. Again, each partner will view the project from a different perspective, and a successful working relationship will involve compromises, most often in favour of the partner paying the bills.

Whatever level of publication you choose for your archives, the effort should be one that supports the work of the archives as a whole and is reflective of the quality you wish to have associated with your institution.

Classes, Seminars and Workshops

For many archivists, the term 'user education' is synonymous with classes, seminars and workshops. Indeed, these activities are among the most rewarding of all user education programs for they are usually enjoyed by both staff and participants and measurably increase awareness of the archives within the larger community. These training activities also benefit the archives in less obvious ways. Staff members involved in teaching gain confidence and renewed enthusiasm for their work when they see that it is interesting to others. Slide shows and videos produced as training aids may be adapted for wider audiences. Teaching research methods often leads to more effective reference procedures and improved finding aids, and many useful publications have their origins in handouts for workshops.

Training for In-House Users

As with other user education programs, teaching activities should directly support and facilitate the use of archival holdings and services within the organisation before developing a wider community orientation. Acquisition and reference come to mind as natural areas where regular training sessions can improve the delivery of services to in-house users, such as officers who will be transferring material or using their own records housed in the archives. The purpose of the training would be to inform new staff and agency representatives of their responsibilities in such areas as

- understanding the functions of archives within the organisation
- care and handling archives and records
- conducting records surveys for disposal
- developing and implementing disposal schedules
- donating records to the archives
- transferring records to the repository
- requesting records or information from the archives.

An understanding of the nature of the archives' work, its procedures and documentation can contribute greatly to the smooth operation of these important functions where clients interact directly with archives staff.

Volunteers are another important audience for in-house training. A general introduction to the purpose and overall operation of the archives program is as important for prospective volunteers as it is for new staff, and an orientation session could profitably include individuals from both groups. However, it is important for instructors to remember that volunteers do not have the same accountability as paid staff and to understand that all training sessions which include volunteers must explain and maintain that distinction in a tactful and friendly way. Overall, there is a benefit in training staff and volunteers together as both groups then have a better understanding of the working relationship they will enjoy in future. Some examples of training sessions which could be suitable for volunteers include

- replacing fasteners, refoldering records
- flattening and cleaning documents
- encapsulating materials
- indexing
- conducting oral history interviews
- transcribing/indexing oral history
- assisting reference staff
- photocopying
- preparing bibliographies and special lists
- conducting tours for visitors
- giving talks about the archives
- writing newsletter articles.

Volunteers are an important asset for the archives and should be well informed about the program and its operations. More information about recruiting and managing volunteers will be presented later in this chapter.

Educating the Public

As a complement to and extension of in-house training, the archives should also develop educational activities for outsiders, whether they be members of the public or individuals from a specialised client group. As mentioned earlier, few people have had any opportunity to learn about archives work or original records in the normal course of growing up; therefore, it is in the archives' own interest to plan programs to bridge this gap of experience and to minimise it in the future. Naturally, the type and content of educational offerings will vary according to the purpose of your archives, its scope and its clientele; smaller institutions may work informally, while large ones may have a calendar full of scheduled events. The main point is that an appropriate level of outreach is necessary so that the archives can develop a base of community support from which to grow.

Mini-Classes

The first priority of archival educators must be to convert first-time users into confident, competent researchers as quickly as possible. While this process always requires the archivist to spend some individual time with researchers, the amount of that time and the extent of information conveyed can be modified by using group instruction and self-teaching aids. A number of archives have instituted programs of mini-classes, half-hour sessions conducted at a regular time or when the need arises, to inform readers. The sessions can be conducted at a table in the reading room so that participants can familiarise themselves with the finding aids and facilities. Most classes combine talks and exercises to present basic information on the following topics:

- Introduction to the reading room.
- Using archival sources – general and various types such as newspapers and photographs.
- Research techniques and/or sources for popular fields such as family history.

After a few presentations, the staff will know what works best and can develop basic outlines and handouts for regular use. Instructors can include researchers and volunteers as well as staff to provide a variety of viewpoints and expertise. In this way the classes can reflect the needs of the users and build upon the strengths of the staff and collections.

An individualised alternative or supplement to the mini-classes is to develop an audiocassette program which orients newcomers to the reading room. Modelled on the museum self-tour of exhibits, this instructional aid employs a portable cassette player with headphones and takes the new reader to numbered sites in the reading room. The tape then explains the sources and how to use them, incorporating tasks for the researcher to do to improve his or her understanding before moving on.

Seminars and Workshops

Extending beyond the immediate need to orient and instruct researchers and staff, the archives can also benefit from sponsoring workshops and seminars that provide a more thorough coverage of archival subjects. In a pure sense, seminars differ from workshops in that they are usually directed discussions of issues and ideas, whereas workshops are practical hands-on occasions where participants develop skills and techniques or solve problems. Both of these programs are most effective with groups of up to 20 people.

Possible topics for workshops and seminars are as varied as the range of materials within the archives multiplied by the interests of the intended audience. In other words the choice is vast. However, first ventures should be designed to explore established strengths, both of the collections and of available expertise. A modest half- or full-day program, executed with confidence, will provide a base of success and enthusiasm on which to expand and diversify. Table 11.4 outlines a basic program with mini-classes, workshops and seminars on popular themes. It also gives tips on scheduling, promotion and administration which are at least as important to the success of the effort as having a good topic.

Conferences

Conferences are more comprehensive undertakings than seminars and workshops both in content and in numbers. A program

Table 11.4 Basic Classes, Workshops

	Subject	Administration	Promotion
Mini-Classes			
• Specific how-to's for beginning researchers	Introduction to research process • Using the finding aids • Proper handling of documents • Basic categories of sources and where they are located (documents, maps, newspapers, etc)	• Appoint staff committee to develop a presentation that can be given by several members of staff • Work class into regular workday schedule • Charge no fee • Hold weekly or biweekly classes at regular times for 20–30 minutes	• List in basic brochure about the archives • Post announcement on signboard in reception area • Announce in research areas just before class begins
Workshops/ Seminars			
• Specialised instruction focusing on specific topics or research problems • In-depth perspectives and discussion of selected subject areas	• Researching historic sites, family or community history • Identification and care of historical papers, photographs, graphic materials • Basic conservation • Research on specialist topics (transport, churches, gold, convicts, World War I) • Indexing original records or contemporary sources (newspapers, school magazines) • Significant historical issues and themes	• Plan presentations, demonstrations and how-to activities by staff and/or invited speakers • Prepare handouts • Charge a reasonable registration fee • Preregister participants • Have refreshments • Limit enrolment to 15–25 • Hold quarterly half-or full- day sessions (Saturday for optimum attendance)	• Mail program brochure to archival researchers, historical societies, libraries, high school social studies departments and other appropriate audiences • Send public service announcements to media • Post on sign board and have in reception area • Pass information by word-of-mouth from readers and staff

is usually organised around a theme featuring one or more large general or plenary sessions followed by smaller, more focused presentations, which may be concurrent as well as sequential to allow participants more choices.

Giving a group of new researchers a short introduction to the archives can reduce repetitive questions.

A show of local hospitality is an important complement to a good program, and the larger audience may include out-of-area participants who will need food and accommodation. Special tours, social events and/or entertainments add zest and contribute to the overall quality of experience. However, all of these ingredients – content, venue, and hospitality – must be measured and combined carefully to ensure a balanced result. Too much or too little of any one of them can spoil the overall effect.

Planning a successful conference can involve a considerable commitment of time. The effort is manageable if the work is shared, and good delegation skills are essential for conference coordinators. Most meetings involve planning in two main areas – program content and local arrangements – and it is helpful to select a responsible person to coordinate each of these. Table 11.5 provides a schedule and checklist of activities for basic conference planning. For more detailed information, consult the suggestions for Further Reading at the end of this chapter.

Conference planners must also decide in advance whether or not to publish the proceedings and make the necessary arrangements with authors and printers. Several cautions are worthy of note. Editing verbal presentations into written form is difficult, as is working with multiple authors; persistence and skill are needed to produce proceedings in a timely manner. Conference papers also vary considerably in quality so it may be best to encourage

Table 11.5 Basic Conference Planning Checklist

5–6 months in advance	1	Meet with colleagues and collaborators to discuss the general theme and scope of the conference and solicit ideas for prospective sessions, topics and speakers.
	2	Check calendars of coming events and set a tentative date.
	3	Reserve meeting facilities; book caterers.
	4	Meet again with fellow planners to finalise session topics and speakers. Have an alternate for each prospective speaker in case the first choice is unavailable. Decide whether or not to publish conference papers.
	5	Invite the speakers: • Telephone each speaker to explain the purposes of the conference, the general topic you would like him or her to cover, and the date, time and place of the meeting. Indicate whether there will be an honorarium or reimbursement for travel/expenses. At the very least, speakers should be given complimentary registration, meals and parking. • Send each speaker a letter confirming the invitation and discussing the topics. Have speakers return a form in which they indicate their exact titles (ie how they would like to be listed on the program), give brief descriptions of their presentations and agree to publishing/ typing arrangements.
	6	Send announcements of the event to calendar sections of all appropriate journals and newsletters.
	7	Start a file for each session and event on the agenda. Include correspondence, biographical information about the speakers, session outline forms, and notes on special logistical requirements (eg extra chairs, audiovisual equipment, microphones, transportation).
3 months in advance	8	Prepare a program flyer: • Prepare program copy and artwork. • Get in touch with speakers for any information not yet received. • Ask how long the printer will take to produce finished copies. • Send the text to the printer so the program is in the mail no less than two months before the conference date. • Prepare the mailing list and labels while the program is at the printer.
2 months in advance	9	Mail program flyer.
1 month in advance	10	Confirm arrangements with speakers.
	11	Confirm arrangements for meeting facilities and coordinate final plans for meals, receptions, tours or other conference events.

	12	Visit the meeting site and assign rooms for the conference sessions. Make arrangements to rent audiovisual equipment as needed.
1 week before	13	Complete the preparation and duplication of handouts, assemble registration packets, and do the final check of all arrangements.
1–2 days before	14	Be prepared to transport speakers to and from meeting site and/or accommodation, if needed, and give them a tour of your facility.
During conference	15	Introduce – or arrange for another participant to introduce – speakers at the sessions. Thank speakers personally for their participation.
Shortly after (no more than 1 month)	16	Send speakers a thank you letter, and mail speakers and participants an evaluation form.
	17	Collect evaluation forms and prepare a report assessing the strengths and weaknesses of the meeting.
Within 6 months	18	Edit/publish selected conference papers (optional).

Note: Lead-time estimates are based on the requirements for a substantial metropolitan meeting and may be scaled up or down for other levels of conferences.

selected authors to publish in a refereed journal, noting that the paper was first presented at the conference. In this way the work is published, the conference credited and someone else does the editing.

Activities for Students

Students are among the most important client groups, particularly for school and local community archives. In the writer's view all students above age 16 should have some exposure to the riches of contemporary and original sources as part of their general education. Otherwise, a critical, perhaps unique, opportunity to acquaint them with archives and archival work is lost and the level of community ignorance perpetuated. Few archives are able to cope with mass onslaughts of researchers, particularly of inexperienced ones, as some students may be, and they should not be expected to do so. After all, research is an individual or, at most, a small group activity, and there are ways, other than on-site visits, to have students interact with original sources.

Duplicates, facsimiles and, in some cases, originals of archival materials can be lent or taken to libraries and classrooms where students can examine them and learn to evaluate evidence or pursue a line of research appropriate for their age and level of experience. Local and family history projects provide excellent laboratories for both exploring and for creating documentary sources. Whatever the proposed project, archivists must recognise that their responsibility is to encourage and support the educational effort, not to design or conduct it; the latter is the domain of the professional educator. Supporting and encouraging activities may include the following:

(a) Developing policies, plans and procedures which
- establish and nurture an appropriate level and scope of interaction between the archives and the education system
- facilitate the use of archival sources and services by educators and students.

(b) Giving presentations to groups of educators to make them aware of the archives and its holdings and
- identify materials related to course curricula
- explain the terms under which materials can be made available
- suggest ways teachers and students can use source materials.

(c) Collaborating with educators to give workshops on the use of archival materials in teaching.

(d) Working with educators to
- identify local structures, sites, events or individuals for which there is sufficient documentation in the archives to do a local history research project
- design projects to document community life on a continuing basis combining photography, oral history and archival research.

The policy and planning work is particularly important because it establishes a framework for an ongoing relationship and enables the archives to respond selectively and appropriately to requests for student activities without being overwhelmed. Some questions that archival policy-makers should ask include:

(a) At what grade level should students
- be introduced to primary sources in a classroom setting?
- become involved with individual research projects using archival resources?
- be permitted to do research at the archives and under what conditions?

(b) What types of experiences are appropriate for the archives to provide for students and how should they be managed? What facilities and staff would be required?

(c) How will the products of student work, particularly those of high quality, be used?

The answers to these questions will provide a sound basis for discussion with educators and enable you to determine a level of involvement in student activities that is suitable for your program and resources. Remember, there is no requirement for the archives to cater to every interest group or demand. It is better to do a few things well.

Follow-up Activities

Any learning experience is beneficial in itself and rewarding for the individual who undertakes it, but the result can be even more significant and worthwhile if it is seen as a lasting contribution to be shared and appreciated by others. Students, or anyone for that matter, including volunteers and staff, will invest more time and effort into their work if they know it will be used and enjoyed. For this reason, archival educators should incorporate plans for the use of archival projects into the program design. The type and extent of promotion and use will vary with the nature of the project, but the suggestions given in Table 11.6 below are a good starting point.

Instructional programs, be they in-house training, workshops/seminars, conferences or activities for students, all have one thing in common: they involve people with archives and expose them to the fascination of archival work. The benefits of such involvement are multiple and diverse, ranging from increased staff knowledge and confidence to new recruits for the volunteer workforce; from an index for a series of previously inaccessible records to a major work of local or family history; from a gift of a single photograph to a host of new collections or substantial gifts of funds. Of all the educational programs, these which implant lasting knowledge and skill through involvement ultimately have the most lasting impact and continue to generate benefits in ever-widening circles.

Community Support Systems

'He who has a thousand friends has not a friend to spare' is the opening line of a famous couplet by Ali Ben Abu Talab, and one that archivists are well advised to take to heart.[2] While it is true that ongoing, responsible enterprises must plan their programs within the bounds of the recurrent financial support they receive from their own budgetary authorities, a gift of special funding and assistance from outside community sources is always welcomed and appreciated. The ability to attract and utilise extra equipment, services, personnel and funding is an acquired skill and one which can, with practice, become an important asset for a

Table 11.6 Follow-Up Activities

Type of Project	Ideas for Promotion and Use
Students bring archival materials from home to share with class	• Prepare a series of selected items for small exhibits within the school, local library or archives. • Work with local newspaper or TV station to feature the historic photograph, object or document of the week.
Documenting a local building or community landmark	• Prepare a small exhibit of documents, photographs and/or objects for an appropriate community setting. • Produce a facsimile package of documentary sources for study by future students.
Listing local landmarks and/or structures/sites	• Prepare a series of historic walking tours based upon project research. • Work with local television stations to produce a heritage commercial or background slides for station breaks.
Local or family history research papers	• Give prizes for outstanding papers. • Publish or arrange publication of significant individual work or collections of work. • Encourage researchers to give presentations based on their work to local historical or community groups.

developing archives. However, before hitting the solicitation trail, you must do your homework and adhere to a few basic rules:

• Outside support must always be considered as an extra. It should not be viewed as a requirement for the success of any venture.

• Outside support should only be sought for specific projects of limited duration. Few benefactors are willing to give to general ongoing programs and they prefer to see the results and the gratitude quickly, certainly within the same budget year.

• Develop and maintain a wish list of defined projects, items or areas where special funding or help can be used to maximum effect. The list should describe the commitment required in terms of time equipment, services and funds and should outline the benefits the gift will bring to prospective benefactors and to the archives.

• Before seeking outside support, determine your objectives, themes or messages and requirements (eg conservation) which the project must meet. Flexibility and room for compromise should be an integral part of project planning, but these are the points you must explain and adhere to in negotiations with prospective donors.

- Prospective donors, whether of time, money, equipment, facilities or services, all hope to gain some benefit meaningful to them. Altruism is a nice idea in the abstract, but in the real world donors want to realise some clear benefit for their help. Your job is to find out what they want and build it into the project proposal.

- Philanthropy is a very competitive business. Most donors have limited funds and many requests for them. You must find out what their funding cycle is and get your request in early to ensure consideration. The proposal must be well prepared, succinct and specific.

- Develop and maintain a hit list of funding and support prospects. See that key representatives of these groups/agencies are on the mailing list to receive the archives' newsletter, calendar of activities, and invitations to special events such as exhibit openings.

- Seek a variety of types of support. Money is only one among many possibilities. The archives may benefit equally from a special piece of equipment, a gift of flowers or refreshments, the use of a meeting or conference venue, free publicity or a complimentary brochure. Services which could be donated include graphic design, typesetting, printing, photocopying, word processing, audio or video recording, consultancy (automation, exhibits, fundraising), photography, music, compere or public speaking duties and interviewing.

- Allow plenty of time for the donor to deliver the gift. Many businesses are willing to contribute equipment, facilities or services during their slack periods. If you allow donors to set their own schedule, you will improve your chances of success.

- If at first you do not succeed, do not be discouraged. Seek advice on how you can improve your proposal and/or its timing in the future and identify other sources of support. Potential donors who cannot help you themselves may be prepared to suggest other prospects and may even offer to use their influence to help you on your way.

- Donors or contributors who have given once are fertile ground for additional aid. However, you must proceed with caution as you do not want to over exploit your friends. On the other hand, those who have helped you in the past may want to continue the special relationship and may be offended if they are not asked to do so.

- Show your appreciation in ways which are both appropriate to your institution and meaningful to your benefactors.

- Managing community support and participation well is a demanding task. Designate a capable senior person to manage/handle this important work.

Exploring sources of support within the archives' area of service is a gradual process. Most archivists begin by asking for specific help or funding for a well-defined project or activity such as refreshments for an exhibit opening, folders for a seminar or workshop or guides for an open day tour. The most difficult part of getting started is making that first appeal. Once you have asked and been successful, the task gets easier and your credibility as a worthy cause grows. Offers of assistance may come spontaneously. Attendees at a workshop seeking further involvement with archival sources may offer themselves as prospective volunteers. Community businesses may volunteer their services, facilities and/or equipment for future projects, particularly if they see their competitors gaining valuable publicity for similar contributions. Once the ball is rolling, it will gain momentum and it will be necessary to establish regular and formal structures to manage the support to the archives' best advantage. Possibilities include a volunteer program, a Friends group and a special funding body. These may be separate entities or they may be combined under the overall umbrella of a community relations program. If your archives is part of a larger organisation, there may already be programs for personnel to handle these tasks for you. Many educational institutions, for example, have strong, well-organised alumni groups and may also operate a special trust fund or foundation to manage special grants, gifts and/or income generated by educational and special activities. Research institutions, particularly universities, have development offices or special corporations which seek and manage funds for the benefit of the institution. Your first step then is to investigate the potential use of any existing structures for the benefit of the archives. Tapping these important resources can begin with a meeting to explain your program and present a shopping list of your needs. You need not feel that you are an indigent seeking a handout; rather you are offering these public relations experts another vehicle for receiving and managing community support and will need to set up their own programs. The task is not an easy one and will require considerable time and effort from senior staff to accomplish.

Volunteers

Volunteer services are the lifeblood of many small archives programs. In fact, most would not exist and could not continue without the dedicated efforts of their honorary archivists. The work performed by volunteers covers all archival functions and activities, but experience indicates that the types of assistance outlined in Table 11.7 are helpful and enjoyable for participants.[3]

Table 11.7 Effective Work Performed by Volunteers

Function	Activities
Preservation	Replacing fasteners; refoldering records; flattening and cleaning documents; encapsulating materials
Arrangement and Description	Indexing finding aids, minutes, newspapers, news-letters, oral history interviews; preparing special lists and bibliographies
Reference	Assisting reference staff in supervising use of records; photocopying; registering, orienting new readers; explaining finding aids; restacking information leaflets, reference supplies, tools
Educating and Public Relations	Conducting tours of facilities and exhibitions; writing feature and news articles; giving talks about services, collections and research methods; updating mailing lists; helping with mailouts and special events; staffing special events; proofreading publications
General Administrative Support	Providing clerical assistance (telephone, photocopying, mailing, typing/word processing); administrative arrangements

A frequent beginning step is to develop a volunteer program to coordinate gifts of service to the archives. Volunteer labour, though freely given, is not without cost to the archives program. Recruiting, training, scheduling and supervising of volunteers is essential and this work must be a significant assigned job duty for a responsible staff member. Volunteer help must be viewed realistically. Volunteers are not a substitute for paid staff, and they must not be used by the organisation to avoid its responsibility to provide the archives with reasonable resources. Work by volunteers also requires that clear policies and procedures be devised for each type of work. Volunteers also do not have the same accountability as paid staff and solving problems such as low productivity, poor quality of work and absenteeism must depend more or less exclusively on persuasion and tact. Many problems can be minimised, if not avoided, by setting up clear standards of qualification and performance for volunteers. The status of volunteers should be a distinction which must be earned and maintained. Therefore, it is important for the archives to formulate policies and guidelines for recruiting, managing and terminating persons volunteering to work on its behalf. Some matters to address include

- a formal application process

- a description of the extent of commitment expected from volunteers, including training, standards of performance and attendance
- descriptions of the types of work available for volunteers
- a system for establishing accountability for volunteers, including procedures for evaluating work performance, for assessing suggestions of suitable projects and duties and for resolving problems and disputes
- a clear understanding that all products, resources and funds generated by volunteer labour are the property of the archives to be managed and administered according to its requirements
- an objective and tactful process for terminating volunteers
- an advisory body composed of staff volunteers, managers to assist with the management of the volunteer program, including evaluating ideas for new projects and duties.

Working with volunteers can be very rewarding both in terms of productivity and in the development of management and interpersonal skills. Particularly in a small archives where one archivist may be responsible for everything, a corps of volunteers can be an essential resource, supplying not only labour but also insights, ideas, community contacts and feedback.

Friends Groups

Given nurturing and good management, enthusiastic volunteers may organise and evolve into, or lead the effort to develop, formal bodies known generically as Friends groups. While volunteer programs operate within the archives program and are directly accountable to it, Friends groups are separate entities whose purpose is to rally and focus community support for the archives. Because they are independent, Friends groups can engage in activities that the archives may not be able to undertake, such as raising and retaining money and political lobbying to promote archival courses. On the other hand, Friends groups can be a powerful platform vulnerable to domination by those seeking to change the policies and/or programs, even the personnel, of the archives. Therefore, every care must be taken when the organisation of a Friends group for the archives is proposed. Several measures can help to ensure that the Friends group stays friendly to the archives:

(a) Archives staff should work closely with Friends group organisers to
- embed goals and purposes that fully serve the archives with the basic organisational documents
- limit the terms of service of office bearers and ensure a ratio of new to continuing members in each executive.

(b) Archives staff should be encouraged to become active members of the Friends group, but should avoid a disproportionate representation, particularly as office bearers.

(c) The archives' administration should be welcoming and supportive of the Friends group, but mindful of the limits required to maintain the group's independent legal status. For example, would provision of office space and/or administrative support for the Friends compromise their status?

(d) The archives should maintain regular official communication with the Friends group, both to inform them of activities and needs and to acknowledge and report on the use of their contributions. Individual members of the Friends should be added to the archives mailing list.

(e) Show special appreciation for your Friends group by having some Friends-only occasions.

A well-managed, effective Friends group is a great asset to its beneficiary as the extensive literature in the subject attests. Some of the more popular achievements of Friends groups include

- fundraising for new facilities, renovations and additions
- purchases of major or specialised equipment
- development and/or operation of programs for volunteers
- sponsorship of publications, exhibits, seminars/workshops and special events (films, tours, lectures and parties).

Friends groups provide a direct means for people of many backgrounds to share their enthusiasm and appreciation for archives and to contribute tangibly to the growth of your institution.

Funding Arrangements

Funding for educational activities is a complex area. Part of the complexity lies in weighing the cost associated with such activities against such difficult-to-measure benefits like community awareness, appreciation and cultural enrichment. Responsible planners must always develop budgets for their work and keep good records of their expenditures. Educational work requires a heavy investment of staff time and this cost should be monitored. Estimates should include internal expenses such as mileage, photocopying, postage and equipment maintenance. A carefully devised budget based upon a reasoned estimate of costs will enable planners to make a realistic assessment of their funding needs.

Meeting the costs of educational activities can be done in various ways. A portion of recurrent funds should be set aside for this work, but supplementary sources should be explored as well.

Fees

Some of the costs of educational activities may be recovered by charging reasonable fees or asking for donations from participants.

Fees are particularly appropriate for publications, workshops/ seminars, conferences and other activities offering services above and beyond the normal level. Setting a fee for an event is difficult and requires one to consider a number of factors including the actual costs per participant, what the market will bear, what related institutions are charging and your community service obligations.

Institutions that have income from fees and the sale of publications may wish to establish a special account or fund to support educational activities. Again, this is a specialist area and will

Table 11.8 Hints for Obtaining Special Funding

Overall Strategies

- Find out as much as possible about government and private sources for special funding and the kinds of projects they support.
- Most agencies will have application guidelines and timetables. Study these and plan ahead; many funding bodies take six months or more to review and process requests.
- Assemble your resources locally. Some agencies favour proposals demonstrating evidence of community support which they will then augment or match.
- Be sure that the amount of money you are seeking is worth the effort you are making to acquire it. It may take the same investment to obtain a thousand dollars as it does ten thousand.
- Do not be discouraged if you are unsuccesful on your first try. Fundraising is competitive and becoming increasingly sophisticated. Ask why you were turned down; insights and advice will help you prepare a stronger application for resubmission or for application to another source.

The Funding Proposal

Competitive funding proposals must
- reflect a realistic assessment of the needs and interests of a defined audience
- demonstrate substantial and/or lasting benefits to a significant and/or representative audience
- have realistic goals, realistic within the time frame specified by the funding source (usually one to three years)
- show awareness and consideration of what other institutions are doing/have done to avoid duplication and build on existing strengths
- present evidence of good research and careful planning of program design and implementation
- indicate the involvement of qualified staff and consultants; experienced personnel who are known to be capable performers add weight to any proposal
- include a realistic and authoritative budget and timetable for completing the project
- explain how the project can, or will, be able to serve a variety of needs or be adapted to produce multiple benefits (for example a proposal for an exhibit could include plans for a book on the theme and/or documentary on its production).

Table 11.9 Steps for Documentation and Evaluation

Before	1	Design the evaluation methods and procedures.
	2	Set up a file to receive records documenting the major stages of the project.
During	3	Add key documents to the project file, beginning with plans, schedules and budgets and continuing with correspondence, press releases, receipts and programs.
	4	Distribute evaluation forms to participants, both attendees and staff, and establish a reliable method for ensuring a good return.
Immediately After	5	Meet with project staff.
	6	Complete the project documentation file.
	7	Analyse the evaluation forms.
	8	Prepare a report on the project or event which includes • a description of the project (purpose, background, steps or phases to completion) • a list of project costs, including staff time, copying, supplies and administrative support as well as items which required a direct payment • an assessment of the projects strengths and shortcomings under such headings as scheduling, publicity, program content, local arrangements, audience reaction, results.
	9	A summary for future planners. Should the project be repeated, expanded or abandoned? Record suggestions and insights you consider essential.
	10	File the report and project documentation so that it can be readily retrieved.

require expert advice. While the existence of a special fund does enable the program to be more flexible and responsive to unforseen opportunities, it also has definite disadvantages. It does imply that educational activities pay their own way, which is not often the case. It is also hard to define 'educational' since many such activities are natural extensions of normal archival services. Finally, budget officers and accountants may be concerned about regulating the fund so that it is used responsibly.

Special Funding

Educational activities are usually well defined and limited in duration and, as such, are ideal candidates for special funding from a granting agency, foundation or private/corporate benefactor. While the practice of seeking special funding is not widespread among archival agencies in Australia, it is an area of increasing interest and a few tips on how to go about it are presented in Table 11.8.

Although the suggestions in Table 11.8 were developed for developing proposals for outside funding, they are just as valid for preparing requests for support from internal sources. All financial analysts, regardless of selling, will be impressed with a well-prepared and well-researched request.

Documentation and Evaluation

If education and greater awareness of archives are our goals, we must document our efforts and try to measure our progress towards achieving them. It is also useful to have accurate records and reports to identify projects worth repeating or expanding, to devise future plans and budgets and to highlight both successes and mistakes.

Sometimes it is difficult to rally the energy and/or reserve the time for post-program assessment. One way to ensure that proper reviews are conducted is to build reporting and evaluation mechanisms into the program schedule when it is first planned. The process should be divided into phases which follow the project as it progresses. Table 11.9 (p. 347) provides an example of this process.

Good documentation and evaluation systems are important for the continued success of all archival programs. Without them, planners lack objective information on which to base future decisions and the means to determine whether or not their efforts have been worthwhile. And it is that last word, worthwhile, which evokes a parting thought. We who labour in and with archives know our work is worthwhile, but unless we employ effective means for communicating this knowledge to others, particularly to our managers and major client groups, we will be undervalued, even ignored. Involving yourself in user education and public relations activities is one way you can share and reaffirm your enthusiasm for archives. Seize the opportunity; begin now.

Endnotes

1 More detailed information about the uses and considerations of video production for archives is included in Chapter 14, Created and Compiled Documentation Programs.
2 The full couplet reads: 'He who has a thousand friends has not a friend to spare and he who has one enemy will meet him everywhere'.
3 The success of each of these activities depends upon the archives having clear and authoritative policies, standards and procedures for each type of work. These guidelines must be user-friendly and meet all the requirements for administrative effectiveness, legal accountability and archival principles.

Further Reading

American Association for State and Local History (AASLH), *Technical Leaflets*, AASLH, Nashville, various dates. Some relevant numbers and titles include: no. 34 Walker, J. J. Jr, *Publishing in the Historical Society,* April 1966; no. 39 Derby, C. S., *Reaching Your Public: the Historical Society Newsletter,* January 1967; no. 42, Smith, A. L., *Producing the Slide Show for Your Historical Society,* June 1967; no. 43 Richman, I., *A Guide to Planning Local History Institutes,* August 1967; no. 45 Gignilliat, M., *Reaching Your Public Through the Newspaper,* April 1968; no. 62 Alderson W. T., *Securing Grant Support: Effective Planning and Preparation,* December 1972; no. 124, Adams, G. D., *Working Effectively with the Press: A Guide for Historical Societies,* February, 1980.

Arnett, Michael, *The Fund Raising Ideas Book for Australia and New Zealand,* Shepp Books, Sydney, 1985.

Australian Dictionary of Philanthropy, 6th edn, D. W. Thorpe, Port Melbourne, 1993.

Australian Government Publishing Service (AGPS), *Style Manual for Authors, Editors and Printers,* 4th edn, AGPS, Canberra, 1988.

Casterline, Gail F., *Archives and Manuscripts: Exhibits,* Society of American Archivists, Chicago, 1980.

Dolnick, Sandy (ed.), *Friends of Libraries Sourcebook,* American Library Association, Chicago, 1980.

Eastman Kodak Company, *Planning and Producing Slide Programs,* Publication S-30, Eastman Kodak Company, Rochester, 1978.

Eutick, Mal L., 'On the display of archives', in *Archives and Manuscripts,* 12/3, May 1984, pp. 17–23.

Freeman, Elsie (ed.), *Public Relations for Archivists,* Scarecrow Press, Metuchen NJ, [forthcoming 1993].

Great Library Promotion Ideas, Annual Publication Series, American Library Association, Chicago, 1984 to date. Each 70+ page volume describes public relations programs from the John Cotton Dana Library Public Relations Award competition, including annual campaigns and short-term events, fundraisers and awards for graphic design, public relations training and outreach to special interest groups. Available from ALA Books.

Pardo, Thomas C., *Basic Archival Workshops: A Handbook for the Workshop Organizer,* Society of American Archivists, Chicago, 1982.

Pederson, Ann E. and Casterline, Gail F., *Archives and Manuscripts: Public Programs,* Society of American Archivists, Chicago, 1982.

Sellen, Betty C. and Tarock, Betty J., 'Fundraising Strategies', in *Bottom Line Reader, A Financial Handbook for Librarians,* Neal-Schuman, New York, 1990.

'Supplement: Public Programming in Archives', in *Archivaria,* 31, Winter 1990–91, pp. 91–141. Especially Cook, Terry, 'Viewing the World Upside Down; Reflections on the Theoretical Underpinning of Archival Public Programming', pp. 123–34; and Craig, Barbara, 'What are the Clients? Who are the Products? The Future of Archival Public Services in Perspective', pp. 135–41.

Flynn, E. J. (ed.) *Friends of the Library Resource File,* 3rd edn, Library Promotion Company, Melbourne, 1989.

12 | Using Computers and Document Imaging

David Roberts

Computers and document imaging are useful tools which are becoming more accessible to archivists. They can enable economies in time and space and can make possible the accomplishment of tasks which may once have seemed impossible. They are not a panacea, and will not turn a poor archival system into a good one. They may even make it worse: chaotic records on microfilm are even less accessible than their chaotic originals. Carefully chosen to meet an archives' particular needs, like any other well-chosen tool, they will allow a better job to be done.

The purpose of this chapter is to describe briefly

- the ways in which computers and document imaging can be used for archives work
- how they can be acquired or access to them can be gained
- the advantages and disadvantages which must be weighed in considering the inevitable range of options available
- a number of matters which need to be borne in mind when introducing or using computers or document imaging in an archivist's work.

This chapter is not intended to be an exhaustive examination of the subjects and will neccessarily be brief and practically oriented. For more background and detail, refer to suggestions in Further Reading at the end of the chapter. This chapter cannot be a state-of-the-art guide to equipment. The range of equipment and related products, such as computer software, suitable for archives work is very large and changing all the time. However, we will show the reader what to look for, or rather, how to decide what to look for.

Using Computers

This part of the chapter is concerned with ways in which the archivist can use computers (and other information technology) to help administer an archives operation. While the principles discussed in this part of the chapter are applicable to the use of mainframe and minicomputers, the focus is on microcomputers and microcomputer networks, which increasingly dominate the computing environment within both large and small organisations. Computers also affect archivists in another important way. Computer systems produce records – machine-readable or electronic records – which are increasingly finding their way as archives into the care of archivists. Managing these forms of records is considered in Chapter 13, Managing Records in Special Formats.

There are several broad categories of possible use of computers in archives work

- general administrative tasks
- intellectual and physical control
- management information
- retrieval.

General Administrative Tasks

The archivist can use a wide variety of office automation and business programs to help the general administration of the archives operation, eg

- a word processing program to prepare correspondence (including standard form letters), reports, forms and other documents
- a desktop publishing program to produce guides, newsletters and publicity materials
- a graphics program to produce signs and captions for exhibitions
- a spreadsheet program to keep track of the budget and help manage statistics (a spreadsheet is also useful for laying out organisation charts, as part of administrative history work, and for drawing up family trees)
- a database program for keeping and updating mailing lists, information about clients and for monitoring stocks of supplies.

Specialised packages, such as accounting, project management and presentation graphics packages, can also be valuable for some aspects of archives work.

These kinds of programs will already be in use in the archives' parent organisation, perhaps on a microcomputer or as office automation facilities on a larger computer system or network. In this case it is sensible to take advantage of these existing facilities and of the expertise and experience of their administrators and users, who can show the archivist how to obtain the greatest benefits from using them.

If the archivist needs to buy a microcomputer, many retailers offer bundles of equipment and software designed for small business or domestic use. Typically, these packages include a microcomputer, a dot-matrix printer and a suite of standard software products (word processor, spreadsheet, database – often combined in an integrated program – and perhaps an accounting, drawing or communications program).

In either case using computers for general administration of the archives can bring rapid productivity benefits by enabling the performance of the inevitable administrative tasks of archives work more quickly and effectively.

Intellectual and Physical Control of the Archives' Holdings

The major challenge for the archivist wanting to bring the benefits of computing to his or her operation is to computerise detailed information about the archives' holdings, especially its archival control systems. Most commonly, a database or database management system (DBMS) program is used. Text retrieval programs provide an alternative approach which may by more useful in certain circumstances.

Database Programs

A database program enables a large amount of information to be stored, organised, updated, sorted and retrieved for a variety of purposes. A database consists of any number of records – each record containing a range of information about one thing. For example, a database of information about archival series would contain one record of information about each series.

Each record comprises a number of fields – each field containing a different piece of information, according to a standard structure across the database specified by the user. Thus, in the example of a database of archival series, one field might be for the series' title, one field for the series' date range, one for the series' provenance, and so on. The database of archival series would therefore comprise information about each of the archives' series, organised in a standard way, and capable of being sorted and retrieved in different ways for different purposes.

Today's database programs can be extremely sophisticated. Many are relational databases, comprising a group of related databases, in which information moves and is updated between the databases automatically according to predetermined routines.

Many database programs also feature the ability to search on individual words within text fields, vastly improving the potential retrieval capabilities of archival control systems using such programs.

Database Software Choices

There are a number of database products designed specifically for archives work which can be bought off-the-shelf and used on a microcomputer or a network of microcomputers. The main advantages of choosing one of these products are
- they require little or no programming before they can be used
- many have sophisticated features designed to meet specific archival needs, which would be costly and difficult to design and program yourself
- they have usually been tested and proven in a working archives

Their main disadvantages are that
- they usually cost more than generic database programs of similar size and power, or require the purchaser to buy a particular generic database program beforehand
- a given product may not have features or be useful for some of the particular purposes required, or may have features that will not be used and must still be paid for
- many will only run on a limited range of computers, eg a product designed to run on a Macintosh will not run on an IBM-compatible machine
- they usually reflect the archival practices of the environment in which they were designed, limiting their applicability to other archival environments
- in an in-house operation there may be problems of compatibility with equipment and software used elsewhere in the organisation if there is any need for the archives' system to 'talk' to other systems, eg to receive or send information.

This last disadvantage reflects the continued worldwide lack of standards in archives work, especially descriptive standards. It will inevitably be a major factor in the choice of software product, since changing a whole archival control system and methods to be able to use a given software product is likely to be both prohibitively expensive and most undesirable.

Products like the *Small Archives Control System* (SACS) and *Professional Archivist* include the series system of control which, with its Australian origins, is not reflected in archives software products designed in other parts of the world. SACS runs on IBM-compatible PCs, while *Professional Archivist* runs on Apple Macintosh machines.

Generic database programs, such as *dBASE, Q&A, Paradox* and *R:Base* for IBM-compatibles, or *Foxbase, Hypercard* and

Filemaker for Macintoshes, generally offer more flexibility than purpose-designed products. Some spreadsheet programs also have basic database capabilities. The preparatory work of designing the database structure, reports and other features can require considerable skill, care and time. Using a purpose-designed product will save a great deal of work.

How to Use Databases of Information about Archival Holdings

Database programs, whether off-the-shelf archives programs or generic programs adapted by the user to archives work, tend to be used for a variety of purposes. The following examples show the kinds of records which might make up typical databases. Each type of information is a field in a database structure.

Descriptive Information about Records and their Provenance

As described in Chapter 8, the intellectual control of records needs to cover information at three levels:

- Provenance: identifying and providing administrative history information about the creating bodies or agencies and information about their functions and activities; or biographical notes about people who created the records
- Record series: identifying and describing individual series of records
- Record items: listing and describing the record items which comprise each series.

A database system for descriptive information about records and their provenance also needs to cover these levels, by establishing a database for each level – with each record in the series database, eg containing information about a given series – and relating the databases together. The following is an example database structure for a series description:

EXAMPLE RECORD SERIES DESCRIPTION

SERIES NUMBER (allocated by System): 43

SERIES TITLE: Master set of minutes of meetings of Council

DATE RANGE: 1953–67

CREATING AGENCY: 3, Honorary Secretary; 1964–67: 12, Office of the Secretary

DESCRIPTION: This series consists of bound volumes containing the typed master set of minutes of Council meetings. Meetings were normally held quarterly. The minutes for each meeting are preceded by the Secretary's copy of the agenda papers and followed by a set of agenda papers. The minutes of each meeting are signed by the Secretary and the President.

PREVIOUS RECORD SERIES: 24, President's digest of Council decisions, 1946–53

SUBSEQUENT RECORD SERIES: 55, Files containing minutes and agenda papers from Council meetings, 1967–92

RELATED RECORD SERIES: 44, Index to minutes of Council meetings, 1964-72; 56, President's annotated set of minutes of meetings of Council, 1964-67

This example uses the data elements in SACS. In this example two bodies or agencies have been identified as creating the series successively. That is, this is a multi-provenance series. SACS, being based on the series system of archival control pioneered by Peter Scott and the Australian Archives in the 1960s, allows for the possibility that more than one body may create a record series. This is essential if there has been any degree of administrative change in the history of the records in your holdings. Similarly, SACS allows for the identification of more than one previous, subsequent or related series.

The following example shows a database structure for an agency level description, again using the data elements from SACS:

EXAMPLE OF AGENCY DESCRIPTION

AGENCY NUMBER (allocated by System): 12

AGENCY TITLE: Office of the Secretary

DATE RANGE: 1964–90

ADMINISTRATIVE HISTORY NOTES: The Office of the Secretary was established by a resolution of Council dated 4 March 1964 to appoint a salaried Secretary and an Administrative Assistant. The duties of the Secretary, as defined in the resolution, were to conduct the Association's correspondence and to prepare the agenda and minutes of Council meetings. The first Secretary, Mr Cuthbert Thudbucket, was succeeded by Mr Jeremiah Mudlark in May 1972. Mr Mudlark retired in May 1990, Council establishing the position of Executive Officer to replace that of Secretary at its meeting of 3 June 1990.

CONTROLLING AGENCIES: 1, Council of the Association, 1946–

RELATED AGENCIES: none registered

SUBORDINATE AGENCIES: none registered

PREVIOUS AGENCIES: 3, Honorary Secretary, 1946–64

SUBSEQUENT AGENCIES: 8, Executive Officer and Secretariat, 1990–

Physical Control of Records

A database of information about the physical attributes of records, usually at the level of accessions, can be used for a variety of purposes. The database as a whole can act as an accession register, as in the following example:

EXAMPLE ACCESSION REGISTER RECORD

ACCESSION NUMBER allocated by (System): 21

DATE RECEIVED: 17.10.1992

SERIES NUMBER: 43

SERIES TITLE: Master set of minutes of meetings of Council

DATE RANGE OF ACCESSION: 1953–62

DONOR/TRANSFEROR: Mr Jeremiah Mudlark, retiring Secretary

CONTROLLING PERSON/BODY: Office of the Secretary

QUANTITY: 1.2m

LOCATION: 3/6/1

ACCESS CONDITIONS: Open. Copyright permission to be sought from Secretary

ACQUISITION FILE NUMBER: 1990/17

In this example QUANTITY is a numerical field. In many database programs such fields can be used as the basis for calculations. In this case the system can add the QUANTITY value in each database record, showing the total quantity of the archives' holdings.

A shelf list can be produced from this type of database by running a report, sorted on the LOCATION field, as in the following example:

EXAMPLE SHELF LIST REPORT

LOCATION: 3/6/1

ACCESSION NUMBER : 21

SERIES NUMBER: 43

SERIES TITLE: Master set of minutes of meetings of Council

QUANTITY: 1.2m

In an archives storing temporary as well as permanent records, it is important to know when particular groups of temporary records are due for destruction. In the following example it is assumed that there is an accession register database similar to that above, with the addition of a field for the date when the records are due to be destroyed. This is a date field, enabling the database to be sorted by date when destruction is due or, more usefully, allowing a report to be produced showing accessions now due for destruction.

EXAMPLE DESTRUCTION DUE REPORT

DESTRUCTION DUE: 1.7.1993

ACCESSION NUMBER: 16

SERIES NUMBER: 12

SERIES TITLE: Claims for payment

DATE RANGE OF ACCESSION: 1984–86

QUANTITY: 5.5 m

LOCATION: 7/13/6–7/14/4

Databases Designed for Non-Archival Materials

The archivist working in an institution such as a library or museum may have the opportunity to assess whether the archives should be controlled using the computer system used to control the institution's other materials. The major attractions of such opportunities are that

- because the computer system already exists, the costs associated with computerising information about the archives are reduced
- the control information about the institution's whole collection, comprising archival and other materials, is integrated (this may be particularly valuable where a close connection exists between the archival and other materials, eg a museum with custody of records relating objects in its collection)
- clients' needs may be better served by the availability of a single catalogue or finding aid for the institution's whole collection.

The main drawback is that the computer system is likely to have been designed or chosen for the institution's main kind of holdings – books or objects in the cases of libraries or museums, respectively – and therefore unsuitable or difficult to adapt to archival purposes.

One fundamental issue is the level of control information used. Both library and museum cataloguing practice focus on the level of the individual item: in libraries, on the individual title, monograph or serial; in museums, on the individual object. In archives, intellectual control involves a hierarchy of levels: the agency or person who created the records, the record series, and the record item. It may be difficult or impossible to adapt a computerised control system working at a single level of control to the multiple levels required in archives work.

Another question is how flexible the database structure of the package is. It may well be possible to use some of the fields in a database package designed for non-archival materials, but it will almost certainly be necessary to add some fields and to change the name or size of others. In an in-house archives the archivist may have an opportunity to assess the possibility of using the organisation's computerised records management system for the organisation's archives. The main benefit would be that all of the organisation's records would be controlled by the one system, making it easier to learn and use the system. However, using records management packages for controlling archives presents similar problems to those raised by the use of library or museum packages. In addition records management packages are normally designed to control record items, usually documents and files, within a single record series and may not cope with records comprising a number of series and reflecting different systems of arrangement and control.

Integrating a Database about the Archives' Holdings with Other Programs

Many computing environments enable users to integrate their work in different computer programs by allowing them to use data prepared and stored using one program in another program. For the archivist, this can mean taking data from a database of information about the archives' holdings and using it to prepare guides, newsletters or reports. For example, a user of SACS running under Microsoft Windows on an IBM-compatible PC can 'select' SACS data (eg, a series description) and 'copy and paste' it directly into a Microsoft Windows word processing or desktop publishing document. This kind of capability can provide great savings in time when preparing documents or publications based on information about the archives' holdings.

Text Retrieval Programs

Text retrieval software provides control over textual data, typically word processing or ASCII files. File-indexing programs like *Isys*, *Magellan*, *ZyIndex* and *Sonar* create an index of selected text files, leaving the original files in place and storing only pointers to the files in the index. Text library programs like *Folio Views* draw all the selected files into a single compendium – a text library – which is then indexed. Most text retrieval programs feature a

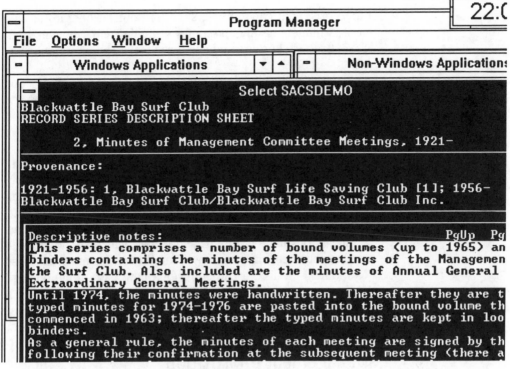

Data can be 'selected' and copied from a database . . .

. . . and 'pasted' into a word processing document.

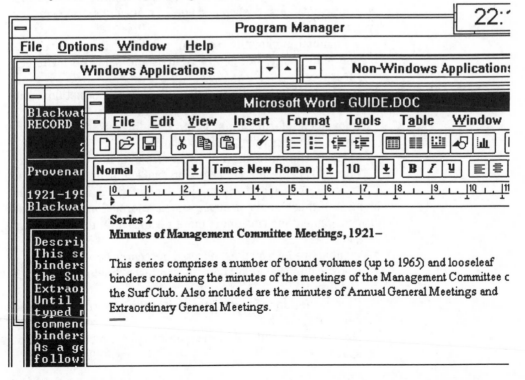

range of search capabilities, such as Boolean operators, wild cards, argument nesting, proximity searching and synonym lists.

Text retrieval programs have three main uses in the management of archives:

- They provide intellectual control over original records and finding aids which have been scanned into digital images and converted into text files using optical character recognition (OCR) software (document image processing and OCR are discussed in more detail later in this chapter).
- They provide a new way to exploit descriptive information already held by the archives in electronic form. Many archives have now been using word processors and microcomputers for some years to produce descriptive documentation, such as administrative histories, series descriptions, inventories of record items and guides, which are available to staff and clients in hard copy form. Where this material is also still held on disk, it can be given a new lease of life through the search capabilities of text retrieval software.
- They provide access to electronic records in ASCII or other text file formats.

Management Information

Management information is the information used by an organisation to support its management decisionmaking and actions. Most organisations develop a range of management information systems, such as

- a financial information system, providing financial reports and statements, budgetary figures and sales performance measures
- a personnel information system, providing information about employees, including their employment history and training
- a logistics information system, including inventory control, production scheduling and distribution
- a marketing information system, covering existing and potential clients, market segments and competitors

An archives may use or establish computerised systems for all or most of these kinds of management information. Some kinds of management information is more peculiar to the archival context, such as

- quantitative information collected in records surveys
- statistical information about the archives' holdings, activities and users
- time series measurements of storage environments and condition reports
- stocktakes and usage of repository space, incuding vacant space.

Users will require initial assistance in retrieving information from an archival computer system but thereafter can carry out their own searches.

A variety of software tools, ranging from familiar spreadsheet programs to sophisticated statistical packages, are available to computerise these kinds of information systems. Some may be drawn from or linked to other information maintained by the archives. An accession register database, for example, may provide the data for statistics about holdings.

Retrieval

Discussion of the use of computers in this chapter so far has been principally concerned with their use by the archivist. Providing a means of retrieval of computerised information by users of the archives can provide a number of benefits to the archivist and to users:

- Users should be able to undertake more comprehensive, sophisticated and effective searches than with manual finding aids.
- Users should also be able to search more quickly.
- Computerised finding aids are generally more likely to be up-to-date than manual, especially printed, finding aids.
- Once they have learned the system, users are likely to need less assistance from the archivist.
- Additional services of benefit to users become possible, such as providing printouts of the results of searches and providing remote access to the system.

It is also important to be aware of some of the limitations of computer-based retrieval:

- Users may come to regard a quick keyword search as sufficient, when more material of relevance could be identified through a traditional provenance-based search.
- Users must be aware of the need to use appropriate search terms. A search of item titles, eg, may be fruitless if the user uses a modern term, instead of terms in use at the time of the creation of the records.

The question of whether users will be able to undertake computer-based retrieval must be decided very early in the process of planning the system. A user-friendly interface becomes even more important than it is if the system is only used by staff. Users need to be able to keep and further develop their search results on screen, especially after a long and complex search. The system needs to be able to provide different levels of access to staff and users so that users cannot alter or destroy data or have access to confidential information. Given that particularly keen users may be expected to spend extended periods using the system, occupational health considerations in the choice and location of equipment and furniture are also important. Explanatory materials will be required and it will be necessary to train users, both in the basic operation of the system and in ways to use it most effectively.

Finally, some users may find it very helpful to be able to use a microcomputer in the search room to take their notes. Many users of archives can now be expected to use a microcomputer at home or at their place of employment, but may not be able to bring a portable computer to use in the search room. Providing a microcomputer for this purpose in the search room may be a good way to make use of a superseded microcomputer which no longer meets the archives' needs. With an adequate word processing package, and perhaps a spreadsheet package for structured information, such a machine will meet a user's needs in the search room. Most modern word processing packages feature conversion utilities, enabling users to save their work in a word processing format which they can use on their own machines. In practical terms users of this kind of service must be permitted to bring floppy disks which they have used on their own machines. For this reason, it is essential that the search room microcomputer have comprehensive and current anti-virus software.

Before Computerising

Using computers, whether buying a microcomputer and software for the archives or making use of existing facilities in the organisation, requires a substantial investment of time and money. This investment will be wasted if the resulting system does not meet the archivist's needs. Before making decisions, careful analysis and planning is necessary. The following steps apply particularly when considering the use of a computer for information about the holdings:

- *Analyse needs.* That is, identify the particular problems to be solved by the use of a computer. By focusing on the problems as the first step, the archivist can decide what the system should do. Then identify the capabilities which are needed to solve the problems. For example, an archives may need to improve its system of intellectual control, but may be small enough to continue to use manual systems to manage repository space and archival processes.

- *Analyse the effectiveness of the present manual system.* Computerising a system which does not work well in manual form will only enhance faults by making them more obvious. Before, not after, is the time to look at how well the various processes are working and clean them up. Here the sins of the past may need to be confronted. In areas such as systems of control and finding aids, the archivist may have inherited several different systems. A choice would need to be made between starting afresh with an up-to-date system suitable for computerising – hoping to convert the earlier material at a later date – or bringing all the documentation up to a consistent standard first of all.

- *Assess software and hardware needs.* There is a variety of software choices available for the general administration of the archives and for managing and using information about the archives' holdings. Choices of software and hardware can be influenced by the environment in which we operate, such as the possibility of using the existing systems in one's sponsoring organisation.

- *Determine the process by which you will computerise.* Should individual archival functions be computerised in turn, or all at once? Can a computerised system of archival control be applied to all the holdings at once or must portions of the collection be covered in stages? Must all the data be keyed or could it be scanned into the computerised system?

- *Assess the effects of computerising on workflows and remaining manual processes.* Using a computer will certainly change the way in which the archives works, but what changes need to be made to the parts of the operation which are not computerised? Who will use the computer? Will the computer system make any other work more difficult? Where will the computer and printer be located?

- *Assess training and documentation.* The training needs of individuals who will use the system will differ, depending on the nature and complexity of the system and the experience of the individuals. Develop and implement a training plan which meets everyone's needs. It is important to document every aspect of the system – versions of software used, description and serial numbers of hardware, maintenance agreements, location of manuals, how to perform tasks not documented elsewhere – anything which someone might need to know if the archivist is not around.

- *Consider backup and disaster recovery.* When using computers for important functions, people quickly come to rely on them and on data stored in the system. Original program disks need to be stored safely and a regime of regular backup of data established so that the organisation can recover quickly from any disaster which may befall the system.

The remaining sections of this chapter are concerned with document imaging, ie the use of a variety of technologies to produce images of records which can be stored, retrieved and used in place of the originals. These sections will focus on the two main methods or technologies: micrographics and document image processing. The former uses photographic processes to produce a miniature image on film, while the latter involves the capture, storage and retrieval of images in electronic form. The similarity of the terms 'document imaging' and 'document image processing' may seem confusing. 'Document imaging' has been chosen here as a simple but accurate description of these methods: both involve the production and use of images of documents for similar purposes in the management of archives and records. 'Document image processing' has been chosen as the most widely accepted term available to describe the latter method.

Micrographics

Micrographics may be defined as the use of photographic processes to produce reduced size images of textual or graphic material on film. This definition requires some modification, since the development of computer output microfilm means that images can be directly transferred to film from a computer without an intermediate or hard copy.

The most common micrographic formats include the following:
(a) 16 and 35 mm roll film. The 35mm roll film remains the most common format for archival microfilming and is normally kept on open reels. Some proprietary systems, particularly those designed for records management application, use roll film in cartridges or cassettes. Jackets comprising transparent sleeves containing strips of roll film are another alternative to open reels
(b) 35mm aperture cards. A single frame of 35mm microfilm is inserted into an aperture or window in a card the size and

A final check is made to 510 rolls of 35mm microfilm, containing New Guinea records from the times of German administration, in the reprography sub-section of the Preservation Services section, Australian Archives ACT Regional Office as part of a large project providing micro-form to all regional offices of Australian Archives and some other countries.

shape of a traditional computer punch card. Information printed on the card enables the image to be identified without the use of special viewing equipment and allows the item to be handled without touching the image.

(c) 35mm slides. Not commonly thought of as a microform, these have some applications in the micrographics industry, such as the reproduction of coloured pictures, maps, or works of art.

(d) Microfiche. This consists of a sheet of film about 105 x 149mm on which a large number of images, normally 60 or 98, have been exposed in a regular pattern of rows and columns. Updateable microfiche also exists but, due to the relative transience of the images produced, it has few archival applications. Microfiche has a number of advantages over roll microfilm:

- A microfiche sheet can be duplicated quickly and inexpensively.
- A particular image can be found more efficiently with less effort.
- More images can be stored in the same space.
- Microfiche readers are cheap and easy to maintain.
- The individual sheets can be stored in ways that provide more convenient access than roll film, eg in holders resembling books.

On the other hand, an error in filming onto microfiche cannot be corrected by splicing in a new frame, as is possible with roll film, requiring the whole fiche to be refilmed. In use, microfiche are easier to misfile, lose or have stolen.

Most publications reproduced in microform appear in the fiche format, while most archival microfilming uses roll film.

Also available now is computer output microfilm (COM), which comprises computer-based data produced directly onto microfilm, normally fiche, without an intermediate paper format. It is already being used by major archives as a means distributing information from computerised finding aids and has much potential for use in archives work.

Why Microfilm?

Archivists are likely to use microfilming for one or more of the following purposes:

- To prolong the life of original records. Even when the greatest care is taken, the repeated handling of original archival material results in damage and eventual destruction. Copying the material on microfilm enables the archivist to remove the originals from active use so that they may be conserved, while still making the records available to researchers in microform.

- To make unique material more widely available. Because archival records are one-of-a-kind, it can be difficult to make them available to everyone who wishes to use them. Microfilm copies make it possible for researchers in different locations to use copies of these records simultaneously. Also some original records may be unwieldy because of an awkward size, shape or mass as in the case of large maps, architectural drawings or very heavy volumes. Microforms are compact, often reducing large or bulky items to a single roll of film which is easy to handle and transport

- To reduce high cost storage. Where the administrative and public areas of an archives are in a high-cost area and low-cost, more secure storage is available in a different location, it may be more efficient to keep the original material in the latter area and to provide access using microfilm copies.

- To protect the security of vital original records. Vital records, such as finding aids or Board minutes are essential to the ongoing work of the archives or its parent organisation. The loss of these records by fire or vandalism could be disastrous, so copying them onto microfilm and subsequently storing the film in a safe, physically separate location helps to reduce the danger (see Table 12.1).

Microfilming (and increasingly electronic imaging systems) is often used in the records management field to reduce the space required for records storage by enabling the original paper records to be destroyed following microfilming. This can be an appropriate solution to the problems of storage and access of active or semi-active records of temporary value. In a program of microfilming records of archival value, the original records are not normally destroyed. Apart from the philosophical problems which would be posed by the destruction of original archival records and the preservation only of microfilm copies, the long-term preservation of microfilm is more problematical than that of most kinds of paper records and requires more specialised and expensive facilities.

Limitations of Micrographics

A microfilming project is an expensive undertaking and is likely to divert considerable resources from other important tasks. The benefits to the archives must be weighed against the cost. As microfilming can be done on a project basis, it may be possible to seek funding from the parent organisation or an outside funding body to undertake a specific microfilming project, leaving the archives' budget unaffected.

As is the case with computers, microfilming is not a panacea for an archives' problems. It will not improve access to poorly organised records and, indeed, may make them even less accessible, since it is generally harder to browse or skim through microforms than through hard copy.

Some types of records are difficult or unsuitable for microfilming. Records in large formats, such as maps or architectural drawings, can only be filmed properly on equipment designed to handle oversized materials. Such equipment is not commonly available outside large metropolitan areas. There are often problems inherent in the records which make them unsuitable for copying onto microfilm, eg where the writing is faint or in inks of various colours, the film may not be legible.

There are also legal matters to consider. Microfilming is another form of copying and is subject to the provisions of the Commonwealth *Copyright Act of 1968* (as amended). The Act is complex and the period of protection varies with different kinds of materials, so it is wise to examine this question in detail at the planning stage of a microfilming project. Copyright protection belongs to the person who created the material (it can also be assigned by that person to someone else, or inherited like other forms of property), and it is not uncommon for custody of material to be legally transferred without conveying the copyright to the new owner. For example, to microfilm the letters written to Sir Robert Menzies by a number of different people, the copyright in each of those letters belongs prima facie to its writer. Sometimes it requires considerable detective work to determine the current owner of the copyright.

To film records of the sponsoring organisation and destroy the records after filming, there are legal requirements that the filming must meet because these records provide evidence of the activities of the organisation. The laws concerning the admissibility of microfilm copies as evidence in court proceedings differ from state to state, so it may help to have legal advice before filming these types of records.

The decision as to the type of microfilm and the size of the image will be greatly affected by the equipment available to view it and whether or not paper copies of individual documents are needed from the film. Microform viewers or readers come in variety of types with a range of features, conveniences, and prices to match. Also consider the cost of supplies and maintenance when making a choice. Again, the rule of thumb is not to pay for capabilities that will not be used regularly. If the archivist anticipates making a number of photocopies from the microfilm, the lease or purchase of a reader-printer can be justified. For duplicate films or for few or infrequent copies, it is possible to use the services of a commercial firm with copying facilities.

How to Have Microfilming Done

The archivist is faced with three main options: a contract with a firm which microfilms records for a fee, the development of an in-house microfilming centre, or a mixture of both.

The use of a commercial microfilming bureau has the advantage that equipment costs are limited to the acquisition of reading, and possibly printing, equipment and to the provision of storage facilities for microfilm. Further, there is no need to acquire or hire the skilled personnel to operate microfilming equipment, which is essential to ensure a professional and legally recognised product. The commercial bureau is also a source of expert advice.

There are several precautions to take when using a commercial bureau for archival microfilming. First the bulk of the filming is likely to be done for short-term business use and does not require archival standards of processing. Hence, it is essential that the required archival standards are stated and understood when drawing up the contract for services. Since the records will leave the archives to be filmed on the premises of the commercial bureau, the archivist should have a detailed list of items sent and be sure that sufficient care is taken for their safety. Some archives send a member of their own staff along with the material to supervise and assist with the filming.

The acquisition of all the equipment and personnel required for a microfilming operation is an undertaking beyond the means of all but the largest archives. To consider this option, the archivist needs to take a number of factors into account. The camera, lights, tables, and related equipment and space needed for microfilming work are very expensive and specialised. While the actual photography may appear to be a simple matter of snapping a shutter, obtaining archival quality exposures requires great attention to technical procedures. For example, various colours of paper require light adjustments; the material must be absolutely flat and properly positioned; faded or damaged material may require special filters to render them legible; and the list goes on.

A microfilming program requires careful evaluation and planning, covering the following seven steps. This sequence assumes the use of a commercial microfilming service. For information about the establishment of an in-house microfilming operation, see the section Further Reading at the end of this chapter.

Choose the Records to be Copied

Conservation, wider access and security were discussed above as some of the reasons why archivists microfilm records. Whatever the purpose of establishing a microfilming program, there are likely to be more records which could usefully be copied than resources will allow. A priority listing of collections or record series which accomplish one or more of these purposes should be drawn up to ensure that the most important work is done. The following table lists some popular microfilming applications for archives. Detailed descriptions of the material should be included to help with estimating the size and cost of the program. Once the list is prepared, it may be worthwhile to contact other archives and libraries to see if any of the materials, especially any published materials, have already been preserved or copied.

Select the Microfilm Format

The choice among roll film, microfiche, aperture cards or other formats will depend on the purpose of the microfilming program, the types of records being copied and the availability of viewing equipment. Microfiche and roll film, eg are particularly suitable for reference copies because they are popular and easy to use. Fiche, in particular, is inexpensive to duplicate. Aperture cards are most commonly used to copy large single items, such as maps and architectural drawings, because a one-to-one relationship can be maintained between the original items and the microform copies. When making a choice among the more common formats, such as 35mm roll film or microfiche, there is the additional advantage of having established standards of quality and a wide range of viewing equipment.

Determine the Film Quality and the Number of Copies

Because archival records and manuscripts are unique and often fragile, there may be only one opportunity to film them and it is essential that the microfilm product be of the highest quality. This standard of excellence is known as archival microfilming. When records are filmed to meet archival standards, it means that

- the original records have been arranged and described as accurately and thoroughly as possible, and that any irregularities or flaws in them have been noted

Table 12.1: Types of Micrographic Applications of Established Benefit for Archives

Archival Records

- Registers, indexes to major series of proven research interest
- Major series of significant agencies (minutes, correspondence, annual reports, newsletter or journal)
- Papers of significant persons (diaries/ journals, correspondence)

Motivation	Benefits	Cautions
• High research demand • Preservation/security of originals • Better service to users in remote areas	• Research by mail is more efficient • Popular indexes can be preserved • Can be sold to other institutions	• Reference demand/ research potential is a major consideration • Legal issues must be resolved • Indexes and finding aids must also be filmed

Archival Records

- Extra large format records: building plans, maps, posters, prints, works of art

Motivation	Benefits	Cautions
• Preservation • Space • Ease of reference	• Less wear and tear on originals, which may be transferred to remote archival storage • Film formats are easier for researchers to handle and offer faster access • Aperture card mount can be coded for automated retrieval	• Coloured inks may require coloured films or colour separations • The reference activity, importance of records, and frequency of changes to originals influence filming decisions • Reader/printers are expensive for extra large formats • Indexes must also be filmed

Publications

- Newspapers and Government Gazettes
- Rare or brittle publications
- Guides, inventories and bibliographies

Motivations	Benefits	Cautions
• Space reduction (gazettes and newspapers) • Preservation (rare and brittle)	• Can be sold to other institutions • Originals may be transferred to remote archival storage for preservation • Increased reference/ research availability for better service to users in remote areas	• Bibliographic search to locate all and best copies (even from other archives and libraries) is essential • Legal issues must be resolved • Indexing desirable for large series

- the film used has a silver halide emulsion on a chemically inert polyester or triacetate base
- the image of the original record reproduced on the film is a complete, true and faithful copy and has been produced to meet the highest technical standards
- the exposed film has been properly processed and all residues have been removed by an especially thorough washing
- the exposed film has been tested and has met the standards for archival quality both technically and as a true copy of the records it duplicates.

It is normal archival practice to produce a minimum of three microfilm copies of each original item. These copies include

- a security or preservation negative on silver halide film
- a negative copy for further duplication known as a duplicating master
- a reference copy.

Use of microfilm, either for reference or for making a further copy, inevitably results in damage which can become extensive over time. For this reason, the security or preservation negative should only be used to produce the duplicating master and thereafter be kept undisturbed in the best conservation environment as security against loss of the original records or of the duplicating master. The duplicating master is used only for making further reference copies and is also stored carefully. The reference copies are for everyday use by researchers and staff.

For the security or preservation negative, the most acceptable medium is black and white silver halide film. This is the only type of film for which archival quality standards exist and which is sufficiently stable, given proper processing and storage conditions, to last for long periods of time. For the duplicating master and for the reference copies, one may use the less expensive, easier to copy diazo or vesicular films which are also more scratch resistant than silver halide. Diazo and vesicular films use different development processes, but are used for similar purposes.

Finally, a choice must be made between a positive or negative image for the copies. Duplicating masters are normally negative; reference copies can be either negative or positive. One advantage of having negative reference copies is that it is easier on the eyes to look at white text on a black background.

Assess the Feasibility and Cost of the Microfilming Project

A microfilming project must be assessed and weighed against the proposed benefits of the filming. The expenses of equipment should be included as well as the labour of preparing and checking the records before and after filming. An outline, such as the following, listing the types of expenses which must be anticipated in a microfilming project is helpful in estimating costs.

(a) Quantity of records to be microfilmed:
- shelf metres
- number of frames (allow 80–100 frames per cm of paper thickness).

(b) Preparation of identification sheets, targets and notes:
- archivist's time to design and fill in
- time to prepare on PC or by hand and print
- stationery costs.

(b) Preparation of records:
- preservation work required
- removal of pins, staples, folds
- final checking of page order.

(c) Filming:
- supervisor's time
- operator's time
- equipment time
- cost of x metres of film at $y per metre length
- cost of any protective treatment or coating required.

(e) Examination of master:
- checking time
- cost of residual chemical testing.

(f) Filming of retakes and additions:
- as for preparation, filming and examination above.

(g) Reassembly of records:
- replacement of pins, etc.
- checking of order.

(h) Transportation:
- of material
- of staff.

(i) Copying:
- cost of copy negative
- cost of copy positive x number of copies required
- checking copies
- cost of residual chemical testing.

Arrange Contract with a Commercial Filming Service

Choosing a commercial service to do the photography, processing and duplicating of microfilms should be done with great care. It is advisable to seek written quotes from firms with proven skills and to enter a formal contract. An essential part of a contract is the specification, which describes the records to be filmed and the qualtiy standards of microfilming to be met. A typical specification should cover the following items:
- *Documents to be microfilmed.* Identify record series, format(s), quantity, approximate size of pages/folios, approximate number of frames, colour of documents (and therefore whether colour testing is required).
- *Camera.* Specify a planetary camera, not a rotary camera.

- *Film*. Specify to meet the *American National Standard Specifications for Photographic Film for Archival Records, Silver-Gelatin Type on Cellulose Estre Base*, PHI.28–1973 or the latest revision thereof; dimensions of film, processed and unprocessed, to meet the specifications set out in USA *Standard Specifications for 16mm or 35mm Silver-Gelatin Microfilms for Reel Applications*, PH5.3–1967, Section 4, or the latest revision thereof; to be 100 feet long, unperforated, and without splices, tears, cuts or holes; at least 50cm to be left at each end of the film to permit insertion into microfilm reader reels; a space of 30cm to left between each series; a space of approximately three frames to be left between each item/file; the film to be surrendered on spools and to be boxed and clearly labelled and identified; before any copies are made, the master negative to be surrendered for checking of image placement, etc, and residual chemicals.
- *Indicators*. All identification sheets, targets and notes to be provided by the client
- *Image placement*. Specify in Simplex fashion in position IB (Comic mode), or IIB for volumes, as recognised by the USA *Standard Specifications for 16mm or 35mm Silver-Gelatin Microfilms for Reel Applications*, PH5.3–1967, Section 5.
- *Ratio reduction*. Specify approximately 11 times.
- *Archival quality*. The archival quality of the film to meet the requirement set by British Standard 1153.1975, *Recommendations for the Processing and Storage of Silver-Gelatin-Type Microfilm*; American National Standard PH4.8–1971, *Methylene Blue Test for Measuring Thiosulphate and Silver Densitometric Method for Measuring Residual Chemicals in Films, Plates and Papers*; the film to receive additional perma-film protection.
- *Conditions of microfilming*. The documents to be filmed on the supplier's premises in the presence of a member of the client's staff; transportation of the documents to and from the supplier's premises to be undertaken by the client; the documents to remain at all times in the supplier's custody.
- *Microfilm copies*. Master negative 35mm; copy negative (to be quoted for separately); X copy positives (to be quoted for separately).

In addition to stating the quality standards that must be met, a contract should make clear how errors in the filming, processing or duplication will be detected, what actions will be taken to correct them and who will pay for them.

Prepare the Records for Filming

Before it can be filmed, the material to be copied must be adequately prepared. This preparation involves:

- *Arranging and describing the material accurately and completely.* Complete arrangement and description of the records minimises the risk of records being out of order or missing. Also, the records will be temporarily passing out of the custody of the archives, which introduces the possibilities of externally caused disturbance, damage or loss of the records. Arrangement and description provides an inventory of records sent to the commercial service's premises, which can be used to ensure that they are later returned complete and in good order.
- *Preparatory conservation work.* Records may require cleaning and flattening before they can be filmed effectively. This kind of preparation can also include the simple but necessary task of removing pins, staples and clips.
- *Preparing and inserting targets and explanatory notes to be filmed along with the records.* Targets provide identifying and technical information and are inserted in the sequence of records prior to filming. Targets indicating the start of the reel, the reel number, the series and item number and title of the records being filmed, the end of the reel and continuation of the series to or from another reel should appear on every reel. These identifying targets should be legible with the naked eye. Specialised targets may also be needed to indicate missing pages, information on the records obscured by the original binding or other problems. Technical targets, such as test charts and information about the reduction ratio used to film the records, may also be prepared. Archivists preparing records for filming must remember that researchers using the microfilm will not have the originals to compare with the film; nor will they necessarily have an archivist with particular knowledge of those records at hand to explain any inconsistencies or legibility problems with the material. The archivist must try to anticipate these needs and provide explanatory notes where necessary to make sure the researcher is fully informed of any factors which might have affected the quality or completeness of the image on the film. Notes may also provide additional descriptive information about the records and a copyright warning.
- *Preparing instructions for the operator.* Remember that the microfilm camera operator is only responsible for producing a technically suitable microphotograph of the material. It is the archivist's responsibility to decide what is to be photographed, to communicate these decisions to the photographer and to prepare the material for placement under the camera. The archivist must provide instructional notes on such matters as what to do with runs of blank pages, when to film covers of

volumes or files and in what circumstances to contact the archives for advice.

- *Packaging the records and preparing them for transport.* The material should be carefully packaged so that the risk of damage in transit is minimised. As noted earlier, it may be considered worthwhile to accompany the material to the firm's premises and even to be present when the filming is done. The archivist also needs to consider the mode of transport to be used. In particular, extremes of heat and temperature need to be avoided, since damage may be caused by the resultant changes in dimension and moisture in the film. Similarly, care must be taken during the return of the original material and the microfilm copies.

Final Check of the Microfilm and the Original Records

Once returned, the original material and the microfilm copies should be checked carefully before paying the bill. To determine technical quality, it may be useful to have the microfilm tested independently by an institutional or commercial lab to ensure that the stipulated standards of processing have been adhered to. If necessary, insist on rewashing, or even refilming with the refilmed frames properly spliced in. Check the microfilm against the originals to ensure that it is complete and in order. Also check the order and condition of the originals before returning them to the shelves.

When handling the master negative microfilm, exercise great care and wear lint-free cotton gloves. Other basic equipment which is useful for a visual inspection of the microfilm includes a lightbench, hand operated film winders, and a magnifying glass.

Storage of Microfilm

There is no point in ensuring that microfilm is made to archival standards if the film is then kept in poor storage conditions. Appropriate storage conditions for film-based materials are discussed in more detail in Chapter 3. At this point, it is useful to note the most important factors which determine the suitability of a storage environment for master archival film:

- *Temperature.* A low temperature (ideally 10°C, but certainly below 21°C, for black and white film; 0°C for colour) prolongs the life of the microfilm image by reducing the rate at which the chemical changes that result in deterioration take place. Changes in temperature, such as the cyclical changes of office air-conditioning, should also be avoided.
- *Humidity.* A low humidity prevents the growth of moulds which eat the emulsion of the film. However, if the humidity is too low, the film base can dry out and become brittle.

Around 30–40% RH is a suitable balance. Good air circulation is also a means of preventing mould.

- *Shelving.* Purpose-designed shelving and drawers should be available for storing microfilm. Alternatively, existing equipment may be adapted.
- *Hazards to avoid.* Microfilm should be kept away from such hazards as heat, light, and water, which could cause damage. For this reason, attics and below-ground storage should generally be avoided.

If storage meeting these conditions is not available to the archives, a larger archives may be able to help by storing the security or preservation negatives.

As well as a suitable storage environment, the containers used for the storage of microfilm are important. Master negative microfilm should be stored on chemically stable polycarbonate or similar reels or cores. Boxes for individual reels should also be made of stable materials, such as polypropylene or made or lined with alkaline buffered paper. Containers should be clearly labelled with identifying information. Colour coding on containers can help underline the status of a particular copy. An growing standard in Australia uses red for master negatives, green for duplicating copies and blue for reference copies.

It is important to monitor the condition of master microfilm so that corrective measures can be taken if it deteriorates noticeably. A random inspection of a small proportion should be made annually.

This strict environment is not required for reference copies. Here emphasis should be placed on proper handling, care in loading and removing from microfilm readers, and keeping reading and printing equipment clean and working well.

Microfilm Readers

A wide range of microfilm viewers or readers is available, new models are being introduced all the time and, given the cost of these machines, it is worthwhile to seek expert advice before making a choice. Colleagues and staff of other archives are a good source of advice on the use of equipment in archival operations. The archivist may want to consider leasing rather than purchasing equipment at first to gauge user demand and satisfaction before making a major investment. Some of the desirable features to seek include

- versatility in terms of the formats of microfilm which the equipment can accommodate (many readers are easily converted between roll film and fiche, or can change lenses for different levels of magnification)
- capacity to adjust the screen's angle and brightness, to suit the needs of different users or changes in location

- quietness and ease of operation, including loading and removing film
- economy of operation, including easy maintenance and reliable, fast repairs.

If a reader/printer is to be chosen, the quality of the hardcopy, the speed of the printing process and the ease or otherwise of routine maintenance, such as the addition of toner, should be investigated. A reader/printer which uses plain paper rather than thermal paper is desirable. Security measures to prevent unauthorised printing and a coin-operated printing operation may also be necessary. Establish a regular cleaning and maintenance routine for the machine, following the supplier's specifications, and protect it from dust with a dust cover.

Having chosen a reader or reader/printer, the archivist must decide where to locate it. Background glare should be avoided, as should light reflected from the screen. A darkened location with down-lighting to enable users to make notes or consult printed materials is ideal. The intermittent noise caused by the operation of a microfilm reader may be distracting both to staff and to other researchers and, therefore, it may be desirable to isolate it. Equally, users should be able to seek assistance easily. The table or bench on which the reader is located should have enough additional work space for a user to take notes. The height of the bench should be chosen to maximise the comfort of the user, depending on the height of the reader's screen. An adjustable chair should also be provided.

While physical access by researchers to archival materials must be strictly controlled, it is possible to be more flexible with microform copies. For example, reference copies may be made available on open access, removing the need to issue them formally. This has the disadvantages that the level of use of microfilmed materials can no longer be accurately monitored and reels may not be returned to their correct places. These problems can be largely overcome by requiring researchers to hand in reels when they have finished with them, to be put back by archives staff, who can also document their use.

Document Image Processing

Document image processing (DIP) is a term applied to a group of technologies and processes whereby an image of a document is captured, stored and retrieved in electronic form.

In recent years document image processing has been used extensively in records management to acquire the same benefits as offered by micrographics technologies – reductions in records storage space, increased security, more convenient access to information – and significant additional benefits, such as

- faster retrieval of document images
- fast and sophisticated searching using retrieval software
- the ability to use modern communication systems to expand access and distribution.

This section will mainly look at document imaging systems sold as complete packages of hardware and software. It is worthwhile noting, however, that 'entry level' imaging capability is becoming increasingly available to microcomputer users.

How Document Image Processing Works

Document images are captured with a scanner, typically producing a digital image using techniques similar to those used in facsimile machines. The images are indexed electronically and stored in mass storage devices, usually optical or magneto optical disks containing thousands of images. Retrieval software is used to enable rapid on-line access to images, which can then be printed or sent by fax or electronic mail. Digitising scanners scan documents at different levels of resolution, normally at 200, 300 or 400 dots per inch (dpi). It is desirable to be able to scan at different levels of resolution to meet the needs of different types of documents. For example, high resolution may be needed for fine lines and handwritng, while lower resolution may be adequate for typescript. Scanners are avalable which can recognise different levels of grey shading – 'grey scales' – or colours. Scanners of different sizes and speeds or designed for different source media – documents, photographs, microforms – are available to suit specific applications. Colour resolution, while adding expense, is highly desirable in archival document imaging applications.

In most document image processing systems the images are stored on optical disks. Digitised images must be stored as graphics files, which are much larger than equivalent text files. Optical disks offer greater storage capacities than magnetic data storage media and are more cost-effective for storing document images. In addition to images some systems store other digital or digitised information, such as computer data, text and sound. All digital optical disk systems use data compression techniques to increase the capacity of their storage devices. Some systems store images in analogue form on optical disks, using the same technology as analogue video disks. This approach is usually used to store images of pictures, such as photographs, because of the huge size of such image files when stored in digital form. The main advantages of storing images in digital form are that

- they can be sent through digital communication networks, such as local area networks and facsimile services
- OCR can be used for indexing them.

Most systems, whether digital or analogue, use Write Once Read Many (WORM) disks. Being a non-erasable medium,

WORM disks are more suitable for records and archives applications than magnetic and the newer rewritable optical media. Some systems offer a choice of storing images in erasable or nonerasbale mode. Many systems provide access to images stored on multiple disks by using one or more 'juke-boxes', robotic mechanisms which automatically load disks into drives. These systems may support one or more disk drives: more than one drive enables users to have access to images from more than one disk simultaneously. Other systems use small desktop drives connected to individual microcomputers and monitors.

Database management software running on a microcomputer, network or mainframe computer is used in most systems for indexing and retrieval of images as well as for related functions such as disk management, security and printing.

When retrieved by a user, an image is displayed on a monitor: high resolution monitors are an essential part of most systems. Portrait-style monitors, enabling a full page to be displayed in one screen, are available with some systems. For archival applications, zoom facilities are very useful, enabling the user to look closely at handwriting or details in drawings and photographs.

A printer is used to produce hard copies of document images when required by a user. The type and quality of the printer depends on the nature and needs of the application. A laser printer, typically printing at 400 dpi of resolution, produces high quality printouts for applications in which the source documents comprise typewritten text, handwriting or line drawings. In one system designed to store images of photographs, a thermal printer produces a hard copy of modest quality, meeting most users' needs, while users requiring copies of reproduction quality can obtain prints or negatives produced through photographic processes.

Being able to connect to a data communications network is an increasingly important feature of document imaging systems.

It is essential to remember that scanning a document produces a digital image of the document. Scanning does not, itself, convert text in a scanned document into computer-readable characters. Thus, the user cannot undertake text-based searches of the contents of scanned documents per se. OCR software can be used with some document imaging systems, and indeed with desktop scanners that are not part of a document imaging system, to 'read' a document's contents, producing a computer text file.

Using Document Image Processing in Archives Work

Fundamentally, the reasons for using document image processing in archives work are the same as those for using micrographics, namely

- to prolong the life of original records

- to make unique material more widely available
- to reduce high cost storage
- to protect the security of vital original records.

The capabilities of document image processing technology provide opportunities for further uses or variations on the uses noted above:

- Document image processing, coupled with OCR techniques and text retrieval software, provides very comprehensive intellectual control over selected records. Certainly, such treatment is costly and would not be justified for one's total holdings, but may provide a desirable level of accessibility to records of very high research value and use and to control records and finding aids.

- Original records and finding aids are generally only available to one user at a time. Multi-user DIP systems enable a number of people to use an image at the same time.

- Archivists working within larger organisations can make images of records available to other parts of the organisation through its data communication network. The same benefit is available in archives operating at more than one site.

- By integrating a DIP system into a communications network with a facsimile capability or connected to an electronic mail service, images can be faxed or mailed to remote users without the need to use a hardcopy.

- In the longer term, images from DIP systems offer great potential for sale on disk to users or other institutions, but this is presently hampered by lack of standards among proprietary systems.

Document image processing offers a number of potential advantages over micrographics in archives work:

- While optical disks require care in handling, they are generally more robust than microfilm. Moreover, in distributed systems in which disks are loaded into centralised players or jukeboxes, the user need not handle the disk at all.

- The ability to 'zoom in' and magnify an image is generally far more flexible and convenient in a DIP system than with microfilm, where changing a lens is often the only means available.

- Where a DIP system is integrated into an archives' or organisation's computer system, high quality laser printers that are already part of that system can be used to print document images. This is likely to be cheaper and more flexible than buying a dedicated microfilm reader/printer.

- Users requesting a copy of a document have the additional option of being given a digital copy, eg on a floppy disk in a common graphics file format such as TIFF.

- The availability of desktop and other entry-level DIP systems means that this technology can be acquired by small archival operations, eliminating the need to use a commercial service. This may be particularly convenient where the DIP system is integrated with the archives' control system, eg with the *Professional Archivist* program, which provides an entry-level document imaging capability.
- As access to images is provided through automated indexing, the physical location of an image on a disk – and therefore the order in which documents are scanned – is far less important than in a microfilming project. While it is still desirable to establish and maintain the original order of records to be scanned, the later insertion of additional documents from the same series presents much less of a problem than with micro-film.

Planning for Document Image Processing

Investigating and planning to use document image processing require a combination of the methods described above for computers and micrographics. This involves a systematic process to cover a careful analysis of needs, identification of a range of possible solutions and their costs, evaluation of options, selection of a solution and supplier, and the development of an implementation strategy.

As in the case of microfilming, the archivist faces the choice of acquiring and using the necessary equipment or of entering into a contract with a commercial service to undertake scanning and image processing and to supply and maintain playback equipment, or a mixture of both. Some commercial suppliers provide a range of associated services, including indexing and cataloguing, production and replication of disks, and consultancy and project management services. Other firms operate as systems integrators, putting together packages of hardware and software and configuring them to meet individual customer needs – and ensuring that they work together.

A number of considerations are need to be taken into account when investigating and planning to use document image processing:

- The flexibility of any system under consideration and its ability to grow in size and functionality will determine its long-term value in meeting the archives' developing needs.
- A degree of choice in each of the hardware and software components of the system or package will ensure not only that it meets the archives' immediate needs, but that it can be improved incrementally.
- How easy the system is to use is especially important if the archives' users are to use it as well as staff.

- The ability of the system to integrate with existing computer systems and data communication networks, as discussed above, can enhance its usefulness in a number of ways.
- The ability to cope with a range of original record formats may be more useful than one designed for a specific format. For example, a system designed for pictorial materials may have a limited future if other types of records are to be covered at a later date.

The size of an archives and its relationship with its parent organisation can have an important bearing on the type of system selected. An archivist working in an organisation which adopts document image processing as a large scale records management solution may be able to have the archives included in that system. In this case it will be important to ensure that the system meets, and does not compromise, the specific needs of the archives. A stand-alone desktop system may be more suitable for a small and fairly independent archives operation, but this is likely to require the archivist to issue disks or other storage media to users in the Search Room, and to ensure their return and safe handling.

An implementation strategy needs to cover a number of considerations:

- A plan will be required concerning the initial capture of images, which will represent one of the largest costs of implementation. This plan needs to include the limits of the initial image capture exercise, the estimated rate at which documents can be scanned and processed and the priority of different series of records and other materials.
- The workflow involved in scanning and image processing must be designed to facilitate the initial image capture work and later or ongoing additions of images to the system.
- Staff and users must be trained in using the system and shown how to get the most from the new capabilities available from it.
- The location of terminals/workstations, especially when available to the archives' users, must be considered. As screen-based equipment, their location should be subject to the same considerations as computers and microfilm readers.

Document image processing can be seen as epitomising the increasing convergence of information management technologies. At one level, it represents a combination of the other two technologies – computers and micrographics – discussed in this chapter. In this sense, DIP involves the use of mass data storage media and computerised control and retrieval techniques to achieve the aims traditionally pursued through the use of micrographics.

At another level, document image processing – along with other developments – is leading archivists on the path to easier access to the holdings of archival repositories. Just as DIP already relies on the fruits of the personal computer revolution, especially for using retrieval software and desktop DIP systems, and on continuing developments in data storage, so it will increasingly exploit the current revolution in data communications. As archives and other centres of documentary information become linked electronically into networks providing access to descriptive and bibliographic data, and as users acquire the means to use these networks remotely, the records themselves – as digital images – will also become accessible through these networks, freeing them from the physical confines of their repositories to an extent never possible before.

Further Reading

Archives Authority of NSW, *Guidelines on Establishing a Microfilming Program (Technical Paper No. 3)*, AONSW, Sydney, 1983.

Archives Authority of NSW, *Microfilming of Records (Technical Paper No. 4)*, AONSW, Sydney, 1983.

Arnold, Bruce and Rowell, Hilary, 'The Australian Archives Records Information Service System (RINSE)', in *Archives and Manuscripts*, 17/1, May 1989, pp. 25–35.

Avedon, Don, *Introduction to Electronic Imaging*, Association for Information and Image Management, Springfield MD, 1992.

Bearman, David, *Archives and Museum Informatics Technical Report No. 4: Automated Systems for Archives and Museums: Acquisition and Implementation Issues*, Archives and Museum Informatics, Pittsburgh PA, 1989.

Black, David, *Document Capture for Document Imaging Systems*, Association for Information and Image Management, Springfield MD, 1992.

Cook, Michael, *Archives and the Computer*, 2nd edn, Butterworths, London, 1986.

Cook, Michael, *An Introduction to archival automation: a RAMP study with guidelines*, UNESCO, Paris, 1986.

Evans, Max and Weber, Lisa B, *MARC for Archives and Manuscripts: A Compendium of Practice*, Historical Society of Wisconsin, Madison WI, 1985.

Faithfull, Fraser, Review of *Professional Archivist*, in *Archives and Manuscripts*, 20/2, November 1992, pp. 275–80.

Green, Adam, *The Development of Policies and Plans in Archival Automation: A RAMP Study with Guidelines*, UNESCO, Paris, 1992.

Hitching, Christopher, *The Impact of Computerisation on Archival Finding Aids: A RAMP Study with Guidelines*, UNESCO, Paris, 1992.

Hoy, Marian and Macknight, Lorraine, 'National Database Cooperation: A Case Study', in *Archives and Manuscripts*, 18/2, November 1990, pp. 231–41.

Keene, James and Roper, Michael, *Planning, Equipping and Staffing a Document Reprographic Service: A RAMP Study with Guidelines*, UNESCO, Paris, 1984.

Kesner, Richard M., *Automation for Archivists and Records Managers: Planning and Implementation*, American Library Association, Chicago, 1985.

Körmedy, Lajos (ed.), *Manual of archival reprography* (ICA handbook series; vol. 5), Saur, Munich, 1989.

Moir, Michael, 'The Use of Optical Disk Technology to Improve Access to Historical Photographs', in *Archives and Museum Informatics*, 6/1, Spring 1992, pp. 5–12.

Sahli, Nancy, *MARC for Archives and Manuscripts: The AMC Format*, Society of American Archivists, Chicago, 1985.

Smith, Helen and Hurley, Chris, 'Developments in Computerised Documentation Systems at the Public Record Office, Victoria', in *Archives and Manuscripts*, 17/2, November 1989, pp. 165–82.

Sung, Carolyn Hoover, *Archives and Manuscripts: Reprography*, Society of American Archivists, Chicago, 1982.

13 | Managing Records in Special Formats

David Roberts

Textual paper records make up the bulk of most archival holdings and consequently continue to be the archivist's major concern. However, archives often include records in special formats, frequently in small quantities, which need to be managed along with those in conventional formats. Moreover, as more organisations and individuals use computers and other information technology as an integral part of their business or work, the nature of the records which are created in the process is changing.

This chapter will provide only a basic introduction to the management of records and related materials in special formats. The focus here is on the management of such records in small quantities within a broader archival collection or operation. The advice presented here, however, will also serve as a brief introduction should the archivist be responsible for a more significant collection of material in one of these special formats.

While reading this chapter, bear in mind that the management of many of these special format materials is the province of other professions – of librarians, museum and gallery curators, film and sound archivists and others. This means that there are considerable bodies of specialised literature and other sources of advice available to help make decisions about dealing with specific formats among archival holdings.

Common Questions

Each of the special formats discussed in this chapter has its own characteristics which will determine much of what the archivist needs to do to manage the material in the archives' custody.

However, the archivist is also faced with similar questions, regardless of the special format concerned.

A fundamental question is whether the special format material should be part of the archival collection at all. Many of the formats discussed in this chapter require specialised storage environments and equipment, preservation measures and means of making them available to users. Many have characteristics which require different descriptive practices either for basic control or to provide users with effective intellectual access to exploit their potential as sources of information. Some have considerably more commercial value than most textual paper records. All of this means that the archivist must decide whether the archival operation will be able to cope with materials in these formats and carry out the responsibility involved in accepting them or keeping them.

The archivist will need to balance the problems raised by materials in these formats against the arguments in favour of keeping them in the archival collection. For example:

- Where the materials are part of a single collection with the same provenance, it would be undesirable to break up the collection and lose the relationship between the different materials and the benefits of enabling them to be studied together
- Where the material otherwise falls squarely within the archives' acquisition policy and complements existing holdings, the benefits for the increased usefulness of the collection may outweigh the problems.

In any case deciding the extent of commitment to the range of special format materials is an essential part of the development of an archival policy, especially the acquisition policy.

Alternatives to managing materials in particular special formats as part of the archival collection include the following:

- Where the archives' parent organisation or institution has alternative locations for managing material in such formats better, for example in its library or museum, it may be preferable to transfer responsibility to them.
- Where the links between the special format material and the rest of the collection are weak or there is no other means available to ensure the material's survival, it may be necessary to propose that it go to another institution better equipped to handle it. In such a case the archivist would need to check the conditions under which it came into the archives' custody.
- In either of the above cases it may be possible to keep copies of the material in the archives so that it is still accessible in conjunction with the related records.

Considering ways of managing some of these special format records, notably moving images, sound recordings and maps and drawings, highlights the tension between the 'media separation' and 'total archives' approaches to these forms of records. The media separation approach argues that the relevant special format records should be managed by specialised custodial institutions, or at least by specialist divisions within larger institutions, using distinct techniques and systems suitable for the particular medium. The total archives approach calls for the integrated management of all forms of archival media, using common techniques and systems as far as possible, while recognising the specific needs of special format records.

Since this chapter is concerned with the management of special format records as archives, we will generally follow the total archives approach.

Photographs

Photographic processes have existed since the 1820s. In the nineteenth century, in particular, a wide variety of processes were used, the results of most of which are now very rare. It is beyond the scope of this chapter to examine those historical processes and the specific types of photographic materials that resulted from them. This section will concentrate on the types of photographic materials most likely to be found in, or to come into the custody of, archival repositories today.

The main physical forms of photographic materials likely to be encountered are

- prints: unmounted, mounted, framed or encased
- negatives: glass plates, unjacketed or jacketed flexible negatives
- transparencies: lantern slides, 35mm projection slides, large slides (usually 4x5" or 8x10").

Appraising Photographs

As with the other formats of records discussed in this chapter, photographs can possess the same kinds of values as conventional textual records. Consequently, we can apply the kinds of appraisal criteria that are discussed in Chapter 6. Note, however, that it is less common for photographs to have *evidential* value than conventional records. They tend to occur in in-house archival operations, where the photographs may show evidence of the structure, personnel, accommodation and so on of the organisation.

The principal values of photographs tend to be *informational*. One of the major strengths of photographs as archives is that they commonly contain a wealth and variety of information that goes well beyond the purposes for which they were originally taken. It must also be emphasised at this point that not all photographs are worth keeping. A significant proportion of the

Photographs generally have great display value.

photographs produced by any organisation or offered to an archives will have insufficient value to justify the expense of keeping and preserving them. The same kind of discipline that is applied to textual records needs to be applied to photographs.

In assessing the informational value of photographs, take account of a number of factors which reflect the particular characteristics of the format:

- *Subject.* Careful thought is required about which subjects have priority, within the context of the acquisition policy.
- *Age.* Nineteenth-century photographs have value as artefacts, illustrating the photographic processes which created them in addition to values in the image.
- *Uniqueness.* There is little point in keeping copies of photographs that exist elsewhere, unless it is clear that this is the original negative or an earlier print of the image. A photograph is particularly valuable if it contains information not available in other formats.
- *Quality.* To be useful for reproduction, a photograph must be of satisfactory quality, ie proper exposure, clear focus, good composition. However, a photograph may not be good enough for reproduction, but still have informational value.
- *Identification.* The more information (about the subject, the photographer, date, location) the better. A completely unidentified photograph is of very little value.
- *Quantity.* It may be too costly to accept or continue to keep a very large group of photographs, and culling or sampling may be necessary. On the other hand, a thorough pictorial record

of a given subject can be more valuable for exploiting the informational values of the material than selected images.

The *provenance* of photographs can be an important factor in their appraisal. It adds meaning to know who created and used the image, and to perform what function. This means that it is necessary to appraise photographs with the same origin together, preferably at the same time as appraising related records in other formats. For example, an individual photograph found on a file should be appraised with and as part of the file, even though the photograph is likely to be separated later for preservation.

It is possible to make some generalisations about the nature of particular types of photographic materials which affect their values. Scientific and technical series of photographs are often repetitive, specific and voluminous; they tend to require culling with careful reference to the related documentation of the processes that they illustrate. The products of commercial photography studios tend to be large collections, often poorly organised and documented. Amateur photography is potentially a huge area, but there can be many problems of technical quality and identification.

It is important that the appraiser of photographs has as strong a background knowledge of the subject area covered by the photographs as possible, so that he or she can recognise features indicating value which might otherwise be missed. It is also helpful to have an understanding of photographic processes and the products of those processes to enable the appraiser to recognise technical or conservation problems and their likely effect on the viability of keeping particular photographs.

Arranging and Describing Photographs

As is the case with other archival materials, the principles of provenance and original order are the basis for the arrangement and description of photographs. Refer to Chapter 8, Arrangement and Description, and Chapter 9, Finding Aids. This section only looks at the characteristics of photographs which require different treatment.

Following these basic archival principles means, in particular, maintaining the relationships between the photographic holdings and archival materials in other formats. There should be no separate, artificial photographic collection. At the same time, it must be recognised that, more than is the case with textual records, archival photographs will be sought and used for a wide variety of purposes, such as the reproduction in publications noted above. Consequently, it is necessary to provide a range of additional means of intellectual access which will help users of the material to find suitable images efficiently. The following are two such means:

- *Indexing*. Index by names of people and localities; by types of images, such as portraits, landscapes, streetscapes; by subjects (using a controlled list of terms). Indexing lends itself well to the use of computer technology, and can be done selectively as resources permit by giving priority to groups or series of photographs most likely to be in demand.
- *Browsing*. Because photographs, by their nature, can be quickly assimilated and assessed by a user looking for specific types of images, it is particularly helpful to enable users to browse through collections of images. This can best be done by providing on open access a set of reference or access copies of all or of selected photographs held by the archives.

This set may comprise prints, kept in drawers or folders; photocopies, similarly filed; or microfilm images. The physical arrangement of this reference set presents the same problem as the arrangements of original archival materials: no specific arrangement will be entirely satisfactory for all purposes. The best approach is to keep the reference set also in original order and to provide general descriptive information and indexes to direct the user to the most relevant parts of the set.

Electronic imaging systems, coupled with computer-based descriptive and indexing tools, are providing convenient and flexible access to collections of photographs and other pictorial materials in an increasing number of archives and libraries. Electronic imaging is discussed in more detail in Chapter 12.

When arranging and describing photographs, the archivist may be dealing with series composed entirely of photographs or series which include photographs among other forms of records. Many photographic series have no original system of control; nor, of course, will an artificial series. However, a series of files including some photographs attached to individual files will probably be controlled at the file level, but the photographs are unlikely to be controlled or numbered. Nonetheless, it is essential to be able to identify each image individually. Where there is no original system of control for the photographs in a series, the archivist must impose one. In the case of photographs within a series of other records, the control numbers imposed must reflect the system of control used in the series as a whole, preferably relating each photograph to the item to which it is attached.

An exception to the rule that photographs must be arranged according to provenance and original order can arise when the archivist undertakes a photographic copying program, as a conservation measure, to produce a reference set of images or to provide copies to researchers. The copying work now and in the future will be made more manageable by applying a running number, normally called a 'negative number', to each image copied irrespective of provenance and series. The negative

A visiting archivist, Papua New Guinean Gabriel Gerry, is shown the storage of photographic records at Australian Archives, ACT.

number is used to control the set of negatives that are used to produce copy prints and can be quoted by a user when ordering a copy of an image. The negative numbering system operates parallel to the normal archival control system based on provenance and original order.

Storing Photographs

In addition to advice about the storage of archival materials generally, which appears elsewhere in this book, we need to note the special characteristics of photographic materials that affect the ways in which they should be stored.

Information on the appropriate range of temperature and relative humidity for the storage of photographs appears in Chapter 3, Preservation. High temperature and humidity accelerate chemical reactions which result in deterioration and encourage the growth of mould. Very low relative humidity can dry out the emulsion layer, resulting in cracking and peeling.

Stability of temperature and humidity is particularly important. Photographs are made up of a sandwich of layers of different materials, which are affected differently by fluctuations of temperature and humidity. Among other problems this can lead to separation of the emulsion layer and the supporting base.

A clean storage environment is especially important for photographs. Insects are very partial to a paper and gelatin sandwich. Deposits of dirt can produce harmful chemical reactions, while abrasive dirt particles can scratch the emulsion layer. The air in the storage area should also be clean as many atmospheric pollutants, particularly in cities, can start or accelerate harmful chemical reactions. The air-conditioning system serving the archival storage area should have effective air-filtering equipment.

Photographs should be stored individually in chemically neutral seamless envelopes, and colour photographs individually in moisture proof plastic packets. Photographic materials, especially prints, can appear in a wide variety of sizes and with different sized mounts and cases. It is often necessary to make custom-sized phase boxes to store photographs of unusual or large size.

Photographic materials in physically fragile forms, such as glass plate negatives, need special care. They should not be stored on mobile shelving. Their storage containers (boxes or drawers) should include rigid dividers to provide support and keep them upright and should be clearly labelled as containing fragile glass.

Moving Images

This section will examine the archival management of moving images, which may be recorded on three main types of physical media

- cine film
- videotape
- optical digital video disks of various types.

While these materials have very different physical natures, their common content – moving images – means that much of their intellectual treatment, including appraisal decisions and arrangement and description, can be similar.

Film is an immensely complex medium. The film production process results in a number of types of film components, including

- the original camera negative
- intermediate or duping components, such as fine grain positives and dupe negatives of black and white film; and interpositives, internegatives, colour reversals and colour separations for colour film

- sound components, including sound negatives with optical or magnetic stripes and separate magnetic tapes, recording dialogue, music and effects, and other components of the sound track, and the final sound mix
- the final release version
- out-takes and cuts which were not used in the final version.

The archivist may need to deal with any or all of these components. This variety of components which may be available for acquisition affects selection and disposal decisions since there is seldom justification for keeping all the components.

Depending on its source and original purpose, film may appear in 8, 16, 35 or 70mm gauge. The physical composition of film is also complex, comprising a series of layers: a base or support layer, an adhesive layer of gelatin, and one or more emulsion layers containing the image. The composition of film will be examined more closely later in the context of its preservation needs.

Videotape may also appear in any of a number of formats, historical or current, including 2" and 1" open reel tapes, 3/4" Umatic cassettes, 1/2" VHS and Beta cassettes, and a variety of recent miniature cassette formats for portable cameras and several obsolete cartridge formats. Despite the fact that the basic composition of magnetic tape has changed little in the last three decades, a major factor in both appraisal and preservation decisions concerning video recordings is the effect of technological change.

In the last decade several video laser disk systems have been developed and released commercially, some of which are intended to be used interactively with the help of a computer.

The focus of this section is on these different moving image media as records and archives. It is necessary to be aware, however, of the work of the 'film archive' community, as distinct from archivists working with moving image records along with records in other formats. The term 'film archive' here refers to the specialised professionals, institutions and techniques devoted solely to managing historical film collections. Archivists responsible for moving image records have much to learn from this community. However, there exist fundamental differences in philosophy and practice between archivists and film archive specialists:

- 'Film archivists', despite their protestations, are concerned almost entirely with cinema productions (and more recently with television output). The conventional archives approach recognises that moving image records may be created in the course of the business of a wide variety of government, business and other bodies, while carrying out many different functions, including training, promotional activities, and scientific and technical research.

- 'Film archivists' place film at the centre of their collections, while related records in other formats, if collected at all, are limited in scope and the status of 'documentation'. Film is removed from its context. The conventional archives approach seeks to preserve an integrated body of related records in different formats which together represent the whole picture.
- 'Film archive' institutions tend to pursue monopolistic and centralist policies concerning the responsibility for preserving a national film heritage. This approach is exemplified in the membership rules of the International Federation of Film Archives (FIAF) and may be contrasted with the membership rules of the International Association of Sound Archives (IASA). These policies do not always account for the valuable work performed by other custodial and research institutions, which hold large or small collections of moving image records among their other holdings and are in a good position to serve their particular clients.

Some specific consequences of the difference between these two approaches are noted in the following sections.

Appraising Moving Images

Much of the literature on appraisal and selection of moving image records comes from the 'film archives' camp. Almost without exception, therefore, this material is concerned with cinema productions to the exclusion of moving image records produced in other contexts, and much of it relates to the methods used by, and really only suitable for, the great national film collections. The approaches described in this literature provide some valuable guidance to archivists in assessing the broad informational values of cinema productions, but otherwise provide us with little assistance.

Many broadcasting archives around the world have developed methods and criteria for selecting television (and radio) program materials primarily on the basis of their value as a resource for future program production, but also for their broader value for research. The approaches used by these bodies offer an insight into the problems of assessing the enormous range of informational values which may be present in moving image records, but, again, are of little practical assistance to archivists working outside the broadcasting area.

Our starting point in considering how to appraise moving image records is the desire to manage them as archives. Thus, the appraisal methods and criteria described in Chapters 5 and 6 provide the basis for the approach to moving image records. The

following additional principles derive from the nature of moving
image records:

- As noted with photographs, moving image records can possess a wide range of informational values – far more than textual records – which can be a persuasive factor in deciding to
  keep them.
- Moving image records are seldom, if ever, created in isolation.
  Moving image records take their place among records in other
  formats which document a process or function of the creating
  body. If it is proposed to keep moving image records for their
  value in documenting that process or function, the related
  records in other formats should also be retained. If they are
  not, the moving image records lose their context and, therefore, much of their value. This principle applies to all types of
  moving image records, including cinema and broadcast
  productions, for which production files, scripts, promotional
  materials and similar records provide an essential complement.
- Moving image records present some of the most difficult
  preservation problems, the solutions to which are inevitably
  expensive. Thus, the cost of long-term preservation, an
  increasingly important appraisal criterion for all forms of
  records, is crucial for moving image records.

Arranging and Describing Moving Images

A fundamental area of difference between the 'film archive'
approach and the conventional archives approach to the archival
management of moving images concerns their arrangement and
description. In the former case the primary level of control and
description is normally the individual film or video production.
Each production is catalogued separately, using methods derived
from library practice.

For moving image records which are being managed as
archives, the principle of provenance, the concept of an archival
series and the relationship between moving images records and
associated records in other media are all important. In this context, moving image records should be arranged according to the
fundamental archival principles of provenance and original order.
They should be described using conventional archival practices
and integrated into the archives' overall control and finding aids
system.

It is particularly important to identify and describe the links
between moving image records and the often wide range of other
forms of records created with them. In the case of film and video
productions, such associated records may include production
files, scripts, musical scores and recordings, distribution records
and promotional materials and ephemera. For film created in the
course of scientific research, their links with the other records
associated with that research – laboratory notebooks, collected

data in paper, electronic or other forms, project reports – must be established and documented if the film is to be of any use.

Equally important for description are the characteristics of moving image records which are not shared with other forms of records. *Inventories of items* or *shelf lists*, for example, should indicate the following for each record item:

- Duration, ie the time taken to play the item
- The number of physical items, such as reels of film, comprising a whole production
- Emulsion type (negative, positive, finegrain, etc.) and gauge (8, 16, 35 or 70mm) of each film item.
- Format and size (eg. 1" or 2" videotape; 1/2" VHS or Beta cassette; CD TV disk) of each video item.
- Black-and-white or colour image.
- Whether a reference copy is available.

Storing and Preserving Moving Images

Film made before about 1950 used a base of nitrocellulose. This nitrate film decomposes inexorably, even under good storage conditions. In the final stages of this decomposition, a recognisable sequence of effects occurs: the image fades; the surface of the film becomes sticky; it forms blisters and acquires a characteristic smell; it softens and separate layers of film congeal into a mass; the mass becomes a brown powder.

Once the emulsion layer starts to soften, nitrate film is particularly inflammable and is even prone to spontaneous combustion. For this reason, film found to be in this condition should be destroyed immediately. Nitrate film which has not reached this stage should be copied at the earliest opportunity. It should also be removed from areas where other film is being stored as the process of deterioration of nitrate film results in the production of gases which are harmful to safety films.

All types of film are subject to gradual deterioration in both the emulsion and base layers. Black and white acetate or safety film is relatively stable. Over long periods of time, however, the acetate base reacts with oxygen and becomes brittle, while chemical processes in the silver emulsion layer cause the image to fade. Colour film presents more difficult problems. The dyes used in colour films fade more quickly and the different pigments disintegrate at different rates. Thus, the colour balance can be lost relatively quickly. Inevitably, colour film cannot survive as long as black and white film, even in the most favourable storage conditions. The presence of residual chemicals in the emulsion layer of both black and white and colour film contributes further to its deterioration. In recent years, vinegar syndrome has been recognised as a danger to holdings of acetate film around the world. Marked by a characteristic vinegar odour caused by the evaporation of acetic acid, vinegar syndrome involves the decomposition of the acetate base, which softens, becomes sticky and finally reduces to a powder.

The most important means of slowing all of these forms of deterioration is to store film in suitable conditions. As noted in relation to microfilm in the previous chapter, a temperature of around 10°C is suitable for black and white film, while a relative humidity of 30–40% represents a good balance between the needs to discourage mould and to avoid brittleness. For colour film, a much lower storage temperature is necessary to retard chemical deterioration to a reasonable extent: 0°C or less. A low relative humidity is necessary in these conditions because of the harmful effects of condensation and freezing of excessive moisture at sub-zero temperatures. A relative humidity of 20–30% is appropriate.

Moving film into and out of such low temperature storage areas requires a period of conditioning. Conditioning the film through two or three intermediate stages between the low temperature and the outside environment minimises the impact of dimensional changes to the different layers of the film and the dangers of condensation. Achieving and maintaining the low levels of temperature and humidity recommended here can be a difficult and costly exercise. One means of solving this problem is to seal the film hermetically, using such equipment as the Swedish Film Institute's *Film Conditioning Apparatus* (FICA). In this kind of system the film is conditioned to an appropriate humidity level and sealed in an inert polymer bag. It can then be stored in the correct temperature, even if the required humidity cannot be achieved in the storage area. The main danger with this system is that it is inconvenient and costly to monitor the condition of film so treated, since it must be resealed every time it is inspected. An essential prerequisite for this kind of system, and indeed for any long-term film storage, is cleaning. A purpose-built film cleaning machine can remove dirt and grease and the most harmful residual chemicals from the surface of the film.

One way of attempting to deal with the more rapid deterioration of colour film is the use of colour separations or tri-separations. This involves making and storing a black and white separation copy of the film in each of the three basic colours – yellow, cyan and magenta – which make up a colour image. These tri-separations can be stored in the same conditions as other black and white film and can be expected to enjoy the same longevity. This technique requires the use of much more storage space than the storage of the original colour film. More importantly, any uneven dimensional changes in the three copies make it impossible to recreate the colour image accurately at a later date.

Film often comes into the archivist's care in steel canisters and on reels which may be rusty and will certainly be prone to rust

over long periods of time. Equally, film may appear in flimsy plastic canisters which will deteriorate and break with time. Before receipt into the archives, or as soon as possible thereafter, film should be transferred into containers and onto cores which promote its long-term preservation: inert, high-impact polycarbonate is the best material for both cans and cores.

Videotape in its variety of formats suffers from the same problems and requires the same storage conditions, as magnetic tape used for sound recordings and computer data. Magnetic tape will be discussed in more detail later in this chapter. The other main concern with the preservation of moving images recorded on videotape is the effect of technological change. Videotapes, cassettes and cartridges accepted into the archives can become effectively inaccessible in a matter of decades or even years when the equipment to replay them is no longer available. The main options here are

- to acquire and maintain playback equipment for each format held, or at least to monitor the existence and availability of such equipment: this option is costly and becomes increasingly difficult as expertise and spare parts cease to be available
- to copy material in older formats to a current format: this is also costly and will need to be repeated as the current format goes out of date. Since video images are still normally recorded in an analogue form on tape, the quality of the image will deteriorate with repeated copying.

Despite the claims of manufacturers, laser-based disks remain something of an unknown quantity as archival media. Their composition, effectively a sandwich of different materials, indicates the likelihood of problems in the long term.

Apart from deterioration over time, the greatest danger both to film and videotape lies in the risk of damage during use. Both the manual handling of film and running it through equipment such as a projector or even a film viewing machine can result in scratches on the emulsion layer, damaging the image. Dirt and grease from hands can also lodge on magnetic tape, producing scratches on the oxide layer and damaging the heads of playback equipment. Simply replaying videotape produces an eventual deterioration of the image.

Consequently, copying is an important means of preserving moving images. In this context, copying has three main purposes:

- to provide reference and duplicating copies so that the original material need not be used for these purposes.
- To provide a security copy in case of loss or damage to the original.
- To preserve the image and sound on a more stable, long-term medium than may be the case with the original material.

Typically, a program of copying of moving image records involves making the following kinds of copies:

- A preservation copy, which also serves as a security copy. In the case of film the preservation copy is processed to archival standards; with video, it should be made in the highest quality format practicable – bearing in mind the effects of technological change – such as one of the high-band broadcast quality formats. The preservation copy is stored with the same care as the original material and is not used for any purpose unless absolutely necessary.
- A duplicating or duping copy. This copy is used to make reference copies or to make copies for clients.
- A reference or viewing copy. This is the copy viewed by clients. In the case of film it may be either a projection print or a video cassette copy.

Making most of these kinds of copies is beyond the means of all but the largest archival institutions. However, many film processing firms and video production services are able to do this work to archival standards.

Having made these different copies, it is essential to ensure that each is easily identifiable from the others. In Australia a colour coding system is widely used: red for preservation copies, green for duplicating copies, and blue for reference copies. This system is applicable to other forms of records for which copying is an important means of preservation, including sound recordings, photographs, electronic media and microfilm copies of paper records. Consistency of practice across all these media is highly recommended.

A booth provides access to video and other 'noisy' media without disturbing other researchers.

Finally, a variety of film restoration techniques exist, including colour correction and the physical repair of torn sprocket holes and broken splices. This work requires skilled staff and specialised equipment.

Providing Access to Moving Images

As is the case with most archival media, providing access to moving images means providing a service at two fundamental levels:
- Enabling the researcher to view the material.
- Enabling the client to use selected material in a film, video or broadcast production.

If your reference copies of film material are in the form of projection prints, a projection room, with screen and projector, or a flat-bed film viewing machine is required. Either of these is an expensive investment and could only be justified in the case of a large collection. For smaller collections of film – and indeed for convenient access in many large collections – video reference copies are suitable. In this case only a video cassette player and monitor are required. To prevent disturbance of other researchers, these may be housed in a separate room or booth, or you could provide headphones. A separate area might be more justifiable if used to provide access to other 'noisy' media as well, such as sound recordings and microfilm, and for researchers who want to use typewriters and portable computers.

Most archives are not equipped to be able to provide a copy of moving image records of sufficient quality for use by a client in a film or television production. In this case the archivist must make arrangements with the client or with a film processing or video services firm for a copy to be made from the archives' duplicating copy.

Copyright in moving image records can be complex. Copyright may exist separately for the moving images, the script and the musical score. The archivist needs to be familiar with the specific provisions of copyright legislation (in Australia the *Copyright Act 1968*) that affect film and video productions and dramatic and musical works.

Sound Recordings

Sound recordings appear in a number of historical and current physical formats, the most common of which can be grouped into three broad categories:

- Phonographic recordings: acetate, shellac and vinyl discs, as well as their predecessor, the wax cylinder.
- Magnetic tape recordings: 1/4" reel-to-reel tapes, cassettes, and digital audiotapes (DATs), as well as their predecessor, the magnetic wire recording.
- Optical digital recordings: compact digital audio disks (CDs).

For most of these formats, there exists a wide variety of technological variations, including mono/stereo, number of tracks, speed of replay and, in many cases, the size of the object and the materials of which it is made. Consequently, the range of equipment and techniques required to preserve the many formats of sound recordings and make them accessible is large. Many of these formats, however, are rare or appear only in certain contexts, for example, 16" acetate discs, which play centre to edge, were used for broadcasting and are unlikely to appear in collections not connected with broadcasting. This means that there is much that the archivist with responsibility for only a small amount of sound material within a broader archival collection can do to manage that material.

Like 'film archive', 'sound archive' is a term which has a taken a special meaning in certain contexts: it refers to the specialised collections, institutions and techniques involved in managing historical sound recordings. Almost a separate discipline, sound archives' work overlaps with archives management and librarianship. For the manager of a broader archival collection which includes sound recordings, the sound archives discipline provides a source for much expertise and experience in dealing with this material.

The term 'sound archive', however, also presents problems for the mainstream archivist. In the context referred to above, it is used to cover historical sound recordings of any type or origin: published recordings, as well as unique material; and commercial recordings originally produced for sale, as well as sound material produced as a by-product of an organisation's activities. Thus, to use a crude analogy, 'sound archives' in this sense represents the sound equivalent of both archives and library materials.

As is the case with other special formats of records discussed in this chapter, the archivist responsible for the management of archival sound recordings is faced with the choice of treating them as archives which possess certain special characteristics, or of treating them as materials fundamentally different from archives and virtually as a separate collection.

In this chapter, as with film, the focus is the kind of sound material that is likely to appear in broader archival collections, ie original, unique, sound recordings produced as a by-product of an organisation's activities.

Appraising Sound Recordings

Like many of the other types of materials discussed in this chapter, sound recordings can possess any or all of the values associated with traditional textual archival materials. Consequently, the starting point for appraising sound recordings is the methods and criteria described in Chapters 5 and 6. In addition sound recordings can have other characteristics which affect their appraisal:

- Published, commercial recordings are more likely to be preserved elsewhere. If so, there is little point in keeping another copy in your collection.
- In an archival collection from a recording company, on the other hand, the master tape recordings and matrices (from which records are stamped) are likely to have archival value.
- Sound recordings often have artistic or cultural value seldom found in textual records.
- Where a sound recording is extensively damaged, so that replay is impossible, there is no point keeping it.
- Item-level selection of sound recordings can be more problematical than textual records: it is more difficult to 'leaf through' the material, and replay may result in damage to the recording.

Arranging and Describing Sound Recordings

The following paragraphs are based on the premise that it is useful to integrate descriptive information about archival sound holdings into the archives' main documentation system and finding aids. To a great extent, it is possible to apply conventional archival descriptive practices to archival sound recordings. It is also necessary to include a range of additional information in the documentation system and finding aids to cope with the special characteristics of sound recordings.

The archivist must identify and document the provenance of the material, in the sense of who made the recording and kept it in its original context, in the same way as with conventional records. With commercial sound recordings, as with publications, it is also necessary to document discographical information about the origin of the recording, such as the publisher, artists and composers.

Similarly, the principle of original order and the conventional concept of a series can be applied to archival sound recordings with little difficulty. As a result of changes over a period of time in sound recording technology, it is possible identify a series comprising recordings in more than one format, for example open-reel tape followed by audio cassette. In such a case, where no other changes to the series took place at the time of introduction of the newer technology, such as a new numbering system, the recordings should be regarded as belonging to the one series.

Two elements common to the description of all forms of sound recordings are
- a description of the physical format of the original recordings, usually at the series level
- the duration, or running time, of each item.

The special characteristics of particular kinds of sound recordings require the archivist to include further information in their description. The precise nature of the information depends on the type of recordings being described. These two examples will illustrate the variety of information that might be required:

(a) A series of spoken word recordings from a radio station:
- title of series of programs
- title of individual program
- date of recording
- date of broadcast
- abstract of segment
- speakers
- people spoken of
- subjects spoken of (using a thesaurus)
- actuality, interview or report?
- existence of script?
- technical quality.

(b) A series of oral history recordings:
- name of subject
- brief biographical note
- date of recording
- place of recording
- name of interviewer
- abstract of interview
- existence of transcript?

The preparation of such specialised descriptions can be a highly complex task, requiring not only a great deal of time but also a specialised knowledge of the relevant subject area. Where such a collection is taken into the archives' custody intact, it is clearly vital to acquire at the same time any existing documentation about the recordings, including catalogues prepared by the creators or original custodians of the material.

As is the case with moving images, it is important to note in the finding aids the existence of copies made by the archives, indicating, for example, that a reference copy of a particular recording is available.

Storing Sound Recordings

In general, good storage conditions for textual records will provide an acceptable basis for the storage of sound materials. Where possible, however, it is desirable to adjust the storage environment to meet the physical characteristics of sound materials.

A drier climate is preferable both for phonographic discs and magnetic tapes (see Chapter 3, Preservation). Where a separate storage area is available for these media within a larger repository, a dehumidifier may reduce humidity to a desirable 40%.

More important than the precise temperature or relative humidity for magnetic media is the stability of the storage area's climate. Unstable conditions encourage 'print-through', a condition wherein the magnetic signal on one layer of tape on a reel becomes imprinted on neighbouring layers and leads to the physical deterioration of the tape's 'sandwich' of layers.

As a general rule, static shelving is preferable to mobile shelving for storing phonographic recordings because the regular movement may result in damage to the surface of the discs or to the physical fabric of the older forms of discs which comprise a core and outer layer of different materials. Shelving suitable for standard archival containers, such as the Australian Archives' Type 1 box, is deep enough for all forms of sound media except 16" transcription disks. Lateral support to prevent warping is essential for phonographic recordings, either by using dividers every 15 cm or so on the shelves or by using purpose-designed boxes, such as the Australian Archives' Type 12 (for 10" and 12" disks) and Type 12A (for 7" disks) boxes. Boxes provide extra protection and make it easier and safer to move recordings in bulk.

Preserving Sound Recordings

Historical sound recording formats tend to be fragile, are easily susceptible to damage and deteriorate over time. Because of their transient nature, much of the preservation practice in this area concentrates on preserving the sound signal, even though the original medium may not survive. Nonetheless, as with other forms of archives, the first of aim of preservation work concerns the preservation of the original medium.

Besides the establishment of a suitable storage environment, the principal active means of preserving sound recordings are copying and reclamation. The two processes are closely connected and are often undertaken together. With sound recordings, the purposes of copying are

- to regenerate the sound signal onto a more stable medium so that it will survive the deterioration of the original medium
- as a security measure in case of damage or destruction of the original medium
- to provide a convenient means of access to the signal that will not damage or endanger the original medium.

As in the case of moving images, a sound copying program involves making the following three kinds of copies:

- A preservation copy, is made onto the most stable available recording medium, at this stage normally a high quality open reel tape. The preservation copy is kept in storage, acts as a security copy, and is not played at all, unless a disaster has befallen the other copies.
- A duplicating or dubbing copy is similarly made on a high quality archival medium, which is used to make or 'dub off' reference copies.
- A reference or access copy is made on a recording medium that is convenient for providing access, normally an audio cassette.

Reclamation is the process of obtaining a satisfactory sound signal from a deteriorating or damaged original recording. It can involve manual repair, but otherwise involves copying and the use of electronic processing to remove excessive unwanted noise. Reclamation includes

- suppression of excessive noise, such as the 'crackle' encountered in replaying old phonographic recordings
- editing out 'fast transients' or 'pops and clicks'
- equalisation to restore the balance of higher and lower frequency signals.

Today much of this work is done with digital recording and editing equipment, which provides greater scope for successful results than working with an analog signal.

Significant ethical problems can arise in sound reclamation and restoration work. Some techniques, especially equalisation, involve making subjective judgments about how the recording ought to sound. There is thus the danger of trying to improve on the original recording. The unwanted noise removed in restoration may be the result of damage and deterioration over the years, but it may also partly reflect techniques and equipment used to make the original recordings, and therefore be very much a part of the original record. Archivists and conservators working in this area must decide what they are trying to achieve with these techniques. The 'conservation' approach aims to avoid adding more unwanted noise during copying, without seeking to remove existing problems. The 'restoration' approach seeks to remove or reduce the faults resulting from the original recording process and later damage and deterioration to produce a signal as close as possible to the sounds originally recorded. The 'conservation' approach is regarded as appropriate for archives work. This is especially so when the very act of copying, and thus preserving the signal, will result in damage or even destruction for the original recording. A good rule is always to make the preservation copy a 'flat' unrestored copy. The desired amount of processing for listening can then be done on another copy without changing the signal irreversibly.

As is the case with other archives conservation work, reclamation work must be carefully documented, particularly because it cannot necessarily be detected otherwise.

Providing Access to Sound Recordings

The approaches outlined in Chapter 10 on access and reference services apply equally to sound recordings. However, it is necessary to note some special considerations relevant to these media.

Generally access is provided in the form of a reference or access copy, usually an audio cassette, to which the researcher can listen in the search room. Headphones can prevent other researchers from being disturbed by the noise, but they can be uncomfortable over extended periods of time. If the size of the sound collection warrants it, a separate room or booth enables researchers to listen to these materials in more comfort.

In certain circumstances a researcher may be permitted to inspect original sound recordings, for example to examine the labels of phonographic recordings. Particular care will be required here to ensure that the recording is handled correctly.

Like moving images and photographs, sound material is often sought for use in productions of many kinds, such as films, television and radio programs and advertisements. To meet these needs, it is necessary to have some means available, either in-house or using a commercial service, to provide the high quality copies that will be required for this kind of use. The copies should be dubbed off the duplicating copy of the recording. Providing such copies can involve significant expense, whether in staff time and materials or in the cost of using commercial services. Reproduction charges should reflect those costs.

As with moving images, copyright in sound recordings can be a complex matter. More than one copyright can exist side-by-side in the one recording, for example, spoken words and background music. The archivist needs to be familiar with the specific provi-

Outsized plans – a special storage challenge.

sions of copyright legislation (in Australia the *Copyright Act 1968*) that affect sound recordings and musical works.

Maps and Drawings

In this section the focus is original maps rather than with published maps, which can be treated as other publications (see below). The term 'drawings' is used here to refer to architectural and engineering design drawings: 'plans' is an imprecise term and is frowned on by the architecture and engineering professions. Artistic drawings will be covered with other works of art (see also below).

Appraising maps and drawings

Generally maps and drawings can be appraised using techniques and criteria applicable to other kinds of records, as described in Chapters 5 and 6. However, it is possible to make a few specific observations about the appraisal of these kinds of records.

It is seldom desirable to appraise maps or drawings individually or in isolation. Where they form part of other records, for example, files, reports or specifications, they will naturally be appraised with them. Separate series of maps and drawings are also likely to be related to other records and should be appraised in conjunction with them.

Maps and drawings comprising or containing unique information should have a higher priority for retention than those which contain in graphic form information that is available elsewhere. Larger-scale maps, ie those covering a smaller area in greater detail, are likely to be of more value than smaller-scale maps.

Architects' models and drawings can combine to provide a comprehensive record of a building.

However, the validity of this generalisation depends on the context and purpose of the map's creation.

Architectural and engineering drawings of existing structures and equipment generally need to be kept at least as long as the structure stands or the equipment is in service. This will meet the possible needs of repair, restoration or sale. The value of architectural drawings may legitimately be related to the value of the building itself, in terms of either its importance to the community or its design and style or its technical innovation. Hence, the work of significant architects may be identified and kept (although it may be many years before their stature becomes apparent) or examples of local or vernacular styles may be selected.

Much architectural work relating to modern buildings involves minor alterations, internal partitioning, and electrical, plumbing and ducting work. The long-term research needs relating to these buildings may well be met without retaining such records. Similarly, detailed drawings of small engineering items, such as bolts, may be so numerous as to make them impractical to keep, with little loss to research. Generally, final drawings are to be preferred over working drawings, unless there is some compelling justification for keeping a complete record of the design process. At the same time, there can be value in the intensive and comprehensive documentation of a particular building or piece of equipment to provide an example of the total work involved in its design and construction.

Finally, older maps and drawings, in particular, are often beautiful things and therefore have an aesthetic value which may justify their retention in spite of other considerations. In addition to their value as art, they are likely to have potential for display and merchandising.

Storing Maps and Drawings

Due to their shape and size, maps and drawings require special storage arrangements. They should be stored flat, either horizontally or vertically. Where they come into archival custody folded or rolled, they should be flattened at an early stage, provided that this can be done without damaging them.

Small maps and drawings can be kept in flat-storage boxes, such as commercially produced map storage boxes or suitable standard archives boxes (such as the Australian Archives' Type 10). Care needs to be taken not to fill such boxes too high, more than a centimetre or so, to avoid the items on the bottom being crushed and to prevent damage when retrieving items from the box. The items can be protected within the box by acid-free folders or interleaving sheets.

There are two main options for storing larger maps and drawings:

- Horizontally, ie in plan cabinets, which are like large filing cabinets containing shallow drawers, each containing a number of maps or drawings.
- Vertically, ie using one of a number of possible storage systems for hanging the items.

Horizontal storage makes good use of available floor space as drawer units can be stacked to heights similar to repository shelving. For large-scale storage, mobile units can be installed. Horizontal storage is flexible, coping well with maps and plans in different sizes, and does not require the use of special hanging attachments or encapsulation of the records.

As with storage boxes, items in horizontal storage can be protected by acid-free folders and interleaves. Using folders is important as removal and return of folders, instead of individual items, prevents the stress and damage that can easily occur otherwise. Again, it is necessary to avoid over-filling each drawer and the archivist should determine a maximum number of items or folders to be placed in a drawer as a part of repository procedures. An appropriate amount of weight, at the same time, can help keep the items flat and prevent curling.

The principal advantage of vertical storage is that it provides easy access to individual maps and drawings. Vertical storage units take up less floor space than horizontal storage cabinets and so can be used in spaces where a cabinet will not fit. In larger numbers they are less effective as vertical storage units cannot be stacked. In some commercial vertical storage systems designed for current or published maps and drawings, a self-adhesive hanger is attached to one edge of the item itself. Clearly, such systems are unsuitable for archival use. In other systems each item is slipped into and hung in a large pocket. The main problem with this is that the item can crumple at the bottom of the pocket under its own weight.

The best approach for vertical storage is to encapsulate each item in a close-fitting pocket of high-grade polyester film, such as Mylar, in turn attached to a hanging strip. Double-sided tape is not suitable for joining the two sides of the pocket, as the map or drawing can easily slip into contact with adhesive from the tape. A low technology solution is to sew the pocket with nylon thread (taking care not to sew the item itself to the Mylar!), but this still involves the risk of perforating the bottom edge of the item if it slips to rest on the sewn line of thread. Ultrasonic welding avoids these problems, but the equipment is costly.

Preserving Maps and Drawings

The advice provided in Chapter 3 on preservation applies to maps and drawings. In this section it is merely necessary to note in brief the principal materials of which maps and drawings are likely to be composed – which affect their preservation needs – and some of the main techniques that are used in their preservation.

Maps and drawings can be the products of a wide variety of physical processes, current and historical. The materials of which they may be composed include
- linen or other cloth
- a wide range of papers, from high quality rag paper to poor pulp-based material
- a variety of photographic processes, including blueprints, electrostatic photocopies and diazotypes
- polyester drafting films
- mounting and framing materials, including cloth, wood and glass.

Information may be recorded on maps and drawings with a variety of inks, pencils, crayons, charcoals, water colours, and adhesive preprinted symbols, in addition to substances associated with printing and photographic processes.

Common techniques used for preserving maps and drawings, most of which require the professional expertise of a conservator, include
- Flattening, where the item is folded or rolled, which may need to be preceded by humidifying

Maps and drawings often require careful surface cleaning.

- Surface cleaning, all too often including the removal of sticky tape
- De-acidification and alkaline buffering
- Repairs to mend tears
- Reinforcement, such as encapsulation, to enable the item to withstand future handling.

Microfilming is a useful means of preserving the information in maps and drawings by providing convenient access to records which are bulky, difficult to handle or particularly susceptible to damage. Microfilming is discussed in Chapter 12. Apart from archival microfilming programs, architectural and engineering firms often microfilm their drawings for the same reasons, and there are obvious benefits in the archivist acquiring these copies at the same time as the original records.

It is useful to note the effect of some of the technological developments in the management of maps and drawings. Many producers of maps now only keep computerised data from satellite, aerial and other sources, which is used to produce one-off maps to meet the needs of a particular client. Even this output may not be in paper form, but may itself be in electronic form or in microform. Similarly, computer-assisted design (CAD) software, coupled with data communication networks, is vastly reducing the number of architectural and engineering drawings produced in the course of design work, especially of working drawings. Increasingly, therefore, the management of modern maps and drawings is becoming another aspect of the management of electronic records.

Ephemera

Ephemera is a term used by archivists, librarians and museum curators to describe a wide range materials, usually printed, which were originally created for a short-term or transitory purpose. Typical examples of ephemera include posters, bus and rail tickets, advertising leaflets and handbills, notices, menus, greeting and post cards. Non-paper ephemera can include objects like badges, souvenir spoons and commemorative crockery.

Ephemera have certain common characteristics:

- They were normally created for a short-term or transitory purpose.
- They are often regarded at face value as junk.
- They are usually printed or photocopies
- They are often small, single documents or objects.

An important question for the archivist to address is whether or not ephemera should be regarded as archives. In a sense, because ephemera do not accumulate naturally in the kind of organic process classically attributed to archives, it is difficult to regard ephemera as archival in nature. However, ephemera may become a useful part of an archival collection in a number of ways, for example

- through their presence in files and other records
- in master sets of ephemeral materials, such as posters
- through collection by the archivist as part of a documentation program.

Appraising Ephemera

Ephemeral materials, perhaps to a greater extent than more formal records, provide glimpses of everyday life – social, cultural and political – and of the values and atmosphere of an era. Thus, their value in an archival collection mainly lies in their ability to complement and extend the more formal archival components of the collection by providing a different perspective on the activities documented in it.

Where ephemeral items do not relate to other materials with the same provenance or already in the archives' custody, their value must be more closely examined. In isolation ephemeral items may have little or no value, especially when weighed against the resources that will be required to document them in the archives' finding aids. On the other hand, a significant accumulation of related ephemeral materials of a given origin can be a rich source for research. Equally, ephemera may be the only surviving record of small or transitory organisations. In these cases their acquisition and retention can be justified.

It is also worth remembering that ephemera are often colourful or otherwise visually interesting, and they tend to have a wider appeal than other forms of records. Their value for display and merchandising may therefore be a major factor in favour of their retention.

In an in-house archives, by their very nature, ephemera are less likely to come into the custody of the archives through normal transfer programs than formal records. Active collecting of relevant ephemera may be necessary to redress the balance.

Arranging and Describing Ephemera

Documenting ephemera within an archival collection requires the archivist to balance a number of competing concerns.

Compared with more substantial records, it may not be worthwhile to commit the resources required for the intensive description and indexing necessary to make ephemera accessible. On the other hand, without adequate attention in the finding aids, individual items of ephemera can easily be put away and forgotten.

Traditionally, librarians have established subject-based 'pamphlet files' as a low-cost, self-indexing method of arrangement. For archivists, the problem with this kind of approach is that it destroys the relationship between the ephemeral materials on the one hand, and their provenance and the records to which they relate on the other. It is recommended that, as far as possible, descriptive information about ephemera be integrated into the archives' control system based on provenance and original order. In doing so, however, the archivist should avoid obscuring the existence and nature of the ephemeral material by grouping it in artificial series and by vague or meaningless terms, such as 'miscellaneous records', in series titles and descriptions.

Storing Ephemera

The wide variety of physical forms in which ephemera may appear means that a given group of records may need to be stored in a number of different places, for example, keeping posters with the archives' holdings of maps and plans. This is necessary and acceptable, provided that such arrangements are recorded in the archives' location control system.

Objects

Most of this chapter is concerned with managing materials which, despite their special formats, are nonetheless records. In this and the next section the focus is materials which may not be records at all.

What is meant by the term 'object' in this context? Is an object a record if it contains information, particularly information which should be preserved? If records are defined as 'documents containing data or information of any kind and in any form, created or received by an organisation or person in the transaction of business and subsequently kept as evidence ...' (see Glossary), it can be seen that what distinguishes an object from a record – besides information – is the purpose for which the latter was created and used.

An object, so viewed, is not normally regarded as a record – unless it forms part of or is attached to a record item or series. For example, a knife is not a record *per se*, but, used as an exhibit in a court case, it becomes a part of the records of that case, along with evidence in more documentary forms. Archivists sometimes find themselves curatorially responsible for objects which are not part of or attached to records, perhaps through a mixed donation of records and objects, perhaps by being given responsibility for a small museum collection by a higher authority.

What is wrong with keeping objects in an archival collection? There may be practical difficulties, such as their size and shape which may make them unsuitable for available storage space. Their composition is likely to present a whole new range of materials to preserve, requiring new expertise and additional cost, perhaps even introducing new sources of danger to the records. Objects cannot easily be described using systems designed for archival materials. Perhaps most importantly, because no-one will expect to find it there, an object of value hidden in an archives will be much less accessible than the same object in an appropriate institution, such as a museum.

The first issue to determine is whether an object should be regarded as part of or attached to a record item or series.

Objects Which Are Part of or Attached to Records

Frequently, the physical nature of an object means that it cannot be stored with the record item or series to which it is attached. In such a case the archivist needs to ensure that the intellectual and physical control documentation for the records preserves the link between the object and the records. For example, the series or record item description should describe the associated object, while the object's location should appear with the location of the series or record item in the location index.

Objects Which Are Not Part of or Attached to Records

As a general rule, the archivist should exclude or remove these objects from the archives, unless there are compelling reasons to do otherwise. If an object is likely to have heritage value, it should be offered to an appropriate repository, most likely a museum. If not, it should be sold or otherwise disposed of.

If it is necessary to keep an object or group of such objects because, for example, it was required as a condition of donation of records, the objects should be kept identifiably apart from the archives. The objects can be linked to the records by references in the latter's control documentation and finding aids. If small in number, a simple system of recording the objects' identification and location will suffice to control them. If larger in number, a museum-style system of registration may be required. In this case the archivist should seek the assistance of people qualified in that field.

Archivists are often critical of members of other professions who try to treat archives in their care as some odd form of book or museum object. Where archivists have control of small collections of non-archival materials, they must be careful not to make the same mistake.

Art Works

Archivists often find themselves with small holdings of art works in their care. Again, they may form part of or be attached to records, or they may have no such connection. Furthermore, some kinds of art works exhibit certain record-like qualities and may be kept for the same kinds of reasons as records. For example, sketches and studies for a painting provide evidence of the creative process in the same way as successive drafts of a work of literature in a manuscript collection. The problems associated with keeping art works in an archival collection are the same as those concerning objects. The archivist must decide whether to keep works of art and, if so, whether they should be treated as part of the archives or as a separate collection.

The most important factor in making these decisions is the connection of the art works with the creator of the records. If the art works were also created by the creator of the records, this is a strong argument in favour of keeping the two, with appropriate links in the documentation and finding aids. Even in this case, however, it may be difficult to justify controlling the art works *as if they were records*. If the works of art were merely collected by the creator of the records, they should be treated like any other possessions. In such a case the possibility of appropriate disposal will most likely depend on the conditions of deposit of the records – the archivist's hands may be tied. This kind of problem can be prevented by careful negotiation before the deposit takes place.

Some kinds of art works may have a strong claim to form part of thematic collections comprising archival and other components. Local studies collections, for example, may well contain archives, art works depicting the local area and other materials. Here, of course, the art is not part of the archives, but stands as a separate element of the collection.

Finally, works of art are of value as part of the collection for display and publicity purposes, even if their retention in the archives cannot otherwise be justified.

Publications

Strictly speaking, by following the definition of records noted above, it must be concluded that publications are not likely to be records where they are not created and kept for the purpose for which records are created and kept. Moreover, publications lack uniqueness, another characteristic of records. However, the situation is not that simple.

Collections of records often contain publications of the body which created the records. Such publications as annual reports and newsletters can be immensely valuable sources of information about that body, its history, functions and structure. Sometimes a master set of publications will have been established by the creating body. Where this has not happened, the archivist may consider assembling an artificial collection of the organisation's publications, which should be clearly identified in the finding aids as such. A second set of all or some of the publications, if available, may form a useful part of the archives' reference library for use by staff and researchers. There is little point, however, in keeping multiple copies of the same publication. In general similar principles can be applied to publications forming part of collections of personal records.

Publications collected and used by bodies often also find their way into archival repositories. The records of an engineering firm, for example, might include a collection of technical reference manuals. As a general rule, it is difficult to justify keeping such materials in the archives. Collections of publications acquired in this way may have significant monetary, cultural or research values, but they are best kept elsewhere.

In the course of their working lives individuals can amass a wide variety of publications, which must be assessed when they form part of a collection of personal records. The records of a research scientist, for example, may include multiple copies of reprints of his or her articles, reprints or copies of articles of colleagues, technical reports, manuals and catalogues for scientific equipment and sets of journals. Generally, again, it is difficult to justify keeping the bulk of this kind of material as part of the archival collection. Exceptions, however, would include annotated copies which form part of the documentation of his or her research and a set of reprints of the scientist's own articles. It may also be that a portion of the publications together represents a consolidated survey of a field of research at a particular time and, consequently, has research value in its own right.

Electronic Records

More than with any other special forms of records discussed in this chapter, electronic records – or 'machine-readable' or 'computer-based' records – challenge archivists to rethink their understanding of what records are and, therefore, how they should be managed. The management of electronic records is an exciting and dynamic area of professional theory and practice. This part of the chapter only skims the surface of a rapidly developing field.

When attempting to define electronic records, it may be tempting at first to think in terms of the physical forms with which we are familiar: computer disks and tapes, digital optical media and mass storage devices such as disk packs. With most of the forms of records we have examined in this chapter, the record comprises both a physical medium or carrier of information and the information itself – and the two are inseparable. With computer data storage media, information is written, altered, deleted and copied routinely. A disk containing certain information one day – or minute – may contain completely different information the next. Certainly, electronic records require a physical storage medium at any instant, but the connection between the information and a given physical carrier is temporary.

Next, it may be tempting to define electronic records in terms of their 'machine-readability'. We have already seen, however, that a number of forms of records, notably sound and video recordings, films and microforms, also require the use of a machine to 'read' their contents. We come closer to the mark when we note that electronic records are products of or connected with computer systems. Other forms of records, however, such as data input sheets and computer printouts share this characteristic but are not regarded as electronic records. Finally, it is necessary to remember the characteristic of all records noted in several other places in this chapter: that records are created or received by an organisation or person in the transaction of business and subsequently kept as evidence of such business.

Together, the following elements provide the basis for a satisfactory working definition of electronic records

* information
* created and used in the transaction of business
* kept as evidence of that business
* capable of being processed in a computer system
* stored at any instant in a medium which requires electronic or computer equipment to retrieve it.

At this stage, it is important to note the role of the 'data archive' community, ie those institutions which assemble research collections of data in electronic form. This data is usually statistical in nature and related to one or more of the physical or social sciences. 'Data archive' collections play an important part in supporting academic, industrial and other research. Much of their experience in dealing with the challenges of preserving and managing information in electronic form is of value to mainstraeam archivists. However, these collections are not normally managed according to established archival principles and are not regarded as archives in the conventional sense.

Appraising Electronic Records

For the purposes of disposal and appraisal, electronic records have many similarities with conventional records:

- They have an identifiable life cycle.
- They are continually being created and should therefore be subject to a regular program of disposal action.
- The criteria by which we assess the value of conventional records during the appraisal process can also be expected to apply to electronic records.

Thus, the approaches discussed in Chapter 6 are relevant to electronic records, both at the strategic and detailed levels. However, there are many aspects of the appraisal and disposal of electronic records which differ significantly from conventional records. The most important are

- appraisal criteria
- appraisal methods
- who should keep electronic archives and in what form, and
- the role of the end user of computer systems in disposal decisions.

Generally, conventional appraisal criteria can be applied to electronic records. Applying some conventional appraisal criteria to electronic records can be difficult. For example, archivists often decide to keep records because of the possibility that they will be required to be presented as evidence in court proceedings. The law relating to the admissibility of electronic records as evidence has differed widely among Australian jurisdictions. Because of the possibility of fraud or misrepresentation in electronic records purporting to provide evidence of particular facts, it has been next to impossible have them admitted as evidence in some jurisdictions; others have required extensive authentication measures, while other jurisdictions have made it easy. Following recommendations by the Australian Law Reform Commission, the Commonwealth and some states have amended their evidence legislation to make the admission of electronic records as evidence easier. At the time of writing, some states are moving in this direction, while others have made no progress.

Besides conventional appraisal criteria, there are some criteria which are of special relevance to electronic records:

- When appraising large databases of survey or measurement-based data that has been processed and analysed, the question arises of which is more valuable: the raw or unaggregated data or the processed or aggregated data. The former lends itself to re-use of the data in different ways; the latter reflects the process by which the study was undertaken.
- If data in electronic form exists, but the documentation which enables the data to be read and used has not survived or is not available to the archives, the data may be entirely unusable, in which case there is no point keeping it.
- If there are grounds for serious doubts about the reliability and completeness of electronic records – if essential data or program files are missing or if physical degradation of the storage media has produced high error rates in reading the data – the value of the data may be sufficiently diminished to make it not worth keeping.
- Because of the cost of preserving electronic records in the long term, possibly including a variety of hardware, software and documentation, cost is increasingly seen as an important criterion in their appraisal.

The most important difference in the method of appraisal between conventional and electronic records lies in the emphasis on the analysis of the systems of which the electronic records form a part. The archivist needs to understand the way in which information flows through a system; the processes by which information is created, duplicated, moved and transmuted in the system; the nature and forms of inputs into and outputs from the system; and the way in which the system and its users relate to the broader functional and informational environment in which they operate. This kind of analysis may require the use of systems analysis techniques and close consultation with system administrators and users as well as records managers. The overview of the system thus developed can then provide the basis for identifying sets of data of enduring value.

The issues which remain the most problematic for appraisers of electronic records concern the form in which electronic records of enduring value should be kept and who should keep them. With conventional records, generally, records become archives and are brought into archival care in the form in which they were created and used. A much greater choice is available to the appraiser of electronic records in terms of physical formats – a variety of digital storage media, printouts, computer output microfiche – and electronic formats, such as the use of ASCII code or more software dependent formats.When keeping electronic records because of their evidential value, it will be desirable to keep the data in a form which will provide an audit trail.

For databases to be kept for their research value, a 'time slice' approach may be more useful.

This very choice, coupled with the rate of technological change in this area, makes it very difficult for the appraiser to specify a format for the archival retention of electronic records which will enable them to be preserved and made accessible well into the future. Thus, this aspect of appraisal is closely linked to the strategies to be adopted for the preservation and accessibility of the material.

Related to this issue is the question of who should keep electronic records. Increasingly, archivists and archival institutions are taking the view that the technological requirements for the long-term preservation and accessibility of most electronic records are beyond their capacity to meet, principally because of the costs involved. Under this view, the solution is to make the organisation creating the electronic records responsible for the ongoing retention and management of electronic records of enduring value. This includes ensuring that such records migrate to new hardware and software in the wake of technological changes and system upgrades. This notion of archivists abandoning custody of electronic records is a radical departure from traditional archival practice and has yet to be proved as a viable long-term strategy.

For archivists in a position to do so, such as those working in an in-house archives, it is highly desirable to build archival considerations into the design of computer systems when new systems or major upgrades are being planned. In this way, electronic records of enduring value which will be created in the system can be identified and the means of preserving them and making them accessible can form part of the system from the start.

Before leaving the appraisal and disposal of electronic records, we need to note the role of the end user in their disposal. The personal computer revolution of the 1980s and the networking revolution of the early 1990s have placed enormous power over information in computer systems in the hands of end users, where once that power was exercised by system administrators. Similarly, when office computers running word processor, spreadsheet and database programs were merely used to produce paper records which then became part of a conventional recordkeeping system, the use of computers had little effect on the role of records managers in disposal. Electronic mail and other technologies which are truly leading us towards the paperless office also contribute to the power of end users over the fate of electronic records in their systems. Archivists need to educate and work with these end users far more than has been the case with conventional records.

Arranging and Describing Electronic Records

In some respects, the arrangement and description of electronic records has much in common with conventional records, notably the archivist's concern to identify and describe the context in which the records were created and used. In other respects, there are major difficulties in trying to apply conventional archival concepts to electronic records. Provenance becomes much less certain when dealing with a system which draws data from a wide variety of sources and is used by people from many organisations. Basic concepts of series and record item are difficult to apply because of their essentially physical bias.

Storing and Preserving Electronic Records

The two fundamental factors which affect the storage and preservation of electronic records are the impermanence of their physical media and the effects of technological change.

The physical media on which electronic records are currently stored present a number of problems for their preservation. Magnetic media, such as tapes, floppy disks, hard disks and disk packs, suffer from many problems, of which the most prominent are that

- the strength of the signal weakens over time
- the physical medium degrades: the binding between the oxide layer carrying the signal and the polyester base deteriorates, so that the layers separate, resulting in oxide shedding
- the media are particularly susceptible to damage due to extremes of temperature and humidity
- dust and dirt on the surface of the tape or disk can cause scratches, resulting in loss of data and head crashes
- irregular packing of tape on a reel can result in damage to the edge of the tape
- layers of tape pressed together over a lengthy period of time can result in 'print-through', whereby the signal on one layer migrates to the next.

Magnetic computer tape is regarded as a better medium for the long-term storage of data than magnetic disks. Measures which prolong the life of magnetic media include storage in a suitable, stable, clean environment; regular cleaning and exercising – preferably annually – using a tape cleaning machine; and making separate copies for security and use.

Alternatives to magnetic media are the many varieties of optical disks which have appeared in the last decade. While they have a number of advantages over magnetic tape, their suitability as archival media has yet to be proved.

Technological change affects electronic records more than any other kind of record and is particularly evident in the rate at which developments and changes in storage media have taken

The process of retrieval of computer tape at the Mitchell Repository, Australian Archives ACT Regional Office – computer storage in a controlled cool environment. Reels are suspended from adjustable racking which is part of a lockable non-motorised compactus unit. The mechanism is not motorised to minimise the risk of magnetic interference with the data.

place. A well-known example has been the move from 8" to 5.25" to 3.5" floppy disks in the space of a decade. The density of data stored on electronic media has also changed inexorably, moving from 800 to 1600 to 6250 bpi (bits per inch) on 1/2" magnetic tape over a similar period.

One solution is to keep a technological museum of tape and disk drives to read and transcribe all the types of electronic records media held by an archives. However, it will be increasingly difficult and costly to maintain this equipment as spare parts and expertise cease to be available. As has already been noted with regard to videotape, this does not appear to represent a viable long-term solution to the problem of technological change. Another approach is to adopt a standard format for the archival storage of data and copy all electronic records in custody to this standard. This is also a costly option and is not immune from technological change. Even a standard format rapidly – in archival terms – goes out of date.

As noted above, archival institutions are increasingly seeking to place a large part of the burden of solving the problems of technological change on the bodies which create electronic records, by requiring them to maintain their data of enduring value and to make it accessible in a technologically current form. This approach is best exemplified in Australia by the Australian Archives' principles for the management of electronic records. This non-custodial approach requires the long term cooperation of the creating body and its successors and does not help when a body ceases to exist entirely. Nonetheless, it represents the most promising solution to the problem of technological change to emerge so far.

A further alternative is to print electronic records out onto paper or microfilm, and thus avoid the problems associated with keeping them in a machine-readable form. However, this defeats one of the main reasons for keeping electronic records: to be able to manipulate the information using a computer as well as just read it.

Providing Access to Electronic Records

Clearly, archivists cannot provide useful access to electronic records in today's search rooms. As already noted, many researchers using electronic records want to be able to process and manipulate the information. The archivist needs to decide what kinds and levels of access and associated services to provide. The options may include
- providing a copy of a whole data file to the researcher
- providing an extract of the data as specified by the researcher
- undertaking data analysis according to the researcher's specifications.

Associated with this issue is the question of how the archives can provide these services in the light of the necessary investment in technology and expertise:
- Does the archives acquire the means to provide the services directly?
- Should some or all services be provided by a computer services firm through a contract with the archives?
- Should the archivist leave it to the researcher to make arrangements with such a firm and provide only the data and necessary documentation?

Many of these services are costly to provide and discretionary in nature. Consequently, most archives need to fit these kinds of services into a framework of charging for services, even if the archives normally provides basic access to its other holdings without charge. Where it is necessary to provide proprietary software along with the data to enable the researcher to process the data, arrangements need to be made to meet copyright obligations.

As data communication networks and services are used more throughout society, there will be increasing demand for archives to make electronic (and other) records available remotely, for example, through dial-up facilities.

The question of who has custody of electronic records clearly has a major impact on the provision of access. The Australian Archives' approach distinguishes between passive access to electronic records – providing access to the data storage medium as an object, with no responsibility for the contents – and active access – electronic access to programs and data. This approach envisages active access to electronic records held by the creating government agency being provided on a networked basis: the Archives would establish intellectual control over the records through its finding aids and provide facilities to allow appropriate access to the agency's current systems. The Archives itself would provide active access directly only to electronic records created by agencies which have ceased to operate and whose functions have not been transferred to another agency, for example the records of Royal Commissions.

Finally, it is necessary to note the importance of privacy considerations in providing access to electronic records. The extent to which government and business organisations use computers to manage personal information and the ability to combine and match data from different sources to produce comprehensive databases mean that extra safeguards are needed to protect privacy when making available electronic records containing such information. Options may include deleting personal identifiers from the data provided to the researcher and performing the analyses on behalf of the researcher. In either case technical feasibility and cost are likely to be be problems.

The Modern Office

This chapter concludes by briefly looking at aspects of the modern office environment, especially office technology now coming into use, and their effects on types of records and recordkeeping.

Electronic trading, or electronic data interchange (EDI), enables businesses to conduct transactions by the electronic transfer of such business documents as purchase orders and invoices. The growth of EDI correspondingly reduces the creation of this vast class of paper records and the need to keep them, if only for a limited time. Similarly, electronic funds transfer (EFT) is having a large impact on the nature and quantity of records created through the transactions of financial institutions and their customers, while the electronic lodgment of tax returns illustrates how this technology can effect government bodies. It appears that these developments will mean more to records managers and providers of commercial document storage facilities than to archivists.

While much business is still conducted by the exchange of correspondence on paper between organisations and individuals, what happens to a piece of correspondence once it has been received by an organisation is now changing. Organisations are increasingly using document image processing, noted in another context in the previous chapter, to scan incoming documents into digital form. The digital image metaphorically travels around the organisation in the computer system as people work on it and it is available for more than one person to work on at the same time, resulting in increased productivity. Related electronic documents may be linked together into notional files, available on-screen. The original hard copy documents are filed and stored together, rather than circulating around the organisation on subject or case files.

The nature of electronic documents is changing too: with multimedia, information can be presented in many forms in the one electronic document. In addition to textual information and computer graphics, a multimedia document can contain speech, music and other sound, photographs, animation and full-motion video. While largely confined to published products, particularly CD-ROM, at the time of writing, the capacity to produce multimedia documents is increasingly available to businesses and other organisations as a tool for presentations and educational purposes. For archivists, the advent of multimedia blurs the distinctions between conventional records and a number of the special format records discussed in this chapter!

At the personal level, the advent of personal organiser software on microcomputers and of pocket or hand-held personal organiser machines means the end of the diary as a basic record of an individual's working life.

Further Reading

Birrell, Andrew, 'The Tyranny of Tradition', in *Archivaria*, 10, Summer 1980, pp. 249–52.

Cook, Terry, 'The Tyranny of the Medium: A Comment on "Total Archives" ', in *Archivaria*, 9, Winter 1979–80, pp. 141–49.

Cook, Terry, 'Media Myopia', *Archivaria*, 12, Summer 1981, pp. 146–57.

Documents That Move and Speak: Audiovisual Archives in the New Information Age: Proceedings of a Symposium Organized for the International Council of Archives by the National Archives of Canada, K. G. Saur, Munich, 1990.

Photographs

Hendricks, Klaus B., *The Preservation and Restoration of Photographic Materials in Archives and Libraries: A RAMP Study with Guidelines,* UNESCO, Paris, 1984.

Leary, William H., *The Archival Appraisal of Photographs: A RAMP Study with Guidelines,* UNESCO, Paris, 1985.

Ritzenthaler, Mary Lynn, Munoff, Gerald and Long, Margery S., *Archives and Manuscripts: Administration of Photographic Collections,* Society of American Archivists, Chicago, 1984.

Moving Images

Bowser, Eileen and Kuiper, John, *A Handbook for Film Archives,* International Federation of Film Archives (FIAF), Brussels, 1980.

International Federation of Film Archives, *Problems of Selection in Film Archives: FIAF Symposium Kalovy-Vary 21/6/1980,* FIAF, Brussels, 1981.

International Federation of Television Archives (FIAT), *Recommended Standards and Procedures for Selection and Preservation of Television Program Material,* FIAT, Paris, 1981.

Kula, Sam, *The Archival Appraisal of Moving Images: A RAMP Study with Guidelines,* UNESCO, Paris, 1983.

Sound Recordings

Harrison, Helen, *The Archival Appraisal of Sound Recordings and Related Materials: A RAMP Study with Guidelines,* UNESCO, Paris, 1987.

Lance, David (ed.), *Sound Archives: A Guide to Their Establishment and Development,* International Association of Sound Archives, Milton Keynes, 1983.

McMullan, Mary, 'Discography: Objectives and Standards', in *Phonographic Bulletin,* 42, June 1985, pp. 14–25.

Ward, Allan, *A Manual of Sound Archive Administration,* Gower, Aldershot, 1990.

Maps and Drawings

Ehrenberg, Ralph E., *Archives and Manuscripts: Maps and Architectural Drawings,* Society of American Archivists, Chicago, 1982.

Hughes, Samantha. 'The City Engineer's Plans Project', in *Archives and Manuscripts,* 20/2, November 1992, pp. 237–46.

McGing, Angela and Picot, Anne, 'The Conservation of Building Plans Project', in *Archives and Manuscripts,* 16/2, November 1988, pp. 97–118.

Schrock, Nancy Carlson and Cooper, Mary Campbell, *Records in Architectural Offices: Suggestions for the Organization, Storage and Conservation of Architectural Office Records,* 3rd edn, Massachusetts Committee for the Preservation of Architectural Records (MassCOPAR), Cambridge Mass., 1992.

Ephemera

Clinton, Alan, *Printed Ephemera: Collection, Organisation and Access,* Clive Bingley, London, 1981.

Organ, Michael, 'Ephemera in Archives: What to do?', in *Archives and Manuscripts,* 15/2, November 1987, pp. 105–18.

Electronic Records

Bearman, David (ed.), *Archives and Museum Informatics Technical Report No. 13: Archival Management of Electronic Records,* Archives and Museum Informatics, Pittsburgh PA, 1991.

Gavrel, Katherine, *Conceptual Problems Posed by Electronic Records: A RAMP Study,* UNESCO, Paris, 1990.

Kowlowitz, Alan, *Archival Informatics Technical Report: Archival Appraisal of Online Information Systems,* Archives and Museum Informatics, Pittsburgh PA, 1988.

Naugler, Harold, *The Archival Appraisal of Machine-Readable Records: A RAMP Study with Guidelines,* UNESCO, Paris, 1984.

Reed, Barbara and Roberts, David (eds.), *Keeping Data: Papers from a Workshop on Appraising Computer-Based Records, 10–12 October 1991,* Australian Council of Archives and Australian Society of Archivists, Sydney, 1991.

14 Created and Compiled Documentation Programs

Ann Pederson

Introduction

Up to this point, the chapters you have read have been quite specific in their discussion of the factors and steps involved in key archival processes such as acquisition or arrangement and description. This chapter on documentation programs will be more general in its approach, focusing on oral history, video recording, and heritage photography projects and how these activities may complement and support the major archival functions, rather than on giving step-by-step instructions for carrying out each project. The reasons for having this general overview are twofold. First, the archives can undertake an enormous variety of activities under these headings and to attempt to treat even the major types in detail would require several books. Second, several of the activities highlighted, such as oral history or documentary photography, already have a considerable body of how-to literature available which can be perused. Third, it is rather more important to see these programs as supplements to the existing core of archival functions, to be considered only after the essential archival work is progressing well.

What Are Documentation Programs?

Documentation programs are efforts by archives to assemble documents or to record information of historical interest for future research. Not surprisingly, it is often an interest in research that motivates an archivist to sponsor or undertake projects to create, copy or transcribe and organise previously inaccessible sources. Many of these research materials, such as oral or video history tapes, did not exist naturally and have been especially created to fill gaps in the written records. Other documentary sources, such as photographs in private hands or gravestones, already exist, but are so scattered and isolated that they are useless for research unless copied and organised.

The family of activities we are calling 'documentation programs' has three basic branches. The first and most controversial group, created documentation, includes projects which set out to make a special recording of unique information. While we have within this group the previously mentioned oral history and video recordings, we would also incorporate contemporary projects to photograph towns and institutions at regular or critical phases in their development.

The second major branch of documentation activity comprises efforts to re-record or make facsimiles of existing documents and records which are not available to the public. Examples of this work includes the copying, via microfilm, paper, or photograph, of selected official or personal papers (particularly diaries, minutes and letters) and photographs held privately in distant or scattered locations. The key characteristic of this category is that these projects seek to make facsimiles of existing private documents accessible to the public.

A third category, though closely related to the first two, is one comprising projects to transfer information recorded on gravestones, buildings, caves and other public but inaccessible structures to media more usable by researchers. Projects in this category often send out teams of people to transcribe information and/or photograph the structures bearing it for later compilation and subsequent use by researchers. These projects are generally more interested in transferring selected information to a more accessible medium than they are in facsimile reproduction. unless they are recording works of art.

Having enumerated these basic categories, this chapter will proceed to examine each in turn with the goal of establishing some guidelines you might use to conduct them successfully. But first, the following section offers a key piece of advice.

The Need for Planning and Commitment

The first questions an archivist or organisation considering documentation activities should ask are 'what resources are required for such programs?' and 'how will they relate to the other commitments and priorities of the archives and of the organisation as a whole?' If your institution is currently struggling to find the staff, space and equipment to manage its existing collections, perhaps it is not wise to rush into a new venture, particularly one that depends so heavily on having sufficient staff and money to ensure a quality product.

All successful documentation programs require a certain standard of technical and historical excellence. Poor quality recorders, tapes or photographic materials can result in totally wasted efforts because the resulting records are so inferior that they can have only limited use or will last a very short period of time. Over and above materials, it is equally important to have procedures to ensure that the process of selecting and recording the material fulfils the requirements of historical evidence.

Creating the best documentary products using proper materials and techniques is only the first step. Many archivists do these things well, yet end up with poor programs because they did not plan carefully for the final and most important phase of the project – the facilities and staff to maintain and reference the collections. Of primary importance is the preservation of the original recording. This may be difficult, particularly in the case of audio and video magnetic tapes (see the section Video: The Pluses and Minuses below for more detailed explanation). Whatever the media, the original record must be secured, stored and taken completely out of use, except to make a master duplicate which itself is used only to make additional copies for reference use. The expense of proper storage for original audiovisual media and of producing a minimum of two copies (the original, the master duplicate, and a reference copy) per document is considerable but essential. The preparation of indexes and other finding aids also tend to be expensive since photographs and magnetic tapes cannot be easily scanned and summarised. Finally, there is the need to provide and maintain equipment to enable researchers to safely and accurately re-experience the material. Again, this area involves considerable potential expense, especially as advancing technology can quickly render existing equipment obsolete. Over time then, the archives could face the costly prospect of maintaining a museum of machinery to play its media artefacts, if only for further reproduction or transfer to a more contemporary mode. Alternatively, one could form a cooperative with other repositories to ensure that, among the members, the full range of needed equipment and expertise would be available.

A final area that one must consider is the social side of documentation programs. Perhaps more than other types of archival activities, documentary efforts bring you and your staff into very close contact with a variety of citizens of the community. Whether they be interview candidates or volunteers conducting the project, people require considerable instruction, guidance and support if one hopes to produce materials of research quality. However, this direction and control must be flexible and applied with sensitivity. A major goal of the archives should be to generate community

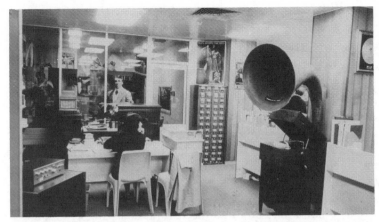

Archives with sound records must also provide the equipment to play them.

interest and involvement. People want to participate, enjoy themselves and feel appreciated; therefore, those responsible for administering the archives must build a very strong component of training, encouragement and monitoring into the documentation program if it is to be successful.

All of these factors – previous commitments, technical quality, good procedures, time, and a desire and willingness to be intimately involved with people – must be considered and accounted for in your decision to undertake a program of documentation activities. The archives should be a source of clear thinking and advice on matters of documentation within the community.

Created Documentation Programs

The search for a way to capture actual events, meetings, performances and encounters so that they can be readily re-experienced has been underway for many years. Always the challenge has been how to replicate the sights, sounds, feelings, and movements of life in process in a long lasting record. In recent times many archives, libraries with local history materials and historical societies have become interested in the concept of 'created documentation programs'. Since most institutions operate under a wide directive 'to collect and preserve the community's valuable historical resources', a number of them have undertaken special activities to *create* records reflecting the present and recent past. Whether such activities are called oral history, modern heritage projects, local history programs, or historical photography, all created documentation programs select persons, places and events in their communities and attempt to capture them using the tape recorder, the camera and, most recently, the video recorder. The resulting products of such recording sessions are magnetic tapes, both audio and video, and photographic negatives and prints which the archivist takes into custody, preserves and makes available for research.

Why Are Created Documentation Programs Special and Controversial?

What makes these records different from the archival materials we have described earlier is the way in which they are created. In the case of created documentation programs, the archivist is the initiator, or in some cases, the actual creator rather than the custodian of the material. He or she may even be said to be orchestrating the quantity and quality of documentation and is thus intervening to produce resources for future history which would not otherwise be available. In short, the archivist is responsible for materials which would never have existed at all without this conscious effort to create a record for posterity.

This type of intrusion into the natural course of events does not harmonise well with traditional archival principles which advocate a much more neutral and objective stance for the archivist. While archivists are obliged to act to ensure that records created in the normal course of an individual's or organisation's active work are identified and preserved, they are cautioned not to interfere or distort this natural process. In contrast, because the archivist is seen as actually generating the records produced by created documentation programs, there is considerable controversy about the appropriateness of such action and about the validity or reliability of historical evidence created in such a 'self-conscious' way. By 'self-conscious' we mean that the records have been produced with the idea that they are 'for history'. Some critics feel that these types of documents may not be as valid as those generated in the course of ongoing business, political or social activity. The rule of thumb is then, whenever possible, to make consciously created records, such as oral history interviews, available in conjunction with a variety of other documents which are more natural by-products of business or personal life. Locating and acquiring letters, diaries, papers and photographs related to the events or persons under study provide the all important reference points from which to test the authority and reliability of the interviews.

Perhaps it would be wise here to digress for a moment to contrast the types of materials we are discussing, ie especially created documents, with audiotapes, photos or videos, which are the products of ongoing work activity. As an example, the regular audio taping of meetings of the city council are made in the normal course of business and capture discussions in progress; therefore, they are a primary documentation of those proceedings. However, if the recordings are interviews with key Aldermen asking their recollections and opinions about what happened in the meeting, they have less authority as evidence. This diminished status reflects the fact that the interviews were influenced by the personal viewpoints of the Aldermen and of the interviewer, particularly if they were recorded much later or if they focus on a specific issue which evolved over time. Such tapes are selected and filtered accounts especially designed to capture definite information and therefore must be used for research with those factors in mind. While audiovisual materials are especially vulnerable to subjective influences, the same filtering is present in paper records. For example the tape recordings of meetings may be summarised into written minutes which delete emotional exchanges, points of discussion and other information important to understanding how a particular problem might have been solved.

Additionally, there are special aspects of sound, video and film media which archivists must appreciate and plan to accommodate. The first is to recognise that these materials capture actual events in progress and therefore intrinsically convey two types of information that written records do not – time and emotion. Because of these additional dimensions such records cannot be summarised, edited or transcribed without distorting the experiences they were created to preserve. Thus, special care must be taken to maintain such records in their complete original form, though copies, transcripts and summaries of their informational contents may be made to facilitate reference use. The second fact to remember is that there is always more than one person involved in creating audio visual records. With written materials, the writer both creates the document and determines its content. However, with audiovisual media, there may be several persons involved – the subject, the interviewer who may or may not be operating the recording equipment, and perhaps others such as researchers, project directors, or technicians. Having multiple creators means that the record can be influenced by several interpretations and viewpoints. It may present the subject or event as interviewed and/or photographed by another person, and this fact should always be recorded and noted when audiovisual materials are used as historical evidence.

Regardless of the issues or debate surrounding created documentation, one thing is certain. More and more institutions and people are becoming involved in created documentation programs. They are tape recording oral reminiscences of the community, making videotapes of local events, drawing or photographing town landmarks, to name only a few such activities. Not only are people involved with creating records, they are also generating excitement and interest in history as a result of them. It is, therefore, very much to the point of our work in this book that we discuss created documentation programs to identify good practices and to discourage those which are unwise or unsound, so that institutions considering such undertakings may make the best use of their scarce resources.

City landmarks should be photographed at regular intervals.

Types of Created Documentation: Photography

Programs centred around photography and historical photographs appeal to many audiences and afford excellent opportunities for involving the public in archival collecting efforts. Photographic documentation projects are of two major types: current or retrospective. The first is discussed in this section as it is a form of created documentation. The second, retrospective heritage photography or projects to rephotograph existing images from the past, is discussed under Compiling Documentary Sources below.

Modern heritage photography usually involves a regular program of taking and obtaining high quality photographs of events, persons, places and activities occurring within the geographic area served by the archives. Such a program offers a number of advantages. First, it generates a regular addition of significant images for the collections. Second, many professional and amateur photographers welcome an invitation to perform such a service in their communities. Third, there are good prospects for arranging joint sponsorships with other organisations such as art schools, camera clubs, or local press associations. Finally, most of the images can be accessioned and used without confusion about ownership, copyright and personal privacy issues because they were taken under archival sponsorship or donated by the photographers.

In addition to receiving full information about the project, all persons taking or obtaining photographs for the archives should be asked to sign an agreement establishing the archives' ownership of the images donated to the institution. The ownership agreement should transfer custody of the image and related rights to the archives, as indicated in the sample in Table 14.1. Copyright is specifically vested in the archives because the work was commissioned by the archives. When taking photographs that include recognisable persons, photographers should ask each subject to sign a release in which the individual consents to being photographed and grants unrestricted use of images in which he or she appears.

The success of these programs depends heavily on the staff's ability to make the photographers aware of the kinds of images that are most useful for historical purposes. For example, the project could focus on local organisations in an effort to create a visual record of the various institutions – economic, social, political and cultural – that shape the character of everyday life. Another approach is to document the buildings, streets, and neighbourhoods that form the physical fabric of the community. As part of this effort, photographers should be asked to submit logs containing all pertinent information about their subjects (ie. date, name, address and other details) so the prints can be properly labelled and catalogued. These records should be maintained on deposit at the archives as part of the project file.

Because such projects involve continuing photographic activity, the staff should work with the photographers in devising a plan for photographing sites, landmarks and similar subjects at regular intervals, perhaps every three to five years. During the rest of the year, project personnel should try to document major events and gatherings by working with local print media personnel or arranging to dispatch a member of the project team to cover selected occasions.[1]

Table 14.1   Photographic Documentation: Photography Agreement Form

I, ..., in consideration of value received, hereby agree to provide to ....(sponsoring institution) the photographic services described below:

I understand that I will be working as a representative of .... (sponsoring institution), and I agree that the ownership of the photographic images produced and all rights thereto are vested in ....(sponsoring institution). I understand that I will receive the following:...

I hereby warrant that I have every right to contract in my own name in the above regard.

....

(Date)   (Photographer's Name)

                                                             ....

                                                             (Name of Representative of
                                                             Sponsoring Institution)

                                                             ....

                                                             (Name of Sponsoring Institution)

Types of Created Documentation: Oral History

Oral history is, perhaps, the best known and most widely practised type of documentation program. A concept difficult to define concisely, oral history is essentially an information gathering technique whereby sound recording equipment is used systematically to capture 'verbatim accounts or opinions of persons who are or were witnesses to or participants in events likely to be of interest to future scholars.'[2] Aural or sound materials lend a colour and dimension that extends information beyond the written page into an involving experience. With sound we know not only what is said, but how. The nuance of the tone and timbre of voice, the urgency and cadence of speaking helps us tune in on the emotional wavelength of the speaker and thereby to come closer to his or her experience. Over the last 20 years, practitioners of oral history have fought for and achieved scholarly recognition at a number of levels. Professional researchers representing fields such as anthropology, sociology, history and literature, among others, regularly produce and consume oral documents in their work. Several Commonwealth research institutions, such as the Australian War Memorial, the National Film and Sound Archive, the National Library of Australia, and the Australian Institute of Aboriginal and Torres Strait Islander Studies, to name only a few, and some major state libraries or archival agencies, notably the Battye Library of Western Australian History, the Mortlock Library in South Australia and the State Library of NSW, have formal programs in oral history which document the work of living Australians. They also accept cohesive collections of audiotapes representing the work of research professionals who have conducted their own scholarly investigations. Persons with an active interest in oral history have formed the Oral History Association of Australia, a branch of an international body, and those institutions and individuals who care for material in aural format, be it verbal, instrumental, or both, may be members of the International Association of Sound Archives (IASA). The reason for mentioning the various institutions and professional bodies is to underscore the fact that aural documentation is a well-established and important discipline which supplements and fills in gaps in traditional paper records. Furthermore, the practice of it is professional and sufficiently widespread that most organisations considering undertaking an oral history program can find qualified persons to advise them.

Good oral history is seldom the child of spontaneity. A successful project requires careful research and preparation at many levels: in selecting the focus of the effort; in choosing the persons to be interviewed; in designing the questions to be asked; in mastering the art of being a good interviewer; and in preparing the materials for long-term preservation and use. The following are some suggestions for achieving quality in all five areas:[3]

- Design the subject and scope of the project with a clear sense of what can be accomplished in terms of information, quality and the potential value of the project for future research investigations.
- Be sure to consider the expense and technical problems involved in the preparation, use and long-term maintenance of the tape products.
- Select and train personnel for the project so that all interviewers are skilled interpersonal communicators who are also well versed in the subject matter to be covered.
- Select good quality, reliable and manageable recording equipment and tapes. If you have volunteer workers conducting the interviews, you should have kits of equipment and tapes for them to use. Even with the best equipment, you will also need backups in case of mechanical difficulties or tape snarls. Use a good quality microphone and invest in special filters to block out extraneous noises. Local broadcasters may be willing to recommend, or even lend, equipment to suit your needs.
- Do your archival and legal homework so that your effort yields long-lasting results and produces taped interviews available for research and quotation. Carefully document the purpose and design of the project, the conditions under which

the interviews were conducted and any factors that might have affected the objectivity of the interviewee's comments.

- Have the interviewer (if not an employee of the archives) and interviewee sign a release in which they agree to participate in the project; to donate their interviews to the archives, together with all literary rights and copyrights; and to permit research use of the interview tapes, transcripts, or other copies. Examples of such agreements appear in Tables 14.2, 14.3 and 14.4.

- Keep the project moving with training, direction, regular progress reports and encouragement. Table 14.5 shows the text of a training leaflet covering many of the basic procedures that ought to be reviewed with all new project personnel.

- Ask interviewees to contribute photographs and written records to the archives. If possible, photograph or videotape subjects at the time they are interviewed (see Table 14.6 for ideas).

- Publicise the project during the phases of its development: conception, planning, progress and results as the materials become available for research.

- Protect original tapes immediately through proper labelling and storage and do not play them except to produce a duplicating master from which additional copies will be made for indexing work or for later reference use.

- To transcribe or not to transcribe, that is the question. Because of the expense of transcription and the loss of information which can be conveyed only by sound, it is recommended that archivists not transcribe but rather prepare notes describing the contents of the tapes keyed to the numerical counter of the tape recorder/player. These notes then serve as a rough index to the tapes.

- Be sure to thank personnel connected with the taping and, if funding permits, enclose a duplicate tape of the interview as a memento of appreciation.

- Consider using copies of project tapes to create slide-tape presentations or public service announcements for radio and television stations. After all, there is no substitute for hearing the spoken word.

Types of Created Documentation: Video

Television has been an integral and increasingly important part of life in industrialised societies for more than 30 years and serves as the major point of contact that most Australians have with events beyond their immediate experience. This powerful electronic window has been praised and criticised on many levels, but few can deny its unique capacity to capture and present events

TABLE 14.2 Oral History: Participant Agreement Form

AGREEMENT TO PARTICIPATE IN THE

....

ORAL HISTORY PROJECT

I, ..., hereby declare my willingness to participate in the .... oral history project, sponsored by .... I understand that the audiotapes from this project will be deposited at the .... (archival repository) as a supplement to the written records of the...................................... ....

I hereby agree to an interview conducted by project personnel during which I will discuss my involvement with .... activities and share my opinions regarding these matters and related issues. I understand and accept the need for forthright and candid discussion and also understand that I will approve, in advance, the subjects to be discussed. It is agreed that I will be given an opportunity to hear the complete interview and to correct or add material in a separate format prior to signing a formal document for archival deposit. Finally, I pledge my cooperation in making the tapes created during the interview available for research use within sound archival guidelines.

....
Preferred Interview Date and Time

Preferred Interview Location:
[ ] Home
[ ] Archives Repository
[ ] Other

....
Signature

....
Name

....
Street

....
City

....
State   Postcode

....
Date

....
Signature of representative of (project sponsor)

TABLE 14.3 Oral History: Donor Form

....
(Name of archival repository)

GIFT OF PERSONAL STATEMENT

BY...
(Name of Narrator/Interviewee)
(Official name of person/organisation/event being documented)

ORAL HISTORY COLLECTION

I, ... (narrator interviewee), hereinafter referred to as the donor, hereby give, donate, and convey to the .... (archival repository) for deposit in the .... (name of collection) Oral History Collection, and for administration therein by the authorities thereof, the audio tape recordings, hereinafter referred to as the material, containing by observations and statements and made on .... (date). This gift is made subject to the following terms and conditions: (tick those appropriate)

[ ] 1 The donor transfers full title of the material and all literary rights, to
.... (name of archival repository)
as of the date of this agreement..

[ ] 2 As donor, I understand that I will have the opportunity to listen to the entire interview when completed and may, at that time and in a separate format, provide additional information, correct errors, and designate any portions as confidential for a specified period of time.

[ ] 3 If, in the future, funding is available to prepare transcripts of the taped interviews, I, as the donor, understand that I will be given the opportunity to read and approve the transcription and may, at that time, provide additional information, correct errors, and designate any portions as confidential for a specified period of time.

[ ] 4 As the donor, it is my wish that access to the material transferred hereunder be as follows:
  [ ] (a) The material may be made available to anyone applying to use the collection.
  [ ] (b) Persons wishing to use the material in the next .... years must have written approval from me or my designee ....
(name of designee) before they may receive access to the material. I understand that I agree to respond to such applications promptly and that it is my or my designee's responsibility to notify ....
(name of archival repository) officials of the current address. After .... years, the material will no longer be restricted.

Gift of Personal Statement of ....
(name of narrator/interviewee)

ORAL HISTORY COLLECTION

A written revision of any terms governing access to the material for research may be entered into by the donor or his designee and officials of the ....
(name of archival repository), if either party wishes to do so.

....	....
Name of Narrator/Interviewee	Name of Interviewer
....	....
Signature of Narrator/Interviewee	Signature of Interviewer
....	....
Street	Signature of (name of archival repository) Designee
....	....
City State Postcode	Date of Agreement
....	....
[ ] Interview Tape Approved	Signature of Narrator/Interviewee
	....
	Date
[ ] Transcript Approved	....
	Signature of Narrator
	....
	Date

that years ago would never have been recorded, much less viewed, in the intimacy of the lounge room. Rapid advances in technology, lower costs and a growing interest in re-experiencing moments in one's own life have made home television recording even more popular than home movies were several decades ago. In fact, electronic equipment and expertise are becoming integrated into our business and personal lives so much so that the videotaping of events and experiences is rapidly overtaking audio recording as the major medium for created historical documentation, and this trend is expected to continue.

Video: The Pluses and Minuses

If we are then to consider undertaking video, as well as oral, history projects, what are the benefits and drawbacks of such an effort?

On the plus side, video recordings undeniably capture human activity far more completely than most other forms of records except for motion pictures. Colour, movement, sound and

(cont. p. 446)

TABLE 14.4   Oral History: Donor Form

GLENELG REGIONAL LIBRARY SERVICE

A. INTERVIEWEE
   I/We, ...(names)
   of,..(address)
   agree to the use of the tape-recorded interview between myself/ourselves and...........................
   ....(name of interviewer) made on....................................
   ....(date) in the following ways:

---

1   The original tape-recorded interview, to be known as the MASTER TAPE will be held in the *State Library of Victoria*.
2   A copy or copies of the Master Tape will be made on duplicate tapes and held by the *Glenelg Regional Library Service*.
3   The *State Library of Victoria* or the *Glenelg Regional Library Service* may prepare or cause to be prepared a transcription of the Master Tape if they so desire.
4   The recording/s, duplicate/s and/or transcript/s may be made available in the *State Library of Victoria* to bona fide scholars.
5   The duplicate tapes and/or transcripts may be made available in any branch of the *Glenelg Regional Library Service* to all persons who would normally be granted use of the *library's* resources.
6   The *State Library of Victoria* may provide further copies of the tape/s
    and/or transcript/s for purposes of historical record, research or private study to other libraries and institutions.
7   The recording/s and/or transcript/s may be quoted in part in published works, broadcasts or public performances provided, in each case, acknowledgment be made to us.
8   Permission to use the recording/s and/or transcript/s in full, in publications, broadcasts, or public performances must be through an initial approach to the *Glenelg Regional Library Service*.
9   After 10 years rights in the tape/s are vested in the *Library Council of Victoria*.
10 *Special Conditions:*

Signed by interviewee:...
Witness (Interviewer):...
Date:..

B. INTERVIEWER
   I, ...(name)
   of,..(address)
   agree that the tape of the interview referred to above may be used as itemised in points one (1) to ten (10) of the previous consent form signed by the interviewee and witnessed by myself as the interviewer for and on behalf of the *Glenelg Regional Library Service*.

Signed: ....
Date: ....
Witnessed: ....
REGIONAL LIBRARIAN
GLENELG REGIONAL LIBRARY SERVICE

Agreement for deposit of a tape-recorded interview for the Oral History Project (1979) conducted by the Glenelg Regional Library Service. Points in italics or in parentheses have been added to show places where you will need to put in names of persons or organisations appropriate for your oral history program.

TABLE 14.5 Oral History: Guidelines for Interviews

Guidelines for Oral History Interviews

1   Select the interview subject. Is it to be biographical, general, or topical?

2   Select the interviewee. You will get suggestions for possible interviewees (narrators) from family, friends, civic groups, teachers, etc. Try to set priorities for who you interview so that your time is used as profitably as possible. If accuracy is important to your project, think about the reliability of the narrator you select. At the same time, do not be so selective that you ignore all but the leading citizens of your community and miss some of the most interesting and informative people.

3   Make initial contact. Initial contact should be made in person, if possible, by the individual who will actually be doing the interview. This is an opportunity to establish rapport with the narrator, but be careful to prevent this first meeting from turning into an interview session *sans* tape recorder. Keep the meeting brief and to the point.

This is the time to tell the interviewee about your project and why you want to interview him or her. Make sure he or she understands how the tapes of the interview will be used. You might also take this opportunity to get the release form signed or at least to tell the interviewee that you will be asking him or her to sign one. Also, point out that you will give him or her the opportunity to review the tape or transcript of the tape to make separate changes or corrections as needed. You might use this time to show the person a list of the kinds of questions you will ask, but use your judgment on this. Do not make the narrator feel compelled to stick to the topics on that list.

4   Pre-interview research. You will be able to ask better questions if you know as much as possible about the person being interviewed and about the subject of the interview. Be careful to use this information only to open questions, not to tell the interviewee your opinion.

5   Prepare a list of interview questions. A list of possible questions will help you move through the interview easily. It will also inspire confidence in beginning interviewers. Keep this list brief and remember to be flexible enough to add other questions or delete prepared ones as you get a feel for the interview. Remember this list is only to help, not to direct or dominate you. And do not read the questions off the sheet!

6   Be sure of your equipment. Practise with the recorder you will be using several times before going to the interview. Practise interviewing a friend or relative so that you will be comfortable in your new role. You might experiment with the pick-up of your microphone and the best place to position it for maximum effectiveness. Also, familiarise yourself with the recording time of the tapes you will be using. Check the recorder before each interview to make sure it is functioning properly, and carry spare tape (and batteries if an electrical outlet is not available) and an extension cord.

7   Pre-interview points. When you arrive at the interview, chat casually with the interviewee for a few minutes while you set up your equipment. Treat the machine casually and make it as unobtrusive as possible so that you do not overwhelm or frighten the narrator with all of your technology. Make sure the recorder is easily visible for you to check the tape occasionally. If possible, cushion the recorder and microphone with a pillow, jumper, etc. to reduce vibrations. Try to minimise outside noises since the recorder will pick up sounds you might not even notice. Be especially alert to air-conditioners, dishwashers, radios, televisions (even in the next room or at the back of the house).

Try to interview only one person at a time, and make sure you talk with him or her in surroundings that will make the narrator feel comfortable. Try to keep away from a lecture-type atmosphere.

Before beginning the actual interview, record a brief introductory statement stating who you are talking with, the date, location and subject of the interview.

8   During the interview. Make notes as you go along so that you can follow up on ideas later. Try to pick up clues on what the interviewee would like to discuss next. You might jot down words or names you are not sure of so that you can clarify them at the end of the interview.

(cont./...)

During the interview ask questions that will allow the narrator to talk freely and at length. Avoid questions that call for one word answers (for example, 'What was it like to grow up in Athens in the 1920s?' rather than 'Where were you born?'). Be attentive, courteous and responsive as the interview progresses. Nod your head and let the narrator know you are following him or her closely. If something is not clear to you, restate it in your own words and ask if that is what was meant. Also remember to check the tape occasionally so that you can turn it over at a convenient break in the conversation. Better to waste a little tape than to interrupt in mid-sentence for a mechanical adjustment.

Watch the time as the interview progresses, particularly with older people. Do not overtire the narrator. Keep the interview within a comfortable length of time such as 1–1 1/2 hours. You can always come back for subsequent interviews so do not feel you have to get it all the first time. If another interview is necessary, make arrangements for it before you leave.

9   After the interview. Be sure to label the tape(s) carefully with the names of the narrator and the interviewer, date, place, topics, etc. before you leave, make sure that the release form is signed and remind the narrator that you will give him or her a copy of the tape and/or transcript for review. Be sure to thank the narrator for his or her time and cooperation.

Very soon after the interview record your own evaluation of how the interview went, ie name of interviewee, physical environment, reaction of interviewee and problems encountered.

Tips for Interviewers (condensed from Willa Baum's *Oral history for the Local Historical Society*, pp. 32–35)

---

1   An interview is not a dialogue, but a chance for the narrator to tell his or her story.

2   Ask questions that require more of an answer than 'Yes' or 'No'. Start with 'Why?', 'How?', 'Where?', 'What kind of ...?'

3   Ask one question at a time and keep the questions brief.

4   Encourage the interviewee to continue talking with *non-verbal* signals, rather than spoken responses. Smiling, nodding and other body language can convey your active interest and appreciation and are not distracting for future listeners as the constant remarks such as 'yes', 'really?' and 'I see ...'.

5   Start with non-controversial questions. If necessary, they can be asked later when you know the narrator better.

6   Do not let periods of silence fluster you. Give your narrator a chance to think of what he or she wants to say before you hustle along to the next question.

7   Do not worry if your questions are not beautifully phrased for posterity.

8   Do not interrupt a good story because you have thought of a question or because your narrator is straying from the planned questions. If the information is pertinent, let him or her continue.

9   If the narrator persists in talking about irrelevant matters, get back on the track with a few leading questions.

10 Do not challenge accounts you think are inaccurate. This could make the narrator angry or defensive.

11 Try to avoid 'off-the-record' information. Try to get permission to record, then let them listen and restrict access.

12 Interviewing is one time when a negative approach can be effective. You might try, 'Despite the mayor's reputation for good works, I hear he was a difficult man to work with. Did you find him so?' The narrator is going to supply useful information either challenging or defending your statement.

13 Do not use the interview to show off your own knowledge, vocabulary, charm or other abilities. Good interviewers do not shine, only their interviews do.

Table 14.6 Don't Forget the Photos!

The person whose recollections you are recording may also have either valuable documentary material in family albums, in suitcases, in boxes under the house or in other places. This material can assist during the interview by stirring memories. It is also a valuable asset for an archival collection, and in any presentation of an ethnic community's history and/or an individual's history.

The following list suggests some of the types of documents which may be found among private papers:

1 **Personal records:**
   Scrapbooks, photographs, diaries, memoirs
   Letters to and from the country of origin
   Documents (eg naturalisation certificates, passports, employment records, trade union and political party tickets, etc).

2 **Government publications and documents:**
   (From country of origin)
   Information about migration (eg pamphlets, newsletters, etc)
   Directories (eg of government agencies, regulations, etc)
   Tourist brochures, posters, school textbooks
   (From Australia)
   Publicity pamphlets and posters about Australia, directed at migrants
   Guides for new immigrants, citizenship booklets
   Letters (eg to and from Australian government authorities about the possibility of immigration; complaints/congratulations to government authorities).

3 **Newsletters, newspapers and journals** (in English and other languages)
   Including ad hoc publications produced on board the ship on the way to Australia, or in holding centres; or by ethnic communities in Australia or elsewhere.

4 **Records of social clubs, welfare associations, political organisations, religious groups, and so on:**
   Minutes of meetings, notices of activities
   Statement of objectives, histories, letters, photographs
   Commemorative programs or publications, membership lists,
   Conference, seminar, workshop, etc, records, news releases
   Personal accounts of activities and involvement

SOURCE: Wilton, Janis and Bollard, Angela, *Balancing the Books; Oral History for the Community*, Ethnic Affairs Commission of NSW, Sydney, 1983, p. 24.

A videotape about the archives can promote wider understanding of its activities.

perspective are a powerful sensory combination for documenting life in progress. Video technology is also becoming cheaper, more portable and easier to use than its film equivalent. Because video recording is an electronic rather than a photographic process, it also offers the benefit of instant replay, making it possible for users to view the quality of their recording on the spot and re-record portions that are faulty. The quality of immediacy also creates in the beholder a greater sense of involvement with actions and events because he or she is watching them as they unfold. A final benefit of video is its popularity. It is literally a household fixture which reaches out to the world; and, since surveys have shown that most people use television as their major source of information and entertainment, it follows that people are potentially more receptive to events and messages presented through this medium.

The negative side of video documentation is also impressive, particularly its instability as a record medium for long-term retention, ie for archives. Video and audio records are created through a process which transforms light and/or sound into electronic pulses which imprint their message magnetically onto a flexible metal oxide coated tape. The information is stored as tiny magnetic arrangements of metal particles which can later be read and replayed. Because the process is magnetic, it is also delicate and can be altered by exposure to other sources of magnetism. Furthermore, the metal particle coating can deteriorate and the flexible tape backing can stretch or grow brittle with age. All of these factors make current videotape an unsuitable medium for recording information which needs to be kept permanently.[4]

A second feature of video technology that is undesirable for archival documentation is the ease with which it can be purposefully manipulated, edited or recorded without a trace. Archival records must have integrity as evidence of reality; and therefore videotape cannot be used for recording information which must stand alone as legal evidence unless very stringent controls and conditions are met, such as those for building security systems.

However difficult these problems of stability and archival integrity are, there is hope that they may be solved in the near future. The new optical digital disk technology which uses lasers to imprint digitised audio and visual information onto an archival quality medium is emerging as a solution. Already commercially available in the entertainment world as prerecorded compact disks or CDs, this technology is gaining popularity though the recording process is still too expensive and complex for small institutions. As costs come down and portability increases, it is possible that smaller archives may transfer their video and audio magnetic tapes to this medium. Still further in the future optical digital disk technology may replace the magnetic medium altogether for the recording of archival information.

The third major area of disadvantage of video for archival documentation relates to the production of videotapes. Few archives are fully equipped for video production largely because such work can comprise only a part of our overall documentary mission and because the technological facilities and expertise are very costly. As sophisticated consumers of professionally produced television programs, we expect the same level of quality in archival audiotapes and videotapes, forgetting that most professional productions are just that, productions with actors, scripts, direction, lights, cameras and retakes, when any of the above is not exactly right. Not at all like real life, which is what archival video attempts to capture. The result is a product that may appear long, monotonous, rambling, with poor or uneven illumination and amateurish camerawork when compared with commercial television programs.

Uses of Video for Archives

Having assessed the pluses and minuses of video technology as a medium for storing archival information, let us turn now to some of the uses it can have for archives. Most of these uses stem from the advantages video possesses ie its capacity to make a multi-sensory record of events in process and its suitability for reaching a wide audience.

Documentation. Despite its technical limitations, video is still a very effective and attractive way to record community personalities, activities or events. Video history interviews are competing with oral history as the popular choice for documenting local identities. Like audio recording, video is now highly portable and brings the additional dimensions of vision and colour to the project. Not only can the person be seen and heard, but so can his or her surroundings and companion photographs, letters and artworks. The video eye can move from the speaker's face to focus on items as they are read or discussed, adding much more information and variety to the interview.

However, video interviews can often be little more than 'talking heads', visually boring, mentally tedious. The staff, equipment and planning involved to excite our jaded viewing palates, ie lights, multiple camera angles, close-ups and insertions of photos or documents, can destroy continuity of thought and intimidate even the most resolute informant. What might have been a relaxed interview becomes a stage set with cues, instructions and concerns about visual interest. Care and balance is needed to retain interest without sacrificing documentary purpose.

Video is also useful to record community or institutional events or to do 'slice of life' documentation. Commemorative events such as centenaries offer re-enactments and parades. Festivals present opportunities to document current public taste and interest in art, music, food and entertainment. 'Slice of life' projects choose a person or occupation and record their activities over time. Examples might include 'A Day in the Life of a Coal Miner' or a video on woodchopping.

Documentary video is also useful for archival management. Video cameras and viewing sets are often important features of a building security system, particularly the reading rooms, though most often these are monitored live by a security guard and only recorded when that person is away from his or her post.

Video can also be used for special problem-solving studies such as documenting the traffic or workflow patterns of visitors, researchers and staff for later analysis and use in the planning of facilities and services.

Interpretation/Outreach. One of the most important and effective uses of video for archives is education, both in teaching research skills and in acquainting users with archival resources and facilities. Since archival materials are unique and must be carefully preserved, they do not circulate like library materials. Since researchers must generally visit the archives to gain access to the materials, it is important that their time be spent as productively as possible, and video can be a great help in several ways. First, a video explaining the purpose and services of the archives, the nature of its holdings and how to prepare a research request can be made available to a number of local libraries and educational institutions. Through video potential researchers can be made aware of the archives and can prepare themselves for their visit so that when they arrive they can spend their time doing research rather than learning their way around. A second and related type of video is the how-to program which provides instruction on research techniques for specialised interests such as family history or historic photographs. These videos make use of the archives' holdings and reference staff to explain the use of archival sources and various approaches and methods which can be employed to solve research problems.

The third type of video is one primarily designed to inform and entertain, with the secondary purpose of raising the level of community interest and appreciation for the archives, its work and holdings. Such programs are the video equivalents of tours, exhibits and publications, and they enable the archives to contact and interest potential users where they live and work. This capability can be very important for archives, such as those of the state or Commonwealth which must serve a large geographical area. Some sample titles of videos which might be undertaken include: *Know Your State Archives*; *Treasures of the Mitchell Library*; *Circular Quay*; *Then and Now* (comparing historic photographs of the area with shots of the present day). Almost any topic that is suitable for a book or exhibit can be videoed; in fact it is a good idea to make a video as a companion to an exhibit or illustrated publication. The video can live on usefully carrying the information to a wide audience long after the exhibit has been dismantled or the book has gone out of print. The possibilities are only limited by the richness of the archives' holdings, the staff's imagination and, of course, its resources.

Getting into Video

As with any other area dependent on technology, video program development requires careful planning, substantial resources and, most of all, expertise. While it is beyond the scope of this chapter to set out a detailed step-by-step list of what to buy and how to produce quality videotape records, it is useful to note the types of activities that you will have to plan to undertake and to point out the options available for incorporating video into your archives program.

In developing a video production capability for the archives, you will be planning and managing resources (staff, equipment, facilities) to support a number of distinct work activities, the most important of which are as follows:

(a) Planning/administering the video program.

(b) Selecting/designing video projects.

(c) Making the video recordings:

- setting up for the recording session (booking/preparing the site/studio; obtaining/producing titles and other graphic illustrations; deploying/checking the recording and lighting equipment; writing/editing narrative; planning/rehearsing content and sequences; obtaining permissions to use any materials covered by copyrights)
- recording the video
- editing the video
- inspecting the completed video.

(d) Preserving the video original:

- making a copy for reference use
- storing the video original and reference copy.

(e) Documenting/cataloguing the videos (master and reference copy) for future retrieval and use.

(f) Using the reference video:
- viewing the reference video
- arranging for copies of all or portions of the reference
- obtaining agreements for further use
- making copies.

(g) Evaluating/monitoring the video program.

As you would imagine, most of these areas require technical expertise well beyond that provided by archival training. Thus, it is best to work in concert with one or more video professionals.

Participation in Created Documentation Programs: The Options

Whether one is planning a video, oral history or photographic documentation program or all three, the options available for incorporating such activities within the archives operation remain the same. The archives can set up its own facility, equipment and staff to undertake such work; however, this option is rarely economically feasible for most archives. An alternative is to contract these activities out to professional firms or consultants who will undertake the work on a project-by-project basis. This option is more attractive since it avoids the heavy cost and ongoing commitment for facilities, equipment and staff.

A third choice is to participate in joint ventures involving other archives and historical agencies such as museums in specific documentation projects. Because such efforts are on a larger scale, they may attract the participation of professional photographers, researcher/writers and radio/television companies as well as outside funding from government or corporate sources.

If documentary production capability seems beyond the resources of your operation (and it is for most small archives), but you would like to include such material in your holdings or use the occasional video as an educational tool, consider the fourth option: becoming a repository for the recordings made by others. This role will limit your commitments to providing safe storage and facilities for viewing the reference copies of the audiovisual materials. There is no need to have in-house copying equipment as this service may be purchased as needed from commercial firms. However, the archives will need to be sure that the researcher has obtained written permission from those who control the rights to the specific recordings and images to be copied before any copies are made.

Whatever participation in video your archives chooses, full, some, or none, the records of this major and powerful form of human communication must be considered in any full-scale archival program.

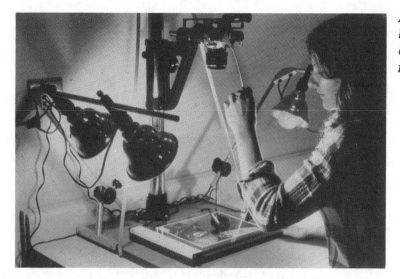

A special stand with lights facilitates accurate copy photography.

Compiling or Rephotographing Historic Images

Programs designed to solicit the donation of original photographs or to copy privately held images for research use can also prove fruitful, particularly when they are done in collaboration with newspapers, local photography studios, or organisations of professional photographers. Yet regardless of whether you are seeking a large collection or a small one, the means of obtaining it will come through contacts with individuals who must somehow be persuaded to join your cause.

As in other forms of field work, success depends on the ability to inspire confidence in one's self and one's institution. The first step is to provide the public with accurate information about the types of images that the archives wants and does not want. Most people will understand a need to be selective; few will understand if you invite any and all donations, only to reject half of them because they are not significant.

Frequently, one donation leads to another. Encourage project participants to suggest the names of other area residents who might be willing to share their images with the archives. And be sure to ask donors if they have written records that might be contributed to the archives as companion pieces to the images. Because the public becomes heavily involved with projects of this type, public relations and careful advance planning for copying project sites are essential. It is vital to document the names and addresses of local sponsors and volunteers and to ensure that you have mailed or personally presented sufficient information in the locality to attract an enthusiastic response. Table 14.7 shows a sample documentation project worksheet which is invaluable for keeping track of the innumerable details of the proposed visit.

Table 14.7   Documentation Project Worksheet

	.... Location .... Dates of visit
DATES OF VISIT... TOWN/CITY:	DISTRICT .... WORK SITE:..
LOCAL COORDINATORS: Name: .... Address: .... Telephone: .... Affiliation: .... Name: .... Address: .... Telephone: .... Affiliation:	Name: .... Address: .... Telephone: .... Affiliation: .... Name: .... Address: .... Telephone: .... Affiliation: ....

SCHEDULE

.... 6 months in advance	Contact President of leading local historical cultural group and invite organisation to participate in the project and to coordinate the local activities.
Confirmation letter sent .... Declined participation NOTES:	
.... 8–10 weeks in advance	Contact leader of local effort to explain logistics of visit and the archives for names of other groups/individuals who might like or need to be involved with the project. Schedule trip to location to meet with the local coordinating committee. Completed: .... <div align="center">Date Initials</div>
.... 5 - 7 weeks in advance	Meet with local committee; explain project fully and show slides; suggest means to publicise and promote project, provide samples of newspaper articles and public service announcements, give local contacts a good supply of project posters and brochures. Check out local accommodation. Completed .... <div align="center">Dates Initials</div>

Visit notes:

....

Maintain frequent contact by telephone
and mail to answer questions and make
sure publicity is reaching the general
public. Line up workers from own staff
and make arrangements for overnight
stay.

Completed: ....

                              Date   Initials

Contact notes:

Staff workers for trip: ....

....

....

Hotel/Motel arrangements:.......................
Local phone number:................................

FIELD REPORT:

No. of people interviewed: ....
Names of local volunteers: ....

Subjects of most interesting images or papers: ....

Visit notes: ....

A retrospective documentation project which copies images
that will continue to be held by their owners presents certain
legal problems for the sponsoring archives. The institution is
receiving not a gift, but rather an opportunity to make film copies
(usually negatives) of unique materials for preservation and
future research use. But what exactly can the archives do with its
copies? The announced purpose of making these images accessible for research certainly implies an intent to make further
reproductions of them, either as reference prints for the reading
room or for sale to researchers. And there is a reasonable certainty
that some of these images will be in demand for publication. Can
the archives legally take such actions and charge fees for services without consulting the owner of the original, who may or
may not also own the copyright to that image?

These are cloudy issues indeed, and they are, as yet, untested
in the courts. The best protection available at present is an agreement between the archives and the owner of the original as to the
use of the copy images. Table 14.8 shows an example of such an
agreement. It is important for image owners to indicate whether
or not they wish their names and addresses to be confidential.

Table 14.8 Photographic Documentation: Image or Reproduction Rights Donation Form

---

CONTROL No. ....
HERITAGE PHOTOGRAPHY PROJECT RELEASE
Terms of Accession:

( ) 1 HISTORIC IMAGE RELEASE
I, ... (name of
owner of photographs) hereby authorise the ....
(name of archival repository hereafter cited as 'the archives' to make a photographic copy
negative(s) from my photograph(s) identified by number in the 'list of items' below. I
understand that once my photograph is rephotographed by the archives, the photographic copy in the possession of the archives becomes a part of its holdings and the use of the
images will be governed by the requirements that apply to the archives. I understand that
I waive all title and rights so far as I possess them to the negative(s) described and to any
future prints or copies produced from it/them.

CONTROL No. ....
( ) 2 DONATION OF PHOTOGRAPH(S) OR PRINT(S)
I, ... (name of owner of photographs or prints)
hereby convey to the ....(name of archival repository)
for deposit in the .... (name of collection if appropriate) and
for administration therein by the authorities thereof, the photographic and/or print material
herein identified in the list of items below. Title to the photographic and/or print material
listed, together with all rights so far as I possess them, shall pass to the
....
(name of archival repository) as of the date of the execution of this Deed of Gift.

CONTROL No ....
DATE: ....

....
Signature of representative
for the ....
....
....
....
(name and address of repository)

....
Signature of donor

ADDRESS: ....
....
....
....

Cross out as appropriate:
I do/do not wish my name and address to
be made available to enquiries about the
material above.

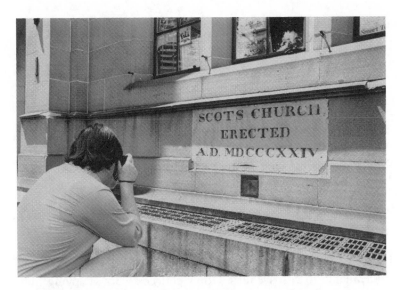

Documenting a historic site includes copying inscriptions.

Some people may not welcome the prospect of being contacted by researchers or photography collectors seeking the originals. By the same token, it is vitally important for project field workers to elicit all pertinent details about the image at the time it is offered for copying. While a contact person is available who may be able to supply the information, ask him or her to date the image and identify the subject or the occasion shown.

Whether the photo project is current or retrospective, a schedule must be set up for processing the films and for describing them for use by the public. Great care must be taken to ensure the quality and longevity of the film negatives, for they are the archival record. Some agencies double-shoot the photograph to create two archival negatives, one for separate security storage and one to use in making reference prints. Proper storage and retrieval systems should be imposed in each case.

Making the collection of images accessible to researchers can be a long and painstaking process. Each image should be subject catalogued and cross referenced. If possible, a contact print of each image should be affixed to the main entry card so that researchers may view the image without having to consult the negative (for details see Chapter 8, Arrangement and Description). Some projects provide a copy of their catalogue cards and contact prints to the local historical societies or libraries serving the areas in which the images were copied. The distribution of this catalogue does much to make the local heritage available locally, and the resulting goodwill facilitates the work of the project.

Whether your images are copied or donated, do not neglect to share your findings with the public. For example, the staff could prepare a 'Historic Photograph of the Week' series in the local newspaper (accompanied by a short caption and credit line mentioning the archives and the name of the donor, with his or her permission). A public exhibit of photographic prints drawn from the project files can also be very effective in arousing community interest.[5]

Compiling Documentary Sources

So far in this chapter we have concentrated upon programs which aim to create information that would not otherwise exist, using audio, video and photographic technology. This section explores a different aspect of documentation: projects to compile widely scattered or obscure existing documents into more convenient and accessible forms. An example of this type of undertaking is the copying of tombstone inscriptions in local cemeteries, providing access in written form to information that would be largely unavailable to researchers. Other sources worth copying and compiling might include the texts on building cornerstones, dedication plates, historical markers, plaques on monuments, and business logos and symbols. Projects to re-record information may not utilise sophisticated technology or specialist skills but they do require careful planning and management to yield optimum results. The following are some of the aspects which must be considered:

(a) Planning/administering the overall program.
(b) Selecting/designing the compilation projects.
(c) Planning the specific project activities:
  • choosing the site/sites to be included
  • breaking the project up into manageable segments (half or full days in sequence)
  • designing the data recording sheets
  • selecting the information to be recorded: full text or specific portions
  • designing the format, sequence, and content of individual entries
  • designing the format and content of the final compilation and its indexes
  • recruiting/training the project personnel (usually volunteers)
  • arranging for transport, supplies, and amenities for project personnel
(d) Conducting the project:
  • transporting project personnel
  • distributing supplies
  • monitoring/guiding progress
  • deploying/maintaining amenities
  • collecting completed data sheets.

(e) Analysing and processing the data sheets into the final
compiled product.
(f) Distributing the compiled product.
(g) Monitoring/evaluating project, product and program success.

These projects have lasting value for the archives, both in
terms of making remote or scattered information available to
researchers in a compact form and as a way of involving the
wider community in heritage activities. Well-planned compilation
projects are rewarding and fun; they bring people together in a
clearly well-defined worthwhile activity that has been organised
into manageable segments. Remember that although the end
product is the ultimate goal, the process of achieving it must
always be through a well-organised sequence of small satisfying
steps for the participants, whether staff or volunteers or both.

In closing, it is desirable to summarise the common benefits
and cautions surrounding documentation programs for archives.
Oral history, videotaping and photographic surveys do supplement and render more human the records of our present and
recent past. The sensory dimensions of such materials bring our
lives back to life in ways ink or paper cannot. But it is precisely
because these documents have such emotional power that the
programs to create them must be carefully planned and executed.
Moreover, documents created for the record raise legal, historical and ethical issues which affect the relationships among
the persons recorded, researchers and the archives' staff.
Properly structured and funded, documentation programs can
become major assets which not only enrich the collections but
also raise community support for the archives as a whole.

Endnotes

1 The material in the preceding section was taken from the author's
work in *Archives and Manuscripts: Public Programs*, Society of
American Archivists, Chicago 1982, pp. 24–25, 78–79.
2 Moss, William W., *Oral History Program Manual*, Praeger, New York,
1974, p. 7.
3 The oral history points and tables were adapted from the author's
work in *Archives and Manuscripts: Public Programs*, SAA, Chicago,
1982, pp. 23–24, 71–77.
4 Caution: Beware of commercial firms offering to take old films and
convert them to video 'to preserve them'. Video is not a safe substitute, and many people have been sorry that they have discarded their
original films. If you have films in your collections (or videos for that
matter) that you want to preserve, consult the National Film and
Sound Archive (NFSA) in Canberra or the Preservation Department
of your State Archives or state library for help. Though they may be
obliged to charge a fee for assistance, their advice will be safe and
authoritative.

5 The discussion of rephotography projects is based upon the author's experience with the Vanishing Georgia Heritage Photography Project of the Georgia Department of Archives and History and was taken from *Archives and Manuscripts: Public Programs*, SAA, Chicago, 1982, pp. 21–25, 80–83.

Further Reading

Charlton, Thomas L., 'Videotaped Oral History: Problems and Prospects', in *American Archivist,* 47/3, Summer 1984, pp. 228–36.

Dick, Ernest J., 'Through the Rearview Mirror: Moving Image and Sound Archives in the 1990's', in *Archivaria* 28, Summer, 1989, pp. 68–73.

Douglas, Louise, Roberts, Alan and Thompson, Ruth, *Oral History: A Handbook,* Allen & Unwin, Sydney, 1988.

Jolly, Brad, *Videotaping Local History.* American Association for State and Local History, Nashville, 1982.

Kula, Sam, *The Archival Appraisal of Moving Images: A RAMP Study with Guidelines*, UNESCO, Paris, 1983.

Leary, William H., *The Archival Appraisal of Photographs: A RAMP Study with Guidelines*, UNESCO, Paris, 1985.

Moss, William and Mazikana, Peter C., *Archives, Oral History and Oral Tradition*, UNESCO, Paris, 1986.

Oral History Association of Australia (South Australian Branch) (comp.) *Oral History Handbook,* revised and extended, 2nd edn, Oral History Association of Australia (South Australian Branch), Adelaide, 1990.

Stielow Frederick J., *The Management of Oral History Sound Archives*, Greenwood Press, New York, 1986.

Thompson, Paul. *The Voice of the Past: Oral History,* 2nd edn, OUP, London, 1988.

Wilton, Janis and Bollard, Angela, *Balancing the Books: Oral History for the Community*, Ethnic Affairs Commission of NSW, Sydney, 1983.

Glossary

Glenda Acland

How To Use This Glossary

The purpose of this glossary is to explain the range of archival and technical terms used by the archival profession and by the chapter authors in the text of this book. It also provides a ready reference for readers to archival terminology. Where the meaning of a particular word is not included in this glossary readers are advised to use the appropriate dictionary meaning of that word. This glossary builds on the valuable glossary in the first edition of *Keeping Archives* which was prepared by Clive Smith.

The following stylistic and methodological notes may help the reader to use the glossary:

- Term headings are in bold.
- Multiple explanations of a given term are indicated by a number with right parenthesis, eg 1); or a letter in parenthesis, eg (n.) for noun.
- A word used within a term definition which is itself defined as a term in the glossary is shown in italics.
- 'see' is used for an exact match on a term, indicating the preferred term.
- Preferred term definitions contain 'also referred to as' cross-references to lesser known or more unusual matches for the terms.
- 'See also' is used for closely related terms which are cross-referenced.

Access

The granting of permission to:

1) use the *reference* facilities of an *archives*;

2) examine and study individual *archives* and *records* or collections held by an *archives*;

3) extract information from *archives* and *records* for research or publication.

Access to *archives* may be restricted or withheld to prevent physical damage to original *records* or to protect confidential information. See also *Access policy*.

Access conditions

The instructions providing *access* to particular *records* and *archives*. See also *Access policy*.

Access policy

The official statement issued by the authorities managing an *archives* setting out which *records* and *archives* are available for *access* and under what conditions. It should be in writing, and should be available to *users* and potential *users*. See also *Access, Access conditions, Archives policy*.

Accession

(n.) A group of *records* or *archives* from the same source taken into archival *custody* at the same time.

(v.) The process of formally accepting and recording the receipt of *records* into archival *custody*.

Accessioning provides basic physical and *intellectual control* over material coming into an *archives*. See also *Deaccession*.

Accession number

The unique number that permanently identifies each *accession*, or part thereof.

Accession register see Register (n.)

Acid-free materials see Archival quality/standard

Acidity

That quality in paper and related material that causes its chemical degradation to the point that it becomes discoloured and brittle and will ultimately fall apart. Usually expressed as pH value below 7. See also *Deacidification*.

Acquisition

The process by which *archives* add to their *holdings* by accepting material as a *transfer, donation*, loan or purchase. See also *Deposit*.

Acquisition policy

An official statement issued by the authorities managing the *archives* which identifies the kinds of materials the *archives* will acquire or collect and the conditions or terms which affect the *acquisition* or *collection* of such materials. See also *Archives policy*.

Active records
Those *records* required for the day-to-day functioning of an *agency* or person. Also referred to as current *records*. See also *Inactive records*.

Ad hoc **disposal authority** see **Disposal authority** (2)

Administrative change
Change made to the organisational structure of an *agency,* or to the allocation of the functions administered by one or more *agencies*. Such changes are, or may be, reflected in the *agency's recordkeeping systems.*

Administrative history
That part of a *finding aid* that describes:
1) the history of an *agency* or a group of related *agencies*, its organisational structure and functional responsibilities; or
2) the highlights of the life and career of a person or family. The administrative history of a person is also referred to as a biographical note.

Administrative value see **Archival value** – *Evidential value*

Agency
A body, business, organisation or institution that creates or manages its own *records* in the course of its business or activities. In the case of large organisations or institutions, subordinate parts such as departments, sections, units, regional or branch offices may be regarded as separate agencies.

Agency description
The *administrative history* of an *agency*.

Aperture card see **Micrographics** – **Aperture cards**

Appraisal
1) The process of evaluating *records* to determine which are to be retained as *archives*, which are to be kept for specified periods and which will be destroyed. See also *Appraisal checklist, Disposal, Destruction.*
2) The monetary valuation of gifts of *records* .

Appraisal checklist
A list of criteria, appropriate to the type and context of the *archival program*, against which all *records* are measured. See also *Appraisal.*

Archival quality/standard
The material properties of *records* media (paper, microfilm) and related supplies (inks, ribbons, fasteners) which make them suitable for creating permanent *records* or *archives*. Such materials must be stable and free of acid (with a pH of 7 or above) or other chemical contaminates. In addition, archival

standard microfilm/microfiche must be exposed and processed to meet standards of technical quality. Also referred to as permanent materials.

Archival value
The values, evidential and/or informational that justify the continuing retention of *records* as *archives*.

Evidential Value. The value for providing evidence of the origins, structure, functions, policies and operations of the person or *agency* that created the *records*. The three major categories of *records* having evidential value are those that:
1) have continuing *administrative, legal* or *fiscal value* for the individual or body that created them, or for any subsequent bodies;
2) record details that may serve to protect the civic, legal property or other right of individuals or the community at large;
3) reflect the development of the creating body, its structures, functions, policies, decisions and significant operations; or which reflect the evolution of the individual's career, interests or activities.

Administrative Value. The value for the conduct of current and future administrative business.

Financial Value. The value for the conduct of current and future financial or fiscal business.

Legal Value. The value for the conduct of current and future legal business.

Also referred to as documentary value, intrinsic value or primary value.

Informational Value. The value for reference or research deriving from the information the *records* contain, as distinct from their evidential value. *Records* and *archives* often contain information that has *reference* or research uses not envisaged by its *creators*.

Also referred to as secondary value.

Historical Value.
1) The value arising from exceptional age and/or connection with some historical event or person.
2) Sometimes used as a synonym for *archival value*, in the sense that 'historical' encompasses other kinds of values.

Archive
1) The whole body or group of *records* of continuing value of an *agency* or individual. See also *Record group* (1).
2) An accumulation of *series* or other record *items* with a common *provenance*, or of a distinct organisation, body or purpose. See also *Collection, Holdings.*

Archives

1) Those *records* that are appraised as having continuing value. Traditionally the term has been used to describe *records* no longer required for current use which have been selected for permanent preservation. Also referred to as permanent *records*.
2) The place (building/room/storage area) where archival material is kept. See also *Repository*.
3) An organisation (or part of an organisation) responsible for appraising, acquiring, preserving and making available archival material.

There are three main types:

Government Archives. A government agency usually with legislative responsibility for providing a centralised archival service for agencies within that government structure.

In-house Archives. That part of an institution or organisation maintained for the purpose of keeping the *archives* of that institution or organisation. An in-house *archives* usually restricts its *acquisition* to *records* generated by its parent institution or organisation or by other closely associated bodies or people. Also referred to as corporate *archives*, dedicated *archives* or institutional *archives*. Other types of *archives* include combined *archives*, clearing-house *archives* and commercial operations.

Collecting Archives. An organisation or part of an organisation that has as its principal function the collection of the *records* of a variety of organisations, families and individuals. Collecting archives are often referred to as manuscript libraries or manuscript repositories.

Archives box

A standard-sized storage container, variable in dimensions and construction used to house and facilitate the handling of archival material. Traditionally they have been made of cardboard (which may be acid-free) which has been die-cut with an integral folding lid, and for *conservation* reasons are held together without the use of glues or staples. Recently boxes have also been manufactured from inert plastic polypropylene.

Archives policy

An official statement broadly but comprehensively outlining the purpose, objectives and conditions that define the scope of archival activities, the authority under which they operate and the services offered to clients. See also *Acquisition policy, Access policy*.

Archival program

A specific ongoing plan or operation to:
1) manage archival *holdings* or an archival *collection*.

2) identify archival material and arrange its *transfer* to an appropriate archival repository.

Archiving

A computing term that has little to do with archival concepts and practices. It refers to the procedure for transferring unappraised non-current information or data from the active system, usually by dumping it onto a computer tape.

Archivist

A person, professionally educated, trained and experienced, responsible for the management or administration of *archives* and/or *records* by appraising and identifying *records* of continuing value, by documenting and preserving *archives* in their context and by enabling and facilitating their continuing use. Traditionally used for a keeper or custodian of *archives*.

Arrangement

The intellectual and physical process of putting *archives* and *records* into order in accordance with accepted archival principles, particularly those of *provenance* and *original order*. If, after detailed examination, the *original order* is identified as a totally haphazard accumulation making the *records* irretrievable (but not an odd, unorderly or difficult arrangement), the archivist may (after documenting this *original order*) impose an arrangement that presents the *records* objectively and facilitates their use. See also *Description, Original order*.

Artefacts

Objects, not being *records*, retained because of their *informational value* or because of their relationship with the *records* or *archives*.

Biographical note see Administrative history (2)

Box list

A basic, preliminary list of the contents of an *archives box* compiled at the time of packing and *transfer* of *records*. It usually includes *item* identifier and date range and is used for control until an *inventory* is compiled. Also referred to as checklist, consignment list or container list. See also *List, Finding aids (1)*.

Cellulose nitrate film

A flexible support or base used for negatives and cine film from *c*.1890 to *c*.1950. It is extremely unstable, self-destructive and represents a major fire hazard as it is highly flammable. By arrangement, nitrate-based film records can be sent to the National Film and Sound Archive for copying.

Checklist see Box list

Class
A group of *documents* or an identifiable sub-division of a *series, record group* or *archive* having common characteristics or the same *archival value*. Sometimes this term is used to mean *series*. Also referred to as disposal class. See also *Series*.

Code of Ethics
The principles of fairness, the standards for behaviour and other rules for the conducting of activities.

Collecting archives see **Archives (3)**

Collecting policy see **Acquisition policy**

Collection
1) An accumulation (usually artificial) of *documents* or *papers* of any *provenance* brought together (sometimes purchased) on the basis of some common characteristic, eg subject or means of *acquisition* or medium. In common use in manuscript libraries and other *collecting archives*. See also *Archive (2), Holdings*
2) An arbitrarily defined unit of *records* or *archives* often used for *personal papers* or *record group*. See also *Papers*.

COM (Computer output microfilm) see **Micrographics**

Computer-generated records see **Electronic records**

Conservation
The physical aspects and processes of *preservation* of original archival materials.
Preventive Conservation. Those measures taken in order to prevent or delay future degradation of *holdings*, eg the provision of environmentally sound and secure storage; the installation of warning devices; the withdrawal, restriction or copying of fragile items. Also referred to as macro-conservation.
Restorative Conservation. Those measures taken to repair or restore damaged or deteriorated archival (and other) material to its original condition. In doing this, it is important that the *evidential value* of the original be retained, and consequently repairs are usually reversible and visible. Also referred to as micro-conservation.
See also *Preservation*.

Conservator
A person, professionally educated, trained and experienced, responsible for the physical *preservation* of archival (and other) materials.

Consignment list see **Box list**

Container list see **Box list**

Contemporaneous finding aids see **Finding aids (2)**

Control records see **Finding aids (2)**

Copyright
The exclusive right, granted by law, of the creator of a work (or his/her assignees or employers) to make or dispose of copies of and otherwise to control the use of a literary, dramatic, musical, artistic or other work. Ownership of copyright in a work does not necessarily pass with ownership of the work itself. The laws relating to copyright are complex and require specialist legal advice.

Corporate archives see **Archives (3)** – *In-house archives*

Created and compiled documentation program
A program of regular activities designed to identify, re-record and possibly create *records* or information for inclusion in the *archives' collections*.

Creator
The person or *agency* which creates, receives and accumulates or otherwise brings into existence *documents* and *records*. See also *Depositor, Donor*.

Cull
To remove selected *documents* from a file or a *series* because they lack *archival value*. Also referred to as stripping or weeding.

Current records see **Active records**

Custody
1) The responsibility for the care of *records, archives* or other material, usually based on their physical possession. Custody does not always include legal ownership, or the right to control *access* to *records*.
2) The physical location of the *records* or *archives*.

Deaccession
The process of removing material from the care and *custody* of an *archives*, either because the material has been reappraised and found to be unsuitable for the *archives' holdings*, or because the legal owner has requested its return, or because it has been agreed to *transfer* it to another *archives*. Deaccessioning is a serious matter which requires careful consideration and *documentation*. See also *Accession*.

Deacidification
The process of eliminating *acidity* in paper and related material, or reducing the *acidity* to a more acceptable level. See also *Acidity*.

Note: Deacidification does not strengthen already embrittled or weak paper.

Deed of gift
The legal agreement between the *archives* and *donor* documenting the terms of a *donation*.

Dedicated archives see **Archives** – *In-house archives*

Dehumidify
The process of reducing the *relative humidity* in the atmosphere, by mechanical or chemical means. See also *Humidification, Humidity, Relative humidity.*

Deposit
An addition to the *holdings* or *collection* of an *archives*. A deposit is usually a *transfer* of material but may also be a *donation* or a loan for either a short-term or an indefinite period. See also *Acquisition.*

Depositor
The person legally responsible for the *records* deposited. See also *Creator, Donor.*

Description
The process of recording information about the nature and content of the *records* in archival *custody*. The description identifies such features as *provenance, arrangement, format* and contents, and presents them in a standardised form. See also *Arrangement, Finding aids.*

Destruction
The physical *disposal* of *records* of no further value, for example by incineration, shredding or pulping. See also *Appraisal, Disposal, Temporary records, Time-expired records.*

Disaster plan
A written procedure setting out the measures to be taken to minimise the risks and effects of disasters such as fire, flood or earthquake, etc, and to recover, save and secure the *vital records* should such a disaster occur. Part of *preventive conservation*. See also *Vital records.*

Disposal
1) The final decision concerning the fate of *records*, ie *destruction* or *transfer* to *archives*. On rare occasions the *disposal* may be by sale or by *donation*.
2) A program of activities to facilitate the orderly transfer of *intermediate* and *inactive records* from current office space into low-cost or archival storage. It includes *surveys*, scheduling and records *destruction*.

See also *Appraisal, Destruction, Disposal authority, Disposal schedule, Inactive records, Intermediate records.*

Disposal authority
1) The *document* authorising the *disposal* of *records.*
2) An *ad hoc* or one-off *disposal* authority is a non-continuing approval, not intended to set a precedent, which provides a particular disposal action for a specific set of circumstances.
See also *Disposal, Disposal schedule.*

Disposal class see **Class**

Disposal sentence
The specification as to whether *records* are to be retained and if so for how long, or when they are to be destroyed. See also *Disposal schedule, Sentencing, Trigger.*

Disposal schedule
1) A systematic listing of *records* created by an organisation or *agency* which plans the life of these *records* from the time of their creation to their *disposal.* A Disposal schedule is a continuing authority for implementing decisions on the value of *records* specified in the schedule.
A *disposal* schedule lists:
  • the *records* created by the *agency;*
  • the *retention period* for each *series* or *class* of *records*;
  • the *disposal sentence* for each *series* or *class* of *records*, specifying whether the *records* are to be retained as *archives* or destroyed;
  • the *custody* arrangements for each *series* or *class* of *records*, specifying when the *records* are to be transferred to *intermediate storage* and/or to *archives.*
2) General disposal schedules cover functions common to a number of *agencies*, typically used by government archival authorities to cover functional areas such as Personnel, Finance and Stores.
3) A recent development in *appraisal* methodology is the view that functional analysis is more efficient than records analysis in producing disposal schedules. The resultant disposal schedules are based on function or activity within function, either across a range of related organisations or to provide a specific *disposal* schedule for a particular *agency* .
See also *Disposal, Disposal authority, Disposal sentence, Disposal trigger, NAP, Sentencing.*

Disposal trigger
In *disposal schedules* the event or activity which indicates that the active life of the *record* is over and the *disposal sentence* can be applied. See also *Disposal sentence, disposal schedule.*

Document
1) Recorded information regardless of medium or form.
2) The smallest complete unit of record material, eg a letter, photograph, report.
See also *Item*.

Document image processing
The technologies and processes whereby an *image* of a *document* is captured, stored and retrieved in electronic form. See also *Image, Optical disk*.

Document trail
The process of producing evidence based on the tracing and tracking of all authenticated sources of recorded information, regardless of medium, on a given matter. See also *Source analysis*.

Documentary value see **Archival value** – *Evidential value*

Documentation
1) The organisation and processing of written *descriptions* of *records* and *archives* for the information of *users*, resulting in *finding aids*.
2) In relation to electronic *records*: The organised set of descriptive *documents* which explains the operating system and software necessary to maintain and use data contained in electronic form.
3) The policies, procedures, forms and reports which provide evidence of the programs, functions, work activities and commitments of an *agency*.

Documentation strategy
A plan to create a continuing mechanism for cooperative *acquisition, collection* and *appraisal* of *records* of significant activities, themes or subjects, involving *records creators*, administrators, policy-makers, technical experts, historians and *archivists*. The process identifies which *archives* exist and which should be created if necessary, for *transfer* to an appropriate custodial institution.

Donation
A voluntary *deposit* of *records*, involving the *transfer* of legal ownership as well as *custody* to the *archives*.
See also *Transfer*.

Donor
A person or organisation who has donated *records* to the *archives*. See also *Creator, Depositor*.

Electronic records
Records capable of being processed in a computer system and/or stored at any instant in a medium which requires electronic or computer equipment to retrieve them. See also *Machine-readable records*.

Encapsulation

The process of encasing a *document* in a polyester envelope, the edges of which are then sealed. The aim is to provide support for a fragile *document* which needs to remain visible.

Ephemera

Items of a transient nature and low value that are expected to have a brief currency. They are usually printed or manufactured in quantity for a specific event or activity and are intended neither to survive the topicality of that event or activity nor to survive as original *records*. They may be retained for their information or as graphic specimens particularly for *exhibitions*. See also *Memorabilia*.

Estray

A record or *document* that has been alienated from the possession of its legitimate custodian.

Exhibition

The use of original archival materials or copies in a display to present ideas which inform or educate the viewer and/or promote the *archives*. See also *Public programs*.

Facsimile

1) A reproduction of a *document* or *item*, that is similar in appearance to, but not necessarily of the same size as, the original.
2) An electronic means of transmitting an exact *image* of a *document* to another location.

File

(n.) An organised unit of *documents*, accumulated during current use and kept together because they deal with the same subject, activity or *transaction* and which may or may not be fastened together with or without a cover.

(v.) The action of placing *documents* in a predetermined location according to an overall scheme of control.

Film-based records see Non-textual records

Financial value see Archival value – *Evidential Value*

Finding aids

1) The descriptive media, published and unpublished, manual or electronic, created by an *archives* or an *archival program*, to establish physical or administrative and *intellectual control* over *records* and other *holdings*. Finding aids lead both *archives* staff and *users* to the information they are seeking from or about *archives*. Basic finding aids include *guides* (general or repository, subject or topical), descriptive *inventories*, *series registers*, *accession registers*, card catalogues, special *lists*, *shelf* and *box lists*, indexes, and, for *machine-readable*

records, software documentation. See also *Description, Guide, Box list, Inventory, List, Location index, Shelf list, Register.*

2) The *registers*, indexes and filing system guides produced by the *agency* or person who created the *records*, also referred to as control records or contemporaneous finding aids.

Fiscal value see **Archival value** – *Evidential value*

Folio
1) A single leaf of paper or page of a *register*, usually numbered only on one side.
2) The number assigned to the leaf or page.

Format
1) The physical medium in which information is recorded or carried, eg paper *files*, computer printout, photographs, *microfilm, machine-readable records*, plans, cards, volumes, etc.
2) A selection of descriptive elements set out in a prescribed manner and sequence so that the resulting description will be standardised for all types of *records*.

Freedom of Information
The right of the public, granted by law, to inspect or otherwise have *access* to *documents* in the *recordkeeping systems* of government, subject to specified exclusions.

General disposal schedule see **Disposal schedule (2)**

Guide
1) A *finding aid* providing summary or broad-level descriptive information about *archives*.
2) A *finding aid* describing the *holdings* relating to a particular topic, subject, period, geographical area, type or category of *archives*.
See also *Finding aids*.

Historical value see **Archival value** – *Historical value*

Holdings
The whole of the *records* and archival materials in the *custody* of an *archives*. See also *Archive (2), Collection*.

Humidification
The process of adding moisture to the atmosphere, usually to correct an excessively dry environment, or to reduce brittleness in paper. See also *Dehumidify, Humidity*.

Humidity
The concentration of moisture in the atmosphere. See also *Dehumidify, Humidification, Relative humidity*.

Hygrothermograph see **Thermohygrograph**

Image
A reproduction of a *document* on media such as film, *microfilm* or *optical disk*. See also *Document image processing*.

Imaging see **Document image processing**

In-house archives see **Archives (3)**

Inactive records
Those *records* no longer required for the conduct of business and which may therefore be *transferred* to *intermediate storage*, archival *custody* or destroyed. See also *Active records, Disposal (2)*.

Informational value see **Archival value** – *Informational value*

Institutional archives see **Archives (3)** – *In-house archives*

Intellectual control
The control established over the informational content of *records* and *archives* resulting from ascertaining and documenting their *provenance*, and from the processes of *arrangement* and *description*.

Intermediate records
Those *records* that are required so infrequently in the conduct of current business that they can be transferred from offices to separate storage areas. Also referred to as non-current records or semi-current records. See also *Disposal (2)*.

Intermediate storage
A low-cost, warehouse-style *repository* or storage area where *inactive* or *intermediate records* are housed and referenced pending their ultimate *destruction* or *transfer* to *archives*. Also referred to as secondary storage. See also *Repository*.

Intrinsic value see **Archival value** – *Evidential value*

Inventory
A basic *finding aid* listing and describing in varying degrees of detail the contents of one or more of the elements of *intellectual control* of an *archives*. See also *Finding aids (1), Inventory of items*.

Inventory of items
A list of all *items* in a *series*, generally including item control number, item title and/or description, date range and item size and quantity. See also *Inventory*.

Item
The smallest discrete unit of record material which accumulates to form a *series* (ie a *file* or part file in a *series* of files; a volume in a *series* of volumes, etc). Sometimes the term is also used as equivalent to *Document* (2). Also referred to as record item. See also *Document*.

Legal value see **Archival value** – *Evidential value*

List
An enumeration of *records* or *archives* for the purposes of establishing control and/or providing information. See also *Box list, Finding aids (1), Shelf list*.

Location index
A *finding aid*, manual or electronic, providing the physical location in the *repository* of all *holdings*. See also *Finding aids (1), Shelf list*.

Machine-readable records
Those *records* created and maintained in such a way that the information they contain is inaccessible without the aid of the appropriate machine, eg sound recordings (both discs and tapes), video recordings and computer tapes and disks. See also *Electronic records*.

Macro-conservation see **Conservation** – *Preventive conservation*

Magnetic tape
A storage medium consisting of a polyester base and a metallic coating on which data is stored by selective magnetisation of the surface of the coating.

Manuscript library/repository see **Archives (3)** – *Collecting archives*

Master record see **Official records (2)**

Memorabilia
Material having sentimental or *historical value* to the creator, the creator's family or to collectors. See also *Ephemera*.

Microclimate
The environment (temperature, *relative humidity* and air movement) contained within a confined space, such as inside an *archives box* or display case.

Micro-conservation see **Conservation** – *Restorative conservation*

Microfiche see **Micrographics**

Microfilm jacket see **Micrographics**

Microfilm see **Micrographics**

Microforms see **Micrographics**

Micrographics
The use of photographic processes to produce reduced-size *images* (usually too small to be read without magnification) of textual or graphic material on high-resolution fine-grain film stock. The following are the more commonly produced *formats*:

Aperture Cards. Cards containing an aperture or window in which is inserted a single frame of microfilm, usually used for mounting images of maps and plans. The cards allow the recording of information about each individual *image* and also allow *images* to be used independently of each other.

COM (Computer Output Microforms). Computer output produced directly as microfilm or microfiche without an intermediate paper format.

Microfiche. A flexible transparent sheet of film, about 105mm by 149mm, containing a number of images sequentially arranged in rows and columns.

Microfilm. A film in roll form, usually 16mm or 35mm in width.

Microfilm jacket. A transparent holder into which individual strips of microfilm, usually 16mm, can be inserted.

NAP
The concept that material can be destroyed according to 'normal administrative practices'. This provides for the routine destruction of drafts, duplicates and publications, with the test that it is obvious that no information of continuing value to the organisation will be destroyed. Originally developed by Australian Archives, the concept is now widely referred to by *archivists*. See also *Disposal schedule*.

Nitrate film see **Cellulose nitrate film**

Non-acidic paper see **Permanent paper**

Non-active records see **Inactive records**

Non-current records see **Intermediate records**

Non-official records
In *government* or *in-house archives, records*, other than *official records*, that are relevant to or reflect the work or interests of individuals or groups associated with the organisational structure of which the *archives* is part. See also *Official records*.

Non-textual records
Items of a pictorial or graphic nature, as opposed to written or textual, eg photographs, films, illustrations, diagrams, plans, etc.

Object see **Artefact**

Office of record
The office held accountable for the documentation of an activity. In *disposal scheduling*, the office responsible for the *record* during its use for the conduct of business. See also *Official records (2)*, *Provenance (1)*.

Official records
1) In *government* or *in-house archives*, the *records* of those *agencies* for which the *archives* has a legislative responsibility or of which it is an organisational part. See also *Non-official records*.
2) In *disposal scheduling*, the copy of the *record* held by the *office of record*. Any other copies of the record can then be destroyed whenever they are no longer required. Also referred to as master record. See also *Office of record*.

One-off *disposal* **authority** see **Disposal authority (2)**

Optical disk
A specially coated disk onto which information is recorded in analogue or digital form by a laser. The information can be retrieved by having a laser read the disk and the result decoded by a microprocessor into sounds or *images*. See also *Document image processing*.

Oral history
A sound recording, or a transcript of an aural *record*, resulting from a planned interview with an individual to systematically capture personal accounts and opinions. See also *Public programs*.

Original order
The order in which *records* and *archives* were kept when in active use, ie the order of accumulation as they were created, maintained and used. The principle of original order requires that the original order be preserved or reconstructed unless, after detailed examination, the original order is identified as a totally haphazard accumulation making the *records* irretrievable (but not an odd, unorderly or difficult arrangement). See also *Arrangement*.

Papers
The accumulation of an individual's *records*, also referred to as personal papers. See also *Collection (2)*.

Permanent materials see **Archival quality/standard**

Permanent paper
Acid-free paper, with a protective alkaline buffer and pH of 8 to 10, containing low levels of undesirable substances such as lignin and acidic sizing. Also referred to as non-acidic paper.

Permanent records see **Archives (1)**

Permanent value see **Archival value**

Personal papers see **Papers**

Physical control
The control established over the physical aspects (such as *format*, quantity and location) of the *archives* and *records* in *custody*.

Preservation
The actions which enable the materials in an *archives* to be retained for as long as they are needed ie the basic functions of storing, protecting and maintaining *records* and *archives* in archival *custody*. See also *Conservation*.

Preventive conservation see **Conservation**

Primary value see **Archival value** – *Evidential value*

Privacy
The right of a living person to be secure from the unauthorised disclosure of or *access* to information contained in *records* and *archives* of a private or confidential nature about himself/herself or his/her immediate family.

Provenance
1) The *agency*, office or person of origin of *records*, ie the entity which created, received or accumulated and used the *records* in the conduct of business or personal life. Also referred to as *records* creator. See also *Records creation, Office of record.*
2) The chain of *custody* which reflects the office(s) or person(s) that created, received or accumulated and used the *records* in the conduct of business or in the course of personal life. Identifying and documenting the provenance of *records* is an essential part of establishing their authenticity and integrity as evidence.
3) In archival theory, the principle of provenance requires that the *archives* of an *agency* or person not be mixed or combined with the *archives* of another, ie the *archives* are retained and documented in their functional and/or organisational context. See also *Respect des fonds.*

Public programs
A planned sequence of community outreach projects and promotional activities which informs the wider community about archival *holdings* and services and involves its members directly in their documentary heritage. See also *User education, Exhibition, Oral history.*

Reading room see **Search room**

Record group
A theoretical unit for the purpose of archival control used to describe:
1) All of the *records* of an *agency* . See also *Archive (1)*.
2) A body of *archives* organisationally and functionally related on the basis of *provenance*.

Record item see **Item**

Recordkeeping system
The principles, methods and processes devised for capturing, arranging and maintaining the *records* of an *agency* or person. See also *Records, Records management*.

Record series see **Series**

Record system see **Recordkeeping system**

Records
Documents containing data or information of any kind and in any form, created or received and accumulated by an organisation or person in the *transaction* of business or the conduct of affairs and subsequently kept as evidence of such activity through incorporation into the *recordkeeping system* of the organisation or person. *Records* are the information by-products of organisational and social activity. See also *Records creation, Recordkeeping system*.

Records centre see **Repository**

Records creation
The act of bringing into existence and/or accumulating *records* and incorporating them into a recordkeeping system. See also *Provenance (1), Records.*

Records creator see **Provenance (1)**

Records management
Activities within the management of the continuum of *records* of an organisation which facilitate the systematic capture, control, maintenance, dissemination and disposition of the *records* of that organisation. *Records* management is primarily concerned with capturing complete, accurate and reliable documentation of organisational activity for current purposes. See also *Recordkeeping system, Records manager.*

Records manager
A person, professionally educated, trained and experienced, responsible for the effective and efficient delivery of *records management* services to meet an organisation's requirements. See also *Records management.*

Records survey see **Survey (2)**

Reference
The range of activities involved in providing information from or about *records* and *archives*, eg making *records* and *archives* available for *access* and providing copies or reproductions of *records* and *archives*. See also *Reference services*.

Reference services
The facilities and services that enable the *user* to use the *archives* and its *records* once *access* to them is approved. See also *Reference*.

Register
(n.) A log or *list* of brief descriptions of matters or things (*accessions*, *series*, letters sent or received, actions taken) usually in a single sequence (chronological or numerical) which serves as a *finding aid* to the matters or things listed. See also *Finding aids* (1).
(v.) The process of formally recording information in a register.

Registry
Literally, an office responsible for maintaining one or more *registers*. Commonly used to denote the administrative unit of an *agency* responsible for the creation, control and maintenance in files of the *active* and *intermediate records* of an organisation.

Relative humidity
The ratio, expressed as a percentage, of the amount of water-vapour present in the atmosphere to the amount required to saturate it at the same temperature. Relative humidity varies with temperature. See also *Dehumidify, Humidity*.

Repository
The building or room, or part thereof, set aside for the storage of *archives* and/or *intermediate records*. Archival repositories are often constructed to meet specific environmental standards designed to ensure the longevity of the *records*. Also referred to as a *records* centre. See also *Archives (2), Intermediate storage*.

Reprography
The full range of processes used to replicate or copy *documents* by optical or photographic means. Reprography includes photocopying, photoduplication, microphotography, photography and the family of printing processes.

Research room see **Search room**

Researcher see **User**

Respect des fonds
Respect for the principle of *provenance* that the *archives* of an *agency* or person are not mixed or combined with those of other agencies or people. See also *Provenance (3)*.

Restoration see **Conservation**

Restorative conservation see **Conservation**

Retention period
The period of time, usually based on an estimate of the frequency of current and future use, and taking into account statutory and regulatory provisions, that *records* need to be retained before their final *disposal*. Sometimes used to indicate the length of time *records* are to be retained in offices before being *transferred* to *intermediate storage*.

Search room
A room or area set aside for supervised consultation of archival materials by authorised *users* with the assistance of the *archives*. Also referred to as reading room and research room.

Secondary storage see **Intermediate storage**

Secondary value see **Archival value** – *Informational Value*

Semi-current records see **Intermediate records**

Sentencing
The act of applying the relevant *disposal schedule* to *records*. See also *Disposal schedule, Disposal sentence*.

Series
Those *records* or *archives* having the same provenance which belong together because:
- they are part of a discernible filing system (alphabetical, numerical, chronological, or a combination of these);
- they have been kept together because they result from the same activity; or
- they are of similar *formats* and relate to a particular function.
A *series* may consist of only one *item*.
Also referred to as record *series*. See also *Class*.

Series number
The unique number that permanently identifies each *series*.

Series register see **Register (n.)**

Shelf list
A list of the *holdings* of an *archives* arranged sequentially in the order of the contents of each shelf. See also *Finding aids (1)*, *List, Location index*.

Source analysis
A synopsis derived from the ascertainment of the *records* relating to a particular function, activity or topic. See also *Document trail*.

Stripping see **Cull**

Survey
The process of gathering information in a systematic and consistent way about *records* in their administrative context. The most common uses of a survey are:
1) An examination of *archives* to ascertain their *provenance, original order* and interrelationships prior to commencing full *arrangement* and *description* processes.
2) An examination of *active* or *intermediate records* noting briefly their nature, systems of *arrangement,* date ranges, quantities, function, physical condition, reference activity and rates of accumulation. This information is used to develop *disposal schedules,* plan *conservation,* or project space requirements, among other uses. Also referred to as records survey.

Temporary records
Records with no *archival value* that can be sentenced for *destruction*. See also *Destruction, Time-expired records*.

Thermohygrograph
A scientific instrument which *records* temperature and *relative humidity* over a period of time, generally daily or weekly. Also referred to as hygrothermograph.

Time-expired records
Temporary records whose nominated date of *destruction* has passed. See also *Destruction, Temporary records*.

Transaction
The process resulting from undertaking a piece of business, or from the interrelationship between or within *agencies,* between people or between an *agency* and a person.

Transfer
The process of changing the physical *custody* of *archives,* generally without changing the legal title of the material. See also *Donation*.

User
A person who consults *records* held by the *archives,* usually in a *search room*. Also referred to as researcher. See also *Reference services*.

User education
The education and training of actual and potential *users* of *archives* in matters such as the availability of material and services, the use of *finding aids*, the use and interpretation of

archives, and the value and importance of *archives* and archival work. See also *Public program*.

User education program see **User education**

Vital records
Those *records* that are essential for the ongoing business of an *agency*, and without which the *agency* could not continue to function effectively. The identification and protection of such *records* is a primary object of *records management* and *disaster planning*. See also *Disaster plan*.

Weeding see **Cull**

About the Authors

Glenda Acland

Glenda Acland is University Archivist and Co-ordinator Records Management and Head of Archives and Records Management Services at the University of Queensland. She was previously foundation University Archivist at the University of Queensland (1982–1988) and an Archivist with the Australian Archives, ACT (1972–1980). She has conducted consultancies both in Australia and overseas. Glenda holds a BA from the University of Queensland. She is a contributor to ASA publications and conferences, has been a member of the ASA's Editorial Board and reviews editor since 1987, a member of various ASA committees including Education and Accreditation and is the Convenor of the Australian Council of Archives' Committee preparing a *Glossary of Australian Archival Terminology*.

Paul Brunton

Paul Brunton is Curator of Manuscripts, Mitchell Library, State Library of NSW and has worked in Australian manuscripts since 1973. He holds a BA from the University of Sydney, and a Diploma in Librarianship from the University of NSW. He is a contributor to several publications on archives and has published on archives management and various aspects of the State Library's Collections, including *Awake, Bold Bligh! – William Bligh's Letters Describing the Mutiny on HMS Bounty* (1989). Paul was book reviews editor of *Archives and Manuscripts* and was a member of the editorial board for the first edition of *Keeping Archives*. He has been an ASA Council member for the past four terms and is both a former ASA Convenor (Sydney Branch) and Federal President (1992–93).

Jennifer Edgecombe
Jennifer Edgecombe is Assistant Archivist at the University of Western Australia and Project Archivist, Supreme Court Records at the State Archives of Western Australia. She was previously Foundation Archivist, Guild of Undergraduates at the University of Western Australia and freelance archivist, including a short time at Australian Archives (Perth Regional Office). Jennifer holds a BA Dip. Ed. from the University of New England and a Diploma in Information Management – Archives Administration from the University of NSW. She is a contributing ASA Committee member (Western Australia Branch).

Ross Harvey
Ross Harvey is Senior Lecturer at the Graduate Department of Librarianship, Archives and Records at Monash University. He was previously Librarian at the Library School of the National Library of New Zealand and in various New Zealand Libraries, most recently the Newspaper Librarian at the National Library of New Zealand. Ross holds a Ph.D from the Victoria University of Wellington and a Diploma NZLS from the New Zealand Library School. He is widely published in musicology, newspaper history and preservation. Recent publications include *Music at National Archives* (University of Canterbury, School of Music, Christchurch, 1991); *Preservation in Australian and New Zealand Libraries* (Centre for Information Studies, Charles Sturt University, Wagga Wagga, 1990; 2nd edn, 1993); *Preservation in Libraries: Principles, Strategies and Practices for Librarians* (Bowker-Saur, London, 1992); and *Preservation in Libraries*: *A Reader* (Bowker-Saur, London, 1992). Ross is joint editor of the Bibliographical Society of Australia and New Zealand *Bulletin* and an Associate of the New Zealand Library Association and the Australian Library and Information Association.

Sigrid McCausland
Sigrid McCausland is University Archivist at the University of Technology, Sydney. She was previously Archives Senior Officer at The Council of the City of Sydney, a tutor in archives administration at the School of Librarianship, University of NSW, Manuscripts Cataloguer at the Mitchell Library, State Library of NSW, and held various positions at Australian Archives (ACT Regional Office). Sigrid holds a BA(Hons) from the Australian National University and a Diploma in Information Management – Archives Administration from the University of NSW. She is a contributor to ASA publications and was editor of Publication Notes of *Archives and Manuscripts* (1987–91). Sigrid has also held various ASA positions, including Management Committee for Local Government Archives Project member (1990–92), Conference Standing Committee member (1989–91), Editorial

Board member (1987–91), NSW Branch Keeping Archives Workshops Committee member (1986–89), Committee of Review member (1985–87), Convenor NSW Branch (1984–85), and Council member (1983–85). She was also a member of the editorial board for the first edition of *Keeping Archives*.

Judith Ellis

Judith Ellis is Managing Director of Archival Systems Consultants Pty Ltd, Melbourne, which provides a range of information management services for public and private organisations in Australia and overseas. She has been an independent records and information consultant for 11 years and a lecturer in archives and records management at four tertiary institutions. Between 1978 and 1981 she held several positions at Australian Archives (Victorian Regional Office). Judith holds a BA(Hons) from the University of Melbourne, an MA(Archives and Records) from Monash University, and membership status with professional associations (MRMA, AIMM). Judith is a contributor of articles and book reviews to *The Informaa Quarterly* and *Archives and Manuscripts* and a presenter of conference papers at various industry forums. She is a member of the Public Records Advisory Council of Victoria and is consultant to the United Nations. She is also an active member of professional associations, including Vice-President of the Records Management Association of Australia (Victoria Branch) and former editor of the national journal, *The Informaa Quarterly*, member of several national ASA committees, and holder of various Branch Council positions since 1980. Judith is general editor for the second edition of *Keeping Archives*.

Sue McKemmish

Sue McKemmish is Deputy Head, Graduate Department of Librarianship, Archives and Records at Monash University. She was previously with Australian Archives (Victorian Regional Office, 1975–83) and the Public Record Office, Victoria (1983–90). Sue holds an MA in History from Monash University and a Graduate Diploma in Librarianship from RMIT. She is contributor to *Archives and Manuscripts* and ASA and RMAA conferences and workshops.

Ann Pederson

Ann Pederson is Senior Lecturer in Archives Administration and Records Management in the School of Information, Library and Archive Studies at the University of NSW, a post assumed in 1981 following a career as Director of Archives, Georgia Department of Archives and History in the US. She holds a BA(Hons) in History from Ohio Wesleyan University and an MA in Research History from Georgia State University. Ann is known for her international editorial and writing achievements, particularly for

Keeping Archives (first edition) as editor-in-chief, for *Archives and Manuscripts: Public Programs* (1982) as co-author, and for *Georgia Archive* (now *Provenance*) as editor and contributor. She has also directed and written several multi-media productions on archival resources and conducted many educational activities (short courses, conferences and seminars). She recently completed a project with Australian Archives to develop a distance education course of study in archives and records management. Ann served two terms on the Council of the ASA (1987–91) and was elected a Fellow of the Society of American Archivists (1990).

Barbara Reed
Barbara Reed is Joint Director of the consulting firm Records Archives and Information Management Pty Ltd, Sydney, a position held since 1989. She was previously with Australian Archives (Central Office and ACT Regional Office) and with the Records Management Section of the University of Melbourne. Barbara holds an MA(Hons) from the University of Melbourne, a BA(Hons) from the University of Sydney, a Diploma in Archives Administration from the University of NSW, and membership status with professional associations (ARMA, AALIA). She is also a registered ASA consultant. Barbara was joint editor of *Keeping Data* (1990) and the *Directory of Archives in Australia* (1992). She is a contributor of articles and book reviews to *The Informaa Quarterly*, *Archives and Manuscripts* and *Records Management Bulletin* (UK). Barbara is a former ASA Council member (1983–87, 1989–91) and ASA Secretary (1985–87).

David Roberts
David Roberts is Manager, Records Management Office of NSW. He was previously Manager, Information Services at Australian Archives (NSW Regional Office); Archivist, Audio-Visual Records; Archivist, Machine-Readable Records; and Assistant Director, Records Data Management at Australian Archives. David holds a BA from the University of Sydney and a Diploma in Archives Administration from the University of NSW. He is a contributor of articles and reviews to *Archives and Manuscripts* and was co-editor of *Keeping Data* (1991). David was Convenor of ASA Standing Committee on Machine-Readable Records (1986–90), ASA Convenor (Sydney Branch), and an ASA Council member (1989–91).

Tim Robinson
Tim Robinson is Assistant University Archivist at the University of Sydney. He was previously College Archivist, Sydney College of Advanced Education; Archives Systems Officer, The Council of the City of Sydney Archives; and Archivist, Society of Australian Genealogists. Tim holds a BA(Hons) from Macquarie University and a Diploma in Information Management – Archives

Administration from the University of NSW. Tim was a member of the editorial board for the first edition of *Keeping Archives*. He is a former ASA Convenor (Sydney Branch), ASA Council member (1985–87), and member of the Executive Committee of the Australasian Council of Archives Inc.

Anne-Marie Schwirtlich

Anne-Marie Schwirtlich is Senior Curator, Printed and Written Records at the Australian War Memorial (Canberra). She was previously Assistant Director of Disposal and Assistant Director of Personal Records and Special Projects at Australian Archives (ACT Regional Office, 1985–88). Between 1978 and 1985 Anne-Marie held several positions within Australian Archives (NSW Regional Office) and in 1983 and 1985 was Lecturer in Archives Administration at the University of NSW. She is a writer of articles for *Archives and Manuscripts* and was co-editor of *Our Heritage: A Directory to Archives and Manuscripts Repositories in Australia* (1983). She is a contributor to ASA workshops and assisted Ann Pederson in the development and delivery of a two-week in-service course 'Managing Archives: An Introduction' (conducted periodically). Anne-Marie is an active ASA member (Sydney and Canberra) and a former ASA Secretary (1983–85), ASA President (1989–90), ASA Vice-President (1990–91), and President of the Australian Council of Archives (1991–92).

Helen Smith

Helen Smith is Senior Archivist – Disposal at BHP. She was previously Corporate Archivist/Manager of Archives and Records at the State Bank of Victoria; Senior Consultant, Development and Consultancy and Manager of Records Services, Public Record Office, Victoria; and a historical researcher at the Australian National University. Helen also has experience as a sessional lecturer in archives and records management, particularly in records disposal and in-house archives/records management programs and in graduate archives administration and business studies courses at the University of Melbourne and Monash University. Helen holds a BA and a Graduate Diploma in Information Management (Archives and Records) from the University of Melbourne. She is both an ASA member and an ASA Education Committee member.

Index